AF835644

Islamic Law, Gender, and Social Change in Post-Abolition Zanzibar

After the abolition of slavery in 1897, Islamic courts in Zanzibar (East Africa) became central institutions where former slaves negotiated socioeconomic participation. By using difficult-to-read Islamic court records in Arabic, Elke E. Stockreiter reassesses the workings of these courts as well as gender and social relations in Zanzibar Town during British colonial rule (1890–1963). She shows how Muslim judges maintained their autonomy within the sphere of family law and describes how they helped advance the rights of women, ex-slaves, and other marginalised groups. As was common in other parts of the Muslim world, women usually had to buy their divorce. Thus, Muslim judges played important roles as litigants negotiated moving up the social hierarchy, with ethnicisation increasingly influencing all actors. Drawing on these previously unexplored sources, this study investigates how Muslim judges both mediated and generated discourses of inclusion and exclusion based on social status rather than gender.

Elke E. Stockreiter is an assistant professor of history at American University, Washington, DC. She obtained her PhD from the School of Oriental and African Studies, University of London, and previously held a position as an assistant professor at the University of Iowa. Her work has been published in peer-reviewed journals, such as the *Journal of Eastern African Studies*, and anthologies, such as *Domestic Violence and the Law in Colonial and Postcolonial Africa*, edited by Emily Burrill, Richard Roberts, and Elizabeth Thornberry.

To Jim Giblin and Omar S. Khamis,
with admiration and gratitude

Islamic Law, Gender, and Social Change in Post-Abolition Zanzibar

ELKE E. STOCKREITER
American University, Washington, DC

CAMBRIDGE
UNIVERSITY PRESS

CAMBRIDGE
UNIVERSITY PRESS

32 Avenue of the Americas, New York, NY 10013-2473, USA

Cambridge University Press is part of the University of Cambridge.

It furthers the University's mission by disseminating knowledge in the pursuit of education, learning, and research at the highest international levels of excellence.

www.cambridge.org
Information on this title: www.cambridge.org/9781107048416

© Elke E. Stockreiter 2015

This publication is in copyright. Subject to statutory exception and to the provisions of relevant collective licensing agreements, no reproduction of any part may take place without the written permission of Cambridge University Press.

First published 2015

Printed in the United States of America

A catalog record for this publication is available from the British Library.

Library of Congress Cataloging in Publication Data
Stockreiter, Elke E.
Islamic law, gender, and social change in post-abolition Zanzibar / Elke E. Stockreiter.
pages cm
Includes bibliographical references and index.
ISBN 978-1-107-04841-6 (hardback)
1. Women's rights – Tanzania – Zanzibar – History – 19th century. 2. Women's rights – Tanzania – Zanzibar – History – 20th century. 3. Civil rights – Tanzania – Zanzibar – History. 4. Justice, Administration of (Islamic law) – Tanzania – Zanzibar – History. 5. Islamic law – Tanzania – Zanzibar – History. 6. Women – Tanzania – Zanzibar – Social conditions. 7. Minorities – Tanzania – Zanzibar – Social conditions. 8. Zanzibar – History – 1890–1964. I. Title.
HQ1236.5.T34S76 2015
305.4209678′1 – dc23 2014034104

ISBN 978-1-107-04841-6 Hardback

Cambridge University Press has no responsibility for the persistence or accuracy of URLs for external or third-party Internet Web sites referred to in this publication and does not guarantee that any content on such Web sites is, or will remain, accurate or appropriate.

Contents

List of Figures and Tables

Figures

Tables

Preface

This project has been both an intellectual challenge and a personal journey, which would not have been possible without inspiration and ample support. The skilful reconstructions of social histories based on legal records from the Islamic world, mostly the Ottoman Empire, provided the inspiration for this study. Being able to use a plethora of Arabic court records from Zanzibar as the basis of this book has been a privilege as much as a reminder of limitations. I would like to thank Marie Miran-Guyon for spurring my curiosity about Islamic court records and helping me to track them down on the Swahili coast. Lynn Welchman kindly offered her expertise in Islamic law when this project was in its dissertation stage, while Jim Brennan kept pushing me to draw broader conclusions. Over the years, Anne Bang and Scott Reese have provided not only great intellectual but also moral support.

I have presented parts of this project to various audiences to whom I owe my awareness of disciplinary myopia and my decision to foreground the law with its technicalities. My sincere thanks extend to Sean O'Fahey, Knut Vikør, Anders Bjørkelo, and Elena Vezzadini for making my sojourn in Bergen a rewarding and delightful experience. At the Zentrum Moderner Orient in Berlin, Katrin Bromber, Kai Kresse, Roman Loimeier, and Marloes Janson provided intellectually stimulating and entertaining company. At the University of Iowa, the History Department has truly lived up to its collegial reputation. Many thanks to all of you! I am particularly grateful for the support from Jim Giblin, whose scholarship, teaching, and modesty I admire greatly. Glenn Penny, Jen Sessions, Jacki Rand, and Marshall Poe dedicated their interest and time to this project, and Paul Greenough offered insightful comments on a chapter. Blandina Giblin, Marie Krüger, and Edward Miner were wonderful colleagues outside the department and enriched my time in the Midwest.

My colleagues at American University also welcomed me collegially and enthusiastically. April Shelford has been the most congenial and scintillatingly witty mentor one can possibly wish for, while conversations with Eileen Findlay, Lisa Leff, Pedram Partovi, Theresa Runstedtler, and Katharina Vester, among others, have been very helpful in adjusting to my new academic home. Among colleagues and friends who have provided inspiring company and support, I would like to thank, in particular, Liz McMahon, Dodie McDow, Feli Becker, Marie Rodet, and Erin Stiles.

In Zanzibar, I am much indebted to the Zanzibar National Archives for their cooperation. My sincere thanks go to the director and all the staff for facilitating my research. Without Omar S. Khamis, who became an invaluable source of support and a dear friend, I would not have been able to complete this project. My special thanks also extend to Bwana Makame Mtwana Haji for his endeavour in making case files appear from the remotest corners of the archives. The archival staff not only provided efficient archival services but also assisted in many of my enquiries. At *Mambo Msiige*, I would like to thank Bwana Rajab Khatib Mwinyi for providing access to the marriage and divorce certificates, as well as Bwana Omar Juma Haji and Zahran Nassor Mauldi for sharing their office with Sh. Mahmoud Mussa, who skilfully embarked on the task of transcribing these certificates.

Whenever around, Abdul Sheriff was very generous with his time and I particularly would like to thank him for help with contacting people and contextualising photos. My sincere gratitude goes to all the interviewees for whom I have created pseudonyms to protect their privacy. My thanks are also directed to Abdulkadir Hashim for generously sharing his material with me. I would also like to express my gratitude to the wives of Omar S. Khamis, Mariam and Zena, and their children.

My parents and friends watched me moving in and out of this project and also moving between countries and continents. I am thankful for the friendships that have endured and cherish memories of those that did not. My gratitude goes especially to Alyssa, Béatrice and Michael, and Antía for their kindness and inspiration and to my parents for their tolerance and trust.

The bulk of the research was carried out with the support of the Arts and Humanities Research Council, UK, the University of London Central Research Fund, SOAS, and the Royal Historical Society, UK. A Norwegian Government Scholarship and an Old Gold Summer Fellowship from the University of Iowa provided funding for this project beyond the dissertation stage. I very much appreciated the professional expertise of the Cambridge University Press editorial team, led by Eric Crahan and Will Hammell. During production, the advice of Minaketan Dash was essential. My thanks also extend to the reviewers and those who contributed without being mentioned by name.

Notes on Transliteration

The transliteration of Arabic words follows the guidelines of the *International Journal of Middle East Studies* (*IJMES*). *Hamza* is transcribed as /ʾ/, although customarily omitted at the beginning of a word, and *ʿayn* as /ʿ/.

My attempts of achieving consistency in the spelling of proper names have been thwarted as they appear with different spellings due to variations in pronunciation and localised forms of names (for example, Fatuma and Asha rather than Fāṭima and ʿĀʾisha) as well as spelling mistakes. I have transcribed the names of the sultans and *kadhi*s in Arabic but have rendered litigants' proper names in Swahili. Names of Arab kin groups may appear in various spellings. For the sake of simplicity, the *nisba*-ending /-ī/, such as in al-Barwānī, is used for both feminine and masculine.

I have been consistent with my rendering of Swahili and Arabic words, but quotes may contain variant forms. Apart from the Arabic "qāḍī" and Swahili "*kadhi*," the reader will encounter the colonial spelling "*kathi*." Following the *IJMES* guidelines, I use shaykh, while other authors use the spelling sheikh, more familiar to Anglophone readers.

I have applied my discretion whether to use a term in English, Arabic, or Swahili. I have opted for "*kadhi*'s courts," since this is the term applied by Swahili speakers. As Swahili versions of legal terms are rarely used, I have provided the Arabic versions. Save for ʿulamaʾ, I have Anglicised the plural of both Swahili and Arabic nouns.

The word "judge" always refers to a British judge, whereas *kadhi* designates a Muslim judge. I have decided to keep the term used in Zanzibari Arabic for slave, *khādim*. *Bin* (Ar. son) and *bint* (Ar. daughter), abbreviated as /b./ and /bt./, were used in the vast majority of the records, such as Taibina bt. Hija, and reflected the Arab and Swahili patronymic use at the time. Names of female interviewees are preceded by Bi, for *bibi*, the term of respectful address for women. For legal reasons, the names of the interviewees are fictitious. Recordings of interviews referenced are in my possession, as are transcripts of the sample of marriage and divorce registers.

It has been my responsibility to decipher and translate the languages that have informed this study. The bulk of the sources are court records written in Arabic that I have translated myself unless indicated otherwise. If a case went on appeal, all documents had to be provided for the judge or magistrate in English. These English documents and transcripts, which I have used to save time, are usually contained in the file. Colonial court staff produced accurate and entirely satisfactory English translations, which exist for HC5 and HC8 cases and for some other cases where I have indicated that the original was in English. Letters by litigants were sometimes written in Ajami, that is, Swahili in Arabic script. I mostly relied on Omar S. Khamis to confirm and correct my reading of these letters. All correspondence between British colonial officers and that directed to them was in English. I delegated the extremely time-consuming task of transcribing the marriage and the divorce certificates to one of the few people in Zanzibar familiar with deciphering Arabic manuscripts: Sh. Mahmoud Mussa. I am most thankful to him for sharing his vast cultural knowledge with me, as well as for his meticulousness and quick adaptation to my research interests.

The Islamic months *Dhū l-Qaʿda* and *Dhū l-Ḥijja* are consistently given in the original documents as *al-Qaʿda* and *al-Ḥajj*; I have corrected these idiosyncracies. For converting hijra dates, I have used a converter provided on the Web, which has a small probability of error of one day, http://www.islamicfinder.org/Hcal/index.php.

Glossary and Abbreviations

If a word is listed in Swahili and Arabic, both versions occur in the text.

Swahili	Arabic	
	bayt al-māl	public treasury
	faskh	judicial dissolution of a marriage
	hadith	accounts of the deeds and sayings of the Prophet Muhammad
	ʿidda	waiting period of three menstrual cycles for women after their divorce, or four months and ten days after their husband's death, to establish pregnancy, in which case this period lasts until delivery
jamaa		person with whom one is connected, such as through friendship or client–patron relations rather than kinship
kabila		ethnic group; race; Arab patronyms, such as al-Harthi or al-Riyami, are called *kabila* in Swahili

kadhi	qadi	Muslim judge
	kafāʾa	concept of equality between the spouses
	khādim/a (m./f.)	slave
khuluu	*khulʿ*	separation of the spouses in which the wife redeems herself from her husband for a material consideration
liwali		provincial governor
	mawlā	slave; client; master; patron
mila		customary law
	mubāraʾa	divorce in which husband and wife release each other from remaining obligations
mudir		person in charge of one of the districts (*mudiria*s) into which Zanzibar was divided under British rule
mwinyi mkuu		ruler of the Hadimu, one of Zanzibar's indigenous groups, who lived in the centre and eastern parts of the island
mwungwana		free, civilised person as opposed to *mtumwa*, slave
ngoma		dance and music performance
	nisba	literally: relation(ship); as an adjective (ending in /-ī/) it indicates people's origin in terms of place, ethnicity, and so on
	sayyid/-a	(term of honour for) a man or woman claiming descent from the Prophet's grandson Husayn; title of the sultan of Zanzibar; master or mistress

shamba		field; plantation
	shariʿa	Islamic law
	sharīf/-a	(term of honour for) a man or woman claiming descent from the Prophet through his daughter, Fatima
	shaykh	honorific title for an elder person or someone learned; a leader
sheha		village or town elder; a political appointee, in charge of a district
suria		concubine; woman of slave status
talaka	*ṭalāq*	divorce pronounced or written by the husband
	ʿulamaʾ	Muslim scholars
ustaarabu		civilisation
uungwana		the state of being free; cf. *mwungwana*
wakf		religious endowment
	wakīl	literally: representative, proxy; in Zanzibar used for lawyers in the *kadhi*'s courts
	wālī	legal guardian; person who gives a woman into marriage
yaya		nanny

Abbreviations

Ar.	Arabic
CUL	Cambridge University Library
*EI*²	*Encyclopaedia of Islam*, second edition
*EI*³	*Encyclopaedia of Islam*, third edition
NAK	The National Archives, Kew, UK
Rs.	Rupees: Zanzibar's currency until 1936
Sh.	shaykh
Shs.	Shillings: Zanzibar's currency from 1936
SOAS	School of Oriental and African Studies, University of London
Sw.	Swahili
ZNA	Zanzibar National Archives

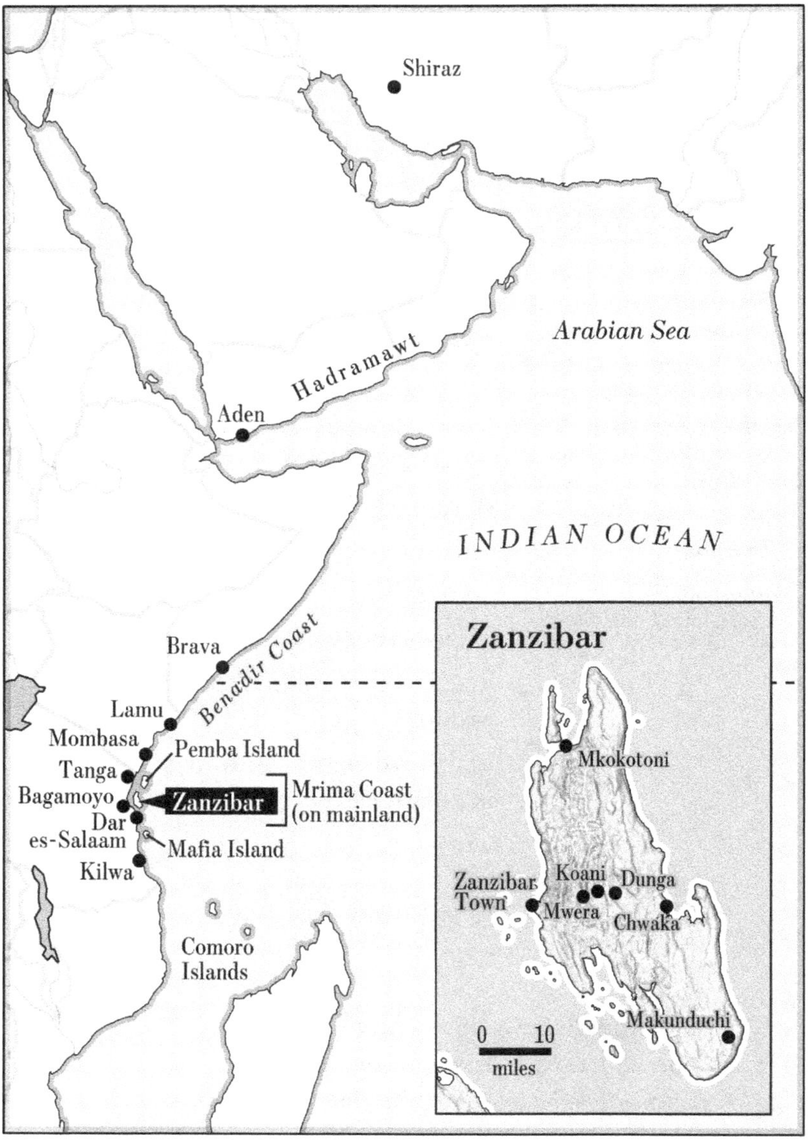

Map of Northwestern Indian Ocean and Zanzibar Island

Introduction

Islamic law and its importance in defining Muslim identity are vigorously debated in various parts of the world today. These debates are underpinned by questions such as whether Islamic law constitutes a threat to non-Muslim populations and is a backlash to modernity and civilisation. They are further driven by fear and misconceptions of its role, both entrenched in the colonial period, in which the Western coloniser imposed reforms on the Islamic legal system in order to eradicate its allegedly draconian, partial, and uncivilised aspects. Since the late nineteenth century, Islamic law has undergone major reforms to make it compatible with a Western-conceptualised, modern judiciary. Against the backdrop of this colonial judiciary, this study uses Islamic courts to map gendered social, legal, and economic agency in Zanzibar Town, a cosmopolitan city on the East African coast during the British colonial period from 1890 to 1963.

In the nineteenth century, Zanzibar Island was a hub in the Indian Ocean trade system and an entrepot for slaves.[1] Its lush environment and reputation as a trading center attracted the Omani Bū Saʿīdī sultans, who established their hegemony over the East African coast by drawing on trade networks linking this region with the wider Indian Ocean world for more than two millennia. A common religion, Islam, and its legal framework buttressed these socioeconomic networks.

[1] Zanzibar and its sister island, Pemba, were both subject to Omani and later British rule. This study is exclusively concerned with the island of Zanzibar.

From the 1830s onwards, the Bū Saʿīdī sultans established in Zanzibar a plantation economy based on the exploitation of slave labour. Using the abolition of slavery as a justification to integrate the island into their empire, the British made Zanzibar a protectorate in 1890. By then, the British perception of Zanzibar as an Arab and a Muslim settler colony was firmly in place. This perception would increase rifts along ethnic identities, between Arabs and non-Arabs, while at the same time fostering the aspiration of the latter towards Arabness. Islamic courts, locally known as *kadhi*'s courts, reveal negotiations for improving and defending socioeconomic status among a wide range of actors, Arabs and non-Arabs, spouses and kin, as well as former slaves and slave owners, in an increasingly ethnicised society.

Islamic Law and the *Kadhi*'s Courts

The *kadhi*'s courts in Zanzibar are the only judicial institution that has operated continuously from the precolonial period to the present day. The law applied in these courts has been Islamic law, or shariʿa. For reasons of convenience we can translate the term "shariʿa" as Islamic law, but shariʿa actually supposes a holistic sociolegal concept in which only a few legally enforceable rules are clearly laid down. In this way, shariʿa is better understood as a total discourse informed by religious, legal, moral, economic, and political discourses, all of which shape it reciprocally. Although the notion of a total discourse is helpful, shariʿa has never ruled all aspects of life of any individual Muslim at a given time. Its purpose is to perpetuate and improve the social order by mediating conflicts rather than punishing individuals, a characteristic of the modern nation-state.[2] Shariʿa is characterised by its adaptability and openness to local and contextual interpretation and has become permeated by customary law in all Muslim societies. The fact that morality and the law are strongly intertwined in Islam accounts for the social embeddedness of shariʿa and its workings.

The term "Islamic law" is actually problematic due to its Western, orientalist roots. Until today, many Western scholars and the general

[2] Wael B. Hallaq, *Shariʿa: Theory, Practice, Transformations* (Cambridge: Cambridge University Press, 2009), 365–66.

public have approached Islamic law as the law of the Other, as a legal system deemed incompatible with modern notions of justice, human rights, and impartiality. Historians of Islamic law, however, have created a considerable body of scholarship that contests these notions of the orientalised Islamic law by understanding shariʿa in its diverse social and historical contexts.[3] This study draws on the malleable discursive traditions of shariʿa at the beginning of British rule and demonstrates how judicial reforms diminished them over the first half of the twentieth century.

The Omani reforms of the judiciary occurred in the context of creating a modern state, which exercised tighter control over its subjects.[4] From the 1820s onwards, the Bū Saʿīdī sultans embarked on the institutionalisation of the judiciary, setting up regular court sessions in

[3] Ibid., 1–2, 10. See, for example, Ghislaine Lydon, *On Trans-Saharan Trails: Islamic Law, Trade Networks, and Cross-Cultural Exchange in Nineteenth-Century Western Africa* (Cambridge: Cambridge University Press, 2009); Shamil Jeppie, Ebrahim Moosa, and Richard Roberts, eds., *Muslim Family Law in Sub-Saharan Africa: Colonial Legacies and Post-Colonial Challenges* (Amsterdam: Amsterdam University Press, 2010); Allan Christelow, "The Transformation of the Muslim Court System in Colonial Algeria: Reflections on the Concept of Autonomy," in *Islamic Law: Social and Historical Contexts*, ed. Aziz al-Azmeh (London: Routledge, 1988), 215–30; Colin Imber, *Ebu's-su'ud: The Islamic Legal Tradition* (Edinburgh: Edinburgh University Press, 1997); Haim Gerber, *State, Society, and Law in Islam: Ottoman Law in Comparative Perspective* (Albany: State University of New York Press, 1994); Brinkley Messick, *The Calligraphic State: Textual Domination and History in a Muslim Society* (Berkeley: University of California Press, 1993); Michael G. Peletz, *Islamic Modern: Religious Courts and Cultural Politics in Malaysia* (Princeton: Princeton University Press, 2002); Ron Shaham, *Family and the Courts in Modern Egypt: A Study Based on Decisions by the Sharīʿa Courts, 1900–1955* (Leiden: Brill, 1997); Iris Agmon, *Family and Court: Legal Culture and Modernity in Late Ottoman Palestine* (Syracuse: Syracuse University Press, 2006); Judith E. Tucker, *In the House of the Law: Gender and Islamic Law in Ottoman Syria and Palestine* (Berkeley: University of California Press, 1998); Margaret L. Meriwether, *The Kin Who Count: Family and Society in Ottoman Aleppo, 1770–1840* (Austin: University of Texas Press, 1999); Leslie Peirce, *Morality Tales: Law and Gender in the Ottoman Court of Aintab* (Berkeley: University of California Press, 2003).

[4] On the absorption of precolonial legal systems by the colonial state, see Lauren Benton, *Law and Colonial Cultures: Legal Regimes in World History, 1400–1900* (Cambridge: Cambridge University Press, 2002); M. B. Hooker, *Legal Pluralism: An Introduction to Colonial and Neo-Colonial Laws* (Oxford: Oxford University Press, 1975); W. J. Mommsen and J. A. De Moor, eds., *European Expansion and Law: The Encounter of European and Indigenous Law in 19th and 20th Century Africa and Asia* (Oxford: Oxford University Press, 1991).

town and rural areas, headed by *kadhi*s, or Muslim judges, and *liwali*s, or local governors. While aiming to make the law more accessible to the population, they started curtailing previously flexible and culturally adapted discursive practices, which spanned the global Muslim community. The Bū Saʿīdī sultans were Ibāḍīs, while the majority of Muslims on the East African coast was Sunni in the nineteenth century. Among the four Sunni schools of law, or legal traditions, the East African coast has followed the Shafiʿi school since the fourteenth century. It was common practice for Muslims, *kadhi*s and litigants, to choose among different legal doctrines. Due to lack of evidence, we can only surmise that this was also practised on the Swahili coast. Archaeological evidence of the coexistence of various Muslim identities, Sunni, Shiʿi, and Ibāḍī from the eighth to the thirteenth centuries, speaks to the historical fluidity of religious practices. Yet after 1845, *kadhi*s had to follow their own school in issuing judgements, meaning that only Shafiʿi and Ibāḍī rules applied. Moreover, the sultans served as appeal institutions. As elsewhere in the Muslim world, the interference of the state was the major cause of the demise of shariʿa in its protean form, epitomised by legal scholars' independence from the political authority.[5] Codification was a key reform tool in the majority of Islamic states, yet not in Zanzibar, where Islamic law has remained essentially uncodified until today.

> Zanzibar was an oriental state, with a well-developed Government, but the local Mahomedan courts were ill-adapted to the adjustment of disputes between nationals of Western powers, and furthermore the establishment of courts in which offences against the slave laws could be dealt with was essential.[6]

Due to the British perception of Zanzibar as an Arab state, Islamic law remained the fundamental law of the protectorate throughout the colonial period. Nevertheless, the British surreptitiously interfered in its application in areas in which they found it incompatible with their

[5] Hallaq, *Shariʿa*, 15–16, Chapter 13; David S. Powers, "Orientalism, Colonialism, and Legal History: The Attack on Muslim Family Endowments in Algeria and India," *Comparative Studies in Society and History* 31, no. 3 (1989): 535.

[6] J. H. Vaughan, *The Dual Jurisdiction in Zanzibar* (Zanzibar: Government Printer, 1935), 9.

standards of justice and morality. Because of the alleged partiality of *kadhi*s, one of the main concerns of the British was to bring subjects of Western nations as well as economically important groups under their jurisdiction. To achieve this aim, they set up ethnically and economically based legal categories of natives and non-natives, reduced the *kadhi*'s sphere of jurisdiction to family or personal status law, bureaucratised the judiciary, and appointed British magistrates and judges to administer Islamic law in the sultan's courts. Prior to 1909, free Muslims who were not subjects of Christian nations could file civil and criminal suits in the *kadhi*'s courts. After 1908, criminal jurisdiction was no longer exercised by the *kadhi*s but by British magistrates. Yet *kadhi*'s courts continuously administered Islamic law in civil matters in the realm of marriage, divorce, and inheritance up to a certain value under dispute to African and Arab Muslim subjects under the sultan's jurisdiction, whereas Indian Muslims were under British jurisdiction.

*Kadhi*s were part of both the classical and modernised structure of the Islamic judiciary. They embodied the long-established Islamic legal tradition of the Swahili coast and constituted an elitist group whose erudition was passed on intergenerationally. Their social embeddedness and role as servants of the law as well as of the community faced new challenges during British rule, which integrated them into the colonial legal apparatus and subjected them to reforms, leading to their alienation from the Islamic legal framework and the people whom they served. *Kadhi*s' attempts to keep individuals in their social positions caused tensions with litigants striving for socioeconomic mobility. Although *kadhi*s enabled individual social mobility, they were more concerned about maintaining the social stability of the community as a whole.[7] Their agency occurred in interplay with the social fabric, political economy, and colonial policies. As the modern colonial state increased bureaucratisation and instigated a shift from community networks towards reliance on the state, *kadhi*s transitioned from orality, which had characterised the legal system for centuries, to scripture.

[7] Cf. Mona Siddiqui, "Law and the Desire for Social Control: An Insight into the Hanafi Concept of *Kafā'a* with Reference to the Fatawa ʿAlamgiri (1664–1672)," in *Feminism and Islam: Legal and Literary Perspectives*, ed. Mai Yamani (Reading, UK: Ithaca Press, 1996), 65, where she uses the concept of equality in marriage as an example for jurists' aim to maintain the social order.

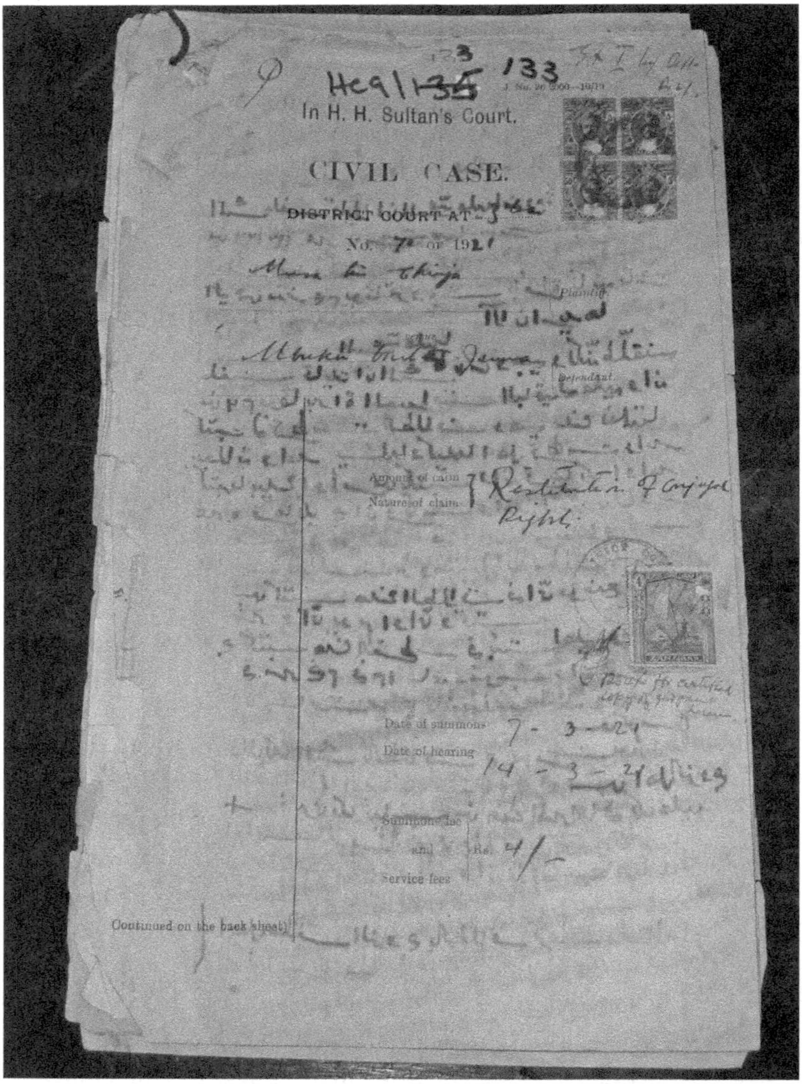

FIGURE 0.1. Cover page of a case file, 1921. The handwriting of the *kadhi*, Sh. Ṭāhir, is bleeding through the verso. Courtesy of ZNA.

It is certainly no coincidence that *kadhi*'s court records became available from 1900, as a decree providing for the keeping of court records was issued in 1899.[8] The presumably earliest preserved records

[8] Decree from Ḥamūd b. Muḥammad, 26 Shaʿbān 1316/9 January 1899, BA14/25, Zanzibar National Archives (hereafter ZNA).

of cases heard by *kadhi*s were contained in a bound, large notebook, dating from February 1900 to June 1903.[9] These neatly written summaries of cases were extremely short if not fragmentary; they did not always record who the plaintiff was and who the defendant was or what the nature of the claim concerned. The value of these entries lies in giving us a sense of who sued whom and of the wide range of issues that was raised before *kadhi*s. Litigants across all social strata sued, for instance, for shares of inheritance and debts, husbands demanded the return of disobedient wives, while some wives sought the dissolution of their marriage because of the husband's impotence or refusal to have sexual intercourse.[10] These usually very short summaries also convey the flexibility of court sessions heard by *kadhi*s at the time, as some defendants used the opportunity to bring counterclaims that the *kadhi* willingly considered.[11]

The *kadhi* first heard the plaintiff and then the defendant, followed by their witnesses in the same order. The burden of proof was on the plaintiff. Islamic law gives preference to proof in the form of oral testimony yet also considers oaths, confessions, and circumstantial evidence. If the plaintiff failed to support his or her claim, the defendant took an oath affirming his or her innocence. Cases in which defendants refused to take this oath were decided in favour of the plaintiff.[12] The office of *wakīl*, or lawyer in the *kadhi*'s courts, was a colonial

9 HC28/29, ZNA.

10 Entry #469, no. 635, 28 Dhū l-Ḥijja 1318/18 April 1901; Entry #490, no number, 11 Muḥarram 1318 [1319]/30 April 1901, HC28/29; HC10/3552, ZNA. Also in a restitution of conjugal rights case, the wife accused the husband of impotence (Entry #330, no. 362, 3 Ramaḍān 1318/25 December 1900, HC28/29, ZNA).

11 During the hearing, the roles of plaintiff and defendant may change. No entry #, no number, 26 Muḥarram 1317 [1318]/26 May 1900; Entry #217, no. 174, 17 Jumādā I 1318/12 September 1900; Entry #404, no. 497, 30 Shawwāl 1318/20 February 1901; Entry #535, no. 780, 27 Ṣafar [1319]/15 June 1901; Entry #584, no number, 13 Rabīʿ I [1319]/29 July 1901; Entry #764, no. 225, 23 Shawwāl [1319]/2 February 1902; Below entry #867, no number, 7 Muḥarram [1320]/16 April 1902; No entry #, no. 5020, 29 Ṣafar [1320]/6 June 1902, HC28/29, ZNA.

12 Oaths are assigned to whom the *kadhi* believes to be the one most likely to know the truth. Socially confirmed truth outweighs truth affirmed by an individual, and truth inferred from evidence is ignored correspondingly. This implies that people who lack witnesses, such as strangers, tend to fail to prove their claim. See Allan Christelow, "Theft, Homicide, and Oath in Early Twentieth-Century Kano," in *Law in Colonial Africa*, ed. Kristin Mann and Richard Roberts (Portsmouth, NH: Heinemann, 1991), 208. Yet legal doctrines are also protective of strangers. See Chapter 5 below.

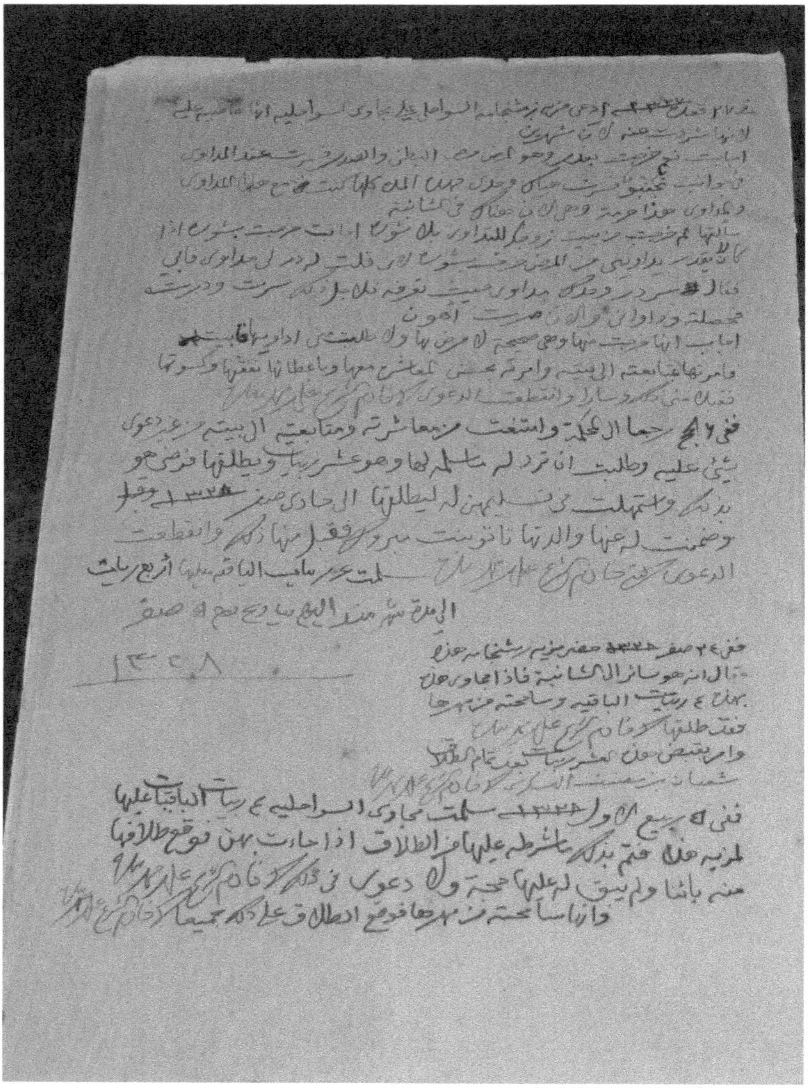

FIGURE 0.2. Last page of the minutes of a case, 1909. *Kadhi* Sh. ʿAlī b. Muḥammad signed *khādim al-sharīʿa*, "servant of the law." Courtesy of ZNA.

innovation dating back to the 1880s. The *wakīl* of either party could ask the litigants and their witnesses questions. Considering these statements and, if provided by the parties, written documents, the *kadhi* arrived at his judgement that he wrote down and read to the parties. In some cases, *kadhis* referred to legal texts of their school of law to justify their reasoning. If a case was heard over a long period, several *kadhis* may have presided over sessions at different dates.[13] When a case went on appeal, its records had to be translated for the judge and it is in these instances that Arabic and English transcripts are available.

Until 1964, the *kadhi*'s court records were exclusively written in Arabic by the *kadhis* themselves, except for the case summaries from 1900 to 1903, which were recorded by a scribe or clerk and often failed to attribute the case to a certain *kadhi*.[14] The *kadhi*'s way of record keeping changed from short summaries in 1900 to 1903 to more formal and standardised records following colonial demands (see Figures 0.1 and 0.2). The length of the cases varied considerably, from half a page to more than sixty pages, with an average of a couple of pages. The length of the records was determined by the nature of the case and the number of witnesses summoned.

When transmitting oral proceedings into written records, *kadhis* functioned as filters in translating and writing down the words of the litigants and witnesses, uttered in Swahili. The *kadhi*'s verbatim record of testimonies indicates the use of jargon and stereotypical formula. Yet longwinded phrasing and the transmission of seemingly irrelevant, unexpected statements attest to the originality and value of this source because of the diversity, intimacy, and, at times, immorality and illegality of its information.[15] The narratives that do not relate to the case balance the bias towards disharmony inherent in the source, which reminds us that people reveal their understanding of social values and norms often only in the context of narrating disputes.[16]

13 In a case heard during 1959 and 1961, three *kadhis* presided over different sessions (HC10/3695, ZNA).

14 HC28/29, ZNA.

15 Cf. Gerber, *State, Society, and Law*, 31; Mahmoud Yazbak, "Minor Marriages and *khiyār al-bulūgh* in Ottoman Palestine: A Note on Women's Strategies in a Patriarchal Society," *Islamic Law and Society* 9, no. 3 (2002): 388.

16 Simon Roberts, ed., *Law and the Family in Africa* (The Hague: Mouton Publishers, 1977), 13. Cf. Kristin Mann, *Slavery and the Birth of an African City: Lagos, 1760–1900* (Bloomington: Indiana University Press, 2007), Chapter 8. A caveat about the sources' focus on conflict is expressed by Ron Shaham, *Family and the Courts*, 20; Kristin Mann, "The Rise of Taiwo Olowo: Law, Accumulation, and Mobility in Early Colonial Lagos," in *Law in Colonial Africa*, ed. Kristin Mann and Richard Roberts (Portsmouth, NH: Heinemann, 1991), 90–91. Since first exploring Islamic court records in the 1970s, historians have attended to their methodological problems, advantages, and liabilities. See particularly Dror Ze'evi, "The Use of

Unlike contemporary Western legal systems, *kadhi*'s courts did not require specialised legal knowledge, a professional mediator, or wealth. They were easily accessible institutions and operated in open space prior to British colonial rule. Given these characteristics, combined with legal doctrines that support the weak and vulnerable, it should be less surprising that marginalised socioeconomic groups were prominent litigants who mostly obtained judgements in their favour.[17] Both genders had equal access to the courts and women were full legal personalities who regarded the notarial work of the courts as essential to the flow of their daily social and economic transactions.[18] The disadvantage they faced towards men in executing these transactions was purdah, or female seclusion, practised by almost all females among higher social strata from the Bū Saʿīdī reign onwards.

After the abolition of slavery in 1897, *kadhi*'s courts were open to all African and Arab Muslim subjects of the sultan. I demonstrate that these courts became fora where freed slaves and their descendants could negotiate socioeconomic participation and, following Jonathon Glassman, could "struggle for citizenship."[19] As the *kadhi*s' task was to preserve social order, they continued to impose restrictive social criteria that equalled varying levels of moral integrity.[20] Although

Ottoman Shariʿa Court Records as a Source for Middle Eastern Social History: A Reappraisal," *Islamic Law and Society* 5, no. 1 (1998): 35–56; Wael Hallaq, "The *qāḍī's diwan* (*sijill*) before the Ottomans," *Bulletin of the School of Oriental and African Studies* 61, no. 3 (1998): 415–36; Beshara Doumani, *Rediscovering Palestine: Merchants and Peasants in Jabal Nablus, 1700–1900* (Berkeley: University of California Press, 1995); Iris Agmon, "Women, Class, and Gender: Muslim Jaffa and Haifa at the Turn of the Twentieth Century," *International Journal of Middle East Studies* 30, no. 4 (1998): 477–500; Leslie Peirce, "'She Is Trouble…and I Will Divorce Her': Orality, Honor, and Representation in the Ottoman Court of ʿAintab," in *Women in the Medieval Islamic World: Power, Patronage, and Piety*, ed. Gavin R. G. Hambly (New York: St. Martin's Press, 1999), 269–300; Judith E. Tucker, *Women in Nineteenth-Century Egypt* (Cambridge: Cambridge University Press, 1985).

17 Cf. Hallaq, *Shariʿa*, 171–73, 187; Judith E. Tucker, *Women, Family, and Gender in Islamic Law* (Cambridge: Cambridge University Press, 2008).

18 Hallaq, *Shariʿa*, 187; Tucker, *Women, Family, and Gender*, 32–33.

19 Jonathon Glassman, *Feasts and Riot: Revelry, Rebellion, and Popular Consciousness on the Swahili Coast, 1856–1888* (Portsmouth, NH: Heinemann, 1995), 23–25.

20 Cf. Hallaq, *Shariʿa*, 167.

former slaves, women from all socioeconomic backgrounds, and the poor used the courts to acquire social legitimacy and participation, litigants were affected by the *kadhi*'s application of Islamic and local norms in establishing social status, in cases, for instance, concerning the appropriate amount of maintenance. Among the criteria determining social status were litigants' descent and free or slave status. Non-Muslims usually addressed the British courts, albeit occasionally they were heard at the *kadhi*'s courts. Both genders thereby consciously defined themselves as Muslim and sought recognition as agents of Zanzibari society. However, with increases in conversion to Islam, the local elite, of which *kadhi*s formed part, started to use ethnicity as distinguishing marker to protect their elitist status in the twentieth century.

Sources and Methodology

This study is the first to be mainly based on the Arabic-language *kadhi*'s court records at the Zanzibar National Archives. They constitute an incomplete set of records whose availability we owe to archivists' decisions and environmental factors. The archives attribute a referential category to a certain court, but this classification is more ambiguous in practice.[21] Ignorant of the number of sources available and their exact nature, I was interested in tracing broader changes and continuities during the colonial period rather than in accounting for detailed fluctuations within a narrower chronological framework. Since criminal cases were no longer adjudicated by *kadhi*s after 1908, I focussed on a random sample of civil cases, which, judging from the nature of

[21] Civil cases heard by *kadhi*s are classified as follows: HC8 (High Court, His Highness the Sultan's Courts) should refer to cases heard at the Court for Zanzibar and Pemba, either originally or on appeal, in which case two *kadhi*s, an Ibāḍī and a Shafiʿi, issued joint verdicts with a judge. HC5 (Civil Appeal Cases) should comprise cases originating from a *kadhi*'s court heard on appeal by a judge. It occurs that the original file has been archived with the appeal file in HC5 but may also have been lost or may still be found as an original *kadhi*'s court case in HC9 (His Highness the Sultan's District Courts – Civil Cases) or HC10 (His Highness the Sultan's Court, *Kadhi*'s Court). HC9 and HC10 contain cases in which *kadhi*'s courts functioned as district courts. Moreover, the numbering of the index has slightly changed. Records may have moved up or down one number, for instance, HC9/82 in 2004 was listed as HC9/81 in 2008.

TABLE 0.1. *Civil Cases Heard in the Sultan's Courts in Zanzibar Town Prior to the Zanzibar Courts Decree, 1923*

Year	Court for Zanzibar and Pemba (Civil Cases, Original and Appellate)	*Kadhi's* Courts	Civil Cases in Zanzibar Town in Total
1911	48	924	not indicated
1912	57	1,372	not indicated
1913	51	733	not indicated
1914	74	612	not indicated
1915	81	674	3,023
1916	76	733	3,025
1917	65	700	2,581
1918	55	503	2,446
1919	65	676	2,842
1920	82	566	2,961
1921	75	711	3,340
1922	59	514	3,486
1923	57	741	3,464
Average	65	728	3,019

Source: Zanzibar Protectorate Administrative Reports, 1915–1923 (Zanzibar: Government Printer, 1916–1924). Data prior to 1911 do not seem to be accessible.

the claim, would potentially yield insights into relationships between spouses, among kin, as well as between former masters and slaves.

Kadhi's courts operated alongside other subordinate courts, but in Zanzibar Town civil jurisdiction over the sultan's subjects up to a certain value under dispute was vested only in *kadhi*s.[22] The appendix lists a table of the cases studied by *kadhi* and year. Tables 0.1 and 0.2 provide the numbers of cases filed at the *kadhi*'s courts in Zanzibar Town per year in relation to the overall number of civil cases in town. Given these statistics, it becomes clear that the number of cases considered in this study represents a tiny fraction of the cases heard by *kadhi*s from 1900 to 1963. Due to the rich yet fragmentary evidence the court records offer, a caveat is in order. My sample serves to highlight the exemplary nature of grievances and allows me to situate

[22] In town, a *mudir*'s court, as existent in the island's *mudiria*s since the 1930s, was only provided for as late as 1957. *Annual Report of the Provincial Administration, 1957* (Zanzibar: Government Printer, 1958), 6.

TABLE 0.2. *Civil Cases Heard in the Subordinate Courts in Zanzibar Town after the Zanzibar Courts Decree, 1923*

Year	*Kadhi*'s Courts	Other Subordinate Courts	Civil Cases in Zanzibar Town in Total
1924	988	2,984	3,972
1925	778	3,781	4,559
1926	661	4,385	5,046
1927	759	4,496	5,255
1928	848	3,892	4,740
1929	656	3,006	3,662
1930	851	3,196	4,047
1931	504	3,554	4,058
1932	260	2,278	2,538
1933	174	2,442	2,616
1934	184	2,181	2,365
1935	243	6,696	6,939
1936	215	2,453	2,668
1937	342	3,986	4,328
1938	228	2,153	2,381
Average	513	3,432	3,945

Source: Zanzibar Protectorate Administrative Reports, 1924–1931 (Zanzibar: Government Printer, 1925–1932) and the *Annual Report on the Social and Economic Progress of the People of the Zanzibar Protectorate, 1932–1938* (London: His Majesty's Stationery Office, 1933–1939). Data on the remaining years covered in this study do not seem to be available.

them in the background from which they arose. My interpretations follow themes along lines of continuity and change rather than simply chronological, while a more extensive sample of cases, more evenly spread over time, might suggest more fluctuations within a chronological framework. During the period studied, the most significant processes were the creation of colonial legal categories bringing Christians and Indian Muslims under British jurisdiction, the bureaucratisation of the judiciary, the reduction of the *kadhi*s' scope of jurisdiction, and the abolition of slavery in 1897.

In addition to court records, a random sample of marriage and divorce certificates, which are available from 1922 and 1925, respectively, has enabled me to outline marriage and divorce patterns. For pragmatic reasons, I have decided to collect the sample in five-year gaps, with a random choice of a few entries each month to arrive at a total of 100 per year up to 1960. Although the marriage registers yield intriguing evidence on guardianship and stipulations, they, together with the divorce registers, constitute a quantitative rather than qualitative data set. The marriage registers contain the names of the spouses, the two witnesses, the wife's guardian in marriage, and the registrar. They also indicate whether the wife was a minor or major and the amount of prompt and deferred dower. The dower is the husband's gift to the wife and legally her property. The divorce registers state the names of the husband, the wife, the two witnesses, and the registrar, the type of divorce, and, if applicable, the amount of the *khul*ʿ, or divorce for a consideration. Both certificates are dated and, unlike the *kadhi*'s court records, they do not give any background to how marriage and divorce arrangements were achieved.

Interpretation and Argumentation

Since the late 1970s scholars from various disciplines have acknowledged the centrality of legal discourses in shaping both the colonial social order and social relationships in sub-Saharan Africa.[23] Yet few scholars have studied African societies through the lens of Islamic law due to an ongoing disciplinary divide between Africanists and Islamicists.[24] Drawing on the rich body of scholarship from both

[23] Scholars who have discussed the use of court records to better understand African, and more precisely colonial, history include Martin Chanock, *Law, Custom and Social Order: The Colonial Experience in Malawi and Zambia* (Cambridge: Cambridge University Press, 1985); John Comaroff and Simon Roberts, *Rules and Processes: The Cultural Logic of Dispute in an African Context* (Chicago: University of Chicago Press, 1981); Margaret Jean Hay and Marcia Wright, eds., *African Women and the Law: Historical Perspectives* (Boston: Boston University, 1982); Sally Falk Moore, *Social Facts and Fabrications: 'Customary' Law on Kilimanjaro, 1880–1980* (Cambridge: Cambridge University Press, 1986); Kristin Mann and Richard Roberts, eds., *Law in Colonial Africa* (Portsmouth, NH: Heinemann, 1991); Richard Roberts, *Litigants and Households: African Disputes and Colonial Courts in the French Soudan, 1895–1912* (Portsmouth, NH: Heinemann, 2005); Simon Roberts, *Law and the Family*; Carol Dickerman, "The Use of Court Records as Sources for African History: Some Examples from Bujumbura, Burundi," *History in Africa* 11 (1984): 69–81.

[24] Notable exceptions are Allan Christelow, ed., *Thus Ruled Emir Abbas: Selected Cases from the Records of the Emir of Kano's Judicial Council* (East Lansing: Michigan State University Press, 1994); idem, "Islamic Law and Judicial Practice

disciplines, I use the *kadhi*'s courts as a valuable and novel prism to reassess and nuance our understanding of the roles of *kadhi*s, gender, and former slaves as well as colonisers' approaches to the judiciary.

The patriarchal Muslim society often serves as an unqualified backdrop against which female agency is set. Since Muslim women are represented through and judged by men, some scholars of Islamic law have argued for the marginalisation of women by making the male experience the norm.[25] However, this conception tells us little about historical gender relations in everyday life. As legal discourse is characterised by a dialectic between theory and practice,[26] it can be used to deconstruct the all-permeating patriarchy. Rather than seeing gender as a strict dichotomy, we should understand gender structures as interacting with the law, which also protects the weak – defined through gender and social status.

The misogynous environment, in which patriarchs such as slave owners, judges, and *kadhi*s curtailed women's roles, allows the historian Laura Fair to highlight Zanzibari women's social and economic agency. In addition, Margaret Strobel's pioneering work on Muslim women in colonial Mombasa consistently perceives women as a subculture to the male dominant culture.[27] While social norms, such as purdah and veiling, hampered the unrestricted social and economic agency of women from upper social strata particularly and made them rely on a male representative, *kadhi*'s court records demonstrate that the supposedly dominant patriarchal ideology did not thoroughly inhibit women's engagement in economic transactions and pursuance of their legal rights as wives and kin in these courts. Women's legal and

in Nigeria: An Historical Perspective," *Journal of Muslim Minority Affairs* 22, no. 1 (2002): 185; Lydon, *Trans-Saharan Trails*; Bruce S. Hall, *A History of Race in Muslim West Africa, 1600–1960* (Cambridge: Cambridge University Press, 2011); Alessandra Vianello and Mohamed M. Kassim, eds., *Servants of the Sharia: The Civil Register of the Qadis' Court of Brava, 1893–1900*, 2 vols (Leiden: Brill, 2006).

25 Tucker, *Women, Family, and Gender*, 28–29.

26 This debate is invoked in most studies of Islamic law. See, for instance, N. J. Coulson, *Conflicts and Tensions in Islamic Jurisprudence* (1969; repr., Kuala Lumpur: The Other Press, 2006); Gerber, *State, Society, and Law*; R. Gleave and E. Kermeli, eds., *Islamic Law: Theory and Practice* (London: I. B. Tauris, 1997).

27 Laura Fair, *Pastimes and Politics: Culture, Community, and Identity in Post-Abolition Urban Zanzibar, 1890–1945* (Athens: Ohio University Press, 2001); Margaret Strobel, *Muslim Women in Mombasa, 1890–1975* (New Haven: Yale University Press, 1979).

economic agency was embedded in Swahili culture and, most importantly, accepted by, in Fair's and Strobel's terms, the dominant male culture. Although women, as well as former slaves and the poor, categories that inevitably overlapped, negotiated their roles, struggling against dominant ideologies that placed women below men, (former) slaves below freeborn, and those without acknowledged ancestry below those with esteemed genealogies, they acted from within a sociolegal context and could successfully draw on legal doctrines to pursue their claims. Contrary to the opinions of Zanzibaris themselves, in the first half of the twentieth century it was not only acceptable but also common to address the court with one's grievances after dispute resolution had failed firstly within families and kin and secondly with elders of the borough or village.[28]

This study demonstrates that the *kadhi*s were advancing women's rights at least from the turn of the twentieth century. Yet what appears as early evidence of female empowerment to the present-day reader was a long-established Islamic right and practice on the Swahili coast. Women across all social strata addressed the *kadhi*'s courts seeking to dissolve their marriage, to claim debts, and to protect their property, with their success in court being contingent on producing evidence satisfactory for the *kadhi*. In her study on dispute discourse in the Kenyan *kadhi*'s courts, anthropologist Susan Hirsch argues that they have offered women avenues to rework gender relations in the post-colonial era, as they shifted away from being patriarchal legal institutions. She accounts for women's success as litigants with *kadhi*s' recent role as upholders of women's claims.[29] Similarly, drawing on

[28] Interviews with Bi Hadiya Rashidi Ali, 13 June 2004; Bi Mwanaidi Makame Ameir, 3 April 2004; Bi Hadija Nasoro Ibrahim, 24 April 2004; Juma Bakari Mfaume, 28 May 2004; Sh. Abdalla Suleiman Jumbe, 24 March 2004.

[29] Susan F. Hirsch, *Pronouncing and Persevering: Gender and the Discourses of Disputing in an African Islamic Court* (Chicago: University of Chicago Press, 1998); see also her "Kadhi's Courts as Complex Sites of Resistance: The State, Islam, and Gender in Postcolonial Kenya," in *Contested States: Law, Hegemony and Resistance*, ed. Mindie Lazarus-Black and Susan F. Hirsch (New York: Routledge, 1994), 207–30. Similar arguments have been provided for Zanzibar by Irmi Hanak, *Gericht-Sprache-Macht: Überlegungen zur Realisierung von Dominanzverhältnissen in und durch sprachliche Kommunikation am Beispiel des Familiengerichts in Zanzibar* (Vienna: Afro-Pub, 1994). For Kenya, see also Beverly B. Brown, "Islamic Law, Qadhis' Courts and Muslim Women's Legal Status: The Case of Kenya," *Journal of Muslim Minority Affairs* 14, no. 1/2 (1994): 94–101.

her ethnographical research at the rural *kadhi*'s court in Mkokotoni, Zanzibar, Erin Stiles has highlighted women's achievement of divorce in the present day, even though they may have to materially compensate their husbands.[30] Once we historicise notions of gender and power, we observe that women in colonial Zanzibar Town actively participated in the legal discourse.

While scholars are often tempted to interpret female participation as subversion, the intention of many women was not necessarily to resist and dominate but to experience and engage through performance, which became increasingly mediated through the *wakīl*. They did not rebel against social norms, such as purdah and arranged marriage, but reshaped their meaning on their own terms.[31] Men rarely questioned women's legal capacity, entrenched in Islamic doctrines, but curtailed it by constructing social norms, such as purdah, whose observation enhanced female respectability. I demonstrate how some women consciously used purdah to preserve their respectability and at the same time engaged in and controlled economic transactions, indicating that they carefully navigated between Islamic doctrines and social norms in pursuing and defending their social and economic mobility.

Following Martin Chanock's lead, research on colonial courts in Africa has stressed the interplay between existing laws, styled as customary law under colonial rule, and colonial laws, arguing that the interaction between elders and colonial officers disadvantaged women, young men, and other marginalised groups.[32] In the Zanzibari context,

30 Erin E. Stiles, *An Islamic Court in Context: An Ethnographic Study of Judicial Reasoning* (New York: Palgrave Macmillan, 2009); idem, "Buying a Divorce in Zanzibar," *ISIM Newsletter* 10 (2002): 33; idem, "When Is a Divorce a Divorce? Determining Intention in Zanzibar's Islamic Courts," *Ethnology* 42, no. 4 (2003): 273–88.

31 Tucker, *Women, Family, and Gender*, 34; Brett L. Shadle, "Bridewealth and Female Consent: Marriage Disputes in African Courts, Gusiiland, Kenya," *Journal of African History* 44, no. 2 (2003): 241–62; Saba Mahmood, *Politics of Piety: The Islamic Revival and the Feminist Subject* (Princeton: Princeton University Press, 2005), 9.

32 Chanock, *Law, Custom, and Social Order*; Margaret Jean Hay, "Women as Owners, Occupants, and Managers of Property in Colonial Western Kenya," in *African Women and the Law: Historical Perspectives*, ed. Margaret Jean Hay and Marcia Wright (Boston: Boston University, 1982), 110–23; Elizabeth Schmidt, "Negotiated Spaces and Contested Terrain: Men, Women and the Law in Colonial Zimbabwe, 1890–1939," *Journal of Southern African Studies* 16, no. 4 (1990): 622–48; idem, "Patriarchy, Capitalism, and the Colonial State in Zimbabwe," *Signs* 16, no. 4 (1991): 732–56.

Laura Fair contends that women, especially poor women, rarely found justice in Zanzibar's colonial courts, with judges preponderantly blaming women for their immoral behaviour.[33] It is now well established that courts in Africa witnessed a surge in popularity during the colonial era. Yet no single group controlled the workings of these colonial courts. Rather, all actors shaped their use.[34] My account of women across the social hierarchy as successful plaintiffs in the *kadhi*'s courts ties in with recent studies, such as those by Richard Roberts and Brett Shadle, who have offered different and more nuanced interpretations of patriarchs collaborating at the expense of marginalised groups. Roberts suggests that women initially flocked to the newly created native courts in the French Sudan as colonial administrators ruled in favour of African women, while Shadle has demonstrated that elders in Gusiiland, Kenya, took women's interests into serious consideration and customary law remained flexible during the colonial period.[35]

A main contribution of this book is to trace the dimensions of female agency and, in particular, to highlight women's economic agency. Unlike in the realm of marriage, in managing material assets Islamic law does not favour a gender.[36] The concept of individual property ownership is intrinsic to Islamic law and provides the basis for economic transactions between spouses and among kin across all social strata. Regardless of their socioeconomic background, some women acted as guarantors for their husbands and also bought from and loaned to their husbands, rather than the other way around, which suggests that these women had a greater economic capacity than their husbands. Seeking to maintain independence from Indian moneylenders,

[33] Fair, *Pastimes and Politics*, 195–209.

[34] Roger Gocking, "British Justice and the Native Tribunals of the Southern Gold Coast Colony," *Journal of African History* 34, no. 1 (1993): 93–113.

[35] Richard Roberts, *Litigants and Households*; idem, "Representation, Structure, and Agency: Divorce in the French Soudan during the Early Twentieth Century," *Journal of African History* 40, no. 3 (1999): 389–410; Brett L. Shadle, *"Girl Cases": Marriage and Colonialism in Gusiiland, Kenya, 1890–1970* (Portsmouth, NH: Heinemann, 2006); idem, "'Changing Traditions to Meet Current Altering Conditions': Customary Law, African Courts and the Rejection of Codification in Kenya, 1930–60," *Journal of African History* 40, no. 3 (1999): 411–31; idem, "Bridewealth and Female Consent," 241–62. See also Carol Dickerman, "African Courts under the Colonial Regime: Usumbura, Ruanda-Urundi, 1938–1962," *Canadian Journal of African Studies* 26, no. 1 (1992): 55–69.

[36] Tucker, *Women, Family, and Gender*, 26.

particularly women from higher social strata borrowed money from kin rather than professional moneylenders. This implies that social status rather than gender was important in shaping Zanzibari women's choices.

The importance of property as a relationship between individuals is manifest in a Muslim marriage with the transfer of dower from husband to wife. The composition and management of marital funds moulded not only the interaction between spouses but also among kin.[37] Since Islamic law attributes the sole role of provider to the husband, at least theoretically, marriage was a way for women to be maintained. Throughout the period under study, elders arranged nearly all marriages, which entitled them to be in charge of the wife's dower even though she was a major and thus financially competent. We see that because of the arranged nature of marriage and social acceptance of divorce, spouses regarded marriage as a temporary union.

Spouses' different perceptions of marriage became manifest in the way of ending marriages. As husbands had to provide the dower after consummating the marriage and had to maintain their wives, they perceived marriage as a material investment. Given the social importance of marriage and the increasing importance of money to social relations, husbands, supported by *kadhi*s, sought to make wives pay for their divorce to obtain money for a new dower. Divorce for a consideration was the preponderant type of divorce in colonial Zanzibar Town, indicating that women from all socioeconomic strata were willing to bear the financial expense of ending their marriage.

The *kadhi* occupied a central role in the bargaining procedures. Chapter 5 contends that, in spite of the British encroachment on the legal sector, the *kadhi* essentially maintained his autonomy in the sphere of family law. I seek to demonstrate that he was not predominantly a collaborator with the colonial government[38] but resisted the colonial encroachment in the sphere of family law by using the Arabic

[37] Cf. Jack Goody, *Death, Property and the Ancestors* (Stanford: Stanford University Press, 1962), quoted in David Warren Sabean, "The History of the Family in Africa and Europe: Some Comparative Perspectives," *Journal of African History* 24, no. 2 (1983): 171.

[38] Anne K. Bang, *Sufis and Scholars of the Sea: Family Networks in East Africa, 1860–1925* (London: Routledge Curzon, 2003), Chapter 8; Randall L. Pouwels, *Horn and Crescent: Cultural Change and Traditional Islam on the East African Coast, 800–1900* (Cambridge: Cambridge University Press, 1987), especially 178–81.

language as a buffer. Because of the formalisation of the judiciary, the *kadhi*'s role of mediator, revealed in court cases of the beginning of the twentieth century, shifted towards stressing the power of the court in the later colonial period. This emphasis on the court seemed to be motivated by *kadhi*s' concerns to distance themselves from colonial legal reforms that contravened shariʿa and that they were obliged to implement. The formalisation also entailed that the public and open character of court sessions in the nineteenth century gave way to private sessions held inside a court building. This shift in space may have diminished yet did not extirpate the role of the *kadhi*'s courts in providing redress to those who otherwise failed to achieve social and economic inclusion.

Colonial officers' approach towards socioeconomic categories was as fluid as the taxonomies of "native."[39] The diversity of approaches on the ground opened avenues of manipulation for the colonised. The colonial government introduced court fees[40] but also provided for suing as a poor person and thus for being exempt from such charges from the 1920s onwards. Chapter 2 argues that *kadhi*s and some colonial officers were concerned to include those who were allegedly excluded: women, slaves, and the poor. The perception and terms of inclusion of each of these groups formed an object of negotiation and constant worry between *kadhi*s and British colonial officers, which over the decades opened loopholes for social and economic participation.

In the nineteenth century, the most important criterion of social status was whether a person was freeborn or slave. At the time, social status largely coincided with economic status, although slaves had possibilities to accumulate wealth. In addition to this dichotomy between free and slave, the elite's notion of "civilised" implied coastal origin, as opposed to "uncivilised" and coming from the interior. In this system

39 On the fluidity of the concept of otherness, see Frederick Cooper and Ann Laura Stoler, eds., *Tensions of Empire: Colonial Cultures in a Bourgeois World* (Berkeley: University of California Press, 1997), 7.

40 The fee for filing a plaint was 2 percent of the amount claimed in 1927 (Explanatory Memorandum, Suits by Poor Persons, by T. S. Tomlinson, 9 February 1927, AB62/30, ZNA). On the use of the courts in Malawi by large numbers of people and regardless of relatively high fees, see Chanock, *Law, Custom and Social Order*, 123–24.

of social stratification, descent was an important criterion. *Kadhi*'s court records reveal "social etymologies,"[41] a person's social status, by listing his or her genealogy. This allowed me to trace the production of social categories and their contestation. With mechanisms of exclusion geared to keep slaves apart from their owners, a long chain of genealogy, with ancestors preferably coming from the Middle East and Persia, bestowed high social status. Slaves countered their stigma as outsiders by becoming fictive members of kin of their masters and adopting respectable names upon manumission, while the notions of illegitimacy and kinlessness, which owners had attached to slaves and slaves partly confirmed by seeking social integration, impeded the inclusion of slaves and their descendants for decades after the abolition of slavery in 1897. Immediately after abolition, freed slaves referred to themselves as Swahili,[42] a term derived from *sāḥil*, the Arabic word for "coast", whereas the continuous use of Swahili suggests that it may have offered a less ethnically defined identity in the late colonial period.

Jonathon Glassman, among others, has accounted for slaves' attempts to counter their exclusion by struggling for participation in local social institutions. This primary form of slaves' resistance was articulated via Islam, *ustaarabu*, or civilisation, generosity, and rituals.[43] I argue that in the twentieth century, this struggle of slaves and their descendants was manifest in claims for inheritance, in which patrons and clients contested access to economic resources. These claims show that although the relationship between patrons and clients outlived abolition in the form of mainly economic relations, an underlying tension persisted decades after slaves had become free subjects of the sultan and legally equal to the freeborn. As masters and slaves occupied positions on the opposite ends of the social hierarchy, Frederick

[41] Ann Laura Stoler, *Along the Archival Grain: Epistemic Anxieties and Colonial Common Sense* (Princeton: Princeton University Press, 2009), 35–36.

[42] Cf. Fair, *Pastimes and Politics*; Frederick Cooper, *From Slaves to Squatters: Plantation Labor and Agriculture in Zanzibar and Coastal Kenya, 1890–1925* (New Haven: Yale University Press, 1980), 159.

[43] Jonathon Glassman, "The Bondsman's New Clothes: The Contradictory Consciousness of Slave Resistance on the Swahili Coast," *Journal of African History* 32, no. 2 (1991): 283–84, 294, 298, 311; idem, *Feasts and Riot*, 95, 267. On slave rituals and slaves' reinterpretation of masters' ideologies, see further Frederick Cooper, *Plantation Slavery on the East Coast of Africa* (New Haven: Yale University Press, 1977), 236–40.

Cooper has argued that the underlying irreconcilable tensions between these two groups increased towards the end of the nineteenth century with the emergence of a planter class. These tensions took shape in differences in descent and religion, although many slaves converted to Islam to attempt to decrease the divide between them and their owners. Slave owners kept the outsider status of slaves alive by denying their ancestry and giving them non-Muslim names distinct from their own.[44]

An ethnic consciousness clearly existed among Zanzibaris in the nineteenth century,[45] when Zanzibar's elite was defined by religion, descent, and social ties. The interpretation and adaptation of ethnic identities was manifest in the fact that some women rejected men on grounds of ethnicity, while others argued for their suitability as husbands despite perceiving them as ethnically unequal. Drawing on this precolonial ethnic stratification, I argue that as Zanzibar's Muslim community became more ethnically diverse in the twentieth century, the Arab elite used ethnicity as a criterion for determining a person's degree of Islamisation. Thus the struggle for inclusion and exclusion characterised Zanzibar's social history in the twentieth century as much as in the nineteenth, with the range of contestants and the parameters of contestation having expanded.

Organisation

This book is divided into three parts. Part I traces the institutionalisation of the legal sector and introduces colonial and Islamic ideologies pertaining to gender, race, and class. It accounts for the two main colonially induced changes in the administration of shariʿa, the establishment of legal categories and procedural changes, which entailed a shift from oral to written culture in the *kadhi*'s courts. It investigates the appeal of these courts, particularly among women and former

44 Frederick Cooper, "The Problem of Slavery in African Studies," *Journal of African History* 20, no. 1 (1979): 124; idem, "Islam and Cultural Hegemony: The Ideology of Slaveowners on the East African Coast," in *The Ideology of Slavery in Africa*, ed. P. E. Lovejoy (London: Sage, 1981), 289.

45 Frederick Cooper, *Plantation Slavery*; Jonathon Glassman, "Sorting out the Tribes: The Creation of Racial Identities in Colonial Zanzibar's Newspaper Wars," *Journal of African History* 41, no. 3 (2000): 395–428.

slaves and their descendants, arguing that these groups could benefit from the competing efforts of *kadhi*s and judges to include the allegedly marginalised. Contrary to previous findings, I demonstrate that *kadhi*s preserved their autonomy in the realm of family law despite the colonial encroachment on the legal system.

Part II mainly draws on the *kadhi*'s court records to discuss social and economic relations between spouses and among kin. As marriage was central to defining social status and arranged by elders, I argue that serial marriage represented the socially accepted norm and divorce featured as a socially acceptable tool to compensate spouses for having no influence on the choice of their partners. The central role of money in social relations appeared by the 1940s with inflated dowers and the predominant practice of women paying husbands for their divorce. The selling and buying, loaning and borrowing, between spouses and kin attest to the social acceptance of female economic agency as well as to the preference among upper social strata of negotiating economic transactions within the family.

Part III focusses on the processes of social inclusion and exclusion, arguing that the nineteenth century exclusionary marker of religion was replaced by ethnicity in the twentieth century, when the economically threatened elite sought to differentiate themselves from immigrants and slave descendants. It suggests that despite the persistence of social and economic relations between patrons and clients into the 1950s, fundamental differences in the attitude of former slaves and slave owners towards their social roles channelled violence.

PART I

1

The *Kadhi*'s Courts Colonised

Until the early nineteenth century, customary law and traditional dispute resolution, such as councils of elders, operated in Zanzibar alongside shariʿa, which gradually came to supersede them. This process faced substantial transformations from the 1820s onwards, when, first, the Omani Bū Saʿīdī sultans and then the British subjected the judiciary to empire-building. While the sultans used the courts to fashion their commercial empire, they also embarked on setting up an easily accessible and flexible Islamic court system serving the entire Muslim population. The *kadhi*'s courts, in which Islamic law was administered, represented local social, moral, and legal values and structures and allowed both the *kadhi*s and the litigants to articulate and negotiate them. The workings of the *kadhi*'s courts, where litigants could obtain formal judgements in accordance with shariʿa, were at the centre of the power struggle between the Omani sultans and the British. Justified by the abolition of slavery, the British aimed to establish their hegemony in the western Indian Ocean. The slave trade, for which Zanzibar was an entrepot, and the presence of Westerners, mostly traders and diplomats originally under the sultan's jurisdiction, offered the British an entry point to the Omani legal sphere.

When Zanzibar became a British protectorate in 1890, the British put into place a visibly formal legal system whose main aim was to entrench colonial rule. This chapter argues that in order to preserve the idea of an Arab state and its Islamic legal system, two key principles operated throughout the colonial period until 1963. One was the upholding of Islamic law as the fundamental law of the protectorate and the other non-interference in the substance of Islamic family law. The combined application of both principles took shape in the arbitrary creation of two sets of courts, which were headed by the sultan and the British Crown, respectively. Yet despite these underlying principles, the colonial state embarked on modernising and restructuring the judiciary in a drive towards modern efficiency, thereby curtailing the application of shariʿa. The colonial government targeted the role of the litigants, the scope of jurisdiction, and nature of procedure.

With the Islamisation of the East African coast, a process that started at least in the eighth century, shariʿa gradually came to be applied alongside customary law and practices. Through travellers' records, such as Ibn Battuta's of the early fourteenth century, we know that Islamic courts have existed for many centuries on the Swahili coast.[1] Due to the dearth of sources, however, it is difficult to picture the workings of these legal institutions. Our understanding of the application of shariʿa, pertaining to questions such as who acted as *kadhi*, who litigated, and where and how court sessions were held, remains very fragmentary prior to British colonial rule, and Bū Saʿīdī rule in particular.[2] As Michael Peletz cautions in his study on shariʿa courts in Malaysia, references attesting to the existence of these courts tell us little about the extent of the *kadhi*'s interaction with the local population and ruler or the extent to which shariʿa was applied.[3] When we visualise the *kadhi*s in the precolonial period, we should imagine them working outdoors as well as at their homes rather than in an actual court building, with their main role being that of a mediator; only if all mediation efforts failed, would they issue a judgement. We also have to bear in mind that Islamic courts were part of a legal system in which tribunals applied customary law on a parallel level.[4]

Not surprisingly, there is no precise information available on how these tribunals functioned and interacted with the *kadhi*'s courts.

[1] Ibn Battuta, *Travels in Asia and Africa, 1325–1354*, trans. and selected by H. A. R. Gibb (New York: Augustus M. Kelley Publishers, 1969), 110–13.

[2] John Gray destroys all hope by saying that "[t]here is literally no information regarding the judicial system in Zanzibar before his [sayyid Saʿīd's] arrival." Idem, *History of Zanzibar from the Middle Ages to 1856* (London: Oxford University Press, 1962), 144.

[3] Peletz, *Islamic Modern*, 26, 62.

[4] On the optional role of courts for conflict resolution, see Hallaq, *Shariʿa*, 160–64.

Consequently, statements such as the one by John Gray, Zanzibar's chief justice from 1943 to 1952, that "Muslim law was the fundamental law of the land"[5] cannot be substantiated by evidence but, in his case, are made in analogy to the judicial system in Mombasa in the 1820s, where a *kadhi*, or *kadhi*s, adjudicated civil and criminal law.[6] Randall Pouwels' confident account of the legal traditions along the Swahili coast holds that customary law was dominant and expanded where Islamic law did not adapt sufficiently to local circumstances. Based on Noel Coulson's elaboration of the continuing prevalence of customary law in Islamised regions, Pouwels deduces for Swahili communities a dialectic between written Islamic sources and local practice, suggesting that if a *kadhi* adopted a customary practice, it could become a shariʿa-sanctioned and established practice.[7] This interpretation presumes an opposition between customary norms and shariʿa, on the one hand, and between the oral and the written, on the other. The interaction of customary laws and Islamic laws has been part of the legal pluralism characteristic of Muslim societies, while an alleged dichotomy between orality and scripture obscures the centrality of the former in Islamic legal discourse.[8] Over the centuries customary laws have become embedded in shariʿa, yet its subordination to the colonial judiciary, which represented a non-Muslim and a competing lawgiver, instigated irreversible structural and substantive changes.[9]

Although the Bū Saʿīdī presence on the East African littoral dates back to the seventeenth century, it was not until 1840 that Zanzibar's prime role as an entrepot in the long-distance trade as well as a producer of cloves made it the seat of the Omani Sultanate. The Bū Saʿīdī sultans were Ibāḍīs, whereas the Muslim majority in Zanzibar, as elsewhere on the Swahili coast, were Sunnis following the Shafiʿi school of law. For Zanzibar Town, travellers report the establishment of formal court meetings from the Bū Saʿīdī period onwards. The American traveller and surgeon Ruschenberger reports that prior to Sultan sayyid

[5] Gray, *History of Zanzibar*, 144.

[6] Ibid., 144–45.

[7] Pouwels, *Horn and Crescent*, 68. Noel Coulson is the author of one of the 1960s classic texts on Islamic law by Western scholarship. See his *A History of Islamic Law* (Edinburgh: Edinburgh University Press, 1964). See further Benton, *Law and Colonial Cultures*, 102–14, for an instructive overview of the fusion of Islamic law and customary law in various parts of the Muslim world.

[8] Cf. Lydon, *Trans-Saharan Trails*, 22.

[9] See Hallaq, *Shariʿa*, Chapter 13.

Saʿīd's settling down in Zanzibar around 1835, his son Khālid, the governor, and three *kadhi*s held court sessions after every afternoon prayer at the fort gates.[10] Shaykh ʿAbdallāh Ṣāliḥ al-Farsī, who was a Shafiʿi *kadhi* in Zanzibar from 1960 to 1967, adds that the Sunni and Ibāḍī *kadhi*s were available at the fort for those who did not want to consult them at their homes, where they might give judgement any time they wished.[11] When sayyid Saʿīd came to Zanzibar, he dissolved this open-air court and declared himself the last instance of appeals against judgements proclaimed by the *kadhi*s.[12] Henceforward, *kadhi*s issued judgements at home or at the sultan's palace. There was a meeting place for *kadhi*s next to the sultan's palace, where they would advise on legal matters and issue documents.[13] Sayyid Saʿīd made further attempts towards regulating the legal system when he proclaimed in 1845 that each *kadhi* had to give a verdict in accordance with the doctrine of his own school of law.[14] Being referred to Shafiʿi and Ḥanafī legal treatises, Assistant Attorney-General J. H. Vaughan was informed that this was the practice in the Indian Islamic courts.[15] This regulation is not a colonial invention, however, as the earliest reference to the provision of appointing a *kadhi* from a different school, who then must

[10] William Ruschenberger, Vol. I, 56, cited in C. S. Nicholls, *The Swahili Coast: Politics, Diplomacy and Trade on the East African Littoral, 1798–1856* (London: George Allen & Unwin, 1971), 278. See also Richard F. Burton, *Zanzibar: City, Island, and Coast*, vol. I (London: Tisley Brothers, 1872), 89; Abdallah Salih Farsy, *Seyyid Said bin Sultan* (Zanzibar: Mwongozi Printing Press, [1942]), 34; Gray, *History of Zanzibar*, 131.

[11] Farsy, *Seyyid Said*, 34. Sayyid Saʿīd provided for Shafiʿi *kadhi*s for the benefit of litigants who did not want to be judged by Ibāḍī *kadhi*s. See Eduard Sachau, "Das Gutachten eines Muhammedanischen Juristen über die Muhammedanischen Rechtsverhältnisse in Ostafrika," *Mittheilungen des Seminars für Orientalische Sprachen*, Afrikanische Studien 1, no. 3 (1898): 7–8.

[12] Nicholls, *Swahili Coast*, 278; cf. R. S. O'Fahey, "The Office of 'Qadi' in Dar Fur: A Preliminary Inquiry," *Bulletin of the School of Oriental and African Studies* 40, no. 1 (1977): 118–19.

[13] Katrin Bromber, ed., *The Jurisdiction of the Sultan of Zanzibar and the Subjects of Foreign Nations* (Würzburg: Ergon Verlag, 2001), 35–36.

[14] Gray, *History of Zanzibar*, 147. The proclamation is cited in Nicholls, *Swahili Coast*, 278.

[15] Vaughan, *Dual Jurisdiction*, 40. On the creation and application of the so-called Anglo-Muhammedan law in India, see Hallaq, *Shariʿa*, 371–83; Hooker, *Legal Pluralism*, 95–101; Michael R. Anderson, "Legal Scholarship and the Politics of Islam in British India," in *Perspectives on Islamic Law, Justice, and Society*, ed. Ravindra S. Khare (Lanham: Rowman & Littlefield, 1999), 65–91.

FIGURE 1.1. View of Stone Town, Zanzibar Town. Courtesy of ZNA.

essentially apply the rules of his own school, is eleventh-century Shafiʿi scholar al-Māwardī.[16]

The application of shariʿa was first established in Zanzibar Town, from where it was expanded into rural areas. In 1844 and 1846, British Consul Atkins Hamerton and French explorer and Navy Captain Guillain, respectively, reported that outside towns the enforcement of law and order remained in the hands of the *mwinyi mkuu*, the ruler of the Hadimu who resided at Dunga in the centre of the island.[17] This implies that customary law rather than shariʿa was applied outside Zanzibar Town. The Hadimu were the most numerous indigenous group who ruled the island prior to the establishment of the Omani Sultanate. The appointment of the *sheha*, or the village headman, lay in the hands of the villagers but depended on the final approval of the *mwinyi mkuu*. There was a tendency prior to the *mwinyi mkuu*'s

[16] Abū Ḥasan al-Māwardī, *al-Aḥkām as-Sulṭāniyyah: The Laws of Islamic Governance*, trans. Asadullah Yate (London: Ta-Ha Publishers, 1996), 102.

[17] Gray, *History of Zanzibar*, 147.

interference to appoint someone from a leading family, meaning that this office tended to be hereditary within one family.[18] This practice also held true for the *kadhi*'s office.

Whereas at the beginning of the Bū Saʿīdī rule local chiefs, who comprised elders, esteemed persons, and headmen of local communities, still functioned as the lawgiver, as judges, and as administrators, the reign of Sultan Barghash (r. 1870–1888) witnessed a shift in dispute resolution from councils of elders to institutionalised shariʿa tribunals. During the reigns of sayyids Saʿīd (r. 1806–1856) and Mājid (r. 1856–1870), elders, who were the first resort in dispute resolution, arbitrated in the boroughs of the town and villages. In town, *kadhi*s are reported to have heard claims by free will and mutual agreement.[19] Under Sultan Barghash, *kadhi*s were introduced into the Hadimu areas and Zanzibar was divided into districts, headed by *liwali*s, the sultan's local governors who also wielded judicial powers.[20] Both *liwali*s and *kadhi*s were directly answerable to the sultan. According to historian A. I. Salim, there was no clear distinction of the scope of jurisdiction between *liwali*s and *kadhi*s in the same town, save that *liwali*s seem to have been assigned more criminal cases than *kadhi*s.[21] With the growing influence of Omani power in local affairs, *liwali*s achieved a more decisive say in the *kadhi*s' appointment, tying *kadhi*s more firmly into the sultan's service.[22] Geographer Garth Myers gives a similar account for Ng'ambo, "the other side" of Zanzibar Town, where Sultan Barghash enhanced the role of the *liwali* in the appointment of *kadhi*s.[23]

The reign of Sultan Barghash was characterised by his cosmopolitan outlook and modernisation, on the one hand, and his autocratisation of the legal sector as well as his support of an Ibāḍī revivalist movement,

[18] Ibid. 165–66; see also Strobel, *Muslim Women*, 29.

[19] Pouwels, *Horn and Crescent*, 134.

[20] John Middleton and Jane Campbell, *Zanzibar: Its Society and Its Politics* (London: Oxford University Press, 1965), 5, 28; J. Spencer Trimingham, *Islam in East Africa* (Oxford: Clarendon Press, 1964), 23.

[21] A. I. Salim, *The Swahili-Speaking Peoples of Kenya's Coast, 1895–1965* (Nairobi: East African Publishing House, 1973), 77, 79.

[22] Pouwels, *Horn and Crescent*, 122.

[23] Garth Andrew Myers, "Reconstructing Ng'ambo: Town Planning and Development on the Other Side of Zanzibar" (PhD diss., UCLA, 1993), 138.

on the other.[24] Under the influence of this reform movement, the sultan embarked on reforming or "purifying" the judicial system whose reputation had suffered from increasing corruption under his predecessor Mājid. His reforms, which entailed the appointment of new *kadhi*s who strictly applied Ibāḍī law and his annulment of verdicts passed under Mājid's reign, were a response to the conversion of Ibāḍī ʿulamaʾ, or scholars, to Shafiʿism.[25] Striving towards a major institutionalisation of the legal apparatus, Barghash increased the salary and status of *kadhi*s.[26] Additionally, he attempted to counter the influence of various Omani groups by fostering his ties to the *kadhi*s and the administrators.[27] While, as elsewhere in the Islamic world, the desire to institutionalise Ibāḍī Islam within a state-judicial apparatus certainly motivated Barghash's efforts, the sultans' increasing grip on the legal sector should also be seen in light of power struggles in Oman and the gradual encroachment of the British in the region. The sultans' growing dependence on the British played a decisive role in their negotiations as these were geared towards maintaining their position within the imperial political economy.

In an important step for Zanzibar's judiciary, and possibly in response to British intentions to infringe on it, the sultans took supreme charge. Sultans served as an institution of appeal for all cases, including those before elders and *liwali*s, and dealt with the most severe cases by personal deliberation. Sultans Saʿīd, Mājid, and, especially, Barghash often rendered judgements themselves. Sultan Barghash spent about

[24] Pouwels, *Horn and Crescent*, 118–19, 122–23, 151, 205–206; Bang, *Sufis and Scholars*, 117–20. Barghash's cosmopolitanism has been accounted for by Jeremy Prestholdt, *Domesticating the World: African Consumerism and the Genealogies of Globalization* (Berkeley: University of California Press, 2008), and by Philip Sadgrove, "From Wādī Mīzāb to Unguja: Zanzibar's Scholarly Links," in *The Transmission of Learning in Islamic Africa*, ed. Scott S. Reese (Leiden: Brill, 2004), 184–211.

[25] Abdul Sheriff, *Slaves, Spices and Ivory in Zanzibar: Integration of an East African Commercial Empire into the World Economy, 1770–1873* (London: James Currey, 1987), 220; Pouwels, *Horn and Crescent*, 116–20.

[26] John C. Wilkinson, *The Imamate Tradition of Oman* (Cambridge: Cambridge University Press, 1987), 239. An English merchant was informed in 1837 that the sultan paid *kadhi*s $15 per month. James Kirkman, ed., "The Zanzibar Diary of John Studdy Leigh, Part I," *International Journal of African Historical Studies* 13, no. 2 (1980): 309–10.

[27] Pouwels, *Horn and Crescent*, 136.

two hours on legal issues every day, passing verdicts and discussing cases with his *kadhis*.[28] Pearce, who became British Resident of Zanzibar in 1914, reports that the sultan sometimes personally listened to the convicted party and as a result released him or her.[29] Based on official records, Pearce notes that sayyid Saʿīd was very reluctant to pass death sentences. In order to avoid causing the death of one of his subjects, the sultan reportedly paid blood money from his own purse to compensate the relatives of the person murdered. The increasing monetarisation of criminal punishment marginalised the application of *ḥadd* punishment during the last years of Sultan Saʿīd's reign.[30] To Pearce's obvious relief, "the mutilation of criminals by cutting off their hands for theft, which was only too frequent an occurrence in the Eastern code of justice, administered under autocratic auspices"[31] was not applied in Zanzibar. This description of how the sultan dealt with criminals shows both the colonial bias against Islamic law and the colonial obsession with the presumed ubiquity of draconian sentences applied by despotic rulers. It was the sensational that caught the colonisers' eye and gave them a pretext for interfering.[32]

British influence on the Bū Saʿīd dates from the end of the eighteenth century, when the Omani state became a serious competitor to the British in India and to British economic interests in the western Indian Ocean. The treaty of 1822, in which the sultan agreed to the appointment of a British agent and his exercise of jurisdiction over English subjects involved in the slave trade, laid the basis for British

[28] Gray, *History of Zanzibar*, 145; Pouwels, *Horn and Crescent*, 135. For Barghash, see Major F. B. Pearce, *Zanzibar: The Island Metropolis of Eastern Africa* (London: T. Fisher Unwin, 1920), 267; and Saʿīd b. ʿAlī al-Mughayrī, *Juhaynat al-akhbār fī tārīkh zinjibār*, 2nd ed. (Muscat, Oman: Ministry of Heritage and Culture, 1986), 327–31, where he provides a meticulous account of Barghash's daily routine.

[29] Pearce, *Zanzibar*, 268.

[30] Kirkman, "Zanzibar Diary Part I," 310; Prestholdt, *Domesticating the World*, 36; Pearce, *Zanzibar*, 115. A similar tendency was noted by an administrator of the Maradi region in Niger in 1913. See Barbara M. Cooper, "Reflections on Slavery, Seclusion and Female Labor in the Maradi Region of Niger in the Nineteenth and Twentieth Centuries," *Journal of African History* 35, no. 1 (1994): 72. The *ḥadd* punishment is only applicable in certain criminal cases and, depending on the crime, provides for the cutting off of limbs, lashing, or stoning. It is questionable to what extent *ḥadd* was historically applied.

[31] Pearce, *Zanzibar*, 115.

[32] Cf. Peletz, *Islamic Modern*, 29.

jurisdiction in Zanzibar.[33] The treaty of 1833, in which the sultan granted American citizens the right to be adjudicated by their own consul, enabled the establishment of consular jurisdiction, in effect sanctioning the interference of foreign powers with the sultan's jurisdiction. The sultan thereby renounced his jurisdiction in cases where his subjects brought suits against subjects of Christian nations, as Western observers detected a bias on the part of *kadhi*s against foreigners in passing judgement on them.[34] This motivated Western powers to establish jurisdiction over their own subjects.

In the second half of the nineteenth century, British encroachment on the legal sector was increasingly justified as an anti-slavery initiative. The treaty of 1873, abolishing the trade in and transportation of slaves, represented another important step in tying the sultan's power to British support. The Slave Trade Prohibition Decree of 1890 provided for the right of slaves to buy their freedom, stipulating that if a slave owner had no heirs, his or her slaves became free. The same decree also provided for the confiscation of slaves in case of mistreatment. The last article of this decree gives the most important clue to the sociolegal disadvantage slaves previously had: they were now entitled to bring claims before *kadhi*s like a *mwungwana*, or a free person.[35]

After the shift from traditional dispute resolution to a centralised, shariʿa-informed mode of settling disputes under the Bū Saʿīd, the British introduced a second wave of modernisation from 1890 onwards. Similarly to other British colonies, changes in the Zanzibari legal system were initiated by the introduction of a parallel system of British courts set up after the sultan had already ceded part of his jurisdiction over certain subjects. Applying the policy of indirect rule, the colonial government aimed at maintaining an amended version of the original judicial institutions rather than radically replacing them. Interference in the local legal system occurred where it contradicted or impeded the aims of the colonial administration as well as "civilised" ideas of

33 Vaughan, *Dual Jurisdiction*, 11.

34 Ibid., 11–12; Gray, *History of Zanzibar*, 201. See further Jagdish S. Gundara, "British Extraterritorial Jurisdiction in Nineteenth Century Zanzibar," *Africa Quarterly* 23, no. 3/4 (1983): 10–27. For a Swahili account of the sultan's scope of jurisdiction, see Bromber, *Jurisdiction of the Sultan*.

35 Decree 15 Dhū l-Ḥijja 1307, BA12/11, ZNA.

FIGURE 1.2. *Liwali*s and *kadhi*s of the sultan's dominions on the announcement of the abolition of slavery, 1907. Courtesy of ZNA.

justice and humanity.[36] The result of this interference was the creation of a new, colonially invented legal substance that only partially reflected customary, Islamic, and common law in their essence. The colonial government gave preference to the law that was used by the ruling class, thus Islamic law, which was consequently adopted as the "fundamental law."[37] This principle was supported by a colonial perception of the virtual absence of customary law, accounted for with the fact that all the "natives" of Zanzibar were Muslim, with a few

[36] See Antony N. Allott, "The Future of African Law," in *African Law: Adaptation and Development*, ed. Hilda Kuper and Leo Kuper (Berkeley: University of California Press, 1965), 220.

[37] See Hamidin Abd Hamid, "Unfinished Business: The Implementation of the Land Titles Ordinance in Coastal Kenya, 1908–1940" (PhD diss., SOAS, University of London, 2000), 5; see also Bang, *Sufis and Scholars*, 129, on the British preference for and equation of Islam with religious institutions.

negligible converts to Christianity.[38] In his study of the judiciary in the Sudan, Abdullahi Ali Ibrahim has argued that the British "relegated Islam to a 'customary law'" in order to construe *kadhis*' sphere of jurisdiction, or civil cases in modern language, as archaic and incompatible with modernity.[39] Also in the Zanzibar Protectorate, British colonial officers regarded Islamic law as customary law, in the sense of the law of the land. Although they saw Islamic law as mostly incompatible with a modern, impartial judiciary, they nevertheless preferred it to unwritten and more archaic Swahili customary laws.[40]

The arbitrary and contradictory lines that the colonial government drew between the two sets of courts, one headed by the sultan and the other by the British Crown, are reflected in the religious and ethnic categories into which Zanzibaris were divided as well as in the different applications of Islamic principles in these courts. Following colonial legal structures in India, the British applied the Indian Penal Code in 1882, and "[f]or certain purposes of the administration of criminal justice Zanzibar was to be deemed a District of the Bombay Presidency".[41] They further drew up legal categories on religious, ethnic, and class-based criteria in order to secure political domination and adjust the economy (resources and labour) as well as power structures to colonial needs.

After the sultan had ceded his right of jurisdiction over Christians as well as Asian Muslims (mainly followers of the Shiʿa and the Ḥanafī school) from as early as 1822, these economically important groups almost exclusively fell under the jurisdiction of the British courts.[42] After the sultan's proclamation in 1845, which ruled that *kadhis* had to follow their own school in issuing a judgement, the sultan's courts only applied Shafiʿi and Ibāḍī rules. This narrowed the variety of legal

38 Report on the Native Administration, [1933], CO 618/55/19, National Archives Kew (hereafter NAK).

39 Abdullahi Ali Ibrahim, *Manichaean Delirium: Decolonizing the Judiciary and Islamic Renewal in the Sudan, 1898–1985* (Leiden: Brill, 2008), 98.

40 See Elke E. Stockreiter, "'British *kadhis*' and 'Muslim judges': Modernisation, Inconsistencies and Accommodation in Zanzibar's Colonial Judiciary," *Journal of Eastern African Studies* 4, no. 3 (2010): 561–65.

41 Vaughan, *Dual Jurisdiction*, 22.

42 J. N. D. Anderson, *Islamic Law in Africa* (1955; repr. with a new preface, London: Frank Cass, 1970), 68.

opinions to those of the two schools to which the *kadhi*s in these courts belonged. Yet we do not know whether and to what extent *kadhi*s previously applied doctrines and opinions from other schools of law. Theoretically, Zanzibaris had a choice when taking their cases to the court of either a Shafiʿi or an Ibāḍī *kadhi*. This choice, however, appears to have been one which the parties could rarely make use of in practice, as, by 1935, only one district was equipped with both *kadhi*s. Unlike *kadhi*s, the judges and magistrates who applied Islamic law in the British courts to British subjects were not confined to the principle of any particular school of Islam, but rather they had to apply the principles of the school to which the litigant belonged. In the case of litigating parties adhering to different schools, the judge applied the rules that he deemed more suitable in accordance with common-law principles of fairness and equity.[43]

In 1890, when Zanzibar became a British protectorate, Islamic law was unrestrictedly applied by Sunni and Ibāḍī *kadhi*s to the sultan's subjects, except in those cases in which the sultan had given up his rights of jurisdiction. One year later, the sultan accepted that consular jurisdiction, originally granted in 1833 and confirmed by a treaty in 1886, might be exercised by other than consular officers. He made further concessions by delegating his jurisdiction in all cases in which British subjects were plaintiffs and the sultan's subjects defendants. Formally, this delegated jurisdiction remained the sultan's jurisdiction; in fact, however, it was exercised by British officers in a court established for this purpose named His Highness Court of Delegated Jurisdiction.[44] The British courts were prepared to administer English, Anglo-Indian, Hindu, and Parsi law as well as Islamic law in the Court of Delegated Jurisdiction,[45] which existed until 1908, when it was absorbed into His Britannic Majesty's Court.

In 1897 and 1899, the British took crucial steps towards the colonial adaptation of the legal sector. The East Africa Order in Council of 1897 ended the period of consular jurisdiction by establishing Her Britannic Majesty's Court, which exercised jurisdiction in cases in which the

43 Vaughan, *Dual Jurisdiction*, 41–42, 64–65.

44 Ibid., 14, 23.

45 Robert Nunez Lyne, *Zanzibar in Contemporary Times: A Short History of the Southern East in the Nineteenth Century* (London: Hurst & Blackett, 1905), 195.

FIGURE 1.3. British court. Courtesy of ZNA.

sultan's subjects were plaintiffs or complainants.[46] In the same year, a decree from Sultan Ḥamūd b. Muḥammad (r. 1896–1902) divided the island of Zanzibar into three districts, Mkokotoni, Mwera, and Chwaka, each headed by a *liwali*, who constituted a district court. The jurisdiction of Zanzibar Town, including Ng'ambo, was cut out from the one of the *liwali* of Mwera and given to the First Minister Lloyd Mathews.[47] The following year, the sultan assigned *kadhi*s to these district courts to hear civil cases to the amount of Rs. 100.[48]

The other decree that initiated fundamental changes to the legal system was the Native Courts Decree of 1899. It was driven by Consul General Arthur Hardinge and provided for a complete reorganisation of the sultan's courts.[49] Given the colonial concern with uniformity,

[46] H. E. Kingdon, *The Conflict of Laws in Zanzibar* (Zanzibar: Government Printer, 1940), 11; Vaughan, *Dual Jurisdiction*, 14.

[47] Decree from Ḥamūd b. Muḥammad, 29 Shawwāl 1314/2 April 1897, BA14/25, ZNA.

[48] Public notification from Ḥamūd b. Muḥammad, 1 February 1898, BA14/25, ZNA.

[49] L. W. Hollingsworth, *Zanzibar under the Foreign Office, 1890–1913* (London: Macmillan, 1953), 164.

this decree enabled the implementation of "native courts" in line with the general order in the East African Protectorate.[50] It established the Supreme Court of His Highness the Sultan as the highest court of appeal in civil and criminal matters. This court consisted of the sultan, an Ibāḍī and a Shafiʿi *kadhi*, and one of the judges of the Court of Delegated Jurisdiction, who was allowed to intervene only upon request. Below the supreme court was the Court for Zanzibar and Pemba, on whose bench sat an Ibāḍī and a Shafiʿi *kadhi* as well as a judge. The latter was not allowed to intervene unless specifically requested by the *kadhis*. The Court for Zanzibar and Pemba functioned as a court of appeal for the district courts. If presided over by a Shafiʿi or an Ibāḍī *kadhi* only, it constituted a district court for Zanzibar Town.[51]

Introducing substantial alterations in procedure, the *kadhi*'s court regulations of 1899 allowed for every witness, regardless of religion and sex, to be heard and for cross-examination. Furthermore, they demanded that reasons be given for all decisions save in petty cases and that the evidence of the witnesses should be recorded for the purpose of appeal. Parties were now encouraged to give written statements of their claims. Further, a memorandum of appeal had henceforward to be filed against which the respondent could argue within a week.[52]

Subsequent reforms targeted the perceived lack of procedure and impartiality in the sultan's courts.[53] The flexibility of the legal system was curtailed considerably by laws that tied the trial of cases to their geographical point of origin. In 1904, it was established that parties were not allowed to take their case to any other than its legitimate district. Thus cases had to be settled where they arose or where the property under dispute was situated. By that time, there were four district courts in Zanzibar – Mkokotoni, Mwera, Chwaka, and the one

[50] Pouwels, *Horn and Crescent*, 176.

[51] Decree from Ḥamūd b. Muḥammad, 26 Shaʿbān 1316/9 January 1899, BA14/25, ZNA. The records classified as HC28/29 at the ZNA are case summaries from the Court for Zanzibar and Pemba when constituted as a district court. We owe the existence of these records to the decree of 1899, which provided for courts to keep records and for Arabic, English, Swahili, Gujerati, and any other local language to be recognised in court.

[52] Regulations for Cadis in His Highness Courts, 1 March 1899, BA14/25, ZNA.

[53] On the strict modes of procedure that *kadhis* have to follow according to Islamic legal literature, see Hallaq, *Shariʿa*, 342–53; Knut Vikør, *Between God and the Sultan: A History of Islamic Law* (London: Hurst, 2005), 173–83.

in town. Consequently, *kadhi*s could hear cases only from the district over which they had jurisdiction. The *kadhi*s in town were allowed to hear only cases from the other district courts on appeal if the appellant produced a letter of appeal from the court of first instance.[54]

British encroachment on the legal sector continued through the Order in Council of 1906, which came into force two years later, making the application of the sultan's decrees contingent on the British agent's countersignature,[55] while the Zanzibar Courts Decree of 1908 altered the jurisdiction of the courts established in 1899. Henceforth in the supreme court, which heard appeals from the Court for Zanzibar and Pemba, the two *kadhi*s had no say in the judgements and thus served as an ironic reminder of the fundamental law of the protectorate. The decree of 1908 established the limit of *kadhi*s' civil jurisdiction as Rs. 500, while the exercise of criminal jurisdiction, to which the *kadhi*s were still entitled according to this decree, did not seem to have existed in practice.[56] Most decisively, it enabled British judicial staff to adjudicate in the sultan's courts. Thus from 1909 onwards, British judges and magistrates applied Islamic law not only in the British courts but also in the sultan's courts, which laid the foundation for assimilating the two jurisdictions.[57]

Between 1908 and 1925, the business in the *kadhi*'s courts was carried out by the four most prominent *kadhi*s of the colonial period, each of whom presided over a *kadhi*'s court in town: the Sunni *kadhi*s Sh. Burhān b. ʿAbd al-ʿAzīz al-Amawī, Sh. Aḥmad b. Sumayṭ, and Sh. Ṭāhir b. Abī Bakr al-Amawī and the Ibāḍī *kadhi* Sh. ʿAlī b. Muḥammad al-Mundhirī. These *kadhi*s also travelled to hear cases in two of the three district courts, as only the court in Mkokotoni had a resident *kadhi*. This was the practice until 1925, when Sh. Aḥmad and Sh. ʿAlī passed away, which caused Chief Justice Thomas Tomlinson to note that "[i]t is becoming more and more difficult to find

54 Proclamation, 3 February 1904, BA14/23, ZNA.

55 Kingdon, *Conflict of Laws*, 14; Vaughan, *Dual Jurisdiction*, 16.

56 The gradual abolition of Islamic criminal law was intrinsic to British colonial policy. See Rudolph Peters, *Crime and Punishment in Islamic Law: Theory and Practice from the Sixteenth to the Twenty-first Century* (Cambridge: Cambridge University Press, 2005), Chapter 4, especially 104–105, 109–25.

57 Decree, 4 November 1908, BA14/26, ZNA; Vaughan, *Dual Jurisdiction*, 27–28, 27n1.

people of the right stamp for the office of Kathi."[58] The Ibāḍī *kadhi* was replaced but the workload among the Sunni *kadhi*s in town now rested on Sh. Burhān and Sh. Ṭāhir.

The increasing workload for the British judicial officers after 1908 was a ground for concern for the colonial authority, as was the inefficiency of the two separate court systems, the so-called dual jurisdiction. Therefore, a commission was set up in 1914 for improving the judicial system as a whole. The implementation of the suggested amalgamation of the dual structures was delayed by World War I but finally came into effect in 1923.[59] Tomlinson, who was appointed as chief justice in 1919, was instrumental in effectuating the Zanzibar Courts Decree and the British Subordinate Courts Order of 1923.[60] These two decrees established the amalgamation of the two court systems, which British colonial officers considered as effectively putting an end to impracticability and injustice. The Court for Zanzibar and Pemba was now replaced by the Sultan's Court for Zanzibar, consisting of one or more judges of the British court. To enhance the efficiency of the legal system, appeals from the *kadhi*s were henceforward considered by judges.[61] *Kadhi*s exercised jurisdiction in suits between "natives" where the subject matter of dispute did not exceed Rs. 500.[62] No clearer definition of the *kadhi*'s scope of jurisdiction was given in these two decrees of 1923. Yet a decree of 1921, conferring civil jurisdiction upon *kadhi*s in the British courts, had defined their jurisdiction as "over Mahommedan natives in matters of personal status, inheritance, marriage, and divorce, and also in all suits of a civil nature in which both parties were natives and the amount in dispute did not exceed Rs. 500/-."[63]

The Zanzibar Courts Decree of 1923 again reaffirmed the position of Islamic law as the fundamental law of the protectorate in civil

58 *Zanzibar Protectorate, Administrative Report, 1925* (Zanzibar: Government Printer, 1926), 1.

59 Vaughan, *Dual Jurisdiction*, 29–30.

60 *Supplement to the Official Gazette Zanzibar 1928*, Vol. XXXVII.-No. 1897, 2 June 1928, 141–42. The Zanzibar Courts Decree, 1923, and the British Subordinate Courts Order, 1923, are listed as Appendix IV and V, respectively, in Vaughan, *Dual Jurisdiction*.

61 *Zanzibar Protectorate, Administrative Report, 1924* (Zanzibar: Government Printer, 1925), 179–80.

62 British Subordinate Courts Order, 1923, section 4, cited in Vaughan, *Dual Jurisdiction*, 118.

63 Vaughan, *Dual Jurisdiction*, 31.

matters.[64] By that time, however, Islamic law had been supplanted by the sultan's decrees, and nothing remained of Islamic criminal law or rules of evidence and procedure except as indirectly upheld by the Oaths Decree of 1917.[65] Although methods of procedure contrary to shariʿa had already been provided for since 1899, the Evidence Decree of 1917 ultimately excluded Islamic rules of evidence from the courts.[66] This decree demanded that all parties were sworn in, hence judgements, which were based on the refusal of a party to take the oath, were prone to be reversed on appeal. In a further step, the Registration of Documents Decree of 1919 required all parties to register documents in order to assert legally enforceable rights.[67]

Regarding the sphere of marriage and divorce, colonial decrees contradicted the principles of Islamic law and constituted innovations, although they meant to contribute towards the convergence of the legal systems in operation. As early as 1915, the Marriage (Solemnisation and Registration) Decree theoretically enabled a Muslim woman to marry a Christian man, made polygyny illegal, and provided for any marriage concluded under this decree to be terminated by judicial decree only. Similarly, the Evidence Decree of 1917 recognised the legitimacy of a child only if it was born fewer than 280 days after the dissolution of the parents' marriage or the father's death, significantly less than under the Shafiʿi school and the Ibāḍī rule, which permit four and two years, respectively. There is, however, no evidence for a rigid enforcement of these provisions. The reforms were not primarily intended to eliminate the discrimination Muslim women faced under Islamic law – a concern that drove many reforms in Muslim countries in the twentieth century – but to impose a greater measure of conformity on Zanzibar's judiciary, taking pressure off the colonial budget and administration as well as exercising tighter control over the colonised. The Marriage and Divorce (Mahommedan) Registration Decree of 1922, providing for the appointment of marriage officers and for marriages and divorces to be registered, should be seen as a similar kind of effort.[68]

64 British Subordinate Courts Order, 1923, section 7, cited in Vaughan, *Dual Jurisdiction*, 106.

65 J. N. D. Anderson, *Islamic Law*, 61.

66 Ibid., 60; Kingdon, *Conflict of Laws*, 12.

67 J. N. D. Anderson, *Islamic Law*, 65.

68 Ibid., 61–62, 70; Vaughan, *Dual Jurisdiction*, 44–45.

Although the colonial government imposed its own legal agenda, its respect for Muslims is illustrated by inheritance laws. Among the enactments that had a direct bearing on social and economic relationships was the Succession Decree of 1917, which established that Muslims be governed by their own personal law and be generally exempt from provisions contrary to shariʿa.[69] Yet an amendment was made entitling the court or the administrator general to order that certain sums be distributed among dependants of the deceased as well as to the spouse in cases in which the *bayt al-māl*, or the public treasury,[70] was entitled to a part of the estate. Thus the possibility was created of both allotting a bigger share of inheritance to the spouse than provided for under Islamic law and including new heirs based on a perceived need.[71]

After the decrees of 1923, additional *kadhi*'s courts were established in Makunduchi and Koani,[72] and changes in the *kadhi*'s scope of jurisdiction only concerned a steady increase in the value under dispute. After the change of currency from rupees to shillings in 1936, the *kadhi*'s jurisdiction was adjusted to Shs. 1,500 and Shs. 750, respectively, in matters relating to personal status, marriage, divorce, and inheritance where the claim did not exceed Rs. 1,000 and, in civil suits, Rs. 500.[73]

Comparing French jurisprudence to Islamic jurisprudence, David Powers has observed that in French legal reasoning, legal subjects correspond to a distinct legal category, whereas in Islamic legal literature, the categories to which legal subjects belong are inconsequential.[74] The colonial and generally Western conceptions of Islamic legal categories, such as a distinction between civil and criminal law, are not

69 This principle of respect and applying Islamic law in matters pertaining to religious institutions was adopted by the British in India in 1772. See Powers, "Orientalism, Colonialism, and Legal History," 555.

70 See *The Encyclopaedia of Islam*, 2nd ed. (hereafter *EI*²), s.v. "*bayt al-māl.*"

71 J. N. D. Anderson, *Islamic Law*, 62–63.

72 *Annual Report on the Social and Economic Progress of the People of the Zanzibar Protectorate, 1931* (London: His Majesty's Stationery Office, 1932), 24, and *Annual Report of the Provincial Administration, 1957*, 5.

73 *Annual Report on the Social and Economic Progress of the People of the Zanzibar Protectorate, 1935* (London: His Majesty's Stationery Office, 1936), 32; *Annual Report on the Social and Economic Progress of the People of the Zanzibar Protectorate, 1936* (London: His Majesty's Stationery Office, 1937), 30.

74 Powers, "Orientalism, Colonialism, and Legal History," 541.

intrinsic to shariʿa. As Wael Hallaq articulated more recently, imperialism invented categories of Islamic legal knowledge. Therefore, the colonial division of Islamic law into criminal and civil, with arbitrary references to personal status as a subdivision of civil law, was a means for accommodating shariʿa into the colonial project. This division does not match Islamic legal conceptions, nor do the varying subject matters adjudicated by the *kadhi*'s courts. The British used this division as a tool to reduce the application of Islamic law to personal status matters, usually marriage, divorce, and inheritance, to which they added *wakf*, or religious endowment, following the *kadhi*s' scope of jurisdiction in India.[75] The blurred boundaries of jurisdiction appeared in court after criminal cases were removed from the *kadhi*s as well as with the regulation that *kadhi*s were disqualified from adjudicating cases above a certain amount of value. This meant that cases of adultery had to be raised at the magistrate's court and that the amount of money claimed needed to be determined prior to the opening of a case. On the one hand, litigants were adversely affected by the restricted scope of the *kadhi*'s jurisdiction, since it implied that they had to travel further and accept the "shariʿa" judgements of a non-Muslim, a judge or a magistrate. On the other hand, the establishment of the British set of courts provided new possibilities in dispute resolution.[76] At least occasionally, individuals could reinterpret legal categories, and judges sitting on appeal may have been more sympathetic to their claims than *kadhi*s. While the litigants were left to explore newly created and continuously amended legal systems, *kadhi*s struggled against as well as with colonial officers in seeking to apply shariʿa on the basis of a socioreligious understanding.

[75] In India, *kadhi*s adjudicated matters pertaining to succession, inheritance, marriage, caste, and religious usage (Hooker, *Legal Pluralism*, 95).

[76] Although this study cannot provide an analysis of litigants' use of the entire legal system, it would be most elucidating to compare the application of Islamic law in the *kadhi*'s courts and the British courts, where judges had to apply the school of law of the litigants, whereas *kadhi*s were bound to apply their own legal doctrines. See Richard Roberts, *Litigants and Households*, 13–20, on the potential of social transformation that litigants created by exploring various legal systems.

2

Race and the Impartial Modern Judiciary

FIGURE 2.1. Fruit market outside the Old Fort. Courtesy of ZNA.

The gateway is the usual intricate barbican. Here in olden times, after the prayers of el Asr (3 P.M.) the governor and three judges, patriarchs with long grey beards, unclean white robes, and sabres in the hand,

> held courts of justice, and distributed rough-and-ready law to peaceful Banyans [Indians], noisy negroes, and groups of fierce Arabs.[1]

In his description of the entrance to the Old Fort in Zanzibar Town in late 1856, the famous explorer Richard Burton depicts the perceived characteristics of Muslim adjudication that would inform the British approach to Islamic law in the protectorate. Burton's passage not only captures colonial categories of race but also illustrates the underlying colonial understanding of where, how, and by whom shariʿa was to be applied. The first bias this description yields pertains to space and the perception that justice is administered at a busy, noisy, and dirty place in the middle of the crowd. Burton's understanding of the properly pristine circumstances in which justice should be rendered obviously jibes at the arbitrariness and dirt he sees in Zanzibar. The lack of official courthouses meant that *kadhis* issued verdicts in a public place as well as in their homes. This absence bothered colonial officials to such an extent that they decided to provide an adequate environment for the esteemed and impartial work of adjudication when they took on overall control of the legal sector. New law courts, housing the British court and the sultan's court, were opened in 1904 and further expanded in 1908. The latter date coincides with the enactment of the decree that restructured the entire court system. The positioning of the court building outside the maze of the narrow streets – an area that the British left to the local population – also indicates that the sultan's courts were now appropriately placed on the colonial map of the town.[2]

This spatial arrangement reflected the power structure of the protectorate. In his proposal for building a veranda to provide means

[1] Burton, *Zanzibar*, vol. I, 89. Cf. Jonathan Miran, *Red Sea Citizens: Cosmopolitan Society and Cultural Change in Massawa* (Bloomington: Indiana University Press, 2009), 202, where he cites a colonial Italian report on Islamic judicial practice in Massawa prior to 1872, echoing Burton's description of corruption and inefficiency in Zanzibar.

[2] On the spatial division of Zanzibar Town, see William Cunningham Bissell, *Urban Design, Chaos, and Colonial Power in Zanzibar* (Bloomington: Indiana University Press, 2011); Myers, "Reconstructing Ng'ambo." On the opening of the court, see *Zanzibar Law Reports*, vol. 1, compiled by Sir William Murison and S. S. Abrahams (London: Waterlow & Sons Ltd.), xi.

FIGURE 2.2. The high court after the revolution. The building was opened in 1904. Courtesy of ZNA.

of communication for the public, lawyers, and other staff between the British courts and the magistrate's court, Chief Justice Tomlinson reveals the philosophy that informed the architecture of the building:

The Court buildings were carried out in two sections. First the British Court was built as a separate unit and subsequently the "Sultan's" [sic] Court.

FIGURE 2.3. Street scene behind the House of Wonders. Courtesy of ZNA.

At the time the distinction between the two jurisdictions was so jealously guarded that I believe that on the original plan there was no provision for any sort of intercommunication between the two Courts, but eventually a door was made from the Assistant Judge's room into the room under the tower.[3]

[3] Chief Justice Tomlinson to British resident, 7 July 1925, AB62/70, ZNA. The expansion of the court building in 1908 brought closer spatial proximity to the two court systems. Thus the decree of the same year was transferred into the architecture of the court (Bang, *Sufis and Scholars*, 164, 236n39).

Apart from Tomlinson's awareness that the design upheld what historian Allan Christelow calls the "spatial segregation of justice,"[4] we should pay attention to his quotation marks questioning the appropriateness of the name "sultan's" court. Tomlinson obviously mocks the designation of what, by 1925, was nothing more than a formal token of the sultan's judicial power. With legislating power in the hands of the colonial government, the label "sultan" was reduced to an instrument for keeping up appearances. Similarly, the sultan's decrees became a tool of colonial rule for modifying Islamic law. Many years later, Islamicist Joseph Schacht provided another piece of evidence for how the spatial arrangement in court reflected shifts in power. In 1953, he noted that in Zanzibar Town the Shafiʿi and Ibāḍī *kadhi*s "sat in corresponding rooms, facing each other, on both sides of the common passage."[5] This arrangement, however, was changed in 1963 to correspond to the actual importance of each *kadhi*, with the Shafiʿi and Ibāḍī *kadhi* sitting for three days and two days, respectively, in the same courtroom.[6]

Returning to Burton, a second assumption inherent in his observation relates to the "patriarchs" who apply "rough-and-ready" justice, symbolised by their sabres. From the Westerner's perspective, the lack of an underlying system of Islamic legal reasoning was compounded by the *kadhi*s' partiality and their proneness to bribery, a "fact" that was cited later by the British in support of limiting Islamic law.[7] Colonial and travellers' reports abound with hints of the corruption of the legal system. In 1844 the first British Consul Hamerton had noted this undesirable state, which Chief Justice Gray apologetically explained by noting that *kadhi*s were inadequately paid.[8] Hamerton's successor

4 Allan Christelow, *Muslim Law Courts and the French Colonial State in Algeria* (Princeton: Princeton University Press, 1985), 38. He thereby refers to the spatial development of Islamic courts from the market place to the judge's house and finally to a courthouse.

5 Joseph Schacht, "Notes on Islam in East Africa," *Studia Islamica* 23 (1965): 117.

6 Ibid.

7 The payment of compensation, such as described for sayyid Saʿīd, may well have been another factor confirming Western impressions of the omnipresent bribery among *kadhi*s. See also Pouwels, *Horn and Crescent*, 81, where he remarks that social rules such as gifts to the *kadhi* were misperceived by Europeans.

8 Gray, *History of Zanzibar*, 145. Gerald Portal notes that also *liwali*s were inadequately paid by the sultan and therefore had to rely on bribes (Portal to Ld. Salisbury, 9 September 1891, FO 84.2149, no. 245, quoted in Hollingsworth, *Zanzibar*, 58).

Rigby confirmed this view eighteen years later, adding that *kadhi*s were not respected by the people.[9] In 1906, A. W. Clarke enquired whether "it would not be possible to get rid of some of the Arab Lewalis [sic] and Kathis, who for the most part are notoriously inefficient and corrupt."[10] Other colonial officers joined in this lament until a dispatch of 1908 reveals that administrators now felt that colonial rule had put an end to *kadhi*s' "old habits of extortion and bribery."[11] Similar disdain was expressed towards the right of appeal to the sultan, which Hamerton acknowledged in 1844 and which Gray called with resignation "the bright spot about the judicial system."[12] What weighed against "this bright spot" was the fact that the sultan was also the only law-making authority. British colonial officers also disapproved of litigants having their judgement reviewed by the *kadhi* of the other school.[13]

After Gerald Portal became consul general, his dissatisfaction with the sultan's disorganised judicial and governmental system led to the complete reorganisation of the administration in 1891 as part of a larger project "to establish the basic trinity of colonial rule: prison, court and barracks."[14] He introduced a separation between the sultan's private revenue and that of the state and appointed British instead of Arab officers. These officers were removable only with British consent and paid out of the sultan's revenues of which Portal was in charge.[15] The institution of the *bayt al-māl* was also a target of reform. It received money from estates without other legal heirs and was administered by the sultan on behalf of the public for welfare and religious purposes. Because of alleged mismanagement under previous sultans,

[9] Gray, *History of Zanzibar*, 146.

[10] Memorandum by A. W. Clarke, 30 April 1906, FO 881/8814, NAK. The same prejudice towards *kadhi*s and *liwali*s is expressed by Hardinge, who felt that Zanzibaris had little confidence in the *kadhi*'s "purity, integrity, or independence" (Hardinge to Ld. Salisbury, 24 October 1898; FO 107.97, no. 333, quoted in Hollingsworth, *Zanzibar*, 163).

[11] Basil Cave to Sir Edward Grey, 26 October 1908, Private papers, Sir John Gray, Add. 7739, box 25, file "Papers relating to Zanzibar," Cambridge University Library (hereafter CUL).

[12] Gray, *History of Zanzibar*, 146.

[13] Hollingsworth, *Zanzibar*, 69.

[14] Bissell, *Urban Design*, 115.

[15] Lyne, *Zanzibar*, 190; Esmond Bradley Martin, *Zanzibar: Tradition and Revolution* (London: Hamish Hamilton, 1978), 40.

this purse was appropriated by the colonial government.[16] During the reign of sayyid ʿAlī b. Ḥamūd (r. 1902–1911), who was a minor when he became sultan and thus had a British first minister acting on his behalf, the Europeanisation of administrative staff began.[17] Yet by 1912, their number was still as low as thirty-four, compared to four in 1891.[18] Jonathon Glassman reminds us that the power of British officials has been overestimated, as many administrative officers actually were Zanzibaris.[19] Although these officers were few in number, their ideologies and initiatives shaped the accessibility of the courts and the outcome of disputes.

The dominant colonial ideology towards Islamic law was informed by the "perceived contrasts between British judicial ideals" and "Zanzibari judicial practice"[20] and presupposed tensions between colonial and Islamic notions of justice. The strength of the Islamic legal system was that it had largely evolved from the local society in which it was applied immediately and thus was, at least in its basics, understandable and, most importantly, accessible to the population. Unlike modern Western laws, Islamic law was not a coercive and a punitive machinery but, within the framework of rooting the Bū Saʿīdī power by expanding Islamic law, aimed to serve the people who, certainly in the pre-Bū Saʿīdī period, were in control of the courts. The colonial bias against the unrestricted application of shariʿa was maintained throughout the colonial period, but its realisation was hampered by the colonial fear of inducing a religious upheaval in the protectorate.[21]

Irrespective of the colonial observer's positive attitude towards the Islamic legal system and knowledge of the subject, he mostly associated shariʿa with irrationality and a lack of evolution and sophistication,

[16] Hollingsworth, *Zanzibar*, 178.

[17] Ibid., 191. The increasing British influence can be traced in the language of the sultans' wills, with Sultan Ḥamūd using English and appointing British executors (Pearce, *Zanzibar*, 271–73; Letter from J. M. Gray to J. N. D. Anderson, 18 September 1950, PP MS 60/1/5, box 1, file 5, SOAS, in which the translations of the wills of sayyids Saʿīd and Barghash are enclosed).

[18] Hollingsworth, *Zanzibar*, 191.

[19] Glassman, "Sorting Out the Tribes," 398.

[20] I have adopted this phrase from Peletz, *Islamic Modern*, 38–39.

[21] Acting Attorney General A. H. Roberts to chief secretary, 21 May 1937, AB12/180; Memorandum, n.d., AB71/4, ZNA.

as well as with injustice in various vague and concrete notions.[22] In a memorandum of 1924, Tomlinson, who was a great friend of the *kadhi*s, termed Islamic law "a very uncertain quantity" as it comprised a maze of conflicting opinions in his view.[23] This patronising tone towards the "native child" was equally reflected in the legal discourse between coloniser and colonised, such as when, earlier in 1901, Consul General Hardinge sought to encourage *kadhi*s to develop some sense of independent responsibility.[24] However, the issues that were at stake and the social relationships into which they played do not permit neat dichotomies, such as Christian–Muslim, domination–subjection, order–chaos, but rather suggest that the motivations of both colonial and local actors were polymorphous, multidimensional, and contradictory.

Although the application of Islamic law originated in a public, open space, shariʿa was characterised by its intimacy – the importance it attaches to the legal person, or individual, and to bringing people back into working relationships as well as establishing the truth through recourse to facts and evidence.[25] In Muslim understanding, only God knows the truth, and *kadhi*s' reference to themselves as "servants of the law" and the practice of concluding cases with "Allah knows best/better than the *kadhi*s" attest to this same underlying principle. The fact that Islamic law is strongly informed by the social environment in which it operates explains much of British notions of its partiality and bribery. As a result of colonial efforts to combat these perceived ills, the *kadhi*'s courts became increasingly alienated from the people and the principles that previously informed them. The Islamic legal system gradually became functionalised through a shift in emphasis from person to role and was integrated into the colonial legal apparatus insofar as the colonial government desired this.[26] What was created was not a merger of customary or common law with shariʿa but a new, undefined legal substance that suited colonial needs to some degree, brought some advantages as well as disadvantages for the litigants,

[22] Cf. Peletz, *Islamic Modern*, 49.
[23] Tomlinson's memorandum, 12 September 1924, AB62/79, ZNA.
[24] Hardinge to Ld. Salisbury, 6 January 1900, FO 2.284, no. 2, quoted in Hollingsworth, *Zanzibar*, 165.
[25] Peletz, *Islamic Modern*, 90.
[26] Cf. Messick, *Calligraphic State*, 195.

and caught the *kadhi*s in an unfortunate position between these two groups of actors. The availability of new legal institutions and paths made going to court attractive in some ways and demands examination as "something more profound than borrowing"[27] between the legal systems and Zanzibaris.

Shortly after the enactment of the Native Courts Decree of 1899 he promulgated, Hardinge was positively surprised by the improved conduct of proceedings and keeping of records at a district court in Pemba. He was told on his visit that the people appreciated these changes, which renewed their confidence in the courts. It is questionable whether changes could be felt and reflected in public opinion only a few months after the decree had been enacted, but Hardinge's discovery obviously emboldened the government's pursuit of further changes in the judiciary.[28]

Perceiving the application of shariʿa essentially in arbitrary and irrational terms, the British strove to create a fixed, legal code, which removed the independence of local scholars in its interpretation.[29] As Muhammad Qasim Zaman argues, under colonial rule, the "conception, according to which the shariʿa is essentially akin to a fixed legal code rather than an ongoing discursive tradition, is central to the conception of an 'Islamic state.'"[30] The original flexibility of the law and its orality mutated into written legal manuals that served as new templates for the interpretation of Islamic law. This new legal substance arose from the British reforms that focussed on the legal apparatus

[27] Richard Rathbone, "Law, Lawyers and Politics in Ghana in the 1940s," in *Contesting Colonial Hegemony: State and Society in Africa and India*, ed. Dagmar Engels and Shula Marks (London: British Academy Press, 1994), 233.

[28] Hardinge to Ld. Salisbury, 6 January 1900, FO 2.284, no. 2, quoted in Hollingsworth, *Zanzibar*, 164–65. On the Benadir coast, the Italians believed that they achieved an improvement in the workings of the *kadhi*'s courts and a considerable reduction in bribery (Vianello and Kassim, *Servants of the Sharia*, 55). For an account of the *kadhi*'s courts in Pemba, see Elisabeth McMahon, *Slavery and Emancipation in Islamic East Africa: From Honor to Respectability* (Cambridge: Cambridge University Press, 2013), Chapter 3.

[29] Cf. Michael R. Anderson, "Islamic Law and the Colonial Encounter in British India," in *Institutions and Ideologies: A SOAS South Asia Reader*, ed. David Arnold and Peter Robb (Richmond: Curzon, 1993), 165–85; Muhammad Qasim Zaman, *The Ulama in Contemporary Islam: Custodians of Change* (Princeton: Princeton University Press, 2002), 21–25. During this process of codification, the original range of legal texts that ʿulamaʾ consulted was reduced considerably.

[30] Zaman, *Ulama in Contemporary Islam*, 32.

and its procedure rather than on the substance of the law.[31] Thus, in appeal cases judges concentrated on assessing whether the *kadhi*s had followed the rules of procedure rather than correctly applied Islamic law. An irreversible shift from oral to written evidence occurred, so, for instance, changes in one's personal status had to be made known to the state.[32] The colonial preference for the written also had the effect of generating sources, although normative and functional, for the workings of the courts.[33]

The colonial focus on tightening rules of procedure and thereby controlling the transactions to which they referred not only implied considerable changes in clerical work, with increasing amount of time and money reserved for litigants, but also affected the relationships between the actors. The mere fact of being a part of the same judicial machinery as the British necessarily brought about spatial contact with the judges and magistrates, as *kadhi*s sought advice, exchanged correspondence, and jointly passed judgements with their British counterparts. *Kadhi* Sh. Ṭāhir, for instance, recorded sending off a copy of the judgement to the registrar, referring to the decree that obliged him to do so.[34] Showing (off?) his ability to accommodate himself to the new rules that surrounded and permeated the application of shariʿa,

31 Cf. Tucker, *Women, Family, and Gender*, 22; David Groff, "The Dynamics of Collaboration and the Rule of Law in French West Africa: The Case of Kwame Kangah of Assikasso (Côte d'Ivoire), 1898–1922," in *Law in Colonial Africa*, ed. Kristin Mann and Richard Roberts (Portsmouth, NH: Heinemann, 1991), 147; Annelies Moors, "Debating Islamic Family Law: Legal Texts and Social Practices," in *Social History of Women and Gender in the Modern Middle East*, ed. Margaret L. Meriwether and Judith E. Tucker (Boulder, CO: Westview Press, 1999), 153.

32 See Moors, "Debating Islamic Family Law," 151; Michael Anderson, "Legal Scholarship," 78–79. Leslie Peirce explores the transformation from orality to text in sixteenth-century divorce cases from the Ottoman court of Aintab (idem, "'She Is Trouble'," 269–300). Also the daughter of sayyid Saʿīd, Salme, noted the strong oral culture in settling affairs and issuing verdicts at her father's court. Emily Ruete, *Memoirs of an Arabian Princess from Zanzibar* (Zanzibar: The Gallery Publications, 1998), 126. Cf. Lydon, *Trans-Saharan Trails*, 22, on the emphasis on orality in Islamic law. Derek Peterson, however, has recently criticised scholarship on courts in Africa for the perceived clash between written, bureaucratised court practice and the fluidity of African orality. Idem, "Morality Plays: Marriage, Church Courts, and Colonial Agency in Central Tanganyika, ca. 1876–1928," *American Historical Review* 111, no. 4 (2006): 983–1010.

33 Sally Falk Moore, *Law as Process: An Anthropological Approach* (London: Routledge & Kegan Paul, 1978), 203.

34 HC9/132, ZNA.

he noted in a judgement of 1921 that he had looked at the law reports by Judge Murison.[35] Considering anthropologist Erin Stiles' observation that *kadhi*s today rarely refer to sources other than the Qur'an and hadith (accounts of the Prophet's deeds and sayings),[36] we must ask why colonial demands for detailed and explanatory records also entailed the *kadhi*s' reference to Islamic legal literature in their judgements. Introduced to Zanzibar by Hadrami scholars, *Minhāj al-ṭālibīn* by the eleventh-century scholar Abū Zakariyā' Yaḥyā b. Sharaf al-Dīn al-Nawawī was the main reference for Shafiʿis, with its main commentary *Tuḥfat al-muḥtāj li-sharḥ al-minhāj* by Ibn Ḥajar al-Haytamī (1504–1567).[37] Among the Ibāḍīs *kitāb al-Nīl*, a comprehensive compilation of Ibāḍī legal doctrines by ʿAbd al-ʿAzīz b. Ibrāhīm al-Muṣʿabī (1718–1808), and its commentary, *Sharḥ (kitāb) al-Nīl* by Muḥammad b. Yusūf Aṭfayyish, were the main legal sources.[38] Shafiʿi *kadhi*s, such as Sh. Ṭāhir, backed up their judgements with reference to the *Minhāj* and its commentaries[39] and so did the Ibāḍī *kadhi*s Sh. Muḥammad b. Khamīs al-Bū Saʿīdī and Sh. Saʿīd b. Rashīd al-Ghaythī with reference to Ibāḍī legal sources.[40] Colonial reforms and a new focus on procedure entailed that British legal staff constantly rebuked *kadhi*s for their irrational and unprofessional adjudication. Thus *kadhi*s decided to substantiate their reasoning in judgements with reference to both Islamic and colonial legal sources.

In addition to incorporating previously unknown rules of procedure, *kadhi*s acceded to the decreasing scope of their jurisdiction. For example, *kadhi* Sh. Ṭāhir refused to continue adjourning cases in 1919 and 1932, in one case because he did not see its merit.[41] In December 1911, he had transferred a case regarding a *shamba*, or plantation, to the Court of Zanzibar and Pemba as the value of the *shamba* under dispute fell beyond his scope of jurisdiction. *Kadhi*s Sh. Aḥmad b. Sumayṭ and Sh. ʿAlī b. Muḥammad, who took over this case, ruled

35 HC9/134, ZNA.
36 Stiles, *Islamic Court*, 191.
37 Bang, *Sufis and Scholars*, 162.
38 C. Brockelmann, *Geschichte der Arabischen Litteratur*, second supplement (Leiden: E. J. Brill, 1938), 892.
39 For Sh. Ṭāhir, see HC5/536; HC9/67; HC9/134; HC10/31, ZNA.
40 See HC10/20 and HC10/2843; HC5/575, ZNA, respectively.
41 HC9/67; HC10/55, ZNA.

against the plaintiff, as the *shamba* had not been duly registered.[42] These attempts at the reversal of the roles between the judge and the *kadhi* took an almost complete form when, between 1958 and 1961, the district commissioner addressed the *kadhi* on behalf of a party, requesting leniency from the court. It was the *kadhi* who reminded the commissioner that the case had been running for two years and that the decree holder was entitled to her rights.[43]

The increasing formality and bureaucratisation of the legal system fostered interaction between the *kadhi*s and colonial officers, on the one hand, and between litigants and court personnel as well as administrative officers, on the other. This formality brought high costs in time, energy, and money for those who were not qualified to appear as a "poor person" in court, as provided for in the Zanzibar Courts Decree of 1908.[44] In order to understand the litigants' approach to the courts, it is necessary to account for the concern of individual colonial officers to ensure access to the Zanzibari legal system. The debate about the poor box and other measures to make the courts accessible to the poor was motivated, first, by humanitarian concerns and, second, by the aim of making the entire legal system more popular among Zanzibaris. Correspondence between colonial officers provides insights into their conflicting attitudes towards helping the poor, as they simultaneously fretted over its costs and the reputation of the judiciary. The registrar of the high court stated in 1946 that if a poor person sued a wealthier one, the latter could easily decline to follow the judgement as "in such cases the longest purse wins, which is a very serious reflection indeed on the reputation of the administration of justice."[45] Moreover, their debates illustrate how the category of race was applied and contested, with some officers trying to make up for and do away with the colonial legal categories that they understood and conceded as fitting badly onto social reality.

42 HC9/12, ZNA. For *kadhi*s explicitly enforcing colonially induced rules of procedure, see also HC10/20; HC10/981; HC10/1156; HC10/1370; HC10/2978; HC10/3001; HC10/3033; HC10/3302, ZNA. Cf. Pouwels, *Horn and Crescent*, 179–80, on how *kadhi*s were affected by colonially introduced measures.

43 HC10/3695, ZNA. See also HC10/3732, ZNA.

44 Zanzibar Courts Decree, 1908, BA14/1, ZNA; cf. Christelow, *Muslim Law Courts*, 38.

45 Registrar Dastur to chief secretary, 16 January 1946, AB62/30, ZNA.

Once the colonial administration had succeeded in establishing a sufficiently bureaucratised legal system, its representatives on the ground realised that this enhanced bureaucratisation partially contravened its functionality. In an explanatory memorandum of February 1927, Chief Justice Tomlinson made clear the need to facilitate civil procedure, regarding the court fees as the primary obstacle for a poor person to file a suit.[46] By 1940, specific rules for appearing as a poor person in court had been established. However, this issue remained a concern of colonial officers and was discussed by the provincial commissioner and the chief justice. The latter made suggestions to further improve the situation, such as by simplifying procedure in the *kadhi*'s courts and by providing legal aid free of charge. The chief justice initiated similar aid with the preparation of documents for people who were not "literate in the language of the court."[47] The result of this debate, the Civil Procedure (Amendment) Rules of 1940, stated that applications for suing or defending as a poor person in the *kadhi*'s courts had to be made in person or in writing. It further assigned to the *kadhi* himself enquiries into the applicant's state of poverty.[48] Although these measures aimed at attracting legally marginalised groups, they demanded from potential litigants a considerable amount of time and the awareness of the existence of these avenues. Moreover, parties had to pass through a number of offices to obtain the certificates entitling them to these privileges.

Colonial officers opened and closed racial boundaries in the sequel to the debate about whether poor persons and/or Africans in general should have access to a free writer. The issue of lost income for the government, if too broad a category of people was included, featured prominently in this debate. The acting chief secretary cautioned against racial distinction, fearing protests from parts of the population.[49] Similarly opposed to the proposition of including Africans only was the acting British resident, anxious about how this might reflect on the government's racial policies.[50] It is worth noting that officials' underlying concern was directed towards the reactions of Arab and Indian

46 T. S. Tomlinson, 9 February 1927, AB62/30, ZNA.

47 Chief justice to British resident, 15 August 1940, AB62/30, ZNA.

48 AB62/30, ZNA.

49 Acting chief secretary to British resident, 20 February 1941, AB62/19, ZNA.

50 Acting British resident to chief justice, 5 March 1941, AB62/19, ZNA.

populations if "Africans only" were entitled to a free writer, given that Africans represented the vast majority. The racial marker was dropped when the Court Petition Writers Rules were enacted in 1941.[51]

By applying economic and racial criteria for access to legal assistance, the British not only brought into being two parallel sets of court systems but also an arbitrary distinction between "native" and "non-native" to which the debates around various decrees attest. What comes to light is an underlying dilemma over whether to "keep the natives native," to "make them better Muslims," and/or to make them progress towards modernisation and Westernisation.[52] The answers to these questions determined who qualified as "native" and who did not. Although a generic definition of "native" in the East African dependencies referred to Arabs and Africans, excluding Indians and Europeans,[53] in practice, colonial officers were unclear as to its definition. In 1924, V. H. Kirkham saw the term "native" as undefined, and he thus concluded that Arabs constituted a separate category.[54] Chief Justice Tomlinson, however, equated "'natives' chiefly with Arabs."[55] After decades of futile discussions of the legal term "native," British Resident Glenday asked the secretary of state for the colonies in 1950 whether "any categorical statement [could] be made regarding our policy?",[56] seeking advice on the status of the Arabs in the Zanzibar Protectorate, still regarded as an Arab state. This dilemma also informed the debate among colonial officers about the expansion of judicial powers, which was discussed around 1924, after the assimilation of the dual jurisdiction.

Colonial discourses about racial taxonomies not only concerned litigants but also court officials. After 1923, *kadhi*s were answerable

51 AB62/19, ZNA.

52 Cf. Peletz, *Islamic Modern*, 58.

53 Hyde to Acheson, 17 December 1931, CO 618/49/1, ZNA.

54 V. H. Kirkham, 15 August 1924, AB62/79, ZNA.

55 Memorandum by Tomlinson, 12 September 1924, AB62/79, ZNA. See also Christopher J. Lee, "The 'Native' Undefined: Colonial Categories, Anglo-African Status and the Politics of Kinship in British Central Africa, 1929–38," *Journal of African History* 46, no. 3 (2005): 455–78; idem, "*Jus Solis* and *Jus Sanguinis* in the Colonies: The Interwar Politics of Race, Culture, and Multiracial Legal Status in British Africa," *Law and History Review* 29, no. 2 (2011): 497–522; James R. Brennan, *Taifa: Making Nation and Race in Urban Tanzania* (Athens: Ohio University Press, 2012), 21–26.

56 Glenday to Creech Jones, 26 January 1950, CO 822/151/5, NAK.

to judges for administrative and appellate purposes, and in the view of Tomlinson, this enhanced their efficiency and limited the number of appeals from their courts. While the entire community appreciated the end of dual jurisdiction, Arabs, he reasoned, benefitted most.[57] Harold Ingrams, secretary to the director of education in Zanzibar during the 1920s, drew up a report throwing light on the efficiency of the legal system and the role of the *sheha*. This report suggests the suitability of Arabs with "miscellaneous knowledge and advanced ideas" for exercising judicial powers.[58] While correspondence between colonial officers in 1924 shows the general tenor of their belief in the "suitability of the Arab" as a judicial functionary, the question turned on whether judicial powers, concentrated on few places and people, should be expanded to serve the population more efficiently. The senior commissioner held that on a small island, people could be expected to proceed to the recognised legal institutions, expressing his opposition to the idea of placing adjudicating powers in the hands of many. At the same time, the senior commissioner appreciated that *sheha*s, perceived as Arab, and elders settled small disputes.[59]

*Sheha*s appear in the court records as witnesses, mediators, and registrars. Their prominence in court was due to their position as headmen of districts or villages and their social knowledge and role as arbitrators. They received court summons and had statutory powers of arrest. In the southern part of Zanzibar, many offences and minor crimes were dealt with by the *sheha*. Colonial officers saw this as an approved irregularity as there were no complaints[60] and encouraged the continuation of traditional forms of dispute resolution as long as they kept the judicial system running smoothly and did not

57 *Zanzibar Protectorate, Administrative Report, 1924*, 180.

58 Administration of the Southern District, AB62/79, ZNA. Cf. Hassan Abdulrahman Mwakimako, "Politics, Ethnicity and Jostling for Power: the Evolution of Institutions of Muslim Leadership and Kadhiship in Colonial Kenya, 1895–1963" (PhD diss., University of Cape Town, 2003), Chapter 3, in which he accounts for how colonial officials introduced racial parameters into the appointment of Muslim leaders in Kenya.

59 Senior commissioner to c[hief] s[ecretary], 25 April 1924, AB62/79, ZNA.

60 Extract from Annual Report on the Southern District, 1923, AB62/79, ZNA. On the roles of other colonial intermediaries, see Benjamin N. Lawrance, Emily Lynn Osborn, and Richard L. Roberts, eds., *Intermediaries, Interpreters, and Clerks: African Employees in the Making of Colonial Africa* (Madison: University of Wisconsin Press, 2006).

compromise its reputation. Chief Justice Tomlinson proposed to give *sheha*s and *akida*s[61] limited judicial powers in criminal jurisdiction, as "[c]ivil work is much more difficult than criminal and civil decrees much more difficult to enforce. [...] Civil cases frequently involve the enforcement of decrees against persons who on family or social grounds are in a position to refuse to obey the authority of such a bench and thus weaken its prestige."[62] Asking "why, for instance, should a Shihiri Arab who is a British subject although a 'native' be in a different position from his not more Asiatic Indian cousin who is a non-native?" and feeling that racial distinctions had become anachronistic, Tomlinson opted for including all subjects, not just the sultan's, under the jurisdiction of these proposed benches.[63] These individual considerations and initiatives gained shape in the British Subordinate Courts (Amendment) Order of 1925.

Despite continuous colonial efforts to control and systematise the legal apparatus and the workings of its officers, the *kadhi*s' adaptation to the new rules of procedure evolved neither gradually nor constantly. The reason for their inconsistent application of rules of procedure was a discrepancy between the shariʿa rules of evidence and witnessing and those of common law. The *kadhi*s were doubtlessly aware of the rules they were obliged to apply but could not avoid continuing to apply their socioreligious and legal understanding.[64] Islamic laws of evidence were not only continuously applied in criminal cases tried in the district courts, as the British Resident Richard Rankine noted in 1933,[65] but also in the *kadhi*'s courts. Although it did not have any bearing on the judgement, the Ibāḍī *kadhi* Sh. Saʿīd b. Rashīd hinted at his preference of proper Muslim witnesses as late as 1952.[66] In a judgement of 1945, *kadhi* Sh. ʿUmar b. Aḥmad b. Sumayṭ rejected a plaintiff's witnesses on the ground that they were not (socially) knowledgeable on the subject, holding that proof could be established

[61] Until 1928, when they were replaced by *mudir*s, *akida*s served in the administrative hierarchy between *sheha*s and *liwali*s.

[62] Tomlinson's memorandum, 12 September 1924, AB62/79, ZNA.

[63] Ibid.

[64] Cf. Peletz, *Islamic Modern*, 91, where he says that *kadhi*s may avoid taking certain actions that are legally justified but socially and morally unacceptable.

[65] R. Rankine to Philip Cunliffe-Lister, 30 June 1933, CO 618/55/19, NAK.

[66] HC10/2843, ZNA.

only from two knowledgeable men.[67] He thereby ignored the Evidence Decree of 1917 that made people, regardless of their religion, sex, and social background, acceptable witnesses in the *kadhi*'s court. However, in a case in 1954, the same *kadhi* found that the court could not hear the application of the defendant's *wakīl*, as the verdict had already been passed, referring the party to the court of appeal.[68] He thereby followed the correct colonial procedure.

Appeal judgements provide ample evidence of the different socio-legal traditions in which judges and *kadhi*s were steeped. When a judge took on the role of a *kadhi*, he seemed to have been unaware of the absurdity of his task to merge Islamic law, which requires *kadhi*s to be Muslim, with common law. Once judges and magistrates had become knowledgeable in shariʿa, at least some, such as Chief Justice John Gray, enjoyed expounding their new erudition, which empowered them to overturn *kadhi*s' judgements on appeal.[69] Studying Islamic family endowments in India, David Powers attributes to British magistrates rigour and zealousness, which exceeded that of *kadhi*s, in enforcing Islamic laws of inheritance. He argues that the application of Islamic laws of inheritance by British judges and magistrates was underpinned by admiration of their uniqueness.[70] Such admiration stemmed from orientalist discourse and was also noticeable among some judges in Zanzibar. In one of his lengthy appeal judgements, for example, John Gray explicitly referred to the "quasi-religious character" of *kadhi*s to explain that shariʿa was an all-encompassing discourse. It is telling that even somebody like Gray, who showed keen interest in Islamic law and was well versed in this subject, continuously grappled with its alleged lack of procedure and of partiality.[71]

The argument about the discrepancies between judges and *kadhi*s does not deny that both shared the goal of issuing righteous judgements, albeit their hermeneutics diverged. The debates about the poor

67 HC10/1435, ZNA. See also HC10/83, ZNA.

68 HC10/2881, ZNA.

69 Judges granted appeals based on the *kadhi*'s error(s) in HC5/536; HC5/582; HC10/47; HC10/64; HC10/1141; HC10/2843, ZNA. Although the *kadhi* was rebuked, the appeal was dismissed in HC10/5533, ZNA.

70 Powers, "Orientalism, Colonialism, and Legal History," 555–56. A discussion of Islamic laws of inheritance follows in Chapter 7.

71 See Stockreiter, "'British *kadhis*' and 'Muslim judges'," 569–71.

box and access to a free writer show common concern among *kadhi*s and judges about the accessibility of courts to potential litigants regardless of their socioeconomic background and, in light of financial considerations, with regard to race.[72] By the time of World War II, colonial officials had yet to find unanimity in their approach to race, while their perception of Zanzibar as an Arab state continuously shaped the categorisation of litigants and court officials. Foregrounding the general accessibility of courts, colonial officers eventually agreed on dropping race as a criterion for free legal access. As judges served the colonial state and used the law to create citizens and subjects, their concerns for an inclusive judiciary could not mask a top-down approach, which challenged egalitarian notions of pluralistic Islamic law and competed with gender agency in the *kadhi*'s courts.

72 Sean Hanretta reminds us that Muslim scholars and colonial administrators had not only divergent but also similar goals. Idem, *Islam and Social Change in French West Africa: History of an Emancipatory Community* (Cambridge: Cambridge University Press, 2009), 139.

3

The *Kadhi*s and Gender

Throughout the colonial period, the *kadhi*'s courts provided possibilities for women both to enhance their social status and to counter the impact of the socioeconomic changes that unfolded on the island at the turn of the twentieth century. Women used the courts to obtain their legal rights as wives, mothers, and daughters; *kadhi*s for keeping up their social status while serving the community; and colonial officers for controlling the local population. Women's aims and options, however, varied according to their social status within Zanzibari society. The decisive dividing marker was their status as slave or free women. Although this distinction was legally abolished by 1909, it continued to play an important role in women's constructions of their identities and their treatment under the law. Legal reforms, designed to serve the aims of colonial officers of keeping control over women rather than improving their lot, affected women both adversely and favourably. As women generally were less knowledgeable about the law than men, the implementation of stricter modes of procedure appeared to be a greater disadvantage for them than for men, whereas the efforts of individual judges to strengthen "the poor and vulnerable" occasionally improved women's chances. From 1899 onwards, the judge provided women with an additional option for redress on appeal, while the *kadhi*s simultaneously continued to enforce women's rights under shari'a throughout the colonial period.

Previous reconstructions of Zanzibari women's lives before 1900 had to surmount a dearth of sources, particularly sources created by women. Swahili literature and Islamic ideologies suggest women's submissiveness to men, whereas folk stories, life histories, court records, and complementary interpretations of Islamic tenets suggest that women possessed significant social and economic agency, prompting a more nuanced understanding of the potentials and limits of their roles. The poem of Mwana Kupona, dictated around 1860, is an example of Swahili literature that is often quoted in support of the wife's duties towards her husband.[1] However, Swahili literature also depicts wives as rebels and adulteresses.[2] On an ideological level, women's subordination depended on "official" Islamic practices, such as seclusion, veiling, and polygyny. Yet there was also a more practically orientated view, pertaining to kinship, local understandings of gendered approaches to managing household resources, and social obligations, which interacted with the "official" view.[3] The tensions between socioreligious ideals and social practice need to be traced within the shifting socioeconomic context to appreciate fully the dynamic of gender relations.[4]

Paradoxically, the concept of patriarchal Swahili societies has helped scholars such as Laura Fair, Margaret Strobel, and Susan Hirsch to stress women's ability to act in a largely misogynous social environment.[5] Fair's argument that cooperation between colonial officers and the local patriarchs, including *kadhi*s, entailed an increasing dominance of men over women is corroborated by research on other colonial legal systems in Africa, suggesting that women and the poor became increasingly alienated from religious, customary, and civil

1 Alice Werner, "The Utendi of Mwana Kupona," *Harvard African Studies* 1 (1917): 147–81. For a discussion of this poem, see Strobel, *Muslim Women*, 84–86, and Ann Biersteker, "Language, Poetry, and Power: A Reconsideration of '*Utendi wa Mwana Kupona*'," in *Faces of Islam in African Literature*, ed. Kenneth W. Harrow (Portsmouth, NH: Heinemann, 1991), 59–77.

2 Jan Knappert, "Social and Moral Concepts in Swahili Islamic Literature," *Africa* 40, no. 2 (1970): 125–36.

3 See Peletz, *Islamic Modern*, 96–97; Leila Ahmed, *Women and Gender in Islam: Historical Roots of a Modern Debate* (New Haven: Yale University Press, 1992), 63, where she points out that the tension between pragmatic and ethical features is traceable in the Qur'an.

4 For an overview, see Rebecca Gower, Steven Salm, and Toyin Falola, "Swahili Women since the Nineteenth Century: Theoretical and Empirical Considerations on Gender and Identity Construction," *Africa Today* 43, no. 3 (1996): 251–68.

5 Fair, *Pastimes and Politics*; Strobel, *Muslim Women*; Hirsch, *Pronouncing and Persevering*.

courts during the colonial period.[6] Rather than stressing the gender divide, I argue that there were continuous attempts by colonial officers and *kadhi*s to support the "weaker sex." As shown in Chapter 2, colonial officers had marginalised groups in mind when they debated the efficiency and suitability of the legal system. The interrelated concepts of patriarchy and women's vulnerability show how women could actually benefit from their vulnerable status. This perception, derived from Islamic ideologies, interacted with women's partly legally disadvantaged position in relation to men. Susan Hirsch argues that women could draw on various discourses, namely Islamic law, Swahili ethics, and cosmology as well as state law, thereby establishing a standard female narrative within a negotiable dominant legal discourse. Similarly, Erin Stiles demonstrates nuances of women's use of the *kadhi*'s court in Mkokotoni. Questioning the usefulness of describing the outcome of court cases in terms of success and failure, she accounts for women's recourse to courts to negotiate divorce and for *kadhi*s' support of women.[7] As the following chapters show, *kadhi*s enforced women's rights as articulated in legal doctrines, such as by ordering husbands to write cheques and divorce papers.[8] In most suits concerning disobedience, the *kadhi* initially ordered the wife to return to her husband, in the expectation of reconciliation, but the outcome of nearly all these suits was a divorce for a consideration. Further, maintenance claims, some of which only concerned the non-provision of clothes, were upheld and enforced, if necessary through attachments of the husband's property, unless he divorced his wife or she obtained a divorce for a consideration.

Although the colonial approach to gender was manifest in individual endeavours rather than a universal colonial doctrine, purdah, veiling,

[6] Fair, *Pastimes and Politics*, 196, 201; Martin Chanock, "Making Customary Law: Men, Women, and Courts in Colonial Northern Rhodesia," in *African Women and the Law: Historical Perspectives*, ed. Margaret Jean Hay and Marcia Wright (Boston: Boston University, 1982), 53–67; idem, *Law, Custom, and Social Order*; Schmidt, "Negotiated Spaces"; idem, "Patriarchy, Capitalism, and the Colonial State"; Mann and Roberts, *Law in Colonial Africa*.

[7] Stiles, *Islamic Court*.

[8] In one case a wife and her child were not ordered to accompany her husband on a potentially dangerous sea crossing to the Mrima coast (Below entry #867, no number, 7 Muḥarram [1320]/16 April 1902, HC28/29, ZNA).

and patriarchy were perennial features in colonial social discourse. While gender segregation and veiling received little attention from Muslim jurists,[9] both practices were central to colonial officers' perception of Muslim women. Their attitude towards Zanzibari women was informed by their bias in favour of the Muslim woman behind the veil as well as against the "uncivilised native." Officers frequently switched between their mission to help the secluded and to control the immoral.[10] Purdah as an institution was frowned upon by colonial officers, because it epitomised the "backwardness" of Zanzibari society. British Resident Pearce, for instance, praised the sultana for setting an excellent example to her female subjects, as she frequently drove out, though closely veiled.[11] Similarly, Vera Davies, the chairwoman of the Ladies Club, remarked in her annual report of 1957 that she was pleased to see many purdah members on the club's sports day.[12] Women's outings were welcomed by British members of Zanzibari society as evidence of their successful "unveiling mission." The colonial patriarchal edifice was built on obvious symbols of male dominance, such as purdah, veiling, polygyny, and the unilateral discretion of the husband for divorce and was exacerbated by Islamic laws discriminating against women.[13] Officers' understanding of patriarchy was a self-fulfilling concept, as the dynamics of gender relations in the family were hidden.

[9] Tucker, *Women, Family, and Gender*, 175.

[10] Cf. Anne McClintock, *Imperial Leather: Race, Gender and Sexuality in the Colonial Contest* (New York: Routledge, 1995), 31; Ahmed, *Women and Gender*, especially 149–52. See also Janice Boddy, *Civilizing Women: British Crusades in Colonial Sudan* (Princeton: Princeton University Press, 2007); Ann Laura Stoler, *Carnal Knowledge and Imperial Power: Race and the Intimate in Colonial Rule* (Berkeley: University of California Press, 2002).

[11] Pearce, *Zanzibar*, 224–25.

[12] Ladies' Club Old Fort, Chairman's Annual Report for the Year Ending 31 March 1957, AB12/70, ZNA.

[13] McClintock, *Imperial Leather*, 240. See also Julia Clancy-Smith, "Islam, Gender, and Identities in the Making of French Algeria, 1830–1962," in *Domesticating the Empire: Race, Gender, and Family Life in French and Dutch Colonialism*, ed. Julia Clancy-Smith and Frances Gouda (Charlottesville: University of Virginia Press, 1998), 154–74. On the imagined suffering of Muslim women, see Haim Gerber, "Social and Economic Position of Women in an Ottoman City, Bursa, 1600–1700," *International Journal of Middle East Studies* 12, no. 3 (1980): 231–44. He strongly questions the applicability of patriarchal concepts to seventeenth-century Bursa.

The perception of gender relations as governed by a patriarchal hierarchy conditioned both scholars' and colonial officers' assumptions about women's socially subordinate status. This assumption, however, reflects a relatively uncritical adoption of the idea of a normative gendered order. On the one hand, the force that the concept of patriarchy has gained owes to the Islamic ideology of women's seclusion, while, on the other hand, it is exacerbated by projecting back present understandings of separated gendered spheres, a female household versus a male world.[14]

From the early nineteenth century, the enslavement of the indigenous peoples of Zanzibar, the Hadimu and Tumbatu, as well as the integration of mainland slaves into Zanzibari society transformed gender relations. Edward Alpers has argued that the commercial expansion under the Bū Saʿīd disintegrated relatively equitable gender relations among the Hadimu and Tumbatu and entailed the marginalisation of women's labour. This argument implies that, prior to Omani reign, women and men were engaged in an equal distribution of labour and that the Omanis negatively affected gender relations. Alpers' argument is enmeshed with another explanatory piece of evidence, the institutionalisation of shariʿa, which reduced the influence of customary law and superseded laws favouring women.[15] Scholars such as Carol Eastman, Margaret Strobel, and Pat Caplan in her earlier work have ascribed to Swahili societies a dichotomy in which shariʿa is defined as a male sphere and customary law as a female sphere.[16] More recently, this dichotomy has been questioned by Allyson Purpura in her thesis on

[14] Arguing against projecting back present practices, anthropologist Kelly Askew has shown innovatively how gender segregation was introduced on the Swahili coast during the nineteenth century. Idem, "Female Circles and Male Lines: Gender Dynamics along the Swahili Coast," *Africa Today* 46, no. 3/4 (1999): 67–102.

[15] Edward Alpers, "'Ordinary Household Chores': Ritual and Power in a Nineteenth-Century Swahili Women's Spirit Possession Cult," *International Journal of African Historical Studies* 17, no. 4 (1984): 680–82. Alpers draws on Pat Caplan's ethnographic studies when he equates customary law with favouring women and shariʿa with being advantageous to men.

[16] Carol Eastman, "Who are the Swahili?," *Africa* 41, no. 3 (1971): 228–36; Strobel, *Muslim Women*; Pat Caplan, "Gender, Ideology and Modes of Production on the Coast of East Africa," *Paideuma* 28 (1982): 29–43. In her article of 1995, however, Caplan revises this original dichotomy. Idem, "'Law' and 'Custom': Marital Disputes on Northern Mafia Island, Tanzania," in *Understanding Disputes: The Politics of Argument*, ed. Pat Caplan (Oxford: Berg, 1995), 203–21.

FIGURE 3.1. Women at a market area. Courtesy of ZNA.

the social relations of Islamic knowledge in Zanzibar Town, in which she argues that both categories overlap and mediate social relations and thus cut across gender "boundaries."[17] There is some appeal in arguments that take customary laws and practices such as spirit possession and ritual performance as forms of protest and compensation for women excluded from Islamic rituals and discriminated against under shariʿa. However, court records demonstrate that the above assumptions have distorted our understanding of gender relations from the Bū Saʿīdī period onwards.

At the turn of the twentieth century, women's socioeconomic status was determined by their free or slave status, their place of residence, and their religion. Although the majority of slaves brought to Zanzibar from the mainland were originally non-Muslim, most gradually

[17] Allyson Purpura, "Knowledge and Agency: The Social Relations of Islamic Expertise in Zanzibar Town" (PhD diss., CUNY, 1997), 251. John Middleton, *The World of the Swahili: An African Mercantile Civilization* (New Haven: Yale University Press, 1992), 119, also cautions against the neat separation of male and female spheres in Swahili societies.

adopted Sunni ideologies and practices. Slave women worked on plantations, as builders, and carried out menial tasks outside as well as inside the household, moving around freely under the supervision of their master or mistress.[18] Women in rural areas, mostly peasants, might have pursued petty trade to provide for the household, regardless of their social and ethnic background. Such rural women may have been less bound by gender segregation than their urban counterparts, particularly women of Arab origin or from households of socially esteemed families, who were less likely to pursue work outside the household.[19] However, this categorisation is anything but rigid. In 1839, the young English merchant Leigh describes Arab women, relations of the sultan, making mats in their house, although it is not certain whether they were selling their handicraft. Moreover, the women in this household were unveiled, which Leigh explains by the absence of men in their home as well as their protection by the sultan.[20] Leigh's observation was probably exceptional, as the experiences that shaped most women in town tended to be restricted to the house, while at the same time women's relationships to other members of both the family and the household characterised their experience irrespective of social background. The overwhelming congruence between social and economic status began to diverge in the twentieth century, leaving women from socially esteemed but impoverished families in previously inexperienced difficulties. Socioeconomic changes affecting relationships within the family and consequently arising grievances could be redressed at the *kadhi*'s courts, whose rulings shaped women's agency and its boundaries.

It appears from the case sample that women were both prominent and often successful litigants throughout the first half of the twentieth century (see Table 3.1). Naturally, court cases do not yield direct information about how female litigants, especially plaintiffs, were perceived by society. Oral sources indicate that filing a suit in court was a last resort in dispute resolution, given that institutions such as elders and *walezi wa mtaa*, or guardians of the neighbourhood, served as

18 The English merchant Leigh describes how slave women were carrying mortar as early as in 1837 (Kirkman, "Zanzibar Diary Part I," 297).

19 See Middleton, *The World of the Swahili*, 24.

20 James Kirkman, ed., "The Zanzibar Diary of John Studdy Leigh, Part II," *International Journal of African Historical Studies* 13, no. 3 (1980): 499–500.

TABLE 3.1. *Female Plaintiffs*

ZNA Court Records	Number of Cases in which the Plaintiff, or one of the Plaintiffs, is Female	Percentage of Female Plaintiffs	Percentage of Female Plaintiffs Winning the Case	Number of Sample
HC5	7	100	43	7
HC8	5	100	0	5
HC9	25	53	76	47
HC10	59	70	71	84
HC28/29	40	63	70	64
Total	136	66	68	207

mediators in most conflicts.[21] When Harold Ingrams was secretary to the director of education in Zanzibar during the 1920s, cases such as theft, assault, and trespassing were mostly settled through mediation and arbitration by the *sheha*.[22] Disputes pertaining to family matters, by contrast, were preferably resolved within the family, as in most other Muslim societies.

To some degree, addressing a court entailed violating local norms of respectability, as it made private affairs public. Questioning our modern dichotomy between public and private, Yaseen Noorani argues that it diverges from early Islamic perceptions of space that were relational and status defined. Space was defined as men being in control of women – a control that was not necessarily manifest in female seclusion and gender segregation, thus concretely delineating space. It was, rather, a symbolic concept that guaranteed social order.[23] This understanding was still reflected in Zanzibari perceptions during early

[21] Interviews with Bi Hadiya Rashidi Ali, 13 June 2004; Bi Hadija Nasoro Ibrahim, 24 April 2004; Juma Bakari Mfaume, 28 May 2004; Sh. Abdalla Suleiman Jumbe, 24 March 2004.

[22] W. H. Ingrams, *Zanzibar: Its History and Its People* (London: H.F. & G. Witherby, 1931), 267.

[23] Yaseen Noorani, "Normative Notions of Public and Private in Early Islamic Culture," in *Harem Histories: Envisioning Places and Living Spaces*, ed. Marilyn Booth (Durham: Duke University Press, 2010), 49–68. On the evolution of the concept of privacy among Sunni jurists, see Eli Alshech, "'Do Not Enter Houses Other Than Your Own': The Evolution of the Notion of a Private Domestic Sphere in Early Sunni Islamic Thought," *Islamic Law and Society* 11, no. 3 (2004): 291–332.

colonial rule, until the British imposed a private–public dichotomy that was first introduced by confining court sessions to an enclosed space and became further entrenched in the course of colonial rule. Judging from colonial court records, the present role of the *kadhi*'s courts, and Zanzibaris' approach to them, this dichotomy engendered a shift in raising and dealing with claims. This affected women more adversely than men, as they perceived it as inappropriate to have to come forward with allegations set down in formal fashion in the plaint. Moreover, the enforced rigidity of procedure entailed the increasing dependency of mostly illiterate women on the men who wrote down their plaint and read it back to them.

Under Bū Saʿīdī reign, physical space had increasingly come to represent strictly gendered spheres, thus moving away from the original symbolism and relationality of gender roles. Yet given the ease with which women from all social backgrounds addressed the *kadhi*'s courts, it is difficult to see that they actually imperilled their respectability in seeking legal redress. The association of women in court with shame may well have been created (by men) as a means of social control. Salme (1844–1924), the daughter of Sultan Saʿīd, noted in her autobiography that there was no reason for a wife to submit to the moods of her husband and that women frequently addressed the *kadhi* in person. However, "custom requires that this right be only put into force in most urgent cases, and vanity has a good share in upholding it, as the veil disfigures women to a degree, and makes them look like walking mummies."[24] The association of women's honour with the veil, and thus with gender segregation, came to be entrenched during Omani rule and primarily affected women of Arab origin and in Arab households. The construction of the social order placed free persons on top and those with Arab ancestors, preferably going back to the Prophet himself, above those of slave and/or mainland, non-coastal origin. Women at the bottom of this hierarchy began to identify the distinguishing markers of seclusion and veiling with higher social esteem and thus began to emulate them.[25]

24 Ruete, *Memoirs of an Arabian Princess*, 105, 107.

25 See Laura Fair, "Dressing Up: Clothing, Class and Gender in Post-Abolition Zanzibar," *Journal of African History* 39, no. 1 (1998): 63–94. On the adoption of veiling as a symbol of women's respectability and social activity, see Hirsch, *Pronouncing and Persevering*, 49–55.

Social background and economic relations between the sexes modified the actual practice of Islam as well as its underlying ideologies and account for the diversity of women's experiences.[26] A careful distinction applies between the spatial creation of gendered spheres, on the one hand, and women's agency, which was regulated by both shariʿa and local norms and predominantly occurred inside the house as well as "behind the veil," on the other. For Mombasa, Strobel argues that women particularly from wealthier backgrounds and in town were more constrained by purdah but had more options to circumvent the constraints it imposed on them.[27] While the daughter of Sultan Saʿīd, Salme, envied lower status women for their freedom,[28] Strobel proposes that husbands from upper social strata exercised less power over women in the privacy of the home than in public. Generally social ideals were less adhered to among lower social strata, which provided women from these strata with greater freedom of movement and suited, or rather was triggered by, their need to contribute to their own and their families' livelihood.[29]

Socioeconomic changes during the nineteenth century suggest the increasing confinement of women to the house and adoption of veiling, which went hand in hand with an Omani-imported, stricter adherence to Islamic practices. By the early twentieth century, gender segregation had become customary among Zanzibari women of all walks of life and manifested itself most in town. After abolition, former slave women were able to construct their identities as free women through clothing and claiming their rights in court, while the colonial government further entrenched changes in work patterns.[30] Strobel argues that British perceptions of the unacceptability of women as manual

[26] Cf. Agmon, "Women, Class, and Gender;" idem, "Text, Court, and Family in Late-Nineteenth-Century Palestine," in *Family History in the Middle East: Household, Property and Gender*, ed. Beshara Doumani (Albany: State University of New York Press, 2003), 201–28; Deniz Kandiyoti, "Islam and Patriarchy: A Comparative Perspective," in *Women in Middle Eastern History: Shifting Boundaries in Sex and Gender*, ed. Nikki R. Keddie and Beth Baron (New Haven: Yale University Press, 1991), 24; McClintock, *Imperial Leather*, 94; Tucker, *Women in Nineteenth-Century Egypt*, 4.

[27] Strobel, *Muslim Women*, 73–76.

[28] Ruete, *Memoirs of an Arabian Princess*, 105.

[29] Strobel, *Muslim Women*, 54–55, 149–50.

[30] See Frederick Cooper, *From Slaves to Squatters*.

workers pushed women to seek employment in domestic service and generally in the informal sector.[31] In early twentieth-century Ng'ambo, women typically engaged in wage labour, whereas during the 1940s and 1950s they were restricted to the home. Throughout the twentieth century, women found it increasingly difficult to get waged jobs in Zanzibar Town. Consequently, they sought income through more respectable, independent forms of employment, which had the advantage of enabling them to combine domestic, child rearing, and social obligations with providing income.[32] This process was also driven by the stigmatisation of paid domestic service, an aftermath of the experience of slavery.

Although a requirement to record litigants' professions appeared in the 1940s, court records are remarkably silent on women's occupations. Probably because of the nature of most cases, in which women tried to prove their economic dependence on their husbands, records rarely state women's means of obtaining income. Arguably, clerks omitted jobs that they did not perceive as decent or favourable for the litigant, while certificates of means attest to women's occupation as simply married or dependant. A small number of women feature as farmers and housewives, while they most commonly appear as having no occupation. Exceptional entries note female traders, plantation owners, and a weeder. Professionalisation and a strict categorisation of income-generating activities were rarely meaningful to men, or to women in particular, as they constituted Western, colonially introduced concepts.

Conceptions of respectability played an important role in the development of women's economic activities. In Mombasa by the mid-1950s, women could engage in a variety of skilled occupations such as dressmaking, nursing, midwifery, and teaching without compromising their respectability.[33] Women's increasing exposure to European and

[31] Strobel, *Muslim Women*, 127, 148–49, 154.

[32] Fair, *Pastimes and Politics*, 33–34. See also Luise White, *The Comforts of Home: Prostitution in Colonial Nairobi* (Chicago: University of Chicago Press, 1990); Grace B. Kyomuhendo and Marjorie K. McIntosh, *Women, Work, and Domestic Virtue in Uganda, 1900–2003* (Oxford: James Currey, 2006), Part II; Marjorie K. McIntosh, *Yoruba Women, Work, and Social Change* (Bloomington: Indiana University Press, 2009), Part III.

[33] Strobel, *Muslim Women*, 115; see also Lynn M. Thomas, *Politics of the Womb: Women, Reproduction, and the State in Kenya* (Berkeley: University of California

Western values and models of behaviour during British rule expanded the roles available to them and, in at least one instance, entailed a clash of values in the sphere of guardianship. The incompatibility of being a proper guardian and going to the cinema comes to light in a case of 1956, in which a grandmother sued the father of her granddaughters for custody. The grandmother, Taibina bt. Hija, described as a woman under purdah, a property owner, and a tailor by profession, stated that she fulfilled her religious duties (praying five times a day and fasting in Ramaḍān) *and* enjoyed frequenting the cinema. For Taibina, indulging in cinema screenings was compatible with being a proper guardian. The *kadhi*, however, held this habit of seeking entertainment against her, as it obviously failed to conform to standards of decency expected of a woman. He ruled that the mother was responsible for the upbringing of children, "[t]herefore if she could not bring up with good character her own son who comes from her own self, how then will she be able to bring up these two girls! And, the mother is the first school where from the child learns manners and character and grows up upon such teachings as she has imparted upon it."[34] Taibina's son was a performer of *ngoma*. In the appeal judgement, whose last pages are missing, the judge says persons unfit for custody were pointed out to him as prostitutes, dancing girls, and persons who do not perform their religious duties. The following page would have continued with this enumeration.[35]

In the first half of the twentieth century, tensions between Islamic doctrines of egalitarianism and social practices of inequality characterised gender relations in Zanzibar Town and drove women to court. These tensions were exacerbated by ideologies of male dominance as well as ethnic and social hierarchy. The ambiguity of women's roles inherent in Islamic doctrines, however, gave women the ability to choose from the roles ascribed to them. Social anthropologist Ziba Mir-Hosseini points to the potential blurring of boundaries between religious and legal dimensions, particularly concerning marriage regulations, which uphold patriarchal ideologies but at the same time allow

Press, 2003), Chapter 2; Elisabeth McMahon and Corrie Decker, "Wives or Workers? Negotiating the Social Contract between Female Teachers and the Colonial State in Zanzibar," *Journal of Women's History* 21, no. 2 (2009): 39–61.

34 HC10/3325, original in English, and HC10/3273, ZNA.

35 HC10/3325, ZNA. Cf. Chapter 6.

alterations.[36] The dialectical relationship between "official" ideologies and local practice is illustrated in a case of 1952, where two witnesses had to confirm Salma bt. ʿAlawi Bunumay's sale of furniture. One witness recognised her voice, but the other needed to see her face, although insisting in court that he did not have the right to see it. When a conflict arose between keeping up the doctrine of sexual segregation through veiling and executing a legal Islamic transaction, the less important of the two needed to give way, which was veiling.[37]

Given the social conventions of purdah and respectability, women from upper social strata particularly preferred to act as legal persons through a representative. However, certain steps, such as taking an oath or giving testimony, demanded the appearance of female litigants in person.[38] In most cases women's representatives were their legal guardians (male relatives or the *kadhi* and, in two exceptional cases, the mother).[39] Representation in court was one of many issues on which the colonial administration imposed its regulations. The Zanzibar Courts Decree of 1908 endorsed the representation of parties by proxy, defined as a near relative of the litigant or her or his master, servant, or general agent. "Near relative" referred to husband, father, son, brother, uncle, or nephew.[40] Thus, the decree reiterated the possible agents according to shariʿa, save that previously a slave could not represent his or her master in court.

In addition to being represented by a male member of the family, it became common among all social strata and among both men and women to employ a lawyer, called *wakīl* in the *kadhi*'s courts. This practice, which Sultan Saʿīd's daughter described as unknown in

[36] Ziba Mir-Hosseini, *Marriage on Trial: A Study of Islamic Family Law*, rev. ed. (London: I. B. Tauris, 2000), 192. See also Fatima Mernissi, *Beyond the Veil: Male-Female Dynamics in Modern Muslim Society*, rev. ed. (London: Saqi Books, 2003), for potentials of and constraints in gender bargains.

[37] HC10/2843, ZNA. Cf. Chapters 7 and 8.

[38] In the *kadhi*'s court at Chake Chake, Pemba, women did not enter the courtroom but spoke through a window (Schacht, "Notes on Islam," 114–15). For other parts of the Muslim world where women among upper social strata preferred to appoint a representative, see Agmon, "Women, Class, and Gender,"490; Tucker, *Women in Nineteenth-Century Egypt*, 96.

[39] See Entry #138, no. 69, 6 Rabīʿ I 1318/3 July 1900, HC28/29, ZNA, where Fatima bt. Muhammad was represented by her mother in a suit for her dower, and HC10/43, where the mother acted as guardian in marriage, which is impermissible according to both Shafiʿis and Ibāḍīs.

[40] Zanzibar Courts Decree, 1908, BA14/1, ZNA.

the midnineteenth century, was established in the 1880s. *Wakīls* were subjected to the same regime of scrutiny and efficiency as all the other holders of posts in the legal system.[41] At least since 1901, in order to represent a party in court, *wakīls* needed a certificate from the sultan and from 1923 onwards a power of attorney.[42] Before colonial reforms made the services of a *wakīl* available for free, from about 1927,[43] a woman from a lower social strata was likely to be represented by her husband or a male relative. Women from more esteemed, upper social strata may have had more than one representative – a *wakīl*, competent in legal issues, and a male family member.[44]

While procedural changes account for the increasing employment of a *wakīl* in the course of the early decades of the twentieth century,[45] the impoverishment of Arab plantation owners may explain the decrease in representation by proxy. Women especially were in a disadvantaged position on account of their ignorance of the law,[46] procedure in particular, and their reliance on representatives who did not keep them informed properly, leading to the likelihood of them being cheated. The trend of lower status women in adopting purdah in order to enhance their respectability can be traced in their imitation of the social convention of the upper class regarding representation in court.[47]

41 A memorandum of 1948 said that only a small number of persons with limited knowledge of shariʿa practised in the *kadhi*'s courts, pointing to the unsatisfactory but long-established practice and people's suffering from their dependence on incompetent *wakīls*. It suggested that the proposed Muslim Institute could train *wakīls* (High court registrar to chief secretary, 23 August 1949, AB62/78, ZNA).

42 Sultan's Decree, 19 June 1901, BA14/25; Rules of Court made under Article 56 of the Zanzibar Order in Council, 1914, AB62/26, ZNA, and section 26 of the Zanzibar Courts Decree of 1923.

43 Sh. Abdalla Suleiman Jumbe believes that people had access to a *wakīl* regardless of their financial means (interview, 26 October 2003).

44 HC9/115; HC10/2843; No entry #, no. 59, 4 Jumādā II 1320/7 September 1902, HC28/29, ZNA. Muhaza bt. Saʿid had two male representatives but no *wakīl* (Entry #492, no. 681, 14 Muḥarram [1319]/3 May 1901, HC28/29, ZNA). Cf. Tucker, *Women in Nineteenth-Century Egypt*, 96, on upper class women's rare appearance in person. On the prominence of powers of attorney in Brava, see Vianello and Kassim, *Servants of the Sharia*, 62–63.

45 Cf. also Agmon, "Women, Class, and Gender," 490–91.

46 Sh. Ahmed Mohamed Saleh Ba Kathir holds that women are generally less knowledgeable on shariʿa matters than men (interview, 27 January 2004). Stiles, however, suggests that Zanzibari women today may be more legally savvy than men (idem, *Islamic Court*, 195).

47 HC9/15; HC9/69; HC9/111; HC9/116; No entry #, no number, date of hearing 20 Ṣafar 1321/18 May 1903, HC28/29, ZNA.

According to one of the most prolific scholars of Islamic legal history, Wael Hallaq, scholarship has ignored "the moral, the religious and to some extent the socio-structural foundations of power, aspects that the modern analysis of power has, perforce, left largely underdeveloped."[48] At the same time, he explains that these under-explored arenas of power structures did not liberate women from the patriarchal legal system that discriminated against them. While we usually describe historical agency in powerful contemporary language, this modern discourse of liberation and empowerment would have meant little to our historical actors and poorly captures their agency. The nuances and versatility of gender demand historicisation, thus reconsideration of the concept of discrimination, and suggest that gender was malleable in Zanzibar at the time. At the official level, the British colonial period saw rigidification of gender roles, likely starting during the Bū Saʿīdī period. In practice, however, gender roles continued to be shaped by social status, descent, and kinship relations and remained relatively flexible.

During the socioeconomic changes after the abolition of slavery in the early twentieth century, the *kadhi*'s courts were a central institution to which women could take their grievances. Although these courts maintained gender spheres, *kadhi*s' judgements were not informed by preference for either gender. The practice of seclusion increasingly became the spatial embodiment of gendered spheres in the twentieth century; it may have hampered but did not disable women's agency. Its lesser form, veiling, on the other hand, became a means for former slave women to enhance their respectability. That neither women's nor men's respectability was imperilled if they addressed the *kadhi*'s courts is shown by the appeal of these courts among all social strata.

[48] Hallaq, *Shariʿa*, 184–85.

4

Litigants and the *Kadhi*'s Courts

Under British–Omani reign, the social order was informed by Islamic ideologies and an exclusivist hierarchical system that, nevertheless, allowed for integration on the basis of common religion, for exploitation if this common feature was lacking, and for involvement with economic partners such as Indians, the chief financial backbone of the sultanate. At the same time, the religiously sustained slave owner–slave relationship lingered on well into the twentieth century, in spite of the implementation of abolition decrees. *Kadhi*'s court records show a struggle for citizenship by those at the lower ranks of the socioreligious hierarchy, demonstrating former slaves' attempts to reverse the social order once the abolition of slavery enabled them to represent their own interests in court.

The fact that the *kadhi*'s courts provided redress for women, and marginalised groups in general, may seem as an idiosyncrasy of these courts but had been intrinsic to their role as important tribunals for dispute settlement since the Bū Saʿīdī reign. In the broader context of the Muslim world, the fact that the *kadhi*'s courts served, within colonially imposed legal categories, the entire population of Zanzibar Town was nothing new or unusual.[1] Most recently, Alessandra Vianello and Mohamed Kassim have shown the popularity of these courts among

[1] See, for instance, Christelow, *Muslim Law Courts*; idem, *Thus Ruled Emir Abbas*; Doumani, *Rediscovering Palestine*; Gerber, *State, Society, and Law*; Peletz, *Islamic Modern*; Shaham, *Family and the Courts.*

all social strata in Brava.[2] According to Judith Tucker, shariʿa courts in nineteenth-century Egypt owed their popular appeal to the fact that they combined elements of elite culture with cultural tradition and social arrangements.[3] In Zanzibar Town, this cultural tradition underwent a process of autocratisation by the ruler from the reign of Sultan Barghash onwards, without, however, thwarting litigants' use of the courts.

Marriage was a main area of contestation in the *kadhi*'s courts. The unequal distribution of rights and obligations between the spouses under Shafiʿi and Ibāḍī laws in part explains wives' decisions to claim their rights in court, in most cases after previous arbitration efforts had failed. The "house of obedience" is the basic concept of a Muslim marriage, providing for the wife's entitlement to maintenance (food, clothes, and proper accommodation) as long as she is obedient towards her husband. In grievances arising in marriage and if wives wished a divorce, some women were compelled to address the *kadhi* both in seeking to obtain their rights and in order to strengthen their bargaining position with their husbands. In breaking- or broken-down relationships, wives asked in court for maintenance and/or the deferred dower, often citing these grounds to petition for a judicial dissolution. Based on at least one of the shariʿa grounds, wives sued for a judicial dissolution of the marriage and the realisation of various conjugal rights, such as proper accommodation, separate accommodation from co-wives, or, their social standing permitting, a servant. Men addressed the court with restitution of conjugal rights claims, often in response to their wives' actions, to get legal support for reestablishing their marital authority; wives tended to counter these attempts with claims of lack of maintenance: the "house of obedience" was thus a highly contested legal concept. Suits between spouses also evolved from a debt other than the dower.

It was common for wives suing for a judicial dissolution of the marriage to cite more than one grounds in order to increase their chances of

[2] Vianello and Kassim, *Servants of the Sharia*. All groups of the population also addressed the African courts in colonial Bujumbura (Dickerman, "Use of Court Records").

[3] Tucker, *Women in Nineteenth-Century Egypt*, 13–14. In Lagos, Mann explored the supreme court records as they yield the voices of slaves, the poor, and women. Idem, "The Rise of Taiwo Olowo," 90.

TABLE 4.1. *Nature of Claims*

Nature of Claim	Number of Cases	Number of Female Plaintiffs	Number of Male Plaintiffs
Guardianship in marriage	4	3	1
Dower (prompt or deferred)	18	18	0
Maintenance	21	21	0
Child custody	5	2	3
Dissolution of marriage	45	45	0
Confirmation of divorce/divorce certificate	7	7	0
Restitution of conjugal rights	36	0	36
Detention of the wife	5	0	5
Paternity	2	1	1
Inheritance	22	15	9
Debt (other than maintenance)/property	35	22	13
Other	6	4	2
Unrecorded	1	0	1
Total	207	138	71

Note: Claims for restitution of conjugal rights and detention of the wife were exclusively filed by husbands, whereas suits for dower, maintenance, dissolution of marriage, and confirmation of divorce were brought by wives only. If more than one grounds was cited in the claim, I have listed the first grounds. In case of female and male plaintiffs suing for inheritance, I have counted both genders. Thus the number of female and male plaintiffs added exceeds the number of cases in this category. In one case, I have not recorded the nature of the claim.

a favourable judgement. With regard to claims on the grounds of failure to provide maintenance, demands for future maintenance appeared in plaints from at least 1916. As maintenance can only be claimed in arrears, this suggests an innovative support of an actual claim for divorce. Children were almost completely absent in claims, indicating that disputes over their guardianship were settled out-of-court.[4] The few cases in which the mother sued on behalf of her child concerned outstanding debts, such as inheritance and maintenance.[5] As for

[4] HC5/561; HC9/67; HC10/64; HC10/3273; HC10/3325, ZNA are rare cases of child custody. Similarly, cases of child custody are absent in the court records of Brava (Vianello and Kassim, *Servants of the Sharia*).

[5] HC10/5569; Entry #58, no number, 24 Dhū l-Ḥijja 1317/24 April 1900; No entry #, no number, 29 Shaʿbān 1320/30 November 1902, HC28/29, ZNA.

inheritance, only lawful children inherit from their father; socioreligiously, illegitimate children belong to the mother only, which explains why paternity could become a contested issue in court.[6] As discussed in Chapter 7, inheritance claims reveal how former masters sought to access shares of inheritance of former slaves, indicating the ongoing tension between these two social groups. Given the importance of having evidence, certificates for divorce, manumission, deeds of sale, and so on, were also the subject of claims.[7]

As in most schools, under Shafiʿi and Ibāḍī laws women need a guardian in marriage. If the guardian withheld his consent, some women sued for his or the *kadhi*'s permission in court, as the lack of the (proper) guardian's consent could lead to the annulment of the marriage.[8] Another type of claim revolved around guardianship and kin detaining the wife. Cases in which the husband accused usually a member of the wife's family of detaining her[9] show the ongoing bond of the wife with her natal family and her capability to draw upon her own social network for support.

The few claims alleging the husband's impotence, two of which were made in 1900 and 1901 and another in 1958, are important reminders of the vast scope of issues that were raised in court and considered legitimate impediments to a happy marriage. If established, *kadhi*s acknowledged women's claims of the husband's impotence or refusal to have intercourse.[10] The complaint of one wife about her husband's

6 HC10/1435; HC10/5569, ZNA.

7 Women sued for a certificate of divorce in HC10/2910; HC10/3695; HC10/5531, ZNA. Salama bt. ʿAli sued for her mother's deed of manumission, a deed for a plot of land, and a paper detailing her father's legacy (No entry #, no number, 7 Shaʿbān 1320/8 November 1902, HC28/29, ZNA).

8 HC5/582; HC10/48; HC10/1156, ZNA. A father sought to annul the marriage of his daughter as he had not given his consent in HC10/2822, ZNA.

9 HC9/136; HC10/3202; HC10/5534; Entry #196, no. 150, 6 Jumādā I 1318/1 September 1900, HC28/29, ZNA. In HC9/122; HC9/129; Entry #771, no. 236, 26 Shawwāl 1319/5 February 1902, HC28/29, ZNA, the relationship between the wife and the person who allegedly detained her is unclear.

10 HC10/3552; Entry #330, no. 362, 3 Ramaḍān 1318/25 December 1900; Entry #469, no. 635, 28 Dhū l-Ḥijja 1318/18 April 1901; Entry #490, no number, 11 Muḥarram 1318 [1319]/30 April 1901, HC28/29, ZNA. Cf. Tucker, *In the House of the Law*, 45. Husbands were generally granted one year to prove their potency. Failing to do so, the wife would be released from the marriage without incurring loss (Tucker, *Women, Family, and Gender*, 93). This also appears to have been the practice in Zanzibar. For the basis of such claims under Shafiʿi law, see L. W. C. van den Berg,

practice of sharing his nights between her and his *suria*, or concubine, also fell into this quite intimate category of claims.[11] Whereas anthropologist John Middleton notes that the personal, private aspect of disputes was stressed when lineage or ward councils were addressed,[12] the *kadhi*'s court records prove that intimate matters were also raised in formal and public legal institutions.

The case register covering the years from 1900 to 1903 provides a valuable array of information detailing who sued whom. Social background is indicated in the lineage of the litigant: people are identified by up to four names (their proper name, their father's and grandfather's name, and a *nisba*), depending on their social standing. That the social status of Jawhar and his wife Maryam Baruti was lower than the one of Saʿid b. ʿAbud Hamid and his wife Fatima bt. ʿAbdallah b. ʿAli Ba Yaʾshut is illustrated by their genealogy or lack thereof.[13] Social esteem is reflected in the terms of address, with *sharīf* and shaykh added after the name of servants or children of the first. Thus the slave Nafasi appears as "*khādima al-sharīf* Aḥmad b. Abī Bakr b. Sumayṭ" and Fatima as "*bint al*-sayyid Ahmad b. ʿAlawi al-Ba ʿAlawi."[14] Additionally, varying sums of maintenance, which Shafiʿi *kadhi*s calculate based on the husband's financial capacity, indicate that all social strata addressed the court. The *kadhi*'s courts did not require specific knowledge or pecuniary reserves from their parties. These courts were accessible to people regardless of their background, exemplifying that neither gender nor social status was a boundary for litigation.

Although individual litigants' motives for going to court varied according to social background and gender, a striking continuity obtains in the framing of claims across all social strata in terms of

Minhâdj aṭ-ṭâlibîn, le guide des zélés croyants, manuel de jurisprudence musulmane selon le rite de Châfi'ī, Arabic text, published at the order of the government, trans. and annotations by L. W. C. van den Berg, vol. II (Batavia: Government Press, 1883), 362–63. These page numbers and those of all subsequent references to Berg refer to the French translation.

11 The *kadhi* did remind the husband of the different legal status between wife and concubine (Entry #432, no. 551, 19 Dhū l-Qaʿda 1318/10 March 1901, HC28/29, ZNA).

12 Middleton, *The World of the Swahili*, 51–52.

13 Entry #330, no. 362, 3 Ramaḍān 1318/25 December 1900 and No entry #, no number, 29 Shaʿbān 1320/30 November 1902, HC28/29, ZNA, respectively.

14 No entry #, no. 82, 17 Dhū l-Qaʿda 1320/15 February 1903 and Entry #755, no number, 14 Shawwāl 1319/24 January 1902, HC28/29, ZNA, respectively.

maintenance, restitution of conjugal rights, debts in general, and inheritance claims. Sayyids as well as former slaves insisted on the reestablishment of their conjugal authority. By the same token, women across the whole social spectrum sued for maintenance and divorce, with suits for debts showing the ramifications of socioeconomic networks within and beyond the family. Omanis and people of Arab origin, real or fictive, *sharīf*s, and sayyids sued and were sued by the socially less esteemed.[15] Likewise, witnesses did not necessarily come from the same social background as the party for whom they gave testimony. Freed male and female slaves acted as witnesses for male and female descendants of their slave owners. The *kadhi* adapted rulings to the litigants' social status with regard to maintenance and also obedience in the case of slaves.[16]

Relationships and social networks occasionally played into litigation. There are indications that women and men from lower social strata drew on personal networks and relationships in order to file a suit and achieve a favourable outcome: an appellant's brother who was the gardener of the judge, an affidavit drawn up for free by a relative, or a free summons for the plaintiff whose father had been a court clerk for many years.[17] Claims were also filed by people who had a connection to the legal system; relatives and household members of *kadhi*s and *wakīl*s appear to have made use of their familiarity with the judiciary.[18] So did the aforementioned Nafasi, *khādima* of *kadhi* Sh. Aḥmad b. Sumayṭ, and Fadila bt. Simba, servant of *kadhi* Sh. ʿAlī b. Muḥammad.[19] Occasionally, there is evidence of litigants' bargaining for the *kadhi* of their choice and pulling various strings

[15] In the seventeenth- and eighteenth-century Ottoman cases that Gerber studied, the litigants were mainly "common people." In 81 of 140 cases the plaintiff and defendant came from the same social stratum. The "social underdog" (as whom he also defines women) initiated cases and mostly won the case (Gerber, *State, Society, and Law*, 56).

[16] Entry #362, no. 443, 10 Shawwāl 1318/31 January 1901; Entry #404, no. 497, 30 Shawwāl 1318/20 February 1901, HC28/29, ZNA.

[17] HC5/312; HC10/2881 and HC10/10, ZNA, respectively.

[18] Zahra bt. Sh. Abdulqadir, represented by her brother, *wakīl* Sh. Hamdan b. Abdulqadir, sued for a debt (No entry #, no. 59, 4 Jumādā II 1320/7 September 1902, HC28/29, ZNA).

[19] No entry #, no. 82, 17 Dhū l-Qaʿda 1320/15 February 1903, HC28/29 and HC9/60, ZNA, respectively.

to achieve their aim.[20] Kasimali b. Idi, for example, addressed the magistrate wishing to appeal against the *kadhi*'s judgement, although the case was not within the magistrate's jurisdiction.[21] It seems that parties were willing to rope in anyone useful to a specific cause.

With the introduction of a judge sitting on appeal from 1899 onwards, litigants obtained an additional mediator who was likely to have an approach that differed from that of the *kadhi*. Thus their options increased, albeit not voluntarily. A few exceptions attest to the loopholes of this arbitrary system, with Zanzibaris breaking through legal categories by contrasting the definitions and categories created by the colonisers with their self-definitions. Court records indicate that Shiʿis, presumably exceptionally, and Baluchis went to the *kadhi*'s courts.[22] Baluchis, usually followers of the Ḥanafī school, thus accepted that they were subject to rules other than those of their legal school. Oral sources suggest that these legal differences rarely mattered to the parties, but court records indicate that they could be turned into grounds for appeal.[23]

Some cases prove that neither the parties nor the *kadhi*s adhered to jurisdictional boundaries. As late as 1954, for instance, a plaintiff from the Comoros (and thus a French subject) sued a mainland resident (a British subject) in the *kadhi*'s court rather than the magistrate's court.[24] Similarly, in two cases of 1901 and 1902, a British (Indian) and German (Tanganyikan) subject, respectively, were sued at the *kadhi*'s court.[25] The latter asked for a review of the case by the *kadhi* of the other school, which at the time should already have been realised as

[20] HC9/34; HC9/66, ZNA. For an example of *kadhi* shopping, see Anne K. Bang, "Cosmopolitanism Colonised? Three Cases from Zanzibar, 1890–1920," in *Struggling with History: Islam and Cosmopolitanism in the Western Indian Ocean*, ed. Edward Simpson and Kai Kresse (New York: Columbia University Press, 2007), 167–88.

[21] HC10/3202, ZNA.

[22] HC10/20; HC10/42; HC10/3555, ZNA, are examples of Baluchis; HC10/3731, ZNA, is a rare example of Shiʿi parties.

[23] Interviews with Bi Halima Abdalla Jafar and members of her family, 13 February, 13 April, and 27 May 2004; Saidi Haji Yusuf, 9 February 2004. See HC10/2843, ZNA, for an appeal because the defendant wanted to be judged by a *kadhi* of her own school, since the Ibāḍī *kadhi* regarded the triple divorce only as a single.

[24] HC10/3097, ZNA.

[25] Entry #634, no number, 2 Jumādā II [1319]/15 September 1901; No entry #, no number, 23 Rabīʿ I 1320/30 June 1902, HC28/29, ZNA.

a petition for appeal. Appeal cases were initiated by men and women from all social strata and normally based on procedural error, the *kadhi*'s failure properly to investigate, or his failure to consider evidence or reliance on the "wrong" evidence. The forerunner of appeals were requests to have the case reviewed by a *kadhi* of the other school irrespective of the fact whether the litigant was initially judged by his or her own *kadhi* or by the sultan. From 1900 to 1903, this form of appeal seems to have been achieved with ease, which implies that the provisions for a proper appeal, laid down by the Native Courts Decree of 1899, were still ignored.[26]

The boundaries of jurisdiction established by British colonial rule were known at least to some litigants, as one losing party denied the *kadhi*'s rights of jurisdiction over a Shiʿi.[27] The fact that shariʿa was still labelled as the fundamental law of the protectorate, and the sultan's courts called as such, did not prevent one witness at the Court for Zanzibar and Pemba in 1909 from viewing the court as a British court.[28] Once the Islamic features of jurisdiction – open, public space, orality, and flexibility – were obscured from parties, the court's designation could not conceal the pivotal legal changes initiated by colonial rule.

The social embeddedness of the Islamic court system implied the easy accessibility of *kadhi*s and their flexibility, manifest in the register of cases from the Court for Zanzibar and Pemba covering the years from 1900 to 1903. In the same session, defendants could and did bring counterclaims that were considered and decided by the *kadhi*.[29] Yet in 1954, *kadhi* Sh. ʿUmar instructed Ame b. Kombo, who sued for restitution of conjugal rights, to file a fresh suit when he claimed to have retracted the divorce whose occurrence witnesses established.[30]

26 Entry #78, no. 966, 10 Muḥarram 1317[1318]/10 May 1900; No entry#, no number, 23 Rabīʿ I 1320/30 June 1902; No entry #, no number, 22 Rajab 1320/24 October 1902, HC28/29, ZNA.

27 HC10/3731, ZNA.

28 HC9/82, ZNA.

29 No entry #, no number, 26 Muḥarram 1317[1318]/26 May 1900; Entry #217, no. 174, 17 Jumādā I 1318/12 September 1900; Entry #404, no. 497, 30 Shawwāl 1318/20 February 1901; Entry #535, no. 780, 27 Ṣafar [1319]/15 June 1901; Entry #584, no number, 13 Rabīʿ I [1319]/29 July 1901; Entry #764, no. 225, 23 Shawwāl [1319]/2 February 1902; Below entry #867, no number, 7 Muḥarram [1320]/16 April 1902; No entry #, no. 5020, 29 Ṣafar [1320]/6 June 1902, HC28/29, ZNA.

30 HC10/3160, ZNA.

As long as *kadhi*s exercised both civil and criminal jurisdiction, the parties did not have to decide which category of suit they would rather pursue. From 1909 onwards, *kadhi*s no longer adjudicated adultery cases, as criminal cases were now adjudicated by magistrates. A few records predating that year, as well as accusations of adultery raised in civil cases after 1908, show the *kadhi*s' neglect of such accusations, with rulings highlighting different aspects of the claim.[31] Although I cannot account for the frequency of this type of claim, Strobel explains the low number of adultery cases in Kenya as the result of the husband's power to divorce his wife outside court.[32] Additional factors, such as the possible stigma of opening such a claim, together with the difficulty of proving it according to shariʿa laws of evidence, may also have contributed to the scarcity of adultery cases.

While the *kadhi*'s courts formally upheld the underlying socioeconomic stratification, at the same time, they served as an arena where people negotiated passage from one social category to another. Social categorisations were highly contested and their boundaries porous. Frederick Cooper holds that patronage and communal membership counted more than ethnicity in nineteenth century Zanzibar and thus that the patron–client relationship was more important than race.[33] Court records from Zanzibar Town show the persistence of patronage, whether in cases of masters exercising authority over (former) slaves and their descendants or in cases of *kadhi*s acting as patrons for men and women seeking integration into Zanzibari society. Both the sultan and colonial officers acted for and were called on by litigants who delegated their struggle for citizenship.

Previous scholarship maintained that solving disputes out-of-court court in an informal manner served the economically and socially marginalised best.[34] *Kadhi*'s court records, however, suggest that a considerable number of women, former slaves, and poor people used every means at their disposal to pursue their rights in these courts. Many former slaves and people of lower social strata, as well as immigrants, went to the *kadhi*'s courts and won. In one case, the fact that Mwana

31 Adultery was not pursued by *kadhi*s in HC5/312; HC9/98; HC10/83; No entry #, no number, 22 Rajab 1320/24 October 1902, HC28/29, ZNA.

32 Strobel, *Muslim Women*, 88.

33 Frederick Cooper, *From Slaves to Squatters*, 158–72.

34 Fair, *Pastimes and Politics*, 207.

Halima bt. Muyi was a stranger from the mainland gained her the empathy of *kadhi* Sh. Muḥammad b. Khamīs al-Bū Saʿīdī and of the judge.[35] Former slaves and immigrants might have been discouraged from addressing *kadhi*'s courts by their relative unfamiliarity with an Islamic legal system. Additionally, the strong social embeddedness of these courts and their reliance on local social networks must have been known to those excluded from, or marginal to, these networks. Yet precisely because of the critical role *kadhi*'s courts played in shaping socioeconomic relations, former slaves in particular but also immigrants used these courts to demonstrate their being part of local society. Also the concept of vulnerability and support of the weak, defined in terms of social status and gender, enabled the marginalised to challenge the established social hierarchy in the *kadhi*'s courts.

In a sense, addressing the *kadhi*'s court was an index of Islamisation and a means of identity creation. *Kadhi*'s courts served as a tool for social integration even as they exposed one's knowledge of Islam to scrutiny by the ʿulamaʾ as members of the ruling elite. Anthropologists John Middleton and Marc Swartz hold that the *kadhi*'s courts played a decisive role in defining parties as Swahili and as Muslim, as people could choose among formal and informal institutions for conflict resolution.[36] Also Schacht noted in 1953 that shariʿa was administered at the choice of the litigants, referring to their choice between Ibāḍī and Shafiʿi *kadhi*s.[37] However, this emphasis on the optional use of courts – meaning a choice within the formal legal apparatus created by the state rather than between formal and informal systems – neglects colonial regulations that clearly defined who might address which court for which subject matter. In 1901

[35] HC10/25, ZNA.

[36] On the role of courts for the social integration of slaves, see Marc J. Swartz, "Religious Courts, Community and Ethnicity among the Swahili of Mombasa: An Historical Study of Social Boundaries," *Africa* 49, no. 1 (1979): 29–40. Middleton, *The World of the Swahili*, 51–52, describes that by addressing the *kadhi*'s court, Swahilis define themselves as Muslim. Moreover, Kuria Mwangi argues that the *kadhi*'s courts played a crucial role in preserving Muslims' rights in colonial Kenya. Idem, "The Application and Development of Sharia in Kenya: 1895–1990," in *Islam in Kenya. Proceedings of the National Seminar of Contemporary Islam in Kenya*, ed. Mohamed Bakari and Saad S. Yahya (Nairobi: Mewa, 1995), 255. For the postcolonial period, see further Hirsch, *Pronouncing and Persevering*, where she argues that courts still serve as focal points for Swahili identification.

[37] Schacht, "Notes on Islam," 117.

Muhammad b. Tabib sought to avoid jurisdiction in one of the sultan's courts by declaring he was a Comorian and thus under French protection, yet such a claim was followed up by thorough investigations by judicial officers.[38] This optional approach to the courts has played a more decisive role in shaping the secular–religious discourse in the postcolonial period. Even though colonial legal categories were prone to circumvention by litigants, *kadhi*s also adhered to these new geographical and substance-related restrictions of their jurisdiction, which resulted in their referral of suits to judges and magistrates.

[38] Charles Eliot to the Marquis of Lansdowne, 8 May 1902, FO 107/118, NAK.

5

The *Kadhis*' Alienation and Autonomy

> In the structure of relationships between politics and religion in Islam, the point of maximum stress is located in the office of qadi, a state-appointed religious judge. In a world which is less than perfect, when political authorities pursue their quest for power as an end in itself, where factions within the community are intent on nothing so much as their own advantage, the qadi has a nearly impossible task. It is no wonder that a popular tradition has it that one day the Prophet proclaimed that a camel could pass through the eye of a needle more easily than a qadi could enter heaven.[1]

Throughout the history of Muslim states, in terms of time and space, this characteristic of the *kadhi*'s office has essentially maintained its universal applicability. From the start of the Bū Saʿīdī reign, *kadhi*s became increasingly tied to the political authority under which they served. B. G. Martin, Randall Pouwels, and, more recently, Anne Bang have explored the lives and workings of the ʿulamaʾ, including

[1] Christelow, *Muslim Law Courts*, 262. See also idem, "The Muslim Judge and Municipal Politics in Colonial Algeria and Senegal," *Comparative Studies in Society and History* 24 (1982): 3–24. For an instructive overview of the historical development of the *kadhi*-ship and court procedure, see Muhammad Khalid Masud, Rudolph Peters, and David S. Powers, "Qadis and their Courts: An Historical Survey," in *Dispensing Justice in Islam: Qadis and their Judgments*, ed. Muhammad Khalid Masud, Rudolph Peters, and David S. Powers (Leiden: Brill, 2006), 1–44. See further Hallaq, *Shariʿa*, Chapter 3; *EI*[3], s.v. "*adab al-qāḍī*".

their relations with the government.[2] Their findings situate individual ʿulamaʾ in local social and intellectual spheres and outline their agency within wider Islamic networks. What remains to be added to this picture is the interaction of these scholars with individuals other than fellow scholars and governmental representatives. Court records particularly offer glimpses of the relationships of *kadhi*s with fellow Zanzibaris and of how *kadhi*s sustained their position as cooperators with the colonial state. Yet despite the fact that changing sociolegal politics had their ramifications in court, *kadhi*s applied a remarkably steady approach to dispute resolution in family matters, while simultaneously functioning as upholders of Islamic legal traditions.

The *kadhi*s who appear in court records available from 1900 to 1963 are relatively few in number, indicating that the official resolution of civil disputes in the *kadhi*'s courts was left to a few individuals, chosen and appointed by the colonial state. As the epigraph above explains, the office of *kadhi* was a double-edged sword. *Kadhi*-ship placed what was often perceived as an unbearable burden on the *kadhi*, with the great possibility of failing his task.[3] *Kadhi*s under Omani sultans declined the office and some resigned prematurely, with or without the sultan's permission. Involvement in the affairs and intrigues of the state seemed unacceptable to some ʿulamaʾ, while it was welcomed by others. The Shafiʿi scholar ʿAbdallāh Bā Kathīr (1860/61–1925), for instance, avoided any government affiliation throughout his life, as opposed to Sh. Burhān b. ʿAbd al-ʿAzīz al-Amawī (1861-1935), one of the most well-known Shafiʿis during the British colonial period.[4]

Kadhi-ships tended to run in certain families, as knowledge generally was preserved within wealthier groups and families, who were able to transmit knowledge intergenerationally. Sh. Nāṣir b. Sālim

[2] B. G. Martin, "Notes on Some Members of the Learned Classes of Zanzibar and East Africa in the Nineteenth Century," *African Historical Studies* 4, no. 3 (1971): 525–45; Bang, *Sufis and Scholars*; Pouwels *Horn and Crescent*. See also Abdallah Salih Farsy, *The Shafiʿi Ulama of East Africa, c. 1830–1970: A Hagiographic Account*, trans., ed. and annotated R. L. Pouwels (Madison: University of Wisconsin Press, 1989); Scott Reese, *Renewers of the Age: Holy Men and Social Discourse in Colonial Benaadir* (Leiden: Brill, 2008).

[3] For an illustrative anecdote of such a dilemma, see Coulson, *Conflicts and Tension*, 58–59.

[4] Bang, *Sufis and Scholars*, 116.

FIGURE 5.1. *Kadhi* Sh. Muḥammad Sālim al-Rawwāḥī on the right. Courtesy of ZNA.

al-Rawwāḥī's father served as Ibāḍī *kadhi* under Sultan Barghash (r. 1870–1888), and he himself became *kadhi* under Sultans Ḥamad b. Thuwaynī (r. 1893–1896) and Ḥamūd (r. 1896–1902).[5] Being a scholar often went hand in hand with pursuing worldly careers as traders, as exemplified by one of the most esteemed and prominent *kadhi*s during the colonial period, Sh. Aḥmad b. Sumayṭ of the Shafiʿi school.[6] The social importance of wealth in Swahili communities also explains why not only the sultans but also scholars strove to obtain assets and busied themselves with worldly transactions.

Islam in East Africa at the turn of the twentieth century was a contested field in which scripture-based traditions contended with oral ones for discursive control.[7] Anne Bang argues that the prominent

[5] Ibid., 136. See Pouwels, *Horn and Crescent*, 80–81, and B. G. Martin, "Notes on Some Members,“ 530, on the intergenerational handing down of knowledge.

[6] Anne Bang explores the life of Sh. Aḥmad in her *Sufis and Scholars*. Doumani points to the preponderance and high esteem of joint religious and commercial careers in the Palestinian context (idem, *Rediscovering Palestine*, 66). Prophet Muhammad himself set the paradigm for this combined businessman-scholar career. See also Pouwels, *Horn and Crescent*, 87, 97, on how wealth often accompanied knowledge.

[7] See Bang, *Sufis and Scholars*, Chapter 7, on the indigenisation of Islam and Pouwels, *Horn and Crescent*. The emergence of scriptualism characterised the Muslim world in the late nineteenth and early twentieth centuries.

scholarly role of relatively recently arrived Hadramis points to a shift from Swahili cultural codes towards Arabic-literate scriptural knowledge, while "knowledge of Swahili language and familiarity with Swahili life still remained a prerequisite for joining the higher ranks of the *ʿulamāʾ*."[8] The detachment of Islamic knowledge from its ideological engagement with descent, social status, and gender should be credited to shaykhs of Sufi orders.[9] As part of the Swahilisation process, Ibāḍī *kadhi*s tended to become adherents of the Shafiʿi school, which aroused suspicion particularly under Sultan Barghash.[10] Most Omanis were Ibāḍīs before 1870, but by 1907 most had become Shafiʿi, and the British faced difficulties in replacing Ibāḍī *kadhi*s.[11]

It needs to be borne in mind that although *kadhi*s became increasingly dependent on the political system under which they served, their office was never their main task as erudite members of their community, which judges noted with concern. Drawing a neat separation between professional and private life does not foster our understanding of *kadhi*s, whose roles exercised outside the court were as important (and more time-consuming) than their work as appointed *kadhi*. Those who were official *kadhi*s acted as mediators; issued legal opinions; dealt with questions relating to prayers, hajj, medicine, and so on; and counselled at home.[12] They listened to the problems of members of their community. Women, who most likely did not have any other trustworthy person available, entrusted *kadhi*s with managing their affairs, though in some cases not entirely to their satisfaction.[13] In

[8] Bang, *Sufis and Scholars*, 103.

[9] See Felicitas Becker, *Becoming Muslim in Mainland Tanzania, 1890–2000* (Oxford: Oxford University Press, 2008).

[10] Both Sh. ʿAlī b. ʿAbdallāh b. Nāfiʿ al-Mazrūʿī (1825–1894) and ʿAlī b. Khamīs al-Barwānī (1852–1885) converted from Ibāḍīsm to Sunnism (Bang, *Sufis and Scholars*, 95).

[11] Pouwels, *Horn and Crescent*, 120. This can also be gleaned from correspondence between colonial officers in the early 1950s (AK1/105, ZNA). The lack of Ibāḍī *kadhi*s was also pointed out to Schacht in 1953 and 1963 (Schacht, "Notes on Islam," 119–20). Ibāḍī *kadhi*s were more numerous in Pemba than Zanzibar, which reflected the distribution of Omani Arabs, many of whom had plantations in Pemba (Farsy, *Seyyid Said*, 34).

[12] Interviews with Sh. Ahmed Mohamed Saleh Ba Kathir, 27 January 2004; Sh. Ibrahim Mtoro and Sh. Hamid Musa Mlomri, 22 December 2003.

[13] Jokha bt. Msellem's petition, 15 May 1938, AX8/2, ZNA. She gave *kadhi* Saʿīd b. Nāṣir al-Ghaythī the power of attorney to manage her *shamba*s while she was on the mainland but felt cheated by him and thus addressed the chief justice.

court, *kadhi*s also appeared as witnesses due to their roles as performing marriages, registering divorces, issuing decrees, mediating, dividing estates, and administering *wakf*s.[14] While being a *kadhi* implies appointment to a government post, any adequately qualified Muslim scholar can issue legal opinions, or *fatwa*s, and thus act as *mufti*.[15] The *kadhi*s explored in this study equally served as *mufti*s for fellow scholars as well as for lay individuals in Zanzibar and from as far afield as North Africa and Arabia. There were also so-called *kadhi*s of the district, knowledgeable esteemed members of the community who resolved grievances locally. What distinguished the *kadhi*s from their contemporaries was the specialised knowledge, usually kept within families of mainly Hadrami, Benadiri, and Comorian origin in the late nineteenth century. In this sense, they were also distinct from *liwali*s and *mudir*s, who were not part of this erudite tradition.

In spite of the colonial creation of a space dedicated to adjudication, the accessibility of the *kadhi* in his home was a local requirement that could not be extirpated by the British. This practice, though, constituted evidence of the *kadhi*'s partiality for the colonial officers. If this overlap of private consultation with official adjudication became known to the judge, he overturned the *kadhi*'s judgement and ordered the retrial of the case. In November 1952, during a divorce suit, Saʿad Msellem al-Riyami obtained a note from the Ibāḍī *kadhi* Sh. Saʿīd b. Rashīd at the *kadhi*'s house, saying that Saʿad's wife had no further claim on him. On appeal Chief Justice G. G. Robinson held it was correct that the *kadhi* revoked this note in court months later, as it was obtained *ex parte* and could not have any bearing on the case.[16] Judges had obvious difficulties in grasping the role of the *kadhi* as shaykh in his community and in coming to terms with the lack of a neat separation of roles. Thus Chief Justice John Gray made the point that if the *kadhi*'s evidence relating to a marriage ceremony was required,

[14] See HC9/12, ZNA, for a *kadhi* as the divider of an estate; HC10/761, ZNA, where Sh. Saʿīd b. Rashīd al-Ghaythī served as both a mediator and witness in court; HC10/761, ZNA, in which case the same *kadhi* was a witness to an allegation of cruelty; HC8/86, ZNA, for *kadhi* Sh. Burhān acting as a witness since he celebrated the marriage.

[15] On the evolution of the distinction between *mufti* and *kadhi*, see Vikør, *Between God and the Sultan*, 170–73, 186–91.

[16] HC10/2881, ZNA, original in English. Cf. Chapters 8 and 9.

the proper course was for the case to be heard at another court, where the *kadhi* could give evidence as witness.[17] The fact that the *kadhi*'s knowledge of people in his community and their affairs could be the basis for legal action was an alien concept for the judge.[18] It must thus be seen as a considerable privilege that after leaving office, the Shafiʿi *kadhi* Sh. Burhān was allowed to give judgements at home. He was, however, told not to interfere with government judgements. *Kadhi* Sh. Ṭāhir was equally granted to give judgements at home towards the end of his life.[19]

The cases forming the basis for this study were decided by no more than thirteen *kadhi*s,[20] with most decisions taken by only four: the Shafiʿi *kadhi*s Sh. Burhān b. ʿAbd al-ʿAzīz al-Amawī, Sh. Ṭāhir b. Abī Bakr al-Amawī, Sh. ʿUmar b. Aḥmad b. Sumayṭ, and the Ibāḍī *kadhi* Sh. Saʿīd b. Rashīd al-Ghaythī.[21] Among these *kadhi*s, the Sumayṭ, the Amawī, and the Ghaythī provide excellent examples of how knowledge, as well as the office of *kadhi*, passed on from one generation to another. The father of Aḥmad b. Sumayṭ had temporarily been *kadhi* in Zanzibar some time in the 1860s. Aḥmad himself arrived in Zanzibar in late 1881 or early 1882 and was probably appointed *kadhi* in 1883 but left the island in autumn 1885 without the sultan's permission.[22] Among the Amawī, Sh. Burhān's father, ʿAbd al-ʿAzīz b. ʿAbd al-Ghanī al-Amawī (1838–1896), held *kadhi*-ships in Kilwa and then in Zanzibar until his retirement in 1894. He was viewed with suspicion by the British due to his insistence that laws should remain

17 John Gray's appeal judgement, 3 August 1943, HC10/1141, ZNA.

18 See Messick, *Calligraphic State*, 176. In civil cases, Shafiʿi *kadhi*s may rule based on personal knowledge (Masud, Peters, and Powers, "Qadis and their Courts," 30).

19 Interviews with Bi Amina Abdulrahman Mahmud, 19 May and 19 June 2004.

20 This number excludes the case sample from HC28/29, ZNA, where the *kadhi* is rarely mentioned.

21 For a distribution of cases among the *kadhi*s, see the appendix. For an introduction to Sh. Aḥmad b. Sumayṭ, Sh.ʿAlī b. Muḥammad, Sh. Burhān, and Sh. Ṭāhir, see Anne K. Bang and Knut S. Vikør, "A Tale of Three *shamba*s: Shāfiʿī-Ibāḍī Legal Cooperation in the Zanzibari Protectorate, Part I," *Sudanic Africa* 10 (1999): 6–11.

22 Bang, *Sufis and Scholars*, 51, 77. See also Pouwels, *Horn and Crescent*, 156–58, on Sh. Aḥmad's relations with the sultans. He supported the British move to terminate the sultan's right as ultimate appellate jurisdiction and was consequently punished to hear petty cases in rural districts. The reform of 1908 brought him back to Zanzibar Town (Bang, *Sufis and Scholars*, 123).

Islamic.[23] The father of Ibāḍī *kadhi* Sh. ʿAlī b. Muḥammad was also *kadhi* under Sultans Saʿīd (r. 1806–1856) and Mājid (r. 1856–1870).

The sultan appointed *kadhi*s based on their scholarly reputation, for which transmission of knowledge, thus the erudition of their teachers, was decisive. As formal training for the office of *kadhi* did not exist, a future *kadhi* obtained his qualification from usually a male family member at home. In scholarly families, from which *kadhi*s generally hailed, male and female children studied the Qurʾan, hadith, theology, jurisprudence, the Arabic language, and literature as well as genealogy and history. *Kadhi*s' education was thus not restricted to jurisprudence but encompassed the Islamic sciences. Often, the quest for deeper knowledge took them to other parts of the Muslim world, especially Hadramawt in the late nineteenth century. Aḥmad b. Sumayṭ, for instance, obtained certificates from various esteemed teachers there. This practice of itinerant learning fostered the integration of Zanzibari scholars into global Muslim scholarship.

The general tenor of previous research on the relationship between the *kadhi*s and the British colonial government emphasises *kadhi*s' striking willingness to cooperate.[24] Although there is no doubt that the sides did collaborate, more remains to be said regarding their interaction. *Kadhi* Sh. Ṭāhir, for instance, was a man of various interests and crafty in communicating with people. He interacted with all sorts of people, among them the British resident.[25] One of his relatives was an interpreter at the court, and Sh. Ṭāhir himself was competent in English.[26] His court records, however, do not hint at his competence

[23] Bang, *Sufis and Scholars*, 94–95; Pouwels, *Horn and Crescent*, 143–44. On the career of Sh. ʿAbd al-ʿAzīz, see also Valerie J. Hoffman, "In His (Arab) Majesty's Service: The Career of a Somali Scholar and Diplomat in Nineteenth-Century Zanzibar," in *The Global Worlds of the Swahili: Interfaces of Islam, Identity and Space in 19th and 20th-Century East Africa*, ed. Roman Loimeier and Rüdiger Seesemann (Berlin: Lit Verlag, 2006), 251–72.

[24] Bang, *Sufis and Scholars*, Chapter 8; Pouwels, *Horn and Crescent*, especially 178–81. See Bang and Vikør, "Tale of Three *shamba*s, Part I" and their "A Tale of Three *shamba*s, Part II," *Sudanic Africa* 11 (2000): 1–24, for the legal cooperation between Ibāḍī and Shafiʿi *kadhis*.

[25] Interviews with Bi Amina Abdulrahman Mahmud, 2 May and 19 June 2004.

[26] Bang, *Sufis and Scholars*, 156. Anne K. Bang sheds light on Sh. Ṭāhir in "Another Scholar for All Seasons? Tahir b. Abi Bakr al-Amawi (1877–1938), *qadi* of Zanzibar, c. 1900–1933," in *The Global Worlds of the Swahili: Interfaces of Islam, Identity and Space in 19th and 20th-Century East Africa*, ed. Roman Loimeier and Rüdiger

in English. Rather, his judgements reveal a versatile scholar whose judgements could fail to reflect colonial ideologies and be overruled on appeal.[27] One of his recorded actions is quite remarkable and his motivation remains elusive. In 1916, he gave Sh. Zahir b. Muhammad al-Jabiri authorisation to act as guardian in marriage whenever no guardian was available.[28] According to al-Shāfiʿī, women must be given into marriage by their male guardian or, in his absence, by the *kadhi* or sultan. Applying the Islamic principle of necessity, Sh. Ṭāhir may have responded to an increasing number of women who wanted to get married but did not have a guardian, thus enabling the integration of recent immigrants who were outside local family networks.

Despite the *kadhi*s' potential for manipulation, there is no evidence that they were routinely corrupt.[29] Apart from being well paid by the government,[30] *kadhi*s such as Sh. Burhān and Sh. Ṭāhir were well-off, sometimes extremely affluent. Sh. Burhān's wealth enabled his son to maintain a high standard of living, with his sole task being to oversee his father's legacy, which consisted of *shamba*s with cloves and coconuts and most likely other real estate.[31] *Kadhi*s Sh. Ṭāhir, Aḥmad b. Sumayṭ, Saʿīd b. Nāṣir al-Ghaythī, and possibly others were also plantation owners and businessmen. From a letter in English, which *kadhi* Sh. Saʿīd b. Nāṣir addressed to the registrar of the high court dated 27 June 1934, it appears that he had leased *shamba*s in

Seesemann (Berlin: Lit Verlag, 2006), 273–88. Ibāḍī *kadhi* Sh. ʿAlī b. Muḥammad was also well versed in English and wrote "a highly original refutation of Christianity based on a thorough reading of the Bible in six different English translations." Valerie J. Hoffman, "The Articulation of Ibadi Identity in Modern Oman and Zanzibar," *Muslim World* 94, no. 2 (2004): 211. A. I. Salim argues that the knowledge of English was a crucial asset for Arab staff in order to maintain their position (idem, *Swahili-Speaking Peoples*, 90).

27 HC5/536, ZNA, original in Arabic and English.

28 HC10/43, ZNA.

29 For an exception, see the case described in Pouwels, *Horn and Crescent*, 123.

30 Bang, *Sufis and Scholars*, 165, 236n42. *Kadhi*s additionally received fees for registering marriages and divorces. On the Mrima coast, the shaykh who contracted the marriage received Rs. 2. See C. Velten, "Sitten und Gebräuche der Suaheli," *Mittheilungen des Seminars für Orientalische Sprachen, Afrikanische Studien* 1, no. 3 (1898): 58. In British Aden, the fees, which the *kadhi*s levied for their services in addition to their governmental salary, accounted for their affluence. Lidwien Kapteijns, "Government Qadis and Child Marriage in Aden: Ethnography in the Aden Archives," *International Journal of African Historical Studies* 37, no. 3 (2004): 404.

31 Interview with Bi Amina Abdulrahman Mahmud, 2 May 2004.

partnership with his brother from 1914 to 1928 but incurred great loss. In 1931, he took out a loan in order to pay his creditors. The balance must have risen to an amount that Sh. Saʿīd was struggling to pay, because his creditors opened a court case that the *kadhi* lost.[32] In some cases, *kadhi*s certainly bore their own economic interests in mind, but it should be considered that the majority of disputes they adjudicated concerned family matters, social and economic, in which it is difficult to see that they were categorically corrupt. This, however, does not deny that *kadhi*s were informed by their social environment and interested in maintaining their individual and group status.[33]

Sh. Saʿīd's letter also shows the relations between the colonial government and the *kadhi*s in social and financial terms, revealing the implicit scope of the *kadhi*'s dependency on his employer. In his letter, he tried to explain what lay behind his defeat in court, stressing the existence of a settlement and his habit of paying off instalments promptly. His goal in this may well have been to avoid losing his job or falling into the disgrace of his employer, which would have eroded his regular source of income. From 1931 to 1941, recommendations by the head of department kept him in office despite his age (he was 50 years old in 1931), as he was seen as an efficient and competent officer. Promotions depended on the *kadhi*'s satisfactory performance. Because the *kadhi*s were officers subject to the scheme for civil servants, the chief justice decided whether it was worth keeping them in certain posts, at the same time considering the increase or decrease of the court's workload. He also proposed any increase in salary, to which the sultan only gave his formal blessing. Thus friendly relations with the chief justice obviously represented a good social investment for *kadhi*s.

Another social-professional level of relations between *kadhi*s and colonial officers appears in form of condolences expressed by the chief secretary to the oldest son of the late *kadhi* Sh. Saʿīd as well as the financial liabilities of the deceased. Sh. Saʿīd had a large family to maintain, including married daughters dependent on his support. After his death in 1942, his family made these financial strains known to the

32 Sh. Saʿid b. Nasir al-Ghaythi to high court registrar, 27 June 1934, AB86/137, ZNA.

33 See David S. Powers, "Kadijustiz or Qāḍī Justice? A Paternity Dispute from Fourteenth-Century Morocco," *Islamic Law and Society* 1, no. 3 (1994): 332–366.

government and applied for a grant. Following the decision of the chief justice, one of the widows and the mother of four of his minor children were granted an allowance, divided according to Ibāḍī law.[34] It could be argued that the Ghaythī's request was an appendix to rights claimed under a colonially disguised form of patron–client relationship. The increasing economic dependency of the *kadhi*s on the state derived from the colonial effort to eliminate their work outside the court. Given their position as colonial officers, *kadhi*s were expected to work according to British standards of efficiency and impartiality. These expectations, however, entailed demands of socioeconomic rights by the client, the *kadhi*, and his dependants from the patron, the colonial state.[35]

While *kadhi*s cooperated with colonial authority on the one hand, there were attempts of resistance on the other. The reason for this was that many ʿulamaʾ preserved close social and economic ties to various groups of the population.[36] Pouwels refers to a report of 1907 that accounts for *kadhi*s being often late and too ill to come to court. He deduces from a similar report pertaining to Lamu that *kadhi*s were torn between obedience towards their British superiors and the established requirements of their society.[37] There are several references to friendships between colonial officers and Muslim scholars, but given both the barrier of language (in most cases officers and *kadhi*s communicated through an interpreter) and their competing positions in the colonial hierarchy, it is questionable whether such friendships served anything but strategic social purposes.[38] Sh. Burhān was on amicable terms with General Mathews, the sultan's first minister from 1891 to 1901,[39] and Chief Justice Tomlinson referred to *kadhi*s Sh. Ṭāhir and Burhān

34 AB86/137, ZNA.

35 On the relationship between the British and ʿulamaʾ in colonial Kenya as a form of patronage, see Hassan Mwakimako, "The *ʿulama*ʾ and the Colonial State in the Protectorate of Kenya. The Appointment of *shaykh al-islam sharīf* ʿAbd al-Raḥmān b. Aḥmad Saggaf (1844–1922) and Chief *Kadhi* Sh. Muḥammad b. ʿUmar Bakore (c. 1932)," in *The Global Worlds of the Swahili: Interfaces of Islam, Identity and Space in 19th and 20th-Century East Africa*, ed. Roman Loimeier and Rüdiger Seesemann (Berlin: Lit Verlag, 2006), 289–315.

36 Cf. Tucker, *Women in Nineteenth-Century Egypt*, 105.

37 Pouwels, *Horn and Crescent*, 191–92.

38 Harold Ingrams, secretary to the director of education, called himself friend of *kadhi* Sh. Aḥmad b. Sumayṭ (Bang, *Sufis and Scholars*, 195).

39 Interview with Bi Amina Abdulrahman Mahmud, 19 June 2004.

especially as friends. In his speech at Tomlinson's farewell party, *kadhi* Sh. Burhān is translated as having said, "[w]e have been fortunate, Sir, to be associated, with Your Honour [Tomlinson] for more than 21 years and during that time we have always found Your Honour to be a just, affectionate, kind and helpful Chief who has continually paid due consideration to all matters in connection with the Islamic Law."[40] But such words were part of a normative social discourse, which could not conceal the gap between their differing approaches to law and *kadhi*s' substantially unrestricted freedom to apply shariʿa rulings in civil cases.

Apart from being both an underpinning public forum and a forum for wielding the power of the state, *kadhi*'s courts based themselves on a theoretical and fundamental presupposition of egalitarianism.[41] In practice, this presupposition was permeated by the *kadhi*'s ideologies of gender, social status, and ethnicity. Each of these factors was compounded or deemphasised by the legal framework and social, economic, and political discourses of the time. *Kadhi*s' rulings in favour of women and socially marginalised groups derive from their close interpretation of Islamic legal literature. Al-Nawawī, for instance, the main source for Shafiʿis on the Swahili coast, records that the *kadhi* must treat two Muslim parties equally. If several litigants ask the *kadhi* to hear their claims and it is unclear who called on him first, or if all of them did so simultaneously, they must draw lots to decide whose claim will be heard first. Priority is always given to travellers, urgent cases, and women's claims, even if these cases were presented belatedly, unless their number is extraordinarily high.[42] Similarly, other literature suggests the promotion of the claim of the "weaker" party, who could be women or the poor – in general, socially marginalised groups.[43] Although Islamic ideologies attribute to women in many respects roles subordinate to male authority, they stress women's responsibility and capability as legal persons.

40 *Supplement to the Official Gazette Zanzibar 1928*, Vol. XXXVII-No. 1898, 9 June 1928, 149–50.

41 See Messick, *Calligraphic State*, 144–45, 153–54.

42 Berg, *Minhādj*, vol. III, 377–79.

43 Messick, *Calligraphic State*, 163–64. Tucker, *In the House of the Law*, 182, also accounts for *kadhi*s' protection of marginalised groups.

The categories that were constantly reshaped and reassessed in court proceedings were social status and ethnicity, because Islamic sources allow for interpretations of these categories to a larger extent than for gender, whose legal roles are more clearly delineated. *Kadhi*s' approaches to these categories prove that they were products of their time, their own socioeconomic background, and ethnic biases.[44] The *kadhi*s' social embeddedness explains why they attached such great importance to litigants' origin, including the social (genealogical and geographical) and, consequently, ethnic origin of parties.[45] Sh. Ahmed Mohamed Saleh Ba Kathir, who served as *kadhi* in Zanzibar during the 1990s, holds that the writing down of ethnic origin goes back to both the Arab system of *kabila*, or patronyms, and the British colonial system and that this practice lacks legal support. Sh. Ibrahim Mtoro, a former chief *kadhi* of Zanzibar, also points out that it is important for the *kadhi* to establish the party's social ties and origin.[46] It certainly mattered to the *kadhi*, as well as the judge, from which social background a person came and thus what degree of esteem and reliability could be attached to him or her. For *kadhi*s Sh. Aḥmad b. Sumayṭ and Sh. ʿAlī b. Muḥammad, for example, the testimony of the *yaya*, or nanny, Bint Farhan was not substantial evidence, while Magistrate Reed saw her as a hostile witness.[47] For the *kadhi*s and the judge, her character and lack of social esteem weighed against her credibility. Yet Sh. Saʿīd b. Nāṣir attached great credibility to the testimony of the mother of Bishara bt. Suwedi Kozi, who was known to him as a "virtuous, trustworthy person."[48] Chapter 9 offers evidence that ethnicity, or notions of belonging, decisively shaped *kadhi*s' understanding of litigants' and witnesses' moral integrity, thus credibility.

44 See Scott S. Reese, ed., *The Transmission of Learning in Islamic Africa* (Leiden: Brill, 2004), 3, where he strongly argues against the still preponderant notion of African ʿulamaʾ "floating in timeless space". Cf. Moore on how judges' perception of their role may affect their decisions (idem, *Law as Process*, 211).

45 Cf. Peletz, *Islamic Modern*, 79, 86.

46 Interviews with Sh. Ahmed Mohamed Saleh Ba Kathir, 27 January 2004; Sh. Ibrahim Mtoro and Sh. Hamid Musa Mlomri, 22 December 2003.

47 HC8/86, ZNA, original in Arabic and English. See also No entry #, no number, 22 Rajab 1320/24 October 1902, HC28/29, ZNA, where the fact that the *kadhi* did not know her witnesses worked against Baya bt. Khamis.

48 HC10/761, ZNA.

Over the course of the colonial period, a shift occurred in the *kadhi*'s conception of his main role from being a servant of his community to being a servant of the colonial state. This process, however, was never complete or without contradiction. The *kadhi*'s alienation is reflected in his language, which increasingly used the term "the court" – the institution re-created and pinned down to an enclosed space under British rule – representing an effort to distance himself from the responsibility of serving the colonial state he never entirely agreed to bear. Concerns shifted away from intimacy, but the social embeddedness of the *kadhi* and his concern for his fellow Muslims remained. The position of the *kadhi* is characterised best by a constant struggle between adherence to the religious ideals and doctrines in which he was entrenched and maintaining his reliability in the eyes of his employer. With the difference between *kadhi* and judge also manifest in language, most *kadhi*s decided to play a game of social disguise that, however apparently successful, seemed "weaker than the house of a spider"[49] once dismantled and examined from various perspectives. The elite position of the *kadhi*s, most of whom were descendants of families who had immigrated to Zanzibar during the nineteenth century, was wiped out by the revolution of 1964, which replaced them by a new type of *kadhi* selected by ethnicity and education.

Court records reveal the dialectic between legal theory and practice and suggest that the main aim of *kadhi*s, albeit circumscribed by the colonial legal framework, remained to restore people to working relationships,[50] thus to achieve a settlement that, in the *kadhi*s' view, enabled each party to live according to local conceptions of shariʿa. While *kadhi*s were clearly embedded in their socioeconomic environment and their judgements wielded power over the litigants, the civil cases portray them as driven by confirming and forging relationships

49 I borrowed this metaphor from a judgement of *kadhi* Sh. Ṭāhir of 1921 (HC9/134, ZNA).

50 Cf. Lawrence Rosen, *The Anthropology of Justice: Law as Culture in Islamic Society* (Cambridge: Cambridge University Press, 1989). Rosen's interpretation of the workings of Islamic courts has been criticised as orientalist. Engin Deniz Akarlı uses the example of the marketplace to show that *kadhi*s' main aim was to maintain harmony in their community. Idem, "Law in the Marketplace: Istanbul, 1730–1840," in *Dispensing Justice in Islam: Qadis and their Judgments*, ed. Muhammad Khalid Masud, Rudolph Peters, and David S. Powers (Leiden: Brill, 2006), 245–70.

that enabled Zanzibari society to adjust to a changing social and economic environment. The notable exception was *kadhi*s' perpetuation of master–slave relations in the context of inheritance claims, explored in Chapters 7 and 9. From 1900 to around 1909, *kadhi*s were little preoccupied with newly defined legal categories or new modes of procedure and other formalities such as record keeping. *Kadhi*s allowed claims to develop their own dynamic once they were heard. Their role as mediators, strongly reflected in the records from 1900 to 1903, diminished over the following decades. However, this impression may be a result of changes in record keeping itself, with the earliest records being short summaries and later verbatim records of each session. From 1910 onwards, *kadhi*s appear to have increasingly adopted a pragmatic stance towards their employer as they began to work jointly with British colonial officers on committees and for public welfare. *Kadhi*s began to adhere to the new boundaries of jurisdiction, slowly adapting to the registering of documents, handing over of fees, and the importance of speeding up litigation processes. Yet at the same time, they had means for resisting colonial encroachment and continued to issue rulings essentially Islamic in their substance. One important buffer was language, since Arabic was the language of the *kadhi*'s court, or at least the language in which the *kadhi* wrote minutes and verdicts. Since *kadhi* Sh. ʿAbdallāh Ṣāliḥ al-Farsī, for instance, is known to have promoted Swahili rather than Arabic as the religious language of Swahili communities, it seems peculiar that he wrote his minutes in this archaic language.[51] If Sh. al-Farsī indeed intended to avoid dependency on Arabic at all costs, as Lacunza Balda suggests,[52] we have to wonder why he maintained the language in his court records, when colonial

[51] See Justo Lacunza Balda, "An Investigation into Some Concepts and Ideas Found in Swahili Islamic Writings" (PhD diss., SOAS, University of London, 1989), 60, 65. Al-Farsī contributed to the popularisation of Islam with his Qur'an translation into Swahili in 1969. For elucidating accounts of al-Farsī's scholarly career, see also F. H. Elmasri, "Sheikh al-Amin bin Ali al-Mazrui and the Islamic Intellectual Tradition in East Africa," *Journal of Muslim Minority Affairs* 8, no. 2 (1987): 234–35; Kai Kresse, "'Swahili Enlightenment?' East African Reformist Discourse at the Turning Point: The Example of Sheikh Muhammad Kasim Mazrui," *Journal of Religion in Africa* 33, no. 3 (2003): 279–309; Roman Loimeier, "Patterns and Peculiarities of Islamic Reform in Africa," *Journal of Religion in Africa* 33, no. 3 (2003): 249–52; idem, *Between Social Skills and Marketable Skills: The Politics of Islamic Education in 20th Century Zanzibar* (Leiden: Brill, 2009), 375–400.

[52] Lacunza Balda, "Investigation into Some Concepts,"227.

FIGURE 5.2. The young Sh. ʿAbdallāh Ṣāliḥ al-Farsī. The picture on the wall shows Sultan Khalīfa b. Ḥārub (r. 1911–1960). Courtesy of ZNA.

rules allowed for both Swahili and Arabic. To colonial officers it could not have mattered if one of them would have disappeared, so it must have mattered to the *kadhi*s, who used Arabic as a buffer against colonial encroachment. Within their restricted boundaries of jurisdiction and unless a case was appealed, Arabic insulated *kadhi*s from interference into their judicial world, whose language kept alive the elitist status of their group.[53]

[53] The disappearance of the Arabic section in the newspaper *Mwongozi* indicates that Swahili increasingly replaced Arabic in the 1950s. See Katrin Bromber, "Who are the Zanzibari? Newspaper Debates on Difference, 1948–1958," in *Space on the Move: Transformations of the Indian Ocean Seascape in the Nineteenth and Twentieth Century*, ed. Jan-Georg Deutsch and Brigitte Reinwald (Berlin: Klaus Schwarz Verlag, 2002), 77. This confirms that *kadhi*s must have had a compelling reason to use Arabic

Conclusion

Part I has shown how the colonial institutionalisation of the judiciary created new legal categories, redistributed scopes of jurisdiction, and brought about procedural reforms. Driven by economic motives and a bias against shariʿa, the British brought Christians and Indians under their jurisdiction and introduced common law-based modes of procedure in the *kadhi*'s courts. After being incorporated into the British colonial legal system, the *kadhi*s at first glance appear hamstrung by the reforms that had been enacted by 1908. Yet if we ask to what extent the colonisers were able to manipulate shariʿa, the answer the *kadhi*'s court records yield is striking. Continuing autonomy within their restricted scope of jurisdiction allowed *kadhi*s to issue rulings in accordance with shariʿa.[54] Doubtlessly, *kadhi*s were hampered by the colonial supervising gaze, with litigants bearing the consequences of their adherence to rigid rules of procedure. The underlying reasoning of their judgements persisted, however, and they were essentially able to uphold their roles as servants of the law and the community. The use of Arabic and the fact that the judge only heard a small number of their cases on appeal attest to this trend.[55] Contrary to previous accounts of the *kadhi*s' cooperative stance towards their employer and judges,

in court records. Cf. Scott Reese, who argues that Benadiri townspeople used the Arabic language to preserve their urban identity. Idem, "Tales Which Persist on the Tongue: Arabic Literacy and the Definition of Communal Boundaries in Sharīf ʿAydarūs's Bughyat al-Āmāl," *Sudanic Africa* 9 (1998): 1–17.

54 Cf. Christelow, "Transformation of the Muslim Court System," for theoretical considerations of the *kadhi*s' autonomy within the Algerian colonial legal system. See also Dickerman, "Use of Court Records," 70, on the autonomy of the courts in colonial Bujumbura.

55 It is difficult to get exact figures of appeals from the *kadhi*'s courts, as prior to 1924 these went to the Court for Zanzibar and Pemba, whose case statistics do not differentiate between original and appellate cases. After 1923, statistics absorb the *kadhi*'s courts among civil appeals from all subordinate courts. Yet the overall number of civil appeals is low. From 1911 to 1923, the number of original and appellate civil cases in the Court for Zanzibar and Pemba ranged between 48 and 82 per year. From 1924 to 1938, the high court heard between 20 to 53 civil cases on appeal from all subordinate courts per year. *Zanzibar Protectorate, Administrative Reports, 1915–1931* and *Annual Reports on the Social and Economic Progress of the People of the Zanzibar Protectorate, 1932–1938* (London: His Majesty's Stationery Office, 1933–1939), respectively. Cf. Shadle, "'Changing Traditions,'" 413–14, where he argues that disputes remained in "African hands," since very few cases went on appeal to European administrators.

kadhi's court records show a more dialectical relationship between autonomy and cooperation, illustrated in the *kadhi*s' dependency on their employer, on the one hand, and the partly irreconcilable differences between the *kadhi*s' and judges' legal ideologies, on the other. The lack of a clear separation between "court" and "out-of-court" is one of the characteristics of shariʿa. This pertains to space as well as to the boundaries of the *kadhi*s' and litigants' roles and constituted a perennial reason for the judge to rebuke the *kadhi* and to overturn his judgement on appeal.

The popularity of the *kadhi*'s courts in Zanzibar Town, as in other parts of the Muslim world, was particularly pronounced among former slaves and women, who addressed these courts to compensate their socioeconomically disadvantaged positions. Aiming to include those whom they perceived as excluded, *kadhi*s and judges competed for litigants. This in turn encouraged the latter to draw on all resources available. While offering avenues of socioeconomic mobility, *kadhi*'s courts also increased tensions among kin, juniors and seniors, former slave owners and slaves, and ethnic groups.

PART II

6

Marriage, Materialism, and Temporary Compliance

Part II explores marriage and its material implications through the lens of Islamic law and changing socioeconomic contexts. This chapter focusses on the legal, social, and moral threads, while the following two chapters investigate more closely the economy of marriage and divorce. The legal tenets described here provided the basis for *kadhi*s to arrive at their judgements in cases pertaining to marriage, such as the wife's claims for maintenance and the dower. Moreover, women seeking to claim their rights from their husbands and bargaining for a divorce creatively explored these tenets. In addition to the Islamic legal framework, the actors were informed by customary norms, such as the presentation of gifts from the groom to the bride's family. These local practices had been reconciled with legal doctrines, were accepted by *kadhi*s, and provided women and men choices and constraints in shaping marital relations.

Anthropologists have outlined that on the Swahili coast, elders preferred to arrange first marriages among kin and equals in rank, whereas subsequent marriages were generally not arranged. They have suggested that subsequent marriages, unlike first marriages, tended to accommodate non-kin and outsiders, as spouses could freely choose each other.[1] The findings for colonial Zanzibar Town suggest otherwise.

[1] Middleton, *The World of the Swahili*, 58, 111, 124; Pat Caplan, *Choice and Constraint in a Swahili Community: Property, Hierarchy, and Cognatic Descent on the East African Coast* (London: Oxford University Press, 1975), 27–28, 138; Pamela

I argue that throughout the first half of the twentieth century, the preference of elders to marry their children to kin or social equals and the Islamic legal principle of *kafāʾa*, the right of the wife and her kin that the husband be her equal, account for an essentially endogamous nature of marriage. This social and ethnic endogamy pertains not only to first but also to subsequent marriages, with the abolition of slavery and, notably, the impoverishment of the Arab oligarchy triggering but a modest opening of marriage networks. As a counterweight to elders' orchestration of marriage, women had recourse to legal doctrines to mould their marriage at least to some extent.

To Marry and to be Married: Gender, Legal Theory, and Zanzibari Practice

Conventional wisdom holds that Swahili women have been excluded from the realm of shariʿa.[2] *Kadhi*'s court records, however, reveal that Islamic legal doctrines offered women tools to negotiate their marriage and thus their social status. Women could actively shape their marriage through guardianship in marriage, by reinterpreting the concept of equality, *kafāʾa* in Arabic, and by inserting stipulations in marriage contracts. Their conscious exploration of legal regulations and differences in Ibāḍī and Shafiʿi doctrines predominantly resulted in favourable outcomes of their claims (see Table 3.1). I provide evidence that even from the earliest years of the twentieth century women articulated their rights towards men in this legal arena, thus offering a historical context to the findings of Susan Hirsch and Erin Stiles

Weaver Landberg, "Kinship and Community in a Tanzanian Coastal Village (East Africa)" (PhD diss., University of California, Davis, 1977), 137, 153, 155, 157.

[2] Carol Eastman, "Women, Slaves, and Foreigners: African Cultural Influences and Group Processes in the Formation of Northern Swahili Coastal Society," *International Journal of African Historical Studies* 21, no. 1 (1988): 1–20; Strobel, *Muslim Women*; Pat Caplan, "Gender, Ideology and Modes of Production," 29–43. Caplan revised her approach in subsequent work, such as her "Cognatic Descent, Islamic Law and Women's Property on the East African Coast," in *Women and Property, Women as Property*, ed. Renée Hirschon (London: Croom Helm, 1984), 23–43; idem, "'Law' and 'Custom'," 203–21. Also John Middleton questions the dichotomy of a female and male sphere in *The World of the Swahili*, 118–19. See further Purpura, "Knowledge and Agency"; Stiles, *Islamic Court*.

that *kadhi*'s courts have become institutions providing Swahili women legal redress in recent decades.[3]

The importance of marriage is stressed in the Qur'an and hadith. Only marriage legitimises sexual intercourse, thus serving to provide sexual fulfilment to both spouses and to procreate. It is a moral obligation for good Muslims and comes into being as a legal contract between two parties, husband and wife, defining their rights and duties as spouses.[4]

Marriage is a watershed in defining women's social status.[5] Under Islamic law, this status is defined in terms of physical factors such as puberty and virginity. Puberty equals majority and the age of nine is generally considered among jurists as the minimum age for girls to be physically mature. The loss of virginity is taken as an indication that a woman is able to act on her behalf and to engage in social activities.[6] Hence girls may have wanted to get married at a relatively early age to participate fully in social life. That girls themselves were aware and proud of having become women can be gleaned from Mwana Khamis bt. Muhammad, who defined herself at the age of fourteen as an adult woman through her menstruation and engagement.[7]

As marriage was a manifestation of moral integrity, defined by normative behaviour of the elite, Zanzibari men and women strove for marital status to achieve respectability. Given the social and moral importance of marriage, men perceived unmarried women as a threat

[3] Hirsch, *Pronouncing and Persevering*, 243; Stiles, *Islamic Court*; idem, "'There Is No Stranger to Marriage Here!': Muslim Women and Divorce in Rural Zanzibar," *Africa* 75, no. 4 (2005): 583.

[4] Tucker, *Women, Family, and Gender*, 41.

[5] The importance of marriage as an indicator of adulthood and the transfer of bridewealth as legitimising marriage are also highlighted in Brett Shadle's study on marriage in colonial Gusiiland, Kenya ("Girl Cases," xxi). Jeremy Prestholdt specifically ties men's acquisition of full personhood to marriage (idem, *Domesticating the World*, 48). On the centrality of marriage in social identities of men and women in the sixteenth-century Ottoman city of Aintab, see Peirce, *Morality Tales*, 229.

[6] Ali bin Hemedi, *Nikahi: A Handbook of the Law of Marriage in Islam*, trans. J. W. T. Allen (s. l.: s. n., 1934), 2. Hemedi largely draws on al-Nawawī's *Minhāj al-ṭālibīn*. See further Fariba Zarinebaf-Shahr, "Women and the Public Eye in Eighteenth-Century Istanbul," in *Women in the Medieval Islamic World: Power, Patronage, and Piety*, ed. Gavin R. Hambly (New York: St. Martin's Press, 1999), 305, on the social freedom women gained in marriage.

[7] HC10/48, ZNA.

and respected them less. Filing for restitution of conjugal rights in 1928, Khamis b. Shahdost alleged that Madina bt. Shambi, with whom his wife, Ganjo, was staying, had a bad influence on her. Madina did not have a husband and, according to Khamis, strangers (Arab, Swahili, and Hindu men) frequented her house. The fact that two other unmarried women were staying at the house compounded Khamis' distrust.[8] Similarly, in a custody case of 1956, the father of the children, Zubeir b. Khamis, a lorry driver employed by the government, described his former mother-in-law, a property owner and dressmaker, as an unsuitable guardian "because she has lived for approximately twenty years without a husband."[9] Terms used in court records such as *fī ḥukm al-zawjiyya*, under the rule of marriage, or *fī l-ʿiṣma*, under the protection (of the husband), also convey the force of marriage and its lack as tantamount to being a prostitute.[10] The tag of prostitute was easily placed on women who were financially and socially independent from men and defying normative behaviour.

Women from all socioeconomic backgrounds sought to raise their respectability by pointing to their marital status. This can be gleaned from a police statement of Pavu bt. Pandu, who admitted to having been ashamed of telling the *kadhi* that she was living with her alleged husband as his lover rather than his wife.[11] Buku bt. Saburi, a former slave, consciously backed up her claim for a share of inheritance by referring to her status as a married woman and the presence of her husband in court.[12] At the upper end of the echelon, Raya bt. Khalfan sought to support her claim for the recovery of money and a house by mentioning that her husband accompanied her to court.[13] This indicates that women were aware of the social importance attached to

[8] HC10/20, ZNA. See also HC10/79, ZNA, where a husband held against his wife that she entered a *bayt ajnabī* (lit. an unfamiliar house). She must have visited a house where none of her relatives or female friends were living. See also Strobel, *Muslim Women*, 138n37, where she refers to a custody case in which the husband accused the wife of frequenting the houses of a Singhalese and a Parsee for prostitution.

[9] HC10/3325, ZNA, original in English. Cf. Chapter 3.

[10] HC10/3295 and HC10/1435, ZNA, respectively.

[11] HC10/3196, ZNA.

[12] HC10/741, ZNA.

[13] HC8/51, ZNA, original in English. Cf. Chapter 7.

marriage and thus sought to portray themselves in court as married women.

Marriage rules are gendered in Islamic law, which conceives of marriage as a complementary rather than an egalitarian partnership. This complementary nature implies different rights and duties for the spouses and is reflected in Swahili, whose speakers conceptualise men as actors and women as recipients: Men actively marry (Sw. *kuoa*), while women are (passively) married (Sw. *kuolewa*). According to al-Shāfiʿī, a woman, unlike a man, can neither conduct her own marriage nor act as a guardian in marriage. She needs a male guardian and her consent to the marriage is not required if, regardless of her age, her father or paternal grandfather gives her into marriage as a virgin.

Under Shafiʿi law, marriage is an oral or written contract concluded in the presence of two free, upright male witnesses. According to Sunna, or tradition, the amount of dower should be stipulated, although this is not necessarily needed.[14] In Zanzibar, contracts seem to have been concluded mostly, if not exclusively, orally.[15] From 1922 onwards, when the colonial government made the registration of marriages compulsory, marriage registers provide evidence of the bride's minority or majority, the amount of dower as well as the names of the guardian and the witnesses, which would serve as evidence in future disputes. It further made the witnesses to the marriage accountable for any violation of the law.[16]

Yet correspondence between colonial officers reveals that the registration of Muslim marriages appeared unsatisfactory. *Mudir*s cast registrars as "a type of people who were not conscious of the accuracy required in spite of repeated explanations and their mistakes

[14] Berg, *Minhādj*, vol. II, 319–22, 375.

[15] Interview with Sh. Abdalla Suleiman Jumbe, 24 March 2004.

[16] On the interaction between society and the registration of marriage in earlier twentieth-century Egypt, see Ron Shaham, "Custom, Islamic Law, and Statutory Legislation: Marriage Registration and Minimum Age at Marriage in the Egyptian Shariʿa Courts," *Islamic Law and Society* 2, no. 3 (1995): 258–81. On child marriages in Zanzibar, see Elke E. Stockreiter, "Child Marriage and Domestic Violence: Islamic and Colonial Discourses on Gender Relations and Female Status in Zanzibar, 1900–1950s," in *Domestic Violence and the Law in Colonial and Postcolonial Africa*, ed. Emily Burrill, Richard Roberts, and Elizabeth Thornberry (Athens: Ohio University Press, 2010), 138–58.

shown."[17] *Kadhis*, who had to verify the suitability of marriage officers and *wakīls*, became aware of the inaccuracy and problems in registering Muslim marriages as well as divorces.[18] Apart from the shortcomings of registrars, the general response to registering marriages seems to have been unsatisfactory. Hence the original stipulation of the Marriage and Divorce Decree of 1935 and 1936, saying that the court would not recognise unregistered marriages, was amended in 1944.[19]

> [T]hat section, by forbidding a court to recognise a marriage or divorce which the parties have failed to register, is too harsh, in that parties may be unable to remedy their omission and so be permanently barred from obtaining through the court such relief as divorce, maintenance, etc., and from establishing a claim to inheritance.[20]

This indicates that only a fraction of contracted marriages were entered into the registers and that the originally stipulated invalidity of unregistered marriages had unforeseen effects. In the early 1960s, individual officers were still debating registrars' inaccuracy, hinting at the government's failure to impose control and desired standards.[21]

On a material level, the dower as an effect of the contract of marriage indicates both women's limitations and options in shaping their marriage. Although the dower "is in Muslim law the gift which the bridegroom has to give the bride when the contract of marriage is made and which becomes the property of the wife,"[22] hence the term dower and not bridewealth, Zanzibari practice appears to have been influenced by bridewealth practices on the mainland. In the first half of the twentieth century, the wife's elders rather than the major wife received the dower. If she was a minor, her dower must have been

17 District commissioner, urban, to senior commissioner, 17 January 1956, AK13/40, ZNA.

18 HC10/84, ZNA.

19 J. N. D. Anderson, *Islamic Law*, 62.

20 Legal Report by Attorney General Hallam Roberts, 14 June 1944, CO 618/81/7, NAK.

21 Town *mudir* to district commissioner, urban, 15 November 1962, AK13/41 and district commissioner, urban, to senior commissioner, 17 January 1956, AK13/40, ZNA.

22 *EI*², s.v. "*mahr*." "Indirect dowry," the transfer of property from the husband, or his kin, for the use of the wife, is the term Jack Goody has proposed for the *mahr* under shariʿa. See Jack Goody and S. J. Tambiah, *Bridewealth and Dowry* (Cambridge: Cambridge University Press, 1973).

received by her guardian as she was not financially competent.[23] By custom the payment of the dower was split into two parts; only one part was paid promptly.[24] For the mainland, there is evidence that husbands wrote a *khatti ya mahari*, a deed of dower, if they did not pay the prompt dower upon marriage, which seems to have occurred frequently. This deed indicated how much dower the husband owed his wife and when the payment was due.[25] As not only the prompt but also the deferred dower is a debt of the husband towards his wife that she can claim any time, Chapter 8 shows that this right was an important tool for women to instigate a divorce. For Shafiʿis, a major woman may ask her guardian to give her into marriage without a dower. If no dower is specified upon marriage, a standard dower (Ar. *mahr al-mithl*) is due, calculated according to the wife's peers.[26] In 1902, Habib b. Saʿid claimed to have married Sheikha bt. Sulayman al-Marhubi for a standard dower, which the *kadhi* confirmed, as Sheikha failed to provide evidence for the higher amount that she held was due to her.[27]

As shariʿa attributes the role of provider to the husband, thereby construing the wife as his dependent, the dower should serve as an emergency resource on which she may draw if he neglects his maintenance duties or divorces her. As elders negotiated the dower on behalf of the bride, she was often unclear about the arrangement. When Mgeni bt. Salim al-Marhubi cited the outstanding deferred dower as one of the grounds on which she sought to obtain a divorce in 1913, the witnesses to the marriage, including *kadhi* Sh. Burhān, who contracted the marriage, were unanimous on the agreement that the remainder of the dower would be due on divorce or death. Thus contrary to

[23] Joseph Schacht, *An Introduction to Islamic Law* (Oxford: Clarendon Press, 1964), 124–25.

[24] Witness in HC9/82, ZNA; Sh. Abdalla Suleiman Jumbe, 24 March 2004. This is in stark contrast to current social arrangements, which do not accept the deferral of the dower (Stiles, *Islamic Court*, 160, 202n16). The current Zanzibari practice stands out as unusual, as it is common practice in the Muslim world to defer at least part of the dower.

[25] Richard Niese, *Das Personen- und Familienrecht der Suaheli. (Ein Beitrag zur vergleichenden Rechtswissenschaft)* (Berlin: Georg Pintus, 1902), 21–22.

[26] Berg, *Minhādj*, vol. II, 384–85. Under Shafiʿi law, criteria such as genealogy, age, knowledge, and virginity determine a woman's standard dower (ibid., 387–88).

[27] Entry #764, no. 225, 23 Shawwāl [1319]/2 February 1902, HC28/29, ZNA.

her understanding of the deferred dower, Mgeni could not claim it in court.[28] While it is obscure why this specific arrangement pertained to Mgeni's marriage contract, it certainly curtailed her bargaining options and recourse to material assets. In addition to imposed restrictions on wives' control of dower, some women indicated that they were too proud to claim the outstanding deferred dower from their husband or his estate. By forgoing their dower and bearing the husband's failure to maintain them as well as their children, they gained in independence and social esteem. Believing in justice in the hereafter, they may have accepted debts rather than sued their husband in court.[29]

Social status affects the spouses' rights and duties, which come into operation once the marriage has been consummated. Wives are entitled to maintenance as long as they are obedient towards their husband. Interpretations of obedience have varied across time and space and were also negotiated by couples individually. There are three levels of maintenance which, according to al-Shāfiʿī, are calculated solely on the basis of the husband's financial capacity – whether he lives in financial ease, with average means, or in dire financial straits. Maintenance entails food, clothes, suitable accommodation, and, if the wife's status demands it, a servant. Sh. Ali b. Hemedi (1891–1957), a Shafiʿi *kadhi* in Tanga, Tanganyika, gives clear instructions that food means foodstuffs and not money and is meticulous in his description of clothes.[30] He may thereby have addressed requests by the wife to receive maintenance in pecuniary form, or generally sought to counter society's strive towards monetarisation.

At least from 1900 onwards, Zanzibari *kadhis* defined maintenance claims predominantly in monetary value, which attests to their acceptance if not encouragement of cash economy.[31] Particularly for maintenance arrears, the *kadhi*s determined the pecuniary value of the husband's debt. Thus if a wife addressed the court with a maintenance claim, she would be granted cash. Also if *kadhi*s ordered husbands to deposit maintenance arrears, including clothes, in court, wives would

28 HC8/86, ZNA, original in Arabic and English.

29 Interviews with Bi Hadiya Rashidi Ali, 13 June 2004; Bi Faida Salim Babu, 26 June 2004; Bi Halima Abdalla Jafar, 13 April 2004.

30 Hemedi, *Nikahi*, 32–34.

31 Only in two cases *kadhi*s defined maintenance also in kind (HC10/25, HC10/31, ZNA).

receive these debts in cash.[32] Additionally, labour migration, which brought many mainlanders to Zanzibar, and the increasing need to earn cash to pay taxes to the colonial government had ramifications in court proceedings. When Kassimali b. Idi responded to the senior *kadhi*'s questions regarding his whereabouts in 1955, he "replied that I went to work as a labourer in order to find the money for my wife's maintenance."[33] Thus if wives filed a maintenance claim in court, they stressed the aspect of marriage as a business partnership and, if their claim was granted, it satisfied a demand for cash.

But *kadhi*s did not exclusively enforce the wife's rights in monetary terms. A *kadhi*, who almost certainly was Ibāḍī, confirmed the wife's right to a servant in addition to maintenance and clothes in 1902, when Salih b. Muhammad and his wife Fatima bt. sayyid Ahmad b. ʿAlawi al-Baʿalawi reached an agreement in court.[34] Moreover, Shafiʿi scholar Hemedi stipulated that kitchen utensils had to be provided by the husband and that the wife was not obliged to do housework. "Cooking, sweeping, pounding, grinding, cleaning, sifting, sieving, washing clothes and utensils, etc., are all the business of the man to do for the woman and she is not required to do any of this except voluntarily out of kindness."[35] In 1931, *kadhi* Sh. Ṭāhir enforced a maintenance claim that the husband denied, arguing that his wife had been disobedient. Sh. Ṭāhir refuted the allegation of disobedience, as the wife had a choice of eating with her husband or on her own. He thereby implied that she was not obliged to cook for her husband.[36]

Virginity, another criterion of women's social status, further defined their rights under shariʿa. Unlike non-virgin women, virgins can be given into marriage by their father or paternal grandfather without their consent under Shafiʿi law, although the girl or woman should be consulted.[37] According to the Ibāḍīs, however, only minor virgins can be married off and they can ask for the dissolution of the contract upon attainment of majority.[38] If a minor virgin is given into marriage, she

[32] For example, HC10/42, ZNA.
[33] HC10/3202, ZNA, original in English. Cf. Chapter 8.
[34] Entry #755, no number, 14 Shawwāl 1319/24 January 1902, HC28/29, ZNA.
[35] Hemedi, *Nikahi*, 34.
[36] HC10/31, ZNA.
[37] Berg, *Minhādj*, vol. II, 322.
[38] J. N. D. Anderson, *Islamic Law*, 71.

will stay with her parents until she attains the age of puberty to prevent the consummation.[39] In Zanzibar Town, this was usually agreed on between the husband and the wife's kin or stipulated. In 1945, for example, a minor daughter was given into marriage by her father on the condition that the husband should not consummate the marriage until her majority.[40] In this case, the wife's absence from the marital home did not count as disobedience. However, the wife was not entitled to maintenance as the marriage had not been consummated.[41] When Mzee b. Hassan, likely a freed slave, sued his wife Safia bt. Mngwali for disobedience in 1902, the *kadhi* was surprised by her obviously young age. Since Safia was a minor, the *kadhi* ordered her to stay with her father and gave her the choice to dissolve the marriage upon majority.[42] Although an Ibāḍī *kadhi* adjudicated this case, it is unlikely that Safia or her husband were Ibāḍīs, and we do not know whether one of the litigants chose to be adjudicated by the Ibāḍī *kadhi*. A Shafiʿi *kadhi*, however, could not have given Safia the option of dissolution upon attainment of majority.

Another criterion for defining social status, and therefore affecting the capacity to contract a marriage, was being free or a slave. Although a male slave could not be given into marriage without his consent, a male or female slave could not insist the master gave him or her into marriage. The master or mistress had to consent to the slave's marriage and let him or her stay with his wife or her husband at night.[43] This was applied when a *kadhi* ordered Binti Baruti to be obedient at night and her husband to provide maintenance at night only because of their slave status.[44] The husband of a slave was obliged to provide food only if his wife stayed with him during the day.[45] When Farashu claimed

39 Berg, *Minhādj*, vol. II, 322.

40 Sample of Marriage Registers, 1945, *Mambo Msiige*. See also Christelow, *Muslim Law Courts*, 125; Marnia Lazreg, *The Eloquence of Silence: Algerian Women in Question* (New York: Routledge, 1994), 102–103.

41 Hemedi, *Nikahi*, 6, 35.

42 The husband had to pay the dower but was exempt from paying maintenance (Entry #842, no. 360, 22 Dhū l-Ḥijja [1319]/1 April 1902, HC28/29, ZNA).

43 Berg, *Minhādj*, vol. II, 337; Hemedi, *Nikahi*, 3, 6.

44 Entry #404, no. 497, 30 Shawwāl 1318/20 February 1901, HC28/29, ZNA.

45 Hemedi, *Nikahi*, 6. On the marriage of slaves, see also Mtoro bin Mwinyi Bakari, *The Customs of the Swahili People. The Desturi za Waswahili of Mtoro bin Mwinyi Bakari and Other Swahili Persons*, ed. and trans. J. W. T. Allen (Berkeley: University of California Press, 1981), 74–75.

that the husband of her slave prevented this slave from working during the day, the *kadhi*s ruled that he could only prevent her from leaving at night.[46]

One of the legal requirements women explored to adjust marital arrangements was the guardianship in marriage. The Shafiʿi school has a strict order of who may act as guardian, giving preponderance to agnates. The father is first in rank, followed by the paternal grandfather and the other nearest agnates. If the woman is a slave, her master acts in this capacity or the guardian of her mistress. Guardianship can also be transferred to the *kadhi* or the sultan in the absence of the immediate guardian.[47] For the Ibāḍīs, the rules differ, as a son can give his mother into marriage.[48] Al-Shāfiʿī gives additional weight to female legal agency in marriage. If an adult woman of sound mind claims that she married such and such under guardianship and in the presence of two witnesses, the marriage is established even if the guardian and the witnesses deny the marriage.[49]

Although Shafiʿi women aiming to contract a marriage are placed under the protection of men, they may interpret the question of guardianship to their advantage. In 1931, after thirteen years of marriage, Mgeni bt. Jaʿfar filed a suit for the dissolution of her marriage on the grounds of its invalidity, as her mother rather than a male guardian had given her into marriage. As discussed in Chapter 5, *kadhi* Sh. Ṭāhir authorised Sh. Zahir to contract the marriage of women with and without their guardian. Mgeni believed the marriage, concluded by Sh. Zahir, to be firm but recently found that it was not. Sh. Zahir testified in court that he had given her into marriage according to her own will and consent as well as the consent of Sh. Ṭāhir. As Mgeni had previously sued her husband for maintenance, clothes, and accommodation, her husband's *wakīl* argued she thereby confirmed the validity of the marriage. Ignoring this point, she explained that she did not have a male guardian who could give her into marriage to her present husband according to shariʿa requirements.[50] Yet the non-availability of a male relative was not an impediment to contracting a shariʿa

46 Entry #362, no. 443, 10 Shawwāl 1318/31 January 1901, HC28/29, ZNA.
47 Berg, *Minhādj*, vol. II, 323–24.
48 J. N. D. Anderson, *Islamic Law*, 71.
49 Berg, *Minhādj*, vol. II, 321; Hemedi, *Nikahi*, 2.
50 HC10/43, ZNA.

marriage, as *kadhi*s and the sultan could give any woman into marriage. Mgeni now sought to back up her claim for divorce by pointing to the absence of a guardian.

Guardianship in marriage was based on the availability of kin and thus tended to expose immigrants who may not have had their immediate guardian available. Yet from 1922 to 1960, samples of marriage registers in Zanzibar Town suggest that women who registered their marriage under an ethnic identity from the mainland or were former slaves were given into marriage by their father or brother as often, if not more often, than by their former master, the *kadhi*, or sultan. Taken at face value, this suggests the presence of their natal kin. If these guardians were "brothers" and "fathers" in the sense of *jamaa*, a group connected through non-biological ties, it attests to the legal awareness of the parties. We do not know whether it was the registrar who translated the kinship ties as legally appropriate or whether this information was provided by the contracting parties themselves. Given that unlawful information entered the historical record, I would suggest that either the women offered these kinship terms, describing their guardian as they saw their relations, or the guardian provided them himself. In the vast majority of cases, we can assume that "father" or "brother" referred to the biological relative.

Across all social and ethnic groups, the father mostly acted as guardian in the marriages registered as well as those disputed in court. At the same time, *kadhi*s acted as guardians for mainlanders and strangers, as well as for women of Arab descent. The sultan similarly was guardian in marriage for these groups of women and for his former slaves and their descendants. Whereas present-day *kadhi*s believe it is shameful for a woman not to have a guardian from her kin,[51] the social and geographical mobility on the Swahili coast in the first half of the twentieth century made scholars and Zanzibari society adopt a different approach to this issue. In 1935, *kadhi* Sh. Ṭāhir registered a marriage in which the wife herself acted as her guardian.[52] Also Buku bt. Saburi, a Ngindo and a former slave, asserted she gave herself into marriage, while her patron claimed he did so.[53] That a

[51] Interviews with Sh. Abdalla Suleiman Jumbe, 24 March 2004; Sh. Ibrahim Mtoro and Sh. Hamid Musa Mlomri, 22 December 2003.

[52] Sample of Marriage Registers, 1935, *Mambo Msiige*.

[53] HC10/741, ZNA.

free, sane adult woman gives herself into marriage is possible according to the Ḥanafī doctrine. Although Shafiʿi *kadhi*s do not seem to have drawn on doctrines of schools other than their own in court, where they were obliged to apply the law of their own school, they may have done so outside court, for instance, when they registered marriages.

As the cases of Mgeni and others suggest, it occurred that unacceptable guardians such as the mother and maternal uncles gave women into marriage. In a case of 1904, Abdurahman b. ʿUthman from the Mrima coast claimed the return of his wife to the matrimonial home. As she was given into marriage by her maternal uncle, who was not a legal guardian in marriage under Shafiʿi law, *kadhi* Sh. Burhān ruled for the return of the dower to Abdurahman and nullified the marriage.[54] In 1902, *kadhi* Sh. Aḥmad b. Sumayṭ annulled a marriage as someone from the *jamaa* of the wife's patron acted as guardian. The wife, Khayzran, further said she had not given her consent to the marriage.[55] In 1905, the *wakīl* of Kweni bt. Majaliwa, a woman from the mainland, explained to the *kadhi* that Kweni's sister had given her into marriage. The sister later refused that Kweni joined her husband, Salmin, as he was a slave and her sister free. However, Salmin's *wakīl*, obviously aware of shariʿa requirements, stated that the father had married Kweni off to Salmin. Examples like Kweni's may indicate that recent converts to Islam and former slaves were less versed in legal doctrines and influenced by matrilinearity. *Kadhi* Sh. Burhān dissolved her marriage, holding that *kafāʾa* was the right of the guardian and the wife.[56]

Kafāʾa, the right of the wife and her kin that her husband be of equal status, is an important requirement of a Muslim marriage. It further demonstrates the adaptability of women's identities, which are tied to their natal families.[57] The interpretation of *kafāʾa* is particularly open to manipulation and, in Zanzibar Town, reflected changes in social and racial definitions. Women interpreted *kafāʾa* in ethnic terms both inclusively and exclusively to protect their status. The guardian

54 HC9/114, ZNA.

55 No entry #, no. 588, 24 Rabīʿ II [1320]/30 July 1902, HC28/29, ZNA.

56 HC9/117, ZNA. Cf. Chapter 8.

57 Tucker, *Women, Family, and Gender*, 45. On the interpretation of *kafāʾa* among the Hadrami diaspora, see Engseng Ho, *The Graves of Tarim: Genealogy and Mobility across the Indian Ocean* (Berkeley: University of California Press, 2006), 150–51, 172–84, 186–87.

has to give a woman into marriage to a man of equal status, unless she agrees to marry a man who does not meet this criterion. If the guardian refuses to marry his ward off, she can address the *kadhi* or sultan, who will marry her to a man fulfilling these criteria, according to her wish.[58] In 1932, when Mwana Khamis bt. Muhammad sued her father for refusing to give her into marriage, *kadhi* Sh. Ṭāhir ordered him to marry her to a man of equal status.[59] The parameters that account for *kafāʾa* according to al-Shāfiʿī are freedom from bodily defects, lineage, probity, profession, and being free in case of non-slave women. Difference in wealth does not constitute grounds for inequality.[60] Hemedi explains equality by status as both spouses being free or slaves and by birth as both sharing their ethnic identity, "as a Swahili is not equal to an Arab."[61] One of the most eminent Shafiʿi scholars in twentieth-century Mombasa, Sh. Muhammad Kasim Mazrui, regards first and foremost religious sincerity but also ethnicity, social status, profession, and even wealth as constituents of *kafāʾa*.[62] Ibāḍīs, however, agree that a non-Arab man is the equal of an Arab woman.[63] Yet this was interpreted differently by Mwana Mkuu bt. Muhammed b. Salum al-Saʿidi in her alleged marriage to Addi b. Juma al-Zarʿa in 1909. Addi, a Tumbatu, claimed she had appointed a *wakīl* to marry her to whomever she wanted. Mwana Mkuu was a divorced Arab woman, a *shamba* owner and patron, to whom the court, the *kadhi*s and the judge, paid considerable respect.[64] Although she was an Ibāḍī, Mwana Mkuu made clear that the lack of Addi's ethnic equality barred her from marrying him. Finding Addi's claim implausible as neither the wife nor her guardian had agreed to the marriage, the *kadhi*s dismissed his claim. The English translation

58 Berg, *Minhādj*, vol. II, 330–32; Hemedi, *Nikahi*, 2.

59 HC10/48, ZNA.

60 Berg, *Minhādj*, vol. II, 332–33.

61 Hemedi, *Nikahi*, 3.

62 Kresse, "'Swahili Enlightenment?,'" 296. On the importance of ethnicity as a qualifier of *kafāʾa* in Mombasa in the 1970s and 1980s, see also Marc J. Swartz, *The Way the World Is: Cultural Processes and Social Relations among the Mombasa Swahili* (Berkeley: University of California Press, 1991), 91. For the Kenyan coast, J. N. D. Anderson observed that by the 1950s, *kafāʾa* was applied according to the texts by all *kadhi*s as regards religion, family, trade, and character (idem, *Islamic Law*, 109).

63 J. N. D. Anderson, *Islamic Law*, 72.

64 At one point, her *nisba* appears as Bū Saʿīdī.

of their judgement reads, "and God forbid from forcing this virtuous woman [into marriage]."[65] The litigant's different social status apparently influenced the *kadhis*' reasoning. Worldly rather than spiritual pedigree was hotly contested in Zanzibari notions of *kafā 'a*.[66]

While the status of being free appears as an important criterion of *kafā 'a* in the years after the abolition of slavery (discussed in Chapter 8 in the context of divorce), ethnicity subsequently became the predominant feature in the conceptualisation of equality, opening new avenues of defining eligible marriage partners. Because of the indebtedness of plantation owners, their daughters and sisters came increasingly under pressure to explore new ways of support. As marriage offered respectability if not financial support, some women became so determined to find a husband that they were willing to waive an essential criterion of *kafā 'a*. In 1949 Asha bt. Awadh, who referred to herself as being of "mixed Arab and African parentage,"[67] wanted to marry Abdalla b. Mfaume, who defined himself as a Bajuni-Swahili. She sued her brother, ʿAli b. Awadh, who had given her into marriage three times previously, for refusing to act as her guardian. Among Asha's former husbands were an Arab-Somali and a Hadrami, but ʿAli refused Abdalla on racial grounds. Asha lived in dire financial straits, saying she depended on friends and stressing "the very great necessity of my getting married."[68] The woman welfare officer Vera Davies described Asha's situation to the *kadhi* as follows:

> The woman [Asha] states that she has no work nor is she supported by her brother or any other relation, so that her method of livelihood appears to be obvious. In view of the circumstances of her life, which probably were unknown to you, perhaps you could persuade her brother to remove his objections to a marriage which would relieve her of the necessity of pursuing that mode of life.[69]

65 HC9/82, ZNA. Cf. Chapter 9.

66 R. S. O'Fahey, "'Small World': Neo-Sufi Interconnexions between the Maghrib, the Hijaz and Southeast Asia," in *The Transmission of Learning in Islamic Africa*, ed. Scott S. Reese (Leiden: Brill, 2004), 286. See also Thomas McDow, "Being Baysar: (In)flexible Identities in East Africa," *The MIT Electronic Journal of Middle East Studies* 5 (2005): 34–42, http://web.mit.edu/cis/www/mitejmes/

67 Asha bt. Awadh to Chief Justice, 16 May 1949, HC5/582, ZNA.

68 Memorandum of appeal by Asha bt. Awadh, n. d., HC5/582, ZNA.

69 Vera M. Davies to *kadhi*, 18 March 1949, HC5/582, ZNA.

Like Zanzibari society, Davies assumed that an unmarried woman could only make a living as a prostitute and that marriage would restore her respectability.

On the question of Abdalla being a suitable match, ʿAli explained that he and his sister were Arabs and, according to shariʿa, a Swahili was not equal to an Arab. For Asha, the criteria of *kafāʾa* were religion and social status or being free. In his judgement, *kadhi* Sh. ʿUmar referred to Asha's own admittance that she regarded a Swahili as not suitable to marry an Arab woman. Due to lack of proof, he dismissed her claim that her guardian prevented her from marrying ʿAli. Asha went to appeal and succeeded. In one of his meticulous judgements, Chief Justice John Gray ruled for the court's consent to the marriage, as it would provide Asha with a respectable way of support.[70]

In addition to guardianship and *kafāʾa*, stipulations in marriage contracts offered ways of individualising them. Although the government forms for registering marriages did not provide for inserting stipulations, parties and marriage registrars drew on this legal provision. Shafiʿis divide conditions into two categories: those that stress the aim of marriage or its rules, such as the wife's right to maintenance, and those that oppose the rules pertaining to marriage. The first category is legally not enforceable but does not affect the validity of the marriage and the dower stipulated, whereas the second category may not only invalidate the dower but also the marriage itself.[71] Ibāḍīs, on the other hand, validate stipulations in favour of the wife.[72] Although stipulations are not enforceable under Shafiʿi law, they can provide a basis for the wife to negotiate her marriage.[73] The records are mostly silent on who initiated the registration of a stipulation. We can assume that the wife, or her guardian, uttered a condition, which was then recorded by either a registrar or a *kadhi*. This demonstrates that women modified marital rights and obligations and that men conscientiously recorded

70 HC5/582, ZNA.

71 Berg, *Minhādj*, vol. II, 382. See also Hemedi, *Nikahi*, 6–7. See further Lynn Welchman, *Beyond the Code: Muslim Family Law and the Shariʿa Judiciary in the Palestinian West Bank* (The Hague: Kluwer Law International, 2000), 156–58, on how the four schools of law classify stipulations.

72 J. N. D. Anderson, *Islamic Law*, 72.

73 Cf. Welchman, *Beyond the Code*, 162.

them in writing. Stipulations were almost exclusively requests by the wife not to be moved to the countryside or to stay in her own house.[74] A guardian and a father, respectively, stated the condition that the wife should not be moved to the countryside.[75] Discussing stipulations providing for husbands not to move the wife upcountry on the nineteenth-century Mrima coast, Jonathon Glassman suggests that the wife's kin stipulated these conditions not to lose their daughter and her children.[76]

In an urban setting like Zanzibar Town, from which every village on the island could be reached in a day's trip, we have to look for motivation other than mere geographical distance from kin. Despite strong familial ties between town and countryside, rural life compared poorly to the appeals of Zanzibar Town, which provided more options of employment and entertainment. Women from the mainland seeking to make a new start after divorce were thus attracted to Zanzibar Town because of its economic opportunities and higher wages than in rural areas. While women who grew up in villages may have moved to town and back to the countryside several times during their lifetime, women from town may not have accepted to leave urban areas.[77] Although life histories usually remain elusive in court records, women who asserted the condition not to move to the countryside seem to have been living in town at least for some time.

Women could be very insistent on a dwelling in town. After thirteen years of marriage during which ʿAli b. Omar struggled to support his wife, Amina bt. Haji, she was unwilling to stay with him in a countryside house and offered to buy her divorce instead.[78] Similarly, Ganjo bt. Mohamedi was adamant on staying in Zanzibar Town,

74 Such stipulations were claimed in HC8/67; HC9/83; HC10/10; HC10/20; HC10/43; HC10/1141, ZNA; interview with Bi Salme Shaban Hilal, 27 April 2004. Shafiʿi *kadhi* Sh. ʿUmar registered the stipulation of a Zigua woman who did not want to be moved to the countryside in 1940 (Sample of Marriage Registers, 1940, *Mambo Msiige*).

75 HC9/83; HC10/1198, ZNA.

76 Glassman, *Feasts and Riot*, 128. Stipulations that the wife should not be moved away from her kin were not peculiar to the Swahili coast. See Tucker, *Women, Family, and Gender*, 49–50.

77 Fair, *Pastimes and Politics*, 16–17, 33–34, 53–54, 173–75, 270–71; Frederick Cooper, *From Slaves to Squatters*, 81; interview with Sh. Abdalla Suleiman Jumbe, 22 June 2004; HC10/20, ZNA.

78 HC10/3302, ZNA.

saying that even if her relatives allowed her to go to Pemba, where her husband was living, she would refuse.[79] The only record of a reason for women's refusal to leave urban Zanzibar cites fear of living in a village and of falling ill.[80] Women's claims for a dwelling in town appear to have become an extravagant demand, which was only supported by the *kadhi*s as a right of the wife to a suitable accommodation in any place.[81] Additionally, some women put oral conditions which expressed their unwillingness to endure marital trouble (Sw. *kutohangaishwa*).[82] However, such conditions were not enforceable. While evidence of stipulations shows *kadhi*s' sympathy towards women's concerns, female access to legal knowledge is a moot point. Stipulations belong to the intricacies of the law rather than the basic practice. Presumably, not many men would have been aware that Ibāḍī law endorses stipulations in the marriage contract. Consequently, few women would have known about these options, let alone about the different status of such stipulations under Shafiʿi and Ibāḍī law. It is thus most likely that they, as well as some fathers and male relatives, acted upon intuition.

A last aspect of the institution of marriage that merits a brief examination is polygyny – a frequently invoked characteristic of a Muslim marriage. While Erin Stiles indicates the frequent occurrence of polygyny in contemporary Zanzibar,[83] there are relatively few references to polygynous marriages in the case sample, only 6.3 percent, which indicates that they were not common in colonial Zanzibar Town. This would correlate with Janet Bujra's findings of a town on the northern Swahili coast in the 1960s and Pat Caplan's indication that only 10 percent of marriages were polygynous in a village on northern Mafia Island in the mid-1960s.[84] At least occasionally, polygyny seems to have disrupted and ended marital relations. In December 1955,

[79] HC10/20, ZNA.
[80] HC8/67, ZNA, original in Arabic and English.
[81] HC8/67; HC10/20; HC10/31; HC10/1141; HC10/1198, ZNA.
[82] Interviews with Bi Mwanaidi Makame Ameir, 3 April 2004; Bi Hadija Nasoro Ibrahim, 24 April 2004; Bi Halima Abdalla Jafar, 13 April 2004; Bi Salme Shaban Hilal, 27 April 2004.
[83] Stiles, *Islamic Court*, 77, 201n9.
[84] Janet M. Bujra, "Production, Property, Prostitution. 'Sexual Politics' in Atu," *Cahiers d'études africaines* 17, no. 1 (1977): 13–39; Caplan, *Choice and Constraint*, 27.

Yusuf Amani travelled to the mainland and left his wife, Hamida bt. Machano, with her kin in the countryside. He returned to Zanzibar in October 1956 with a second wife. After his return, Yusuf failed to provide Hamida with suitable accommodation, separate from her co-wife, and maintenance and let her stay with her family. In September 1957, Hamida sued him for past and future maintenance, her deferred dower, Shs. 60, or divorce. *Kadhi* Sh. ʿUmar accepted Yusuf's claim that he had divorced Hamida and entitled her to maintenance prior to the divorce and her deferred dower.[85] I would suggest that the main reasons for the low rate of polygynous marriages in town were men's difficulties in raising the dower and, as Yusuf's failure to comply with his maintenance duties illustrates, their economic liabilities in a marriage.

Elders and the Orchestration of Endogamous Marriages

It was one of the duties of parents towards their child to find a suitable spouse for her or him. Most parents in Zanzibar fulfilled their duty as soon as their daughter was physically ready and before their son himself considered taking a wife. Thus boys were married off in their early teenage years and girls even earlier.[86] At the beginning of the twentieth century, the main concern of elders and parents was to control the sexual behaviour of their children and to forge ties that met the interests of the family.[87] As Pat Caplan and John Middleton have shown, Swahili marriages served elders' strategies of augmenting

85 HC10/3447, ZNA. For further evidence on polygyny causing the end of marriages, see HC9/134; HC10/2881; HC10/3302, ZNA.

86 Velten, "Sitten und Gebräuche," 56. The age of fifteen for boys, which Velten indicates for the Swahili coast, is also a reasonable guideline for Zanzibar (ibid., 60). This age is described for Uzi Island in the south of Zanzibar (Private papers, Sir John Gray, Add. 7739, box 1, file "Uzi Island: its land tenure and other customs. Extracts from a report by Mohammed Abeid el-Haj, 1851," CUL), and by Burton, *Zanzibar*, vol. I, 426.

87 For a description of marriage and its rules, see Velten, "Sitten und Gebräuche," 60–63. In Palestine, families of high social standing also closely supervised marital arrangements. See Judith E. Tucker, "Ties That Bound: Women and Family in Eighteenth- and Nineteenth-Century Nablus," in *Women in Middle Eastern History: Shifting Boundaries in Sex and Gender*, ed. Nikki R. Keddie and Beth Baron (New Haven: Yale University Press, 1991), 242.

property and power. There was a strong preference for marrying relatives so family ties would not spread too far.[88] Caplan argues that only a small number of marriages may be termed hypergamous on Mafia Island. Particularly, families who wielded power practised exclusionary marriage. The reasons given for the preference of kin marriage were familiarity, stability, and to prevent the splitting of property.[89] Court records as well as marriage and divorce registers from Zanzibar Town suggest that this was practised by Arab, Tumbatu, and Hadimu families and, to a lesser extent, among former slaves and immigrants. Generational hierarchy thus strictly defined exercise of social control, with elders wielding power over male and female juniors.

Given that parents initiated marital ties and that spouses were socially inexperienced in adult tasks and duties, newlyweds initially stayed with a member or members of kin, usually the father or mother, particularly in rural areas.[90] This parental observation should guide the couple and entrench the parameters expected of a good marriage. In the case of cousin marriage among Arabs, the husband would stay in the house of his wife, with his paternal or maternal uncle.[91] In a contemporary rural Zanzibari context, Erin Stiles observes that new couples live virilocally. If the wife is sent home to her kin, this indicates that the husband divorced her.[92]

As marriage strategies aimed to assure and enhance socioeconomic positions, marriage in notable Arab families was preferably concluded between cousins. Wealth was thus consolidated and redistributed among the poorer group of the family through inheritance.[93] If the

[88] Caplan, *Choice and Constraint*, especially 29; Middleton, *The World of the Swahili*, 121, 185. Interviews with Bi Fadhila Mohamed Hasan, 30 March 2004; Bi Maua Azizi Mbarak, 16 March 2004; Bi Aziza Sharif Issa, 26 April 2004. Drawing on fieldwork in Lamu and Zanzibar, Middleton has described in detail marriage between stone town members and country town members, respectively (idem, *The World of the Swahili*, especially Chapter 5 and 58). He stresses the great variety of marriage patterns along the coast but also highlights their coherence (ibid., 112).

[89] Caplan, *Choice and Constraint*, 28, 137–38.

[90] Personal communication with Omar S. Khamis, 6 May 2004; interviews with Seif Hemedi Musa, 7 May 2004; Rashid Omar Sharif, 9 April 2004; Sh. Abdalla Suleiman Jumbe, 24 March 2004.

[91] Middleton, *The World of the Swahili*, 133.

[92] Erin Stiles, "'There Is No Stranger to Marriage Here!,'" 588.

[93] Middleton, *The World of the Swahili*, 112, 123; Landberg, "Kinship and Community," 111. Marriage strategies among Hadramis are analysed by Françoise Le

spouse was not a cousin, he or she usually was a member of the same or another Arab patronymic group. Among the Hadimu and the Tumbatu, this preference could include classificatory cousins who were linked through their grandfather or even great-grandfather. Although there was no pooling of assets between spouses, being married to a richer kin implied that these assets were available on a favourable yet contractual basis for economic ventures.

Elders arranged first marriages for daughters and sons according to this aim, save among slaves and ex-slaves.[94] While Middleton holds that subsequent marriage partners were freely chosen, oral sources suggest that even subsequent marriages may have been orchestrated, though rather on behalf of women than men.[95] Men appear to have increasingly married below their status in subsequent marriages, whereas evidence of women being of higher status than their husbands is scarce.[96] Social norms and the concept of *kafāʾa* account for this, as a woman cannot raise the status of her husband but rather loses her status if that of her husband is below hers. Based on this decisive distinction in gender, Frederick Cooper describes marriage as "the testing ground of social distinctions," in which any notion of slavery precluded social respectability and ethnic identities fostered exclusion.[97]

Guennec-Coppens, "Qui épouse-t-on chez les Hadrami d'Afrique orientale: Les réseaux d'alliances," in *Les Swahili entre Afrique et Arabie*, ed. Françoise Le Guennec-Coppens and Pat Caplan (Paris: Karthala, 1991), 145–62. In her data, endogamous and exogamous marriages constitute about 50 percent each. Hadrami men account for slightly less endogamous than exogamous marriages, whereas it is the other way around for women. See further Colette Le Cour Grandmaison, "Rich Cousins, Poor Cousins: Hidden Stratification among the Omani Arabs in Eastern Africa," *Africa* 59, no. 2 (1989): 181, on how Omanis' preference of marrying within the same patronymic group shifted to forming marital ties with different patronymic groups. Cf. Kristin Mann, *Marrying Well: Marriage, Status and Social Change among the Educated Elite in Colonial Lagos* (Cambridge: Cambridge University Press, 1985), 92, on the crucial role of marriage in the consolidation of the elite in Lagos.

94 Cf. Fair, *Pastimes and Politics*, 98, on the aim and arrangement of women's first marriages.

95 Middleton, *The World of the Swahili*, 123–24; interviews with Bi Mwanaidi Makame Ameir, 3 April 2004; Bi Faida Salim Babu, 22 March 2004; Bi Hadija Nasoro Ibrahim, 24 April 2004; Bi Mwajuma Mzee Mhina, 17 March 2004. See also Stiles, *Islamic Court*, 75–78.

96 Cf. Caplan, *Choice and Constraint*, 137–38.

97 Frederick Cooper, *Plantation Slavery*, 264. Cf. R. E. S. Tanner, "Cousin Marriage in the Afro-Arab Community of Mombasa, Kenya," *Africa* 34, no. 2 (1964): 132.

Ethnicity, or *nisba*, was a decisive marker of eligibility as a spouse. While previous research has stressed the importance of marriage in assimilating migrants in other parts of the Swahili coast, which mainly occurred through women's subsequent marriages,[98] marriage and divorce registers suggest that Zanzibar Town was a stronghold of endogamous marriages. This seems to have left social aspirants with the sole option of adapting their ethnic identities. Laura Fair has accounted for the fluidity of ethnic identities with the relationships between African women and Arab as well as Asian men.[99] These relationships, however, were liaisons rather than marriages, which indicates the social unacceptability of "mixed race" relations. As Michael Lofchie observed, it was after the increasing indebtedness of the Omani oligarchy that intermarriage of poor Arabs with indigenous Africans occurred.[100] This suggests that women's, or rather elders', choice of partners was determined by economic criteria in the absence of a common ethnic background.

At the turn of the century, many slaves and ex-slaves defined themselves as Swahili, as changing their ethnic identities turned out to be a remedy that enabled social integration. As the twentieth century progressed, an increasing number of Shirazis registered their marriages and divorces. Claiming descent from the Persian city of Shiraz invoked Arabness and raised respectability. This indicates that the Shirazi identity not only provided a useful tool for obtaining land but also enhanced marriage options from at least the 1940s onwards.[101] In the census of 1931, 40,891 identified themselves as Shirazi and 2,434

98 Glassman, *Feasts and Riot*, 127–28; Landberg, "Kinship and Community," 7–8, 157, 165, 175; idem, "Widows and Divorced Women in Swahili Society," in *Widows in African Societies: Choices and Constraints*, ed. Betty Potash (Stanford: Stanford University Press, 1986), 122–23.

99 Fair, *Pastimes and Politics*, 97–99, 209–23.

100 Michael F. Lofchie, *Zanzibar: Background to Revolution* (Princeton: Princeton University Press, 1965), 77–78. On the polemics of racial intermarriage, see Jonathon Glassman, *War of Words, War of Stones: Racial Thought and Violence in Colonial Zanzibar* (Bloomington: Indiana University Press, 2011), 137–44.

101 During the 1930s, many Tumbatu, Hadimu, and mainlanders registered as Shirazi. In *From Slaves to Squatters*, Frederick Cooper explores in detail how economic change triggered the redefinition of social, thus ethnic, identities. See also Fair, *Pastimes and Politics*, 28–55; Abdul Sheriff and Chizuko Tominaga, "The Ambiguity of Shirazi Identity in the History & Politics of Zanzibar," *Christianity and Culture* 24 (1990): 1–37. For a revised interpretation of changes in ethnic identities, see Glassman, *War of Words*.

as Comorian of a total population of 235,428 in the protectorate.[102] Thus Shirazis constituted a considerable proportion of the town population, about 17.37 percent. It was almost exclusively the bearers of Shirazi and Comorian identities who could permeate social and ethnic boundaries of marriage. Even though they seem to have been considered suitable marriage partners by all other ethnic groups, they rarely intermarried. A clear indication of social mobility would have been marriages between Shirazi men and Arab women, yet these seem to have been extremely rare. Legal requirements coupled with local interpretations of *kafāʾa* (see Hemedi above) made it difficult for men to marry above their status and fostered endogamy.

By 1960, the vast majority of Arab men and women still married among themselves, which speaks for the continuously arranged character of their marriages. At the lower end of the ethnic hierarchy, former slaves and ethnic groups from the mainland also largely remained within their marriageable boundaries. Apart from the flexibility that the adoption of Comorian and Shirazi identities entailed, mainlanders, Hadimu, and Tumbatu were curtailed by their ethnic identities that impeded them from marrying Arabs or Indians, save when Arab or Indian men chose to marry among them.[103] Endogamous marriages predominated at the turn of the twentieth century as much as towards the end of the colonial period. Whereas Arab matches were tailored as ethnically exclusive, inclusivity, which was much desired by former slaves, Hadimu, Tumbatu, and mainlanders, only could be achieved by climbing the ethnic hierarchy and occurred rarely.

Dower and the Materialisation of Social Power

Against the well-explored backdrop of Swahili consumerism and increasing integration into the global economy during the nineteenth century, marriage provides a lens to study the transfer of property and objects, represented in the dower and the trousseau, the items that a wife brought to the marital home. Court records are largely silent about the trousseau, but occasional references confirm what elders describe:

[102] BA34/3, ZNA.

[103] On sexual relations between Africans and Asians in Tanganyika, see Brennan, *Taifa*, 128–36; for Lamu, see Patricia W. Romero, *Lamu: History, Society, and Family in an East African Port City* (Princeton: Marcus Wiener, 1997), 181.

It often consisted of furniture (always a bed), household items, and possibly jewellery.[104] These items, however, were not provided by the wife's elders, nor did they comprise heirlooms but were newly acquired and paid for from the dower provided by the groom. This implies that elders used the dower to acquire customary items, thus reducing the costs of giving a daughter into marriage. Exceptionally, in wealthy families, the bride received objects from her elders, who added to the dower. This pertained to the first marriage only in most cases.[105] Although these items, like the dower, were the property of the wife, she could not control their acquisition. In more recent decades, the bride has become more explicit in defining the nature of the dower. Sh. Abdalla Suleiman Jumbe observed in court that some wives aim to "see the dower," meaning they are less interested in money, "which leaves no memories," than in objects.[106] By custom, until today, the wife brings household items and furniture to the marital home.

Marriage marked women's entry into social adulthood, while it offered men the opportunity to demonstrate their financial ability and social control. Given the importance of objects and display, Zanzibari custom required that proposers not only provided a considerable dower but also offered gifts to the immediate relatives of the bride.[107] These customary gifts expressed the respect that the husband-to-be had to pay towards his in-laws, thus, the elders. As parents arranged the marriage of their sons, they may have provided the dower.[108] The

[104] In some Muslim societies trousseau was more substantial than dower, thus enabling wives' financial independence. See Yossef Rapoport, *Marriage, Money and Divorce in Medieval Islamic Society* (Cambridge: Cambridge University Press, 2005), 13–22; Tucker, *Women, Family, and Gender*, 153.

[105] Interviews with Bi Amina Abdulrahman Mahmud, 2 May and 19 May 2004; Bi Salme Shaban Hilal, 27 April and 25 May 2004; Juma Bakari Mfaume, 28 May 2004; Bi Hadiya Rashidi Ali, 13 June 2004; Bi Mwanaidi Makame Ameir, 24 June 2004; Bi Fadhila Mohamed Hasan, 11 June 2004; Bi Faida Salim Babu, 22 March 2004; Bi Hadija Nasoro Ibrahim, 17 June 2004; Bi Maua Azizi Mbarak, 9 June 2004; Bi Rehema Abbasi Rajabu, 11 May 2004; Bi Halima Abdalla Jafar, 27 May 2004; Bi Aziza Sharif Issa, 26 April 2004; Seif Hemedi Musa, 7 May 2004; Rashid Omar Sharif, 9 April 2004; Sh. Abdalla Suleiman Jumbe, 24 March 2004.

[106] Interview with Sh. Abdalla Suleiman Jumbe, 24 March 2004.

[107] On the nature of these gifts, see Velten, "Sitten und Gebräuche," 60; Hemedi, *Nikahi*, 10; Ingrams, *Zanzibar*, 234; Private papers, Sir John Gray, Add. 7739, box 1, file "Uzi Island: its land tenure and other customs. Extracts from a report by Mohammed Abeid el-Haj, 1851," CUL; HC10/79, ZNA.

[108] Interviews with Sh. Abdalla Suleiman Jumbe, 24 March 2004; Juma Bakari Mfaume, 28 May 2004; Seif Hemedi Musa, 7 May 2004.

FIGURE 6.1. Interior of a house. Courtesy of ZNA.

family of the wife may have added to the dower to cover the costs of the celebration, which rose in accordance with the family's aspiration to show lavishness and could become a competition in outdoing one another.[109] Parents' instigation of marriage entailed financial liabilities, such as the feast and dower, but culturally empowered them to dispose of their daughter's dower. Given the weak sociolegal position of female minors, their guardian received the dower on their behalf and thus had the opportunity to decide how it should be spent, whether furniture was to be acquired and how much he was going to invest in material items and hand over to the bride. This principle may have been modified when the wife had gained sufficient social experience and was advanced in age, meaning she was aware of her dower arrangements and could not be deceived easily.[110]

109 Interview with Omar Barwani, 27 December 2003.

110 That minor wives could not receive their dower themselves was expressed by a *wakīl* in 1942 (HC10/1010, ZNA). Bi Halima Abdalla Jafar, who was about forty years old when she married, received her entire dower from the hands of her brother (interview, 13 February 2004). Cf. Annelies Moors, *Women, Property*

The role of elders as custodians of dower cut across the social hierarchy and ethnic identities, including at least one mistress, who kept the wife uninformed about her dower.[111] Women may have believed that the dower, which was handed to them upon marriage, was their entire dower, so they forfeited the remainder upon divorce or the husband's death. Bi Salme, for instance, asserted that her father received the entire dower prompt, but her marriage certificate reveals that the husband only paid a third.[112] The Islamicist J. S. Trimingham observed that disputes over compensation upon divorce were due to various payments when the marriage was contracted.[113] Court records indicate that wife and husband rarely seem to have had a different understanding regarding the stipulated amount of dower in Zanzibar Town.[114] These various payments and ensuing disputes to which Trimingham refers very likely comprised not only the dower but also the husband's gifts towards his future in-laws and the trousseau.

The dower as an "advance gift,"[115] paid in full upon marriage to the wife, constituted a relatively low percentage of the registers' sample (see Table 6.1). The deferred dower should provide security to the wife by deterring the husband from repudiating her and make material assets available to her upon his death or divorce. As Mgeni's case above demonstrates, it was both Shafiʿi and Ibāḍī practice to claim the deferred dower upon divorce rather than any time.[116] Another reason for the customary splitting of the dower was its high amount, usually worth several months of income. The Swahili proverb, *mke ni*

and Islam: Palestinian Experiences, 1920–1990 (Cambridge: Cambridge University Press, 1995), 95–96. R. E. S. Tanner also describes that wives take their dower in subsequent marriages. Idem, "The Relationships between the Sexes in a Coastal Islamic Society: Pangani District, Tanganyika," *African Studies* 21, no. 2 (1962): 80. Even presently, parents take a part of the dower, if not the entire dower, and many women are unaware of their first dower (Stiles, *Islamic Court*, 162).

111 HC10/15, ZNA.

112 Interviews with Bi Salme Shaban Hilal, 27 April and 25 May 2004.

113 Trimingham, *Islam in East Africa*, 139.

114 Wife and husband disagreed on the amount of dower in HC10/1010; Entry #764, 23 Shawwāl [1319]/2 February 1902, HC28/29, ZNA.

115 Rapoport, *Marriage, Money and Divorce*, 53.

116 This is explicitly mentioned in HC8/86, ZNA. Sh. Muḥammad Sālim al-Rawwāḥī also refused a wife's request for the remainder of her dower as she was still married to her husband (HC10/3295, ZNA). See also J. N. D. Anderson, *Islamic Law*, 72–73.

TABLE 6.1. *Dower Payments in Zanzibar Town*

Year	Entire Dower Paid	More than 50% Paid	50% Paid	Less than 50% Paid	Dower not Indicated	Number of Sample
1925	13	25	20	40	3	106
1930	15	20	26	29	9	118
1935	18	19	25	34	4	100
1940	5	23	22	43	7	100
1945	7	26	27	38	3	101
1950	8	19	29	43	1	100
1955	19	36	18	27	0	100
1960	23	38	14	25	0	100
Total	14	26	23	35	3	825

Source: Sample of marriage certificates from *Mambo Msiige*. Numbers are given in percentages; due to rounding, totals may not equal 100 percent.

nguo, which literally means "a wife is clothes," hints at the financial burden marriage imposed on husbands. Exploring the social logics of consumerism in nineteenth-century Mombasa, Jeremy Prestholdt notes that "[w]eddings, while forums for displaying a groom's ability, were also scenes of his material depletion."[117]

Although we should not take the payments recorded in the marriage and divorce registers at face value, they capture dimensions of social and material relations.[118] If an uneven sum of dower registered suggests the husband's financial limits and the negotiations involved, at least up to the 1930s, mostly immigrants from the mainland and ex-slaves seem to have provided the dower under these conditions. They registered uneven amounts of which they paid any affordable fraction prompt. In 1925, a husband from the Mrima coast registered a dower of Rs. 76 for his wife, a former slave. He paid Rs. 20 prompt. In 1930, a Nyamwezi (?) husband gave his wife, a Tumbatu, Rs. 12 of her dower worth Rs. 30, and a Ngoni married a Nyasa for Rs. 31, which the register claims she received immediately.[119] To register a high amount of dower may have boosted the esteem of the bride's family and, as long as the prompt dower was relatively low, did not threaten the husband's

[117] Prestholdt, *Domesticating the World*, 48.
[118] Cf. Rapoport, *Marriage, Money and Divorce*, 54–55.
[119] Sample of Marriage Registers, 1925 and 1930, *Mambo Msiige*.

resources. The deferred dower may have remained an eternal debt if the marriage lasted until the death of either spouse, while the wife commonly offered or agreed to forgo all debts upon divorce, as discussed in Chapter 8.

While fractions of dower may indicate differences according to social status, these differences did not coincide with the prompt payment of the entire dower. Neither the immediate transfer of the entire dower nor its amount was congruent with social standing. Not surprisingly, the highest sums were stipulated among Arab families, while spouses of slave descent were among those with the lowest amounts. Yet the vast majority of marriages indicate that the amount of dower was not tied to social status or ethnicity, indicating that these criteria did not determine the value of the dower. Assumptions that the value of the dower hinged on who acted as guardian have to be discarded. *Kadhi*s as well as fathers and brothers gave women into marriage with high amounts of dower. Equally, fathers often accepted a low amount of prompt dower. What can be gleaned from this diversity of data is that social status increasingly diverged from economic status, as members of families with Arab *nisba*s started to register low and uneven amounts of dower.

Although the background of the dower arrangements remains elusive in the registers, the increasing variety of amounts clearly emerges. In 1922, the registered amounts ranged between Rs. 20 and Rs. 300, with the sample comprising only thirteen different amounts. In 1930, its variety had increased to twenty, with Rs. 12 at the bottom and Rs. 2,000 at the top. By 1940, twenty-six different amounts appear in the sample, slightly reduced in 1945 and 1950, and back in range in 1955 and 1960. Amounts at the upper end of the scale gradually rose, with Rs. 100 (Shs. 100 from 1936 onwards)[120] remaining the amount wives had most frequently registered. As for the prompt and deferred payment of the dower, Table 6.1 shows that in 1940, 1945, and 1950 the prompt payment of the entire dower dropped considerably. This was triggered by the general economic difficulties that affected Zanzibaris in the post-war-1940s. The negative ramifications on the population were compounded by a drought threatening crops

[120] From January 1936 onwards, shillings replaced rupees. Rs. 1 was worth Shs. 1.5.

and food production.[121] The low in paying the entire dower prompt, reflected in the samples of 1940, 1945, and 1950, coincided with a slight rise in payments of less than 50 percent, which suggests that men faced difficulties in raising the dower they blamed elders inflated at the time.[122] The lower numbers in paying 50 percent and less than 50 percent prompt in 1955 and 1960 correlate with higher numbers in paying the entire dower and more than 50 percent prompt, indicating the shift in the post-independence period towards paying the entire dower upon marriage.

It is important to note that the vast majority of registered marriages are not first marriages of the wife. Given that first marriages were exclusively arranged and that, unlike in other places on the Swahili coast, even these subsequent marriages were largely conducted within the same ethnic and social strata, this emphasises further that Zanzibar Town was a stronghold of endogamous marriages. Since the amount of dower was contingent on the "qualities" of a woman, she generally received a higher dower in her first marriage,[123] which is confirmed by the few entries of first marriages in the marriage registers. As even the dower of subsequent marriages was high, men must have been struggling considerably to provide the one of mostly unrecorded first marriages.

Conclusion

As generational hierarchies dictated social relations, this chapter has argued that the role of elders as matchmakers and their application of the concept of equality account for the endogamous nature of not only first but also subsequent marriages in Zanzibar Town. We

[121] See Anthony Clayton, *The Zanzibar Revolution and Its Aftermath* (London: Hurst, 1981), 23; Samuel G. Ayany, *A History of Zanzibar: A Study in Constitutional Development, 1934–1964* (Nairobi: East African Literature Bureau, 1970), 21–22; Norman R. Bennett, *A History of the Arab State of Zanzibar* (London: Methuen, 1978), 241–42. The economic crisis preceded the 1940s but is not born out by the sample prior to this period.

[122] See Elke E. Stockreiter, "Materialism, Contention, and Rebellion: The Changing Demands on Marriage in Colonial Zanzibar," in *Domestic Tensions, National Anxieties: Global Perspectives on Modern Marriage Crises*, ed. Kristin Celello and Hanan Kholoussy (Oxford: Oxford University Press, forthcoming).

[123] Ingrams, *Zanzibar*, 234.

better understand the ramifications of this exclusionary practice by approaching marriage as the only socially accepted form of partnership. The constraints imposed upon women and men to marry into families other than among ethnic and social equals must have played their part in catalysing rifts in Zanzibari society, which emerged over the course of the first half of the twentieth century and culminated in the revolution of 1964. Elders' appropriation and inflation of the dower further shows that their material interests outweighed those of juniors and that material assets were mostly in the hands of the elders.

The dialectic of customary law and shariʿa indicates that women benefitted from the latter, while the former worked to the advantage of elders. Countering the power of elders, women could effectively draw on the concept of equality, stipulations, and guardianship to mitigate their passive role in marriage and dower arrangements. Guardianship in marriage further indicates that interpretations of legal doctrines may have differed among social groups. Women who may have become Muslims recently or lived among non-Muslims before arriving in Zanzibar reinterpreted legal doctrines in their own right in order to shape their marriage once their agency was no longer restricted by elders. *Kadhi*s were in a delicate position, in which they had to abide by colonial rules and at the same time enable the flow of social relations amidst the influx of immigrants, a large population of slave descent, and the increasing indebtedness of the population.

7

Property, Debt, and Inheritance

Studies on Muslim societies generally and the East African coast specifically have construed purdah and misogynous Islamic ideologies as major obstacles for female economic agency.[1] This view was purported by colonial officers who imparted a metropolitan understanding of gendered economic roles onto the colonised. As property disputes were common by the nineteenth century and meticulously recorded in the *kadhi's* courts from at least 1900 onwards, they offer a more nuanced and revised, albeit incomplete picture of gendered economic roles. The frequency of these disputes pertained to all social strata and both genders, thus implying a level of ease and familiarity by the litigants and the court.[2]

Women's roles as property owners and heirs were enshrined in Islamic law and very rarely, if at all, questioned on the basis of gender by any of the local actors. Women and men across the social hierarchy loaned as well as borrowed money; husbands relied on their wives as agents, guarantors, and executors, which suggests that networks between spouses and among kin crucially enabled economic mobility. Society's attitude towards women's economic agency did not noticeably change during the first half of the twentieth century, but colonial

[1] Glassman, *Feasts and Riot*, 42–45; Strobel, *Muslim Women*, 58–73.

[2] Cf. Peirce, *Morality Tales*, 193, where she speaks of a "comfort level." Court cases show that women's ability to enforce the Islamic law of inheritance was not merely theoretical but real (Gerber, "Social and Economic Position of Women," 233; Vianello and Kassim, *Servants of the Sharia*, 35).

decrees and the bureaucratisation of the judiciary entailed enhanced scrutinising of documents and written evidence. The shift towards the written made the illiterate, women but also men, bound to lose out to the literate. Although women's reliance on male representatives may have occasionally hampered their legal and economic agency, it cannot be universally understood as undermining their agency.

Property negotiations reveal discourses of inclusion and exclusion between freed slaves, as well as their descendants, and former patrons throughout the first half of the twentieth century. *Kadhi*s shaped this discourse as they played an important role in distributing shares of inheritance along patron-client ties, thus upholding their sociolegal tradition. An additional field of contestation in the realm of inheritance was the preference of cognates under customary law and agnates under Sunni laws. Litigants who were less familiar with *kadhi*s' exclusive application of shariʿa rules of inheritance brought futile claims as cognatic heirs.

Marital Economies: Between Legal Ideal and Social Reality

By the 1860s, the emergence of an Omani oligarchy and plantation-owning class had resulted in an increasing gap between rich and poor, reflected in the architecture and spatial structure of Zanzibar Town.[3] Their practice of female seclusion, later adopted by other social groups, made travellers and scholars believe that women in these wealthy circles lacked economic agency. Sources on women's participation in economic activities before the establishment of the British Protectorate are scarce, yet both court records and recent scholarship suggest women's active engagement beyond the household from 1890 onwards.[4] Although Laura Fair has interpreted the approaches of

[3] On the geography of Zanzibar Town, see Myers, "Reconstructing Ng'ambo"; Bissell, *Urban Design*; on the political economy of the plantations, see Frederick Cooper, *From Slaves to Squatters*; Sheriff, *Slaves, Spices and Ivory*.

[4] Thomas McDow has demonstrated women's involvement in large-scale trade in the nineteenth century. See his "Arabs and Africans: Commerce and Kinship from Oman to the East African Interior, c. 1820–1900" (PhD diss., Yale University, 2008), ProQuest (ATT 3317172). The role of women in economic transactions, such as moneylending, in Pemba has most recently been demonstrated by McMahon, *Slavery and Emancipation*. See also Fahad Ahmad Bishara, "A Sea of Debt: Histories of Commerce and Obligation in the Indian Ocean, c. 1850–1940" (PhD diss., Duke University, 2012), 186–87; Miran, *Red Sea Citizens*, 144, 149.

individual British officers towards shariʿa as largely undermining women as property holders and conceiving them as property of men,[5] *kadhis* actually did not question women's ability to accumulate and manage property. They enforced the husband's role as a provider in court with no exceptions, while the colonial assumption that Muslim, or, rather, Arab, women did not generate income manifested itself in an increasing segregation of economic roles. The monetarisation of social relations and the arising opportunities to invest in property, with most property acquired on mortgage, account for tensions in marital relations that spouses had to weather.[6] If we situate the ownership of property in the discourse on the patriarchal Muslim and Zanzibari family, it becomes clear that the evidence of women buying and selling property within and beyond the family calls for a reassessment of the concept of patriarchy.

At the turn of the twentieth century, women's source of wealth came, firstly, through inheritance, secondly, through marriage in form of the dower, and additionally through work in the case of poorer and former slave women. Women from higher social strata usually acquired substantial property through inheritance, thus bringing considerable capital into marital unions. A vast number of women were in charge of property substantial enough to make them financially independent.[7] Former slaves and economically less privileged women were more dependent on their labour to obtain property. While women's access to property differed according to their social background, all socioeconomic groups could explore serial marriage as a way of obtaining property.

Under Islamic law, individual property ownership provides the basis for many economic partnerships between the spouses, as any pooling

[5] Fair, *Pastimes and Politics*, 201–206.

[6] Moors argues for Palestine that the greater emphasis on men as providers resulted from an interplay of processes such as commoditisation, labour division, work migration, and local constructions of gender (idem, *Women, Property and Islam*, 254).

[7] The wife of the merchant Tippu Tip was a wealthy property owner unlike him at the beginning (Frederick Cooper, *Plantation Slavery*, 68–69). One could speculate whether she lent him money to start his trade. Drawing on studies from sixteenth- to nineteenth-century urban Turkey, Aleppo, and Cairo, Leila Ahmed asserts women's ownership of property and engagement in commercial activities. Yet based on the same evidence, she concludes that the number of women who were financially independent of male relatives was minute (idem, *Women and Gender*, 110–12).

of assets only exists on a voluntary basis.[8] The legal ideal further assigns the provider role exclusively to the husband, while in reality the wife rarely relies solely on this right. Based on her fieldwork on Mafia Island, Pat Caplan notes that poverty drives women to consolidate the little money they (can) make with the husband's money.[9] Oral sources, however, suggest that Zanzibari women from lower socioeconomic strata did not necessarily pool incomes.[10] Although spouses may have pooled money for their children, they held jointly acquired property in a strictly regulated coownership. Regardless of their economic background and conscious of their role as sole providers, men seemed to be more inclined than women to accept the consolidation of property, indicating a divergence between legal ideal and social reality.[11]

By the turn of the twentieth century, women from Arab families engaged in selling and buying property but also relied on their families' and husbands' maintenance.[12] When this support became unreliable due to the economic difficulties that were rampant among Arab planters and traders by the 1930s, their wives and sisters needed to provide for themselves. Their choices ranged from petty trading and selling their property to marrying, and if necessary, below their status (see Chapter 6). Arab women mainly generated respectable income by selling food and property, while most Hadimu and Tumbatu women were farmers and their crops were consumed by the family rather than sold.[13] When women earned money as potters, they used it for building

[8] This strict division between the husband's and wife's property was evident in 1943, when Sh. ʿUmar had to determine whether a donkey, seized to pay off a debt, was the property of Khamisa bt. Fundi or her husband (HC10/1122, ZNA).

[9] Caplan, *Choice and Constraint*, 16–17.

[10] Interviews with Bi Fadhila Mohamed Hasan, 30 March 2004; Bi Mwanaidi Makame Ameir, 3 April 2004; Bi Maua Azizi Mbarak, 16 March 2004; Bi Hadiya Rashidi Ali, 13 June 2004; Bi Faida Salim Babu, 22 March 2004.

[11] Interviews with Juma Bakari Mfaume, 28 May 2004; Sh. Abdalla Suleiman Jumbe, 24 March 2004; Seif Hemedi Musa, 7 May 2004.

[12] In some places on the Swahili coast, like Pate, freeborn women whose plantations collapsed after abolition invested their wealth in homes (Strobel, *Muslim Women*, 132). Yet real estate transactions in Mombasa suggest that women held a relatively small share of property (ibid., 65). In Massawa, transactions of buying and selling involved women from elite rather than lower status families (Miran, *Red Sea Citizens*, 149).

[13] In Mombasa, farming was an acceptable source of income for slaves and freeborn women. Women of mainly slave origin worked as *ngoma* dancers and midwives (Strobel, *Muslim Women*, 133).

and buying items falling outside the husband's maintenance duty, that is, anything other than food, essentials for hygiene, and a specified amount of clothes.[14]

Husbands' provision of maintenance encountered increasing difficulties over the course of the colonial period due to a changing socioeconomic context, which shaped spouses' understanding of their economic relations. The post-abolition economy of the colonial state left planters struggling to provide favourable terms for attracting workers, former slaves exploring offers of menial jobs and squatting on their ex-master's land, and traders readjusting to new trade networks after the collapse of long-distance trade with the interior. The trade in and acquisition of commodities and luxury items to reinforce social power characterised Swahili societies since their incipience and gained new momentum in the nineteenth century with demands for funds to buy objects and assets. The abolition of slavery and its ramifications on the economy entailed the increasing inadequacy of the husband's role as sole provider as well as elaborate explorations of networks of borrowing and mortgaging to cover both husbands' need to provide and women's drive to accumulate.

Although court records rarely provide the context for indebtedness, they reveal that men in each socioeconomic group struggled to make ends meet. The colonial economy entrenched a new circle of indebtedness and perpetual mortgaging,[15] while restricting certain groups from access to property, land particularly, and from economic participation other than envisioned by the colonial state. Following colonial perception, at the upper end of the racial scale, landownership was in Indian and Arab hands, with Arab plantations mortgaged to, and thus owned or rather under usufruct by, Indians. At the lower end of this racial pyramid of indebtedness, former slaves bought, sold, and mortgaged *shamba*s to their former masters to achieve a certain degree of economic independence. They also bought houses and land with money borrowed from Indians, to whom the property was then mortgaged.[16] As buyers rarely claimed ownership but rather usufruct

[14] Interview with Bi Maua Azizi Mbarak, 16 March 2004.

[15] For a novel account of the complex systems of credit and debt in the northwestern Indian Ocean during colonial rule, see Bishara, "Sea of Debt."

[16] See Frederick Cooper, *From Slaves to Squatters*, Chapters 2–4, for a detailed analysis of these processes.

in return for credit advanced, property ownership generally constituted a form of mortgage to circumvent Islamic law prohibiting interest.[17] Within these networks of dependency, men and women sought to obtain funds by relying on spouses and kin to avoid indebtedness to outsiders. Thus in cases in which husbands misappropriated the property of their wives, debts may have played as great a role as men's ambition to spend and accumulate beyond their individual economic means.[18]

To account for economic relations between spouses in Zanzibar Town, we have to consider the local practice of accumulating property in conjuncture with the social opportunities this practice provided particularly for freed slaves. Being or becoming a landlady was an important indication of a woman's socioeconomic status and her respectability. After the abolition of slavery in 1897, women explored the growing economic niches in town. Women from the mainland seeking to make a new start after divorce were attracted to Zanzibar Town because of its economic opportunities, high wages, and possible ease to obtain real estate.[19] In the first two decades after abolition women bought property in urban Zanzibar to promote their social and economic independence. Buying, owning, and managing property did not put their respectability at stake. On the contrary, women's property investments were a means to transform unrespectable economic activities such as prostitution and taints of slavery into respectability.[20]

Former slaves, who had conducted business on behalf of their owners, continued to engage in buying and selling property after their manumission. Male ex-slaves also used their wives' freedom of movement to make them their representatives. Women like Asha bt. Mbwana, who had worked in domestic service for an Indian for twelve years, could save enough money to invest in property. Asha clearly had a coownership in mind when she offered her husband's

17 Bishara, "Sea of Debt," especially Chapter 2.

18 The highest number of records in the *kadhi*'s courts at Brava from 1893 to 1900 concern debts (Vianello and Kassim, *Servants of the Sharia*, 61). Although Vianello and Kassim do not question the reasons for this, we can surmise that consumer and economic patterns similar to those in Zanzibar account for people's indebtedness.

19 Frederick Cooper, *From Slaves to Squatters*, 81; Fair, *Pastimes and Politics*, 155.

20 See Bujra, "Production, Property, Prostitution"; White, *The Comforts of Home*.

agent, his maternal uncle, to pay the remainder of the price of a house that the uncle should buy on her husband's instruction. Her intention of investing into property is backed up by her renovation of the house as well as by a testimony of her employer, whom she had asked for an advance of her wages.[21] The agency of a third person as a messenger or guarantor is characteristic of socioeconomic networks. Trustworthy relatives often functioned as messengers and guarantors, but when husbands sought to obtain funds to pay off debts, some preferred to involve non-family members.[22]

Husbands struggled to provide for their wives and to pay off debts, obviously being short of funds. Wives could thus pressure their husbands if they fell behind in providing maintenance.[23] Whereas wives rarely borrowed from their husbands, husbands commonly borrowed from their wives or pawned their property.[24] While suits for debts indicate conflict and tension in the couple's interests, the spouses' pooling of income was based on achieving a common aim (which is usually not indicated in the records) and constituted a token of love from the

21 HC9/69, ZNA. For an example of a former slave couple who built a house in partnership, see Entry #[806], no. 283, 10 Dhū l-Qaʿda 1319/19 February 1902, HC28/29, ZNA.

22 For examples of husbands selling their wife's property to a third party, see HC10/54; HC10/58, ZNA. Similarly, Omar b. Mwana seems to have sold a house he held in coownership with his wife to a third party to pay off a debt. He was indebted either to his wife or the woman to whom he sold the house (HC9/69, ZNA).

23 In 1901, Salima bt. Yusuf sued Suleiman b. Madai for Rs. 68, the wage of her *khādima* for six months, rent for her house for five years, and maintenance. Her husband, on the other hand, sued her for Rs. 120 that he gave on her behalf as security to an Indian. She, however, alleged that this was her dower (Entry #584, no number, 13 Rabīʿ II [1319]/29 July 1901, HC28/29, ZNA). See also Entry #764, no. 225, 23 Shawwāl [1319]/2 February 1902, HC28/29; HC10/3537, ZNA.

24 For husbands being indebted to their wives, see No entry #, no number, 8 Ramaḍān 1320/8 December 1902; No entry #, no number, 7 Shawwāl 1320/6 January 1903; No entry #, no number, date of hearing 20 Ṣafar 1321/18 May 1903, HC28/29; HC9/60, ZNA. See also Strobel, *Muslim Women*, 67n68, for cases in which husbands borrowed money from their wives. Husbands' indebtedness to their wives was also common in medieval Cairo, Jerusalem, and Damascus (Rapoport, *Marriage, Money and Divorce*, 25) and Ottoman Aintab (Peirce, *Morality Tales*, 209). A rare example of a Zanzibari wife being indebted to her former husband was Sigata or Sijata, an ex-slave and a property holder. In 1902, she came to court acknowledging that she had to pay Rs. 21 and a half to her ex-husband, Suwed, *khādim* of Suleiman b. Saleh al-Bahrani. She gave him her house in Saateni, Zanzibar Town, as security (Entry #920, no number, 25 Ṣafar 1320/2 June 1902, HC28/29, ZNA).

wife towards her husband.[25] Richard Roberts makes the crucial point that affection played a huge role in marital ties in addition to the mutual benefits that the spouses gained from the exchange of gender-specific tasks and services.[26] By acting as guarantors, wives showed support and affection for their husbands. In 1930, Panya bt. Maftah guaranteed for her husband's debt of Rs. 97 and therefore stayed in Zanzibar so he could travel to Mafia Island. Alas, her husband died without leaving any property and she had to pay back his debt.[27]

Differences in women's social status and the divergence of social and economic status during the course of the twentieth century made them increasingly engage in economic transactions to obtain more social power. Additionally, they could use real estate either as alternative accommodation, if the one the husband provided was below their social standard, or as an escape from his authority.[28] Furthermore, husbands could oversee the *shamba*s of their wives. However, wife and husband may have had a diverging understanding of property ownership and management.

In 1908, Raya bt. Khalfan sued the representatives of her late husband, Salem b. Hamed, for money and a house from her husband's estate. The English transcripts of the case give us insight into the economic relations between Raya and her husband, through whom she executed economic transactions. As she observed purdah, her husband built two houses for her, looked after her *shamba*, and arranged the picking of cloves. One of her houses was rented to a Bohora on her instructions. A few months before her husband's death, she had deposited with him Rs. 450, the amount her clove crop yielded. The separation of the spouses' assets was executed meticulously. When Raya asked for Rs. 100, her husband gave her a receipt for Rs. 350 that were still deposited with him. In her testimony, she indicated her high social standing by purdah, by observing the period of mourning (during which a Muslim woman is not supposed to leave the house) and by the fact that her new husband accompanied her when she filed the

[25] On the voluntary pooling of income, see also Tucker, *Women in Nineteenth-Century Egypt*, 98. On class and gender framing women's contradictory opinions about sharing property with their spouse, see Moors, *Women, Property and Islam*, 6.

[26] Richard Roberts, *Litigants and Households*, 196.

[27] HC10/54, ZNA.

[28] See Strobel, *Muslim Women*, 91; HC10/2881; HC8/67, ZNA.

suit. She thus subtly stressed the social necessity of depending on her husband as agent, at the same time making clear on whose instruction he acted.[29] Women like Raya used their male agents consciously for their own aims, maintaining a delicate balance between these aims and respectability as a key factor of social and economic power. We should thus analyse female dependency in the context of navigating between these two complementary types of power. Women's legal and economic agency exercised through male representatives, both from among their kin and slaves, was a social construction that occasionally thwarted their aims but did not generally undermine their agency.

Women's reliance on their husband as representative and the ideal of upholding purdah and respectability at times exacerbated women's vulnerability to deception. Women could face threats from officials as well as family members who wanted to seize their property.[30] In 1917, Aisha bt. Mabruk, possibly a former *suria*, bought for her three children a *shamba* from her husband, Msellem b. Hussein. He not only divorced her after the sale but also sold her a *shamba* that was mortgaged with an Indian with the consent of the latter. Msellem sold the *shamba* above its value, indebting his stepchildren to the Indian.[31] In another case of 1913, Mgeni bt. Salim b. ʿAbdallah al-Marhubi claimed that her husband pretended to sell her his *shamba* but actually took Rs. 460 from her and mortgaged his *shamba* to her below its actual value. As Mgeni was illiterate, she only discovered the fraud when the alleged deed of sale was read to her.[32] Illiteracy enhanced vulnerability, with some husbands attempting to control their wives' income and property, while the fact that spouses did not jointly own property enabled women's social and economic mobility. Additionally,

29 HC8/51, ZNA. Cf. Chapter 6. Women presented their observance of the *ʿidda* after the husband's death as an impediment to take charge of their share of inheritance from his estate (HC5/312, ZNA). In 1940, a *mudir* reproached a woman, who had observed her *ʿidda*, for not coming to the probate department herself since this was the usual procedure (HC10/741, ZNA). Bakari remarked that women could only observe the death *ʿidda* if they could afford to stay inside the house (idem, *Customs of the Swahili*, 80).

30 See Jokha bt. Msellem's petition, 15 May 1938, AX8/2; HC5/229; HC8/86; HC10/59; HC10/741; HC10/3073; HC10/3284, ZNA. See also Strobel, *Muslim Women*, 61–62, where she refers to a case in which the *kadhi* seems to have played a dubious role.

31 HC9/20, ZNA.

32 HC8/86, ZNA. See also Strobel, *Muslim Women*, 58–59.

upholding their social esteem and purdah led to women's deliberate reliance on a representative, which could work against their interests. Particularly women of lower social strata, who used the accumulation of property to move up the social ladder,[33] imitated the convention of appointing a male representative deliberately. At the same time, the concept of vulnerability was effectively explored by women and also by men when they were in similar situations. The writer's or pleader's sense of vulnerability may actually have been dramatised to influence the hearing positively.[34]

The nature of the property women owned could disadvantage them further. Jewellery constituted an important source of property and investment for women in addition to real estate. Yet it was easily seized by husbands, whose property was primarily real estate and could only be confiscated by women through the court.[35] In 1956, Amina bt. Haji gave her husband, ʿAli b. Omar, all her jewellery, worth Shs. 1,000, which he then sold to provide for their maintenance. According to ʿAli, Amina owned *shamba*s and houses, while he was without property and earned his living as a tailor. He had to provide for three children and a second wife with an income of about Shs. 150 or Shs. 30 per month.[36] Because Amina maintained her husband, he could afford two wives. Her willingness to share her property with her husband and to maintain him must have been motivated by affection.[37]

[33] Strobel, *Muslim Women*, 64, 73.

[34] See Jokha bt. Msellem's petition, 15 May 1938, AX8/2; HC5/312; HC10/59; HC10/2881, ZNA. Age also accounted for vulnerability (HC10/1122, ZNA). Cf. Strobel, *Muslim Women*, 60; Rapoport, *Marriage, Money and Divorce*, 23–24.

[35] On the importance of jewellery for women in Lamu to raise their social esteem, see Patricia W. Romero, "Possible Sources for the Origin of Gold as an Economic and Social Vehicle for Women in Lamu," *Africa* 57, no. 3 (1987): 364–76. Margot Lovett also argues that Ha women's assets were their jewellery as the majority of them lacked access to land. Idem, "Elders, Migrants and Wives: Labor Migration and the Renegotiation of Intergenerational, Patronage and Gender Relations in Highland Buha, Western Tanzania, 1921–1962" (PhD diss., Columbia University 1996), 52–54.

[36] These considerably diverging amounts of income are quoted in two certificates of poverty provided by ʿAli, indicating that these documents could obviously be manipulated (HC10/3302, ZNA).

[37] HC10/3302, ZNA. The husband also seized the wife's jewellery in Entry #342, no. 304, 21 Ramaḍān 1318/12 January 1901; Entry #683, no. 58, 1 Shaʿbān 1319/13 November 1901, HC28/29; HC10/3631; HC10/3695, ZNA. For women suing their husbands for stolen property, see Strobel, *Muslim Women*, 47–48, 133.

The common characteristics of civil cases in the early colonial period were a frequently travelling husband, an intricate economic relationship between the spouses involving more than one type of property, and a wife seeking to obtain a divorce, in the course of which the couple's socioeconomic partnership becomes, at least partly, revealed.[38] The marriage between Muhammed b. Hamed al-Barwani and Rabia bt. Muhammed b. ʿAli al-Barwani was a successful economic partnership for about thirteen years. Muhammed managed his wife's property (real estate) and at the same time he pursued his business, which involved frequent travelling. When she sued him for rent for seven years in 1911, a total of Rs. 1,680, he claimed to have left her the produce of his *shamba* and cows for maintenance. Typical of actors at the time, Muhammed expected his wife to look after his property during his lengthy absence, during which she was free to move between her own, her family's, and her husband's houses. The couple had stayed in Rabia's house by mutual agreement, which may have made it easier for the husband to oversee her *shamba*s, including the selling of cloves. When for some unrecorded reason her expectations of her marriage fell short and she got tired of him, she turned their previous arrangement, from which both spouses profited, into a suit for maintenance and rent. Muhammed in turn argued that he had not claimed payment for the management of her property and that her management of his property was unsatisfactory. When a relationship had broken down, the individual tasks and favours rendered were listed by each spouse and sought to be accounted for. Rabia had obtained freedom of movement (her husband did not seem to mind in which property she stayed) and a manager of her property while accepting an absent husband and some responsibility for his *shamba*.[39]

Husband and wife constituted the basis of many economic activities such as joint ownership, selling and buying of property, and, often without the spouse's agreement, giving her or his property as

38 See, for example, No entry #, no number, 26 Muḥarram 1317 [sic, 1318]/26 May 1900, HC28/29, ZNA. Although men tended to have more geographical mobility than women, legal records attest to women's geographical mobility.

39 HC8/67, ZNA. The unresolved case between Sharifa bt. Suleiman al-Mundhuri and Sultan b. Salem b. Hashil of 1916 hinged on the same issues: his management of her two *shamba*s for the past eleven years and arrears of maintenance; additionally, she claimed the value of her donkey (HC8/102, ZNA).

security.[40] These transactions enabled spouses to preserve and enhance their social status but at the same time disrupted their relationship if debts remained unpaid. The frequency with which wives loaned money to their husbands ties in with men's complaints about the inflated dower recorded from the 1940s onwards, whereas women's ability to loan attests to their continuous financial independence. Because wives frequently acted as money lenders, we may draw the conclusion that, regardless of their socioeconomic status, they were better off than their husbands. Borrowing money from one's spouse did not involve Indian moneylenders, while it simultaneously strained relationships, as unhappy wives could sue their husbands for outstanding debts with the final aim of getting a divorce.[41]

Socioeconomic Networks among Kin and Social Groups

Three processes moulded the access to and management of property in the first half of the twentieth century. The first process was the high geographical mobility of Zanzibari society, which opened opportunities for sending money but at the same time affected the management of property negatively.[42] The second process was the reliance on trustees during legal minority, which frequently exposed minors to mismanagement of their property. The third process, the colonial interference in the sphere of property ownership, was manifest in colonial decrees pertaining to guardianship and resulted in restricting Africans from property ownership. This was part of the colonial state's endeavour to take over the role of individuals and the community as guarantors, as Martin Chanock has argued. Thus colonial decrees in Zanzibar sought to restrict the scope of Islamic law pertaining to the rights of guardians over the custody of persons and property of minors. Generally these decrees intended to curtail the free disposal of adults over their property and to put men in charge of female property.[43]

[40] Cf. Tucker, *Women in Nineteenth-Century Egypt*, 100.

[41] See Tucker, "Ties That Bound," 242, on reinforcement of marital ties through spouses' mutual indebtedness.

[42] Also further up the coast, in Brava, a considerable part of the population seems to have been highly mobile (Vianello and Kassim, *Servants of the Sharia*, 31).

[43] Martin Chanock, "A Peculiar Sharpness: An Essay on Property in the History of Customary Law in Colonial Africa," *Journal of African History* 32, no. 1 (1991): 76, 80–81, 87; J. N. D. Anderson, *Islamic Law*, 92.

The Majority Decree of 1917 brought the age of majority for Muslims to 18 or 21, ensuring that the property of Muslim women and men was under their guardian's management for longer than until the age of puberty, as provided for under shariʿa. Litigants applied the shariʿa understanding of legal minority and were unaware that the colonial legislator had provided otherwise. In a similar vein, the Arab and African Guardianship Decree of 1927 prevented Africans and Arabs under the age of 25 from acting as guardians and receiving property from their guardian.[44] This suggests that the colonial government partly applied the category of race and partly the one of legal minority in its attempts to restrict certain groups of the population from property ownership.

During the late 1920s, the property of Maryam bt. Delwa was entrusted to a chain of relatives and misappropriated before she reached her legal majority. As she was a minor, Maryam's husband handed her dower over to her paternal uncle, who then entrusted her property to the father of her husband. After the death of his father, Maryam's husband left her property with Indians. Someone (it is not clear whether the husband or the person in charge of Maryam's property at the time) then sold it to Maryam's mother-in-law. By the time Maryam sued for divorce in 1931, gold and silver jewellery and furniture were all that remained.[45] Interestingly in her case, movables rather than real estate proved unalienable.

Seeking to control property transactions, the colonial administration tried to instil the concept of property ownership particularly in ex-slaves. It interpreted their previous rights to buy land and hold property strictly, aiming to abolish the flexible arrangements between patrons and clients regarding labour and usufruct of land.[46] Moreover, the compulsory registration of documents, first provided for in 1892, disadvantaged illiterate litigants, mostly women and the poor.[47] When *kadhi*s enforced the decrees pertaining to the registration of documents,

[44] See, for example, HC10/42; HC9/12, ZNA, on how the Majority Decree of 1917 worked to the disadvantage of minors. If one of the heirs had reached majority, he or she could take over the property and the possibility of mismanagement was reduced (HC10/59, ZNA). See also J. N. D. Anderson, *Islamic Law*, 63.

[45] HC10/42, ZNA.

[46] See Frederick Cooper, *From Slaves to Squatters*, 69–84.

[47] BA14/25, ZNA.

women rather than men tended to lose property because of their lack of property deeds.[48] Although Laura Fair convincingly argues that women were declared inapt property managers under colonial rule and that *wakf* dedications were alienated from the poor in the protectorate,[49] *kadhi*'s court records do not suggest women's categorical marginalisation in property ownership. Islamic law and colonial decrees guaranteed and to some extent inhibited women's acquisition and management of property.

Islamic law entrenched women's right to inherit and to buy and sell property, but social norms often impeded women to use these rights without a male agent. Hence, most women under purdah and women who wanted to uphold their respectability necessarily or preferably conducted economic transactions with spouses and kin. Husbands also relied on kin to provide for their wives, while brothers preferred to borrow money or buy property from their sisters. Messengers and guarantors were essential actors in the fulfillment of economic transactions, which grew more diverse the lower one's social status was. Ex-slaves drew as clients on their patron's economic capacity by using him or her as guarantor, buyer, or seller.

The complexity of suits regarding property ownership and inheritance was enhanced by the coexistence of shariʿa with *mila*, or customary law. Although the issue of land ownership lies beyond the scope of this chapter, there is evidence suggesting that *mila* predominated in the realm of landownership and particularly among people who grew up in rural areas.[50] In town, and among Hadrami and Omani lineages, patrilineal descent groups determined property ownership, whereas in rural areas property rights could be claimed cognatically,

48 See, for example, HC9/12; HC10/3325, ZNA, where women had no deeds of the *shamba*s they inherited.

49 Fair, *Pastimes and Politics*, 123–29.

50 In rural areas, land was owned by a kin group, a village, or a descent group. In some areas, men acquired their rights of land usage and building through their wives; in others, inheritance was exclusively established matrilineally. A. H. J. Prins, *The Swahili-Speaking Peoples of Zanzibar and the East African Coast (Arabs, Shirazi and Swahili)* (London: International African Institute, 1961), 62. See also Justin Willis, *Mombasa, the Swahili, and the Making of the Mijikenda* (Oxford: Clarendon Press, 1993), Chapter 5, on the correlation of Islamic and Nyika landownership systems in Mombasa.

by male and female descendants of a great-grandfather through both lines.[51] As explained below, in the *kadhi*'s courts, the denial of illegitimate children's rights to their father's estate and the favouring of paternal male relatives tended to puzzle litigants, in whose social practice Islamic doctrines were blurred with customary norms.

Economic transactions in colonial Zanzibar were preferably negotiated along the lines of kinship, based on both individual basis and utilitarian interpretations of property ownership. Women sold property to members of their family and bought property from them.[52] Brothers and sisters frequently appear as key economic partners. As Leslie Peirce has argued in an Ottoman context, women renounced on real capital in order to gain social capital through the protection of male relatives, notably brothers.[53] In 1952, the economic relations of an extended Hadrami family in Malindi, Zanzibar Town, were determined by their daughter, Salma bt. ʿAlawi Bunumay, whose absent husband, sayyid Saleh b. ʿAlawi b. Shihab, had successfully applied for the attachment and sale of her furniture. Yet the lack of two years' maintenance from her husband had forced Salma to sell her furniture to her brother, Muhammad,[54] who fulfilled sayyid Saleh's neglected maintenance duties. As Muhammad now wanted to marry, it was his sister's turn to provide support. The coincidence of Salma's need to provide for her child and to pay off debts with her brother's marriage not only shows how members of kin supported each other but also demonstrates that the time when support was claimed might not have suited both parties.[55]

The support that sisters provided brothers by lending them money so that they could raise the dower must have become crucial during the later colonial period, when the cost of getting married rocketed. Before or in 1934, Hamadi b. Islam borrowed money from his sister

[51] Middleton, *The World of the Swahili*, 102. Yet he argues that the concepts of patriliny and matriliny cannot fully capture inheritance patterns in stone towns (ibid., 135).

[52] See also Gerber, "Social and Economic Position of Women," 233.

[53] Peirce, *Morality Tales*, 227.

[54] This sale was witnessed by two male witnesses and recorded (see Chapter 3).

[55] HC10/2843, ZNA. Cf. Chapter 8. See also HC10/59, ZNA, for the sale and purchase of property between brother and sister because of his forthcoming marriage. A clear division of property between a husband and the mother of his ex-wife is further recorded in HC10/3004, ZNA.

Mwana Huru and her husband, Abud b. Yuslim, to cover his marriage expenses. Mwana Huru was Hamadi's guarantor and agent in paying his debt. Hamadi jointly owned a hut with his sisters, Mawlidi and Mwana Huru. Their inheritance was tied in real estate, and none of them seemed to have the funds to pay the other heirs. Mwana Huru had taken over the house as she was a major at the time. When she got married, her husband moved into her coowned house, whose ground rent was paid by her and her brother. To expand the range of economic actors, Mwana Huru had a daughter, presumably from a previous marriage, who contributed to the house from her dower. Obviously, the house was treated as an investment by various individuals and family units who lived in it. In 1937, when his suit of debt against Hamadi remained to be settled in court, Abud divorced Mwana Huru. When the coowned house was sold to pay off Hamadi's debts to Abud, the other sister, Mawlidi, deposited the necessary amount to set the sale of the house aside.[56] Although the joint ownership of property clearly entailed tensions and the risk of losing one's share if one of the shareholders incurred a debt, it appeared that many members of the community preferred to have business partnerships with kin and in-laws, whom they considered more trustworthy than strangers.

While socioeconomic networks between relatives account for the majority of women's transactions, there is evidence of women's economic transactions with men of a non-barred degree of marriage.[57] This was more pronounced among former slave women and their descendants but also practised among women from Arab background. Both women and men could draw on efficient networks of economic agents. Friends and relatives served as messengers of money and were entrusted with property, enabling its buying and selling. In these networks, Indians (Shiʿi Muslims and Hindus) feature as money lenders among non-kin. However, for economic and social reasons, higher status women rarely borrowed money from Indians.[58]

[56] HC10/59, ZNA, original in Arabic and English.

[57] Entry #87, no. 676, 17 Muḥarram 1317 [sic]/17 May 1900, HC28/29; HC10/62, ZNA. See also McMahon, *Slavery and Emancipation*, 149–50; Gerber, "Social and Economic Position of Women," 234.

[58] For examples of these patterns of money lending and transfer, see HC9/20; HC9/69; HC10/42; HC10/981, ZNA. I have not come across evidence that higher status women borrowed from Indians but would not rule out completely its occurrence. It was, however, certainly rare.

FIGURE 7.1. Store selling manufactured household items. Courtesy of ZNA.

The increasing availability of manufactured goods nourished consumer patterns that needed to be financed.[59] Indian moneylenders and businessmen in general sought to tie as many debtors as possible into their networks to create dependency, thereby enhancing their positions as powerful patrons and social and economic control.[60] People's eagerness to engage in property transactions was generated by a competition to out-do one another in ownership and display. For slaves, it was a compensation for deprivation, for former slave owners a display

[59] See Prestholdt, *Domesticating the World*, Chapter 4; idem, "On the Global Repercussions of East African Consumerism," *American Historical Review* 109, no. 3 (2004): 755–81; Frederick Cooper, *Plantation Slavery*, 75; idem, *From Slaves to Squatters*, 96; McDow, "Arabs and Africans." For a general discussion regarding the consumption of food and clothes, see Fair, *Pastimes and Politics*, 41–55. On clothing more specifically, see idem, "Dressing Up."

[60] Pearce, *Zanzibar*, 242; Prins, *The Swahili-Speaking Peoples*, 70. See also Mann, *Slavery and the Birth of an African City*, Chapter 8, where she argues that owners, and perhaps husbands, used credit and debt to exercise control and pressure dependants.

of continuing power as patrons, and for women, regardless of their social background, it generated credit as much as it enhanced respectability. In addition to continuous economic ties between patrons and clients, former slaves and masters perpetuated and transformed their mutual social duties (see Chapter 9).

Prior to the abolition of slavery, the possibilities slaves had to accumulate money and to access land depended on their relationship to their owner. Islamic tenets encourage piety and generosity and applied in the struggle for citizenship along the Swahili coast, this allowed slaves to accumulate assets. Masters let slaves pursue their own economic activities and gave them access to the land they cultivated. Slaves were also considered in their master's will and *wakf*s were set up on their behalf. This was notwithstanding the considerable coercive economic power owners had over slaves. Masters could inflict corporal punishment and give slaves, and even their spouses, as security. In turn, slaves generally could not incur debts without the knowledge of their masters. If there was written evidence, slaves were allowed to borrow money without their master's authority, but slaves themselves became liable to compensation. These economic activities demonstrate how slaves used their owners to achieve independence from them.[61]

Opportunist ventures and conflicting understandings of ties between former masters and slaves come to light in an intriguing court case of 1959. Mbasho bt. Kasim filed a case against the *sheha* of Mkokotoni, Mohamed Sheha or Shah,[62] for taking possession of her father's *shamba*s ten years ago. She had to maintain a large family, seven children between the ages of thirteen and twenty-five, and lacked income. Based on her vague knowledge of her late father's wife, Mwajuma bt. Mambo, "a lunatic who had disappeared about a decade ago," she claimed her share of inheritance from two *shamba*s and goats, which her father supposedly inherited from his wife. The alleged confiscator of Mwajuma's property, *sheha* Mohamed Sheha, dated her disappearance considerably earlier, in 1936, and suggested that this former slave of his family was a leader of a Sufi order.[63] It remains elusive whether

[61] See Bakari, *Customs of the Swahili*, 176; Frederick Cooper, *Plantation Slavery*, 234–36.

[62] Both versions occur in the file.

[63] HC10/3732, ZNA, original in Arabic and English.

she actually was a leader of an order, but this interpretation seems convincing as many former slaves became Sufis. Women particularly were attracted to Sufism, offering them ways to act as religious leaders that so-called mainstream Islam failed to provide.[64] Most strikingly, this interpretation was advanced by a man who presented Mwajuma's participation in Sufism as a commonly known and accepted fact. Mbasho's and Mohamed's diverging interpretations doubtlessly reflected their contradictory aims, as she sought to access the property that he tried to defend.

Mohamed Sheha defined himself in the English statement of defence as a person closely connected to Mwajuma and her parents – a euphemism for their master–slave relations. His ancestor had donated land to seven slaves for dwelling, farming, and picking coconuts. This plot of land was meant to revert to the descendants of the donor after the death of the last donee, Mambo, Mwajuma's father. This donation accounts for Mbasho's claim that the property was now in the hands of Mohamed Sheha. Following the typical pattern of economic relations between patrons and clients, this *shamba* had been partly leased by Mwajuma's father to Mohamed Sheha for a period of two years and by her (on behalf of her father?) to the same for a period of six months.[65] While this case illustrates how the continuous relations between former slaves and masters hinged on credit and debt, it also attests to slave status rather than gender being a criterion in entitlement to inherit.

The networks Zanzibaris drew on in the processes of buying and selling hint at both the brevity and ambiguity surrounding ownership of property. To some degree, gender and social status were decisive in choosing economic partners. For women from higher social strata husbands and relatives were obvious choices. Former slaves primarily explored ties to their patrons and Indian moneylenders and, secondarily, to kin. By the turn of the twentieth century, women sued and

[64] For a female slave who became the leader of the Qadiriyya order in the Lake Malawi region, see François Constantin, "Le saint et le prince: Sur les fondements de la dynamique confrérique en Afrique orientale," in *Les voies de l'islam en Afrique orientale*, ed. François Constantin (Paris: Karthala, 1987), 87–88. See also Felicitas Becker, *Becoming Muslim*, 79–80, 196, 284.

[65] HC10/3732, ZNA. See also Glassman, "The Bondsman's New Clothes," 290–91, on slaves' land use.

were sued for property. With sparse evidence from the nineteenth century, it is difficult to portray economic activities of Omani and Hadrami women, whom Margaret Strobel finds to be less economically active than other ethnic groups in Mombasa prior to the collapse of the plantation economy. Starting from the first decade of the twentieth century, and possibly earlier, women from originally wealthy backgrounds had to find new ways of securing their economic status, which accounts for their frequent appearance as sellers and buyers of property. Although the actors' relations and aims often remain elusive, the outlined patterns of buying and selling clearly attest to economic interactions between men and women across ethnic identities and socioeconomic strata.

Inheritance and the Invention of Ancestry

Disputes over property articulate underlying tensions along the lines of socioeconomic differentiation and were strongly affected by descent. Given that property ownership was shaped by ethnicity and social status, it is worth considering the ratio of the population in these terms. In 1924, 90,000 of a native population of over 180,000 in Zanzibar and Pemba appear as slave descendants. The census of 1948 established that 37,404 women and men claimed mainland origin in Zanzibar and 13,873 in Pemba. With 51,277 people of a population of 264,162 on both islands, the percentage of those whose ancestors were enslaved or were labour migrants was far from negligible.[66] The African population on Zanzibar Island comprised 118,652 men and women.[67] When former masters and former slaves left estate, essential discourses of exclusion and inclusion were negotiated in court. In the post-abolition era, inherent and unresolved contradictions in colonial and Islamic legal discourses of patron–client relations diverged further.

Islamic laws of inheritance allocate shares in a complex manner, and in the context of this chapter, a brief summary of their basic principles should sufficiently guide the reader.[68] Muslims can only

66 Frederick Cooper, *From Slaves to Squatters*, 83; AB33/13, ZNA.

67 BA34/5, ZNA. The racial definitions applied in this census were Arab, African, European, Indian, Goan, and other.

68 For a detailed elaboration, see N. J. Coulson, *Succession in Islamic Family Law* (Cambridge: Cambridge University Press, 1972). For an instructive summary, see Meriwether, *The Kin Who Count*, 154–56.

dispose of one third of their estate by will and may appoint executors, who are charged with the partition of the estate and supervised by a *kadhi*.[69] Gender was not a criterion in the appointment of executors, as women across the social hierarchy functioned before and during the colonial period in this capacity.[70] The costs of the burial and debts of the deceased are paid first. Then the shares are paid to the heirs who are entitled to a fixed share, the immediate relatives – children, spouses, sisters, brothers, and parents – to whom the Islamic system of inheritance gives priority. Fixed shares are allotted to these heirs in a complicated system of shares, with women receiving half of men's shares. The favouring of relatives from the father's side, the agnates, constituted an antithesis to the preference cognates receive under customary law. A disadvantage of this allocation of shares was "the excessive fragmentation of landed property to which the multiple rights of numerous heirs frequently gives rise,"[71] which could be circumvented if heirs bought and sold shares of coheirs.[72] Moreover, cousin marriage was an approved method to inhibit the division of a large estate. Stipulations further served to bypass gender differentiation, for instance, when a wealthy Arab woman entered into her will that her grandchildren's share in the estate should be divided equally between male and female.[73] Some parents might have also left gifts to their daughters to mitigate this discrimination.

Wakfs were another way of circumventing shariʿa regulations,[74] as was asking one's children to keep property as joint property (Sw. *shirika*). Although *shirika* was not recognised by shariʿa, this customary practice ensured that property remained undivided. *Shirika* only

[69] On the mainland, this regulation was superseded by customary law that allowed that half of the estate be regulated by will. C. H. Becker, "Materialien zur Kenntnis des Islam in Deutsch-Ostafrika," *Der Islam* 2 (1911): 2.

[70] The wives of Sultan Saʿīd and Barghash, respectively, are prominent examples. In 1900, Moza bt. Mhina al-Yaʿrabi had a power of attorney over her father's legacy, which she then may have passed on to her brother (Entry #78, no. 966, 10 Muḥarram 1317 [sic, 1318]/10 May 1900, HC28/29, ZNA). See also HC10/981, ZNA.

[71] J. N. D. Anderson, "Recent Reforms in the Islamic Law of Inheritance," *International and Comparative Law Quarterly* 14, no. 2 (1965): 354.

[72] Cf. Miran, *Red Sea Citizens*, 254; Powers, "Orientalism, Colonialism, and Legal History," 567. In Aleppo, women sold inherited property to family members to purchase other property or to invest in different assets (Meriwether, *The Kin Who Count*, 168).

[73] Strobel, *Muslim Women*, 64–65.

[74] Rapoport, *Marriage, Money and Divorce*, 27–28.

lasted for one generation, as its division was obligatory if one of the holders died.[75] As for the institution of *wakf*, the Wakf Validating Decree of 1946 followed the Indian model but included the kindred of founders as well as their families, children, and descendants.[76] It applied only to Arabs and Africans. Shafiʿi *wakf* dedications to a specific person and his or her heirs entitled males and females to equal shares, with beneficiaries including the grandchildren generation.[77]

As the family has a central place in Islamic systems of inheritance, parents and children are reciprocal heirs and owe each other material support when necessary.[78] Thus, paternity is one of the contested constructions of family. Only legitimate children and those acknowledged by their father inherit their social status and ethnicity through him. Children born out of wedlock are regarded as the mother's child only and deprived of crucial rights, such as a lawful guardian in marriage as well as inheritance from the father and paternal relatives.[79] A father may acknowledge paternity belatedly, any time he wishes, perhaps, as Shafiʿi scholar Hemedi notes, because he wants to inherit from his child. Claims in which family members sought to disown each other frequently occurred in coastal Tanganyika, implying that money was at stake and formed the core of social relations by the 1930s.[80]

Most importantly in the Zanzibari context, the group of heirs entitled to inheritance, after those with fixed shares and agnates had received their share, was the manumitter, or patron, and his or her paternal relatives.[81] In 1900, Fatima bt. Yusuf b. Rashid al-ʿAjami, whose *nisba* indicates Shirazi identity, sued Bint Hussun or Hissun for her share of inheritance from the latter's mother. The *kadhi* confirmed Fatima's claim and allowed Bint Hussun to pay her debt in instalments. Without further hints of the litigants' relationship and relying on genealogy as evidence of social status, it can only be an early recorded

[75] See Caplan, *Choice and Constraint*, 44.
[76] J. N. D. Anderson, *Islamic Law*, 64.
[77] On the differences between Shafiʿi and Ibāḍī *wakf*, see further ibid., 77–78.
[78] See Tucker, "Ties That Bound," 244.
[79] Suits for shares of inheritance on behalf of children do not seem to have been frequent. For rare examples, see Entry #367, no number, 15 Shawwāl 1318/5 February 1901, HC28/29; HC10/5569, ZNA.
[80] Hemedi, *Nikahi*, 25.
[81] See Schacht, *Introduction to Islamic Law*, 169–74.

case of a mistress suing for the estate of her (freed) slave.[82] As shown in this section, and further through the lens of the ethnicisation of social relations in Chapter 9, the application of this feature of shariʿa rules of inheritance left former slaves and their descendants baffled and enraged. The persistent enforcement of these rules created considerable tension in a climate of increasing social unrest.

Zanzibari society associated illegitimate descent with slaves, which was a powerful tool to inhibit their socioeconomic participation. In the struggle for social recognition, descent was a particularly sensitive issue that could drive slave descendants further towards exclusion rather than bring them closer to the inclusion to which they aspired. An inheritance case heard on appeal in 1924 left Aisha bt. Baraka devastated as it raised the illegitimacy of her late husband, a former slave. Referring to the Qurʾanic verse stipulating the punishment for wrong accusation of adultery, her *wakīl* argued that witnesses had defamed the mother of her late husband in order to deprive Aisha of her share in her husband's estate. While Sh. Ṭāhir made no indication of depriving the widow of her fixed share, he held that the Qurʾanic verse exclusively referred to the accusation of adultery and could not be understood to nullify testimonies of witnesses in other cases. He ruled that the issue of adultery could not be pursued further, as the accused was dead. Yet the question of illegitimacy, derived from slavery, affected his judgement. As he regarded the deceased as an illegitimate son, he established the absence of agnatic heirs and thus granted the plaintiff, a maternal cousin of the deceased, a share in the estate.[83]

Members of Arab and higher status families were generally aware of Islamic rules of inheritance, suing immediate relatives and agnates, whereas representatives of lower social strata tended to seize opportunities to inherit from aunts, uncles, and cousins of second and third degrees. Although the number of estate cases I have considered only allows me to draw tentative conclusions, there may be indications that women and men of mainland origin as well as from rural areas claimed shares of inheritance from cognates when the likelihood of receiving a share was very small.[84] These claims may hint at either the plaintiff's

[82] Entry #162, no. 94, 2 Rabīʿ II 1318/29 July 1900, HC28/29, ZNA.
[83] HC5/312, ZNA, original in English.
[84] HC5/547; HC10/1335; HC10/2840; HC10/2906, ZNA.

predominant identification through matrilineal rather than patrilineal descent or his or her identification through both lines of descent, which anthropologists consider to be the practice of lower status Swahili but not Arabs.

Customary duties served as a pretext for claiming inheritance and to support such claims. The person who paid for the burial or nursed the deceased during his or her illness usually expected to be included among the heirs.[85] Such customary notions influenced how litigants and *wakīl*s, though not *kadhi*s, perceived the relation of litigants to the deceased. *Kadhi*s only considered if plaintiffs were entitled to inherit according to shariʿa rules of inheritance,[86] while litigants referred to customary norms and their understanding of shariʿa to strengthen their claims.

In 1944, Mwana Mgeni bt. Pandu, a Shirazi without occupation, sued for a share of the estate of her maternal uncle Muhammad b. Saʿid, a Comorian. She claimed to be the daughter of the sister of the deceased. Muhammad had taught the children of Mwana Mgeni, who paid Shs. 70 for his burial, believing she was the heir and claiming the return of this amount if she were not entitled to inherit. As *kadhi* Sh. ʿUmar demanded proof of this expense, she brought two witnesses, her son, whom Sh. ʿUmar therefore disqualified as witness, and someone who refused to take the oath before giving testimony. Failing to comply with procedural rules, the *kadhi* dismissed her claim for the expense. As for the share in the estate, he ruled that among maternal relatives, "the heir is the one who preceded the heir." The defendant, who was the son of the paternal uncle of the deceased's mother, was closer related to the deceased than Mwana Mgeni, the daughter of the daughter of the paternal uncle of the deceased.[87]

Narratives of ancestry, in which stories of immigration unfolded during bargaining processes for social and economic participation in court, were contested in claims of inheritance.[88] If, as in the case below

85 HC5/575; HC10/55; HC10/1335; HC10/3033, ZNA.

86 For an example in which the burial gave rise to a claim for inheritance, see, for example, HC10/55; for such claims being raised on the basis of sick care, see HC10/741; HC10/3033, ZNA.

87 HC10/1335, ZNA.

88 See, for example, HC10/1370, ZNA, which tells the story of the arrival of Comorians in Zanzibar.

heard on appeal in 1939, witnesses referred to stories they heard outside Zanzibar, their testimonies were weak for the *kadhi*, for whom they amounted to hearsay and local knowledge was preeminent. Decisive in this case also was the fact that relations and affinity among slaves were usually hidden from masters,[89] whose beliefs of kinlessness and illegitimacy served to exclude slaves from social participation. Members of kin might have enabled slaves to mobilise networks other than those of patrons, whereas illegitimacy further stigmatised slaves. Hence, slaves' claims to have siblings were treated suspiciously in court.

Mlange bt. Ngoro and her maternal aunt, Yasmin bt. Kahunga, filed a suit for inheritance from their late full brother and maternal nephew, respectively, in 1938. *Kadhi* Sh. Saʿīd b. Nāṣir al-Ghaythī removed Yasmin from the case, since there was a relative entitled to a fixed share, a sister. He was further unconvinced as to the plaintiff's name. Mlange produced a document in the name of Bint Gowe but refused to provide receipts for rent to confirm her name as Bint Ngoro. The defendant's *wakīl* accused her of having made her name agree to the name of the deceased's father. To understand the actors' concerns, it is worth quoting from Sh. Saʿīd's judgement at length:

> We say that it has been established herein by evidence and by the aforesaid document that the deceased in question herein originally came to Zanzibar in Sheikh Hamed bin Mohamed el Marjebi's [alias Tippu Tip, a well-known slave and ivory trader] company and lived under his care and that he was looking after and bringing up his son Juma bin Hamed bin Mohamed. If we consider Rashid bin Hamed's and Masud bin Hamed's evidence in this case we shall see that if we reject their evidence on the grounds that they are biassed [sic] against the plaintiff [Mlange] because they had demanded Shs. 120/- from her so that they might help her in this case and that when she refused to pay them they became her enemies and made her lose her dues to the Probate Department and lose hope of her right, we say this idea is rejected inasmuch as their brother Juma bin Hamed was brought up and cared by [sic] the deceased and that Juma bin Hamed left children. Incidentally, the two witnesses [Rashid bin Hamed bin Mohamed and Masud bin Hamed bin Mohamed el Marjebi] stated that the deceased himself used to say that he would be succeeded by his grandchildren, the said Juma's children. If these witnesses were to favour any one [sic] in respect of the deceased's estate they were sure to fabricate and

[89] Interview with Bi Mwanaidi Makame Ameir, 3 April 2004.

give some evidence in favour of their brother Juma's children in respect of the deceased's estate so that Juma's children might get some thing [sic] therefrom because the two witnesses are related to them and perhaps their property may revert to them by inheritance. This consideration weighs heavily in favour of the view that Rashid and Masud are telling the truth in their evidence which is preponderant in this case. I am satisfied with [sic] and accept it and I hold it to be the truth. God be praised.[90]

Sh. Saʿīd's wordy elaboration reveals the divisions that characterised Zanzibari society by 1938. His euphemistic description of a former slave as beloved member of the family certainly clashed with Mlange's perception of her status as slave. In their memorandum of appeal, Mlange and Yasmin accused the *kadhi* of failing to consider evidence provided by the head of the Wamanyema Community and two other witnesses, who all knew the late Rehani b. Ngoro from Manyema country, a region now divided between the eastern Democratic Republic of Congo and western Tanzania. Rather, the *kadhi* relied on witnesses who had only known the deceased since his arrival in Zanzibar.[91] Mlange's allegation suggests more than merely a desperate attempt to access property. By the late 1930s, the communities of various ethnic groups were firmly established and Zanzibaris' social and ethnic consciousness became highly sensitised. These sensitivities arose from the paradox of being legally free yet being a slave in the eyes of society – *kadhi*s and judges in the context of inheritance. Attempts to access property tended to fail because of *kadhi*s' allocation of inheritance shares to former slave owners and litigants' ignorance of Islamic inheritance laws or lack of satisfactory evidence.

Throughout the colonial period, *kadhi*s continued to uphold masters' rights to inherit from their slaves, thereby contributing to the entrenchment of fundamental differences in patrons' and clients' understanding of their mutual rights and duties. As access to property was a contested field, slave descendants filed claims for shares of inheritance, contending with patrons for property and credit. In 1953, Mwatumu bt. Thabit sued for the entire estate of her paternal

[90] Judgement of Saʿid b. Nasir, HC5/547, ZNA, original in English. This translation authentically conveys the longwinded phrasing and elaborate arguments of *kadhi*s in Arabic.

[91] HC5/547, ZNA. A case that invoked similar issues, heard in 1945, is explored in Chapter 9.

great-grandmother Mema bt. Ibrahim, who was, in fact, a freed slave of her grandfather. She emphasised her entitlement to inherit by referring to the fact that she had nursed Mema during her lengthy illness and covered the funeral costs as well as other expenses. *Kadhi* Sh. ʿUmar added Mwatuma's brother and sister as plaintiffs; the sister, however, asked to be removed from the suit as she did not consider Mema as her grandmother. The brother did not appear in court and it remains elusive whether he also asked to be removed from the plaint. The defendant Khamis b. Ahmed claimed that Mema was the full sister of his mother. Although Sh. ʿUmar accepted the degree of kinship between Khamis and the deceased, he entitled Mwatumu to the entire estate, as she was an agnatic heir with a fixed share of inheritance. Applying the Shafiʿi rules of inheritance, Sh. ʿUmar gave precedence to the descendants of the manumitter over kin a decade before Zanzibar obtained its independence.[92]

Conclusion

This chapter challenges the common understanding of patriarchal order as an impediment to women's economic agency. Clearly, economic agency in colonial Zanzibar Town was more complex than the blanket argument of patriarchy suggests. In the eyes of *kadhi*s and Zanzibari society, men and women were equally apt property managers, although access to property and its nature were partly gendered. Zanzibari women from all socioeconomic backgrounds invested in diverse assets, such as real estate, whose management is often seen as incompatible with purdah. Both movable property and real estate could be seized, the first usually more easily. Women's ownership of highly prized real estate thus indicates their ability to climb the property ladder and their awareness of immovable property being a more reliable asset than movable property.

The most disadvantageous development to property ownership and management were colonial decrees that were partly gendered and racialised. Both genders could face challenges in their economic

[92] HC10/3033, ZNA, original in Arabic and English. Frederick Cooper and Margaret Strobel also refer to cases in which masters claimed the inheritance from their former slaves according to shariʿa (Frederick Cooper, *Plantation Slavery*, 236; Strobel, *Muslim Women*, 51).

capacities due to illiteracy, unfamiliarity with colonial laws, geographical mobility, and, in the case of women, purdah. At the same time, it was the scale of movements of men and women among all social strata that enabled economic transactions in the northwestern Indian Ocean. Although purdah and illiteracy entailed a degree of dependency on male agents, some women deliberately relied on agents and constructed purdah to enhance their respectability. While individual ownership of property under Islamic law enabled male and female economic agency in response to socioeconomic changes, the fact that men and women found ways to circumvent Islamic laws of inheritance, allocating women only half the share of men, proves that these legal doctrines were not immutable and that Zanzibaris shaped the law as they saw fit.

Social status was a distinguishing marker in economic networks. Even though the actors' relations and objectives tend to remain obscure, the outlined patterns of buying and selling clearly show economic interactions between men and women across ethnic identities and socioeconomic strata. The preference of creating economic networks between spouses and among kin to avoid Indian moneylenders seems to have manifested itself more among women, who sometimes preferred to invest in social capital – ties with male kin particularly, and higher social strata.

These intricate economic networks were woven into the commercialisation of social relations. Due to the wider range of actors in the struggle for accumulating assets in the post-abolition era, patrons sought additional ways of exclusion and of regaining access to resources. Patron–client relations could become unsettled when *kadhi*s ruled in favour of patrons in estate cases decades after abolition, applying Islamic rather than colonial law and confirming the exclusion of former slaves and their descendants as well as their inferior status. With ethnicisation heavily influencing both *kadhi*s' and litigants' agency, while gender constituted a relatively uncontested field in property relations, the *kadhi*'s courts both mediated and generated discourses of exclusion and inclusion.

8

Bargaining for Divorce

To historicise Zanzibari divorce means to write against Western, Christian-influenced perceptions and to avoid projecting present understandings onto historical actors. Unlike Christian ideals, Islamic precepts embrace the option of divorce, although, according to a hadith, divorce is the most reprehensible of all permissible things. In characteristically pragmatic fashion, Islamic law suggests the termination of marital relations if a spouse, or both spouses, no longer wishes to remain married.[1] In addition to this key juridical principle, the Qur'an not only acknowledges the possible necessity to end a marriage for good but also offers the following remedy to husbands: "If you wish to replace one wife with another, do not take any of her bride-gift [that is, dower] back, even if you have given her a great amount of gold."[2] This provision for remarriage indicates the non-stigmatisation of serial marriage and discourages the husband from demanding material compensation for divorcing his wife. Zanzibari husbands, however, rarely heeded the advice to divorce their wives for free.

As contemporaries and scholars observed, the Swahili coast had a high divorce rate.[3] In colonial Zanzibar Town, the pragmatic attitude endorsed by the Qur'an and Islamic jurisprudence, coupled with

[1] See Tucker, *Women, Family, and Gender*, 84.

[2] Qur'an 4:20.

[3] Landberg, "Kinship and Community," 167–68; Françoise Le Guennec-Coppens, "L'instabilité conjugale et ses conséquences dans la société Swahili de Lamu (Kenya)," in *Transformations of African Marriage*, ed. David Parkin and David Nyamwaya

the practice of arranged marriages, made divorce a means of social mobility and individual agency. *Kadhi*s supported the dissolution of marriages that had irreconcilably broken down. They helped husbands to retrieve the dower in order to remarry by holding wives, whom they found unwilling to reconcile, accountable in material terms. Men clung to their wives not only in an affectionate but also in a materialist way, since they perceived marriage as an investment. In the first half of the twentieth century, marriage was characterised by monetarisation, with women and men experiencing its impact differently upon divorce.

Women's ability to obtain a divorce, for which this chapter accounts, is not unique to colonial Zanzibar Town. Divorce patterns from the Middle East have shown that Muslim women have actively and successfully – if obtaining a divorce may be termed "success" – negotiated their divorce in court.[4] Their success has been explained by the interplay between female agency, social practice, and the flexibility of Islamic law rather than by wives' perseverance, which most scholars have portrayed as Swahili women's main contribution to achieving a divorce.[5] As for colonial courts in sub-Saharan Africa, Martin Chanock's seminal study on the creation of customary law argues that the collaboration between colonial officers and elders marginalised women and the poor from the legal systems in Malawi and Zambia.[6] His approach has henceforth been applied in other colonial African settings and has also become more nuanced.[7] An account of creative

(Manchester: Manchester University Press, 1987), 238; Gabrielle O'Malley, "Marriage and Morality: Negotiating Gender and Respect in Zanzibar Town" (PhD diss., University of Washington, 2000), 79.

4 See, for example, Amina El Azhary Sonbol, introduction to *Women, the Family, and Divorce Laws in Islamic History*, ed. Amina El Azhary Sonbol (Syracuse: Syracuse University Press, 1996), 1–20; Abdal-Rehim Abdal-Rahman Abdal-Rehim, "The Family and Gender Laws in Egypt during the Ottoman Period," in *Women, the Family, and Divorce Laws in Islamic History*, ed. Amina El Azhary Sonbol (Syracuse: Syracuse University Press, 1996), 96–111; Meriwether, *The Kin Who Count*; Rapoport, *Marriage, Money and Divorce*; Tucker, *Women in Nineteenth-Century Egypt*; idem, *Women, Family, and Gender*.

5 Fair, *Pastimes and Politics*; Hirsch, *Pronouncing and Persevering*; Sarah Mirza and Margaret Strobel, eds., *Three Swahili Women: Life Histories from Mombasa, Kenya*, trans. S. Mirza and M. Strobel (Bloomington: Indiana University Press, 1989).

6 Chanock, *Law, Custom and Social Order*; idem, "Making Customary Law."

7 See, for example, Jean Allman and Victoria Tashjian, *"I Will Not Eat Stone": A Women's History of Colonial Asante* (Portsmouth, NH: Heinemann, 2000); Barbara Cooper, *Marriage in Maradi: Gender and Culture in a Hausa Society in Niger,*

female agency in negotiating divorce in court ties in with Brett Shadle's recent sociohistorical study on Gusiiland, Kenya, in which he provides evidence how fluid interpretations of customary law enabled women and young men to advance their interests against predominant views.[8]

The first two sections of this chapter introduce the legal options of divorce and their practice in Zanzibar Town in the first half of the twentieth century, highlighting the interplay of custom and legal doctrines. The final section looks more closely into the actors' negotiations of divorce, the strategies of wives and husbands, and *kadhi*s' roles in dissolving marriages. Given the restricted grounds on which a wife can file for the dissolution of her marriage under Shafiʿi and Ibāḍī laws, claims for dower and maintenance debts were apt female strategies to end a marriage for good.

Dissolving a Muslim Marriage: Legal Options and Constraints

One of the frequently invoked characteristics of Islamic legal doctrines is the husband's right to unilaterally repudiate the wife, without giving any cause and turning to court. This is known as *ṭalāq* in Arabic or *talaka* in Swahili. Discourses by non-jurists on *ṭalāq* may be oblivious to the fact that this is only one of three preponderant types of divorce under Islamic law.[9] Another common type of divorce is *khulʿ*, in which the wife offers her husband compensation if he is unwilling to repudiate her. Further to that, the wife may petition for a divorce based on at least one of the legal grounds of her school of law. This third type of divorce, *faskh* or judicial dissolution, can be achieved only by a *kadhi* in court. A technical *faskh*, however, may imply that the wife does not receive debts from her husband, such as maintenance and the deferred dower.

According to al-Shāfiʿī, the unilateral repudiation, *ṭalāq*, is valid if a sane adult husband explicitly pronounces it even though he does not intend it. If he phrases the repudiation in implicit terms, he has to intend

1900–1989 (Portsmouth, NH: Heinemann, 1997); Dorothy L. Hodgson and Sheryl McCurdy, *"Wicked" Women and the Reconfiguration of Gender in Africa* (Portsmouth, NH: Heinemann, 2001).

8 Shadle, "'Changing Traditions'." For a useful overview of literature on this topic, see idem, "Bridewealth and Female Consent," 242–44.

9 Five other much less commonly applied types of divorce are introduced below.

the divorce for it to be valid. Any doubt about the occurrence of the *ṭalāq* must be interpreted as confirming the marriage. The husband can pronounce up to three *ṭalāq*s either separately or one immediately after the other. After the third *ṭalāq*, the divorce becomes irrevocable and he can only take his wife back after the occurrence of an intervening marriage of the wife with another man and with a new contract.[10] The issue of intervening marriage is complex and if scrutinised in court, it attests to the couple's legal knowledge as well as the *kadhi*'s values of shariʿa. In 1902, Shafiʿi *kadhi* Sh. Aḥmad b. Sumayṭ ruled for the invalidity of an intervening marriage to which the wife had not given her consent (her consent was necessary as she was not a virgin) and in which case the guardian was not lawful.[11] When Abdalhafith b. ʿUthman admitted in 1902 that he had repudiated his wife ten times, a *kadhi* registered that she would not be permissible for him without an intervening marriage.[12] The *kadhi* thereby reminded Abdalhafith that his tenfold repudiation resulted in an irrevocable divorce.

For a *ṭalāq al-sunna*, or repudiation in compliance with tradition, the husband has to divorce the wife during her ritual purity.[13] After its pronouncement, the wife enters into *ʿidda*. *ʿIdda* is a legal obligation and serves to establish whether the wife is pregnant. It lasts for three menstrual cycles for free women, two for slaves, or until delivery. The husband is obliged to maintain the wife during her *ʿidda*.[14] During the *ʿidda* of the first and second divorce, the husband has the right to revoke the divorce. According to al-Shāfiʿī, it is not necessary that two witnesses attest to the retraction of the divorce, which the husband has to perform verbally, but it is desirable in case a dispute arises over the occurrence of the retraction.[15] When ʿAbdallah b. Sheilab, a Shirazi and scholar, sued for the return of his wife, Khadija bt. Suleiman, a Manyema and housewife, to the marital home in 1952, she countered that he had divorced her. As two witnesses confirmed that ʿAbdallah

[10] Berg, *Minhādj*, vol. II, 343–44, 425, 446.
[11] No entry #, no. 588, 24 Rabīʿ II [1320]/30 July 1902, HC28/29, ZNA.
[12] Entry #771, no. 236, 26 Shawwāl 1319/5 February 1902, HC28/29, ZNA.
[13] Ritual purity is required for Muslims to fulfill religious duties, such as praying. Sexual activity, urination, defecation, sleep, menstruation, and childbirth lead to ritual impurity and require ablution.
[14] Hemedi, *Nikahi*, 26–31.
[15] Berg, *Minhādj*, vol. II, 471; Hemedi, *Nikahi*, 21.

had retracted the divorce, *kadhi* Sh. ʿUmar ruled for Khadija's return to her husband.[16] If the divorce is not revoked, the marriage ends when the wife has completed her *ʿidda*.

As no codification has tackled the husband's discretionary powers of divorce in Zanzibar, a triple divorce in a single session counted, and still counts, as irrevocable.[17] Uttering a repudiation more than three times, as in the case of Abdalhafith above, counted as triple and irrevocable. Women had room for manoeuvring, since Ibāḍīs consider a triple divorce in succession as single and revocable, seen by legal reformers as a successful method to curtail the husband's right to repudiation.[18] This reform is based on the underlying assumption that the wife wishes to remain married, which was not universally applicable. Salma bt. ʿAlawi Bunumay had been married to sayyid Salih b. ʿAlawi b. Shihab for about five years when he went to the Benadir coast in April 1951. He left Salma at her father's house in Malindi in town. Shortly after his arrival, he sent a letter to Zanzibar saying he had given her a triple divorce but later retracted the divorce as three witnesses confirmed. When the Ibāḍī *kadhi* confirmed Salma's marriage, she was outraged, as she would have been divorced under her own, the Shafiʿi, school. Determined to get a divorce, she appealed to the high court and in further instance to the court of appeal for Eastern Africa in Nairobi, which confirmed her divorce.[19] Divorce by letter, such as between Salma and Salih, occurred when husband and wife stayed in separate towns and villages, often due to labour migration.[20]

Literacy and scriptualism, the epitome of *ustaarabu* in the later nineteenth century, may also have been expressed in divorce papers

[16] HC10/2833, ZNA. See also HC5/536, ZNA.

[17] Hemedi, *Nikahi*, 14–21.

[18] Cf. J. N. D. Anderson, "Reforms in the Law of Divorce in the Muslim World," *Studia Islamica* 31 (1970): 47–48. For an analysis of the options created by divorce reforms in early twentieth century Egypt, see Ron Shaham, "Judicial Divorce at the Wife's Initiative: The Shariʿa Courts of Egypt, 1920–1955," *Islamic Law and Society* 1, no. 2 (1994): 217–57.

[19] HC10/2843, ZNA. Cf. Chapters 3 and 7.

[20] See Hamed bin Saleh El-Busaidy, *Ndoa na talaka* (1958; repr., Nairobi: East African Literature Bureau, 1962), 30; cf. Aharon Layish, *Divorce in the Libyan Family: A Study Based on the* sijills *of the* sharīʿa *Courts of Ajdābiyya and Kufra* (New York: New York University Press, 1991), 41–42.

through which men stressed their belonging to Islam, generosity, and social superiority.[21] The high status of written documents, which John Middleton describes, has to be situated in the social struggle between those embodying Arabness and those striving towards it. To provide one's wife with proof of divorce appears to have been an act of respect and was essential if women wanted to remarry. Despite the fact that under Shafiʿi law the mere pronouncement of divorce renders the divorce valid, the issuing of divorce papers was established in Zanzibar at the turn of the twentieth century. In 1906, Sifiru bt. Hussayn produced a letter which stated that ʿUmar b. ʿUthman had divorced her once, that she had received her entire dower, and might take all her furniture from his house whenever she wanted.[22] In 1909, Jawhar b. Almas al-Habashi responded to his wife's request for a divorce by saying they would have to go to court. He handed a divorce paper to his wife two days after the divorce.[23] Another divorce paper, dated 14 Rajab 1335/6 May 1917, said in Swahili, "To Munshaykh b. Ahmad and Sudi b. Mwinyi Kombo: Mwana Ngaza bt. Mwinyi Kombo has got a child that I do not know at all and I gave her a single divorce. Muhammad b. ʿAli."[24] Although these examples do not allow deducing how widespread this practice was, they attest to the consciousness of some husbands of providing the wife with evidence. Today it is the norm that husbands issue divorce papers.[25]

In addition to the possibility of husbands providing wives with a divorce paper, the official divorce certificate became an important piece of evidence for women to establish their status as divorcees and to ascertain the validity of a new marriage. In the *kadhi*'s courts, the Marriage (Solemnisation and Registration) Decree of 1915, providing for any marriage concluded under this decree to be terminated by judicial decree, and the succeeding decree of 1922 enabled women to sue for their divorce certificate. Furthermore, the Marriage and Divorce (Mahommedan) Registration Decree of 1935 provided for the

[21] Cf. Middleton, *The World of the Swahili*, 27, 191. On the practice of issuing divorce papers, see also Niese, *Personen- und Familienrecht*, 25.

[22] HC9/125, ZNA.

[23] HC9/97, ZNA. Jawhar's name suggests slave origin.

[24] HC10/48, ZNA. Papers, either for *ṭalāq* or *khul*ʿ, were also issued by husbands prior to 1922 in HC9/66; HC9/112; HC9/134; HC10/1010, ZNA.

[25] Stiles, "'There Is No Stranger to Marriage Here!,'" 584.

registration of the retraction of a registered revocable divorce.[26] Aware of the importance to have proof of being divorcees, both Mayasa bt. Musa and Rufume bt. Khamis sued in 1959 and 1960, respectively, for an official divorce certificate as the husband had only provided an unofficial paper.[27]

Although Muslim women are disadvantaged towards men in seeking a divorce, their legal capacity is entrenched in the other two most common ways of ending a marriage, *khul*ʿ and judicial dissolution, *faskh*. Only the wife herself, not her guardian, has the right to seek the annulment of her marriage. Wives may petition the court for a *faskh* on the grounds of defects of the husband (such as impotence or incurable or infectious diseases) and his wilful non-provision of maintenance, according to the Shafiʿi school, as well as cruelty, according to Ibāḍī rules.[28] Cases of cruelty are an important indication of the *kadhi*'s support of women's claims.[29]

According to both Shafiʿis and Ibāḍīs, the wife is entitled to *faskh* if the husband has failed to provide maintenance for three consecutive days. The wife receives support by the law, as she is believed on oath if she claims not to have been maintained and the husband cannot prove the opposite.[30] If a judgement stated that the husband was obliged to provide maintenance, the wife secured a divorce if she could prove that he had not complied with this order. The *kadhi* would then dissolve the marriage.[31] After marrying a second wife, Saʿad Msellem drove Zayana bt. Saʿid b. Suleiman out of his house and stopped supporting her. Ibāḍī *kadhi* Sh. Saʿīd b. Rashīd al-Ghaythī entitled Zayana to all conjugal rights and provided for a *faskh* if the husband failed to comply with the judgement. When Sh. Saʿīd inspected the house that

26 Legal report by Acting Attorney General J. H. Vaughan, 16 December 1935, CO 618/65/7, NAK.

27 HC10/3695 and HC10/5531, ZNA.

28 Hemedi, *Nikahi*, 5; Berg, *Minhādj*, vol. II, 361–62; J. N. D. Anderson, *Islamic Law*, 73.

29 Cf. Christelow, *Muslim Law Courts*, 90; see Stockreiter, "Child Marriage and Domestic Violence," 141–44.

30 Hemedi, *Nikahi*, 35–37.

31 On the grounds of lack of maintenance, Shafiʿi and Ibāḍī *kadhi*s ordered a *faskh* in HC9/72; HC9/84; HC10/15; HC10/42; HC10/1276; HC10/2792; HC10/2881; HC10/3001; HC10/5570, ZNA. The option of *faskh* was provided for in HC10/10; HC10/31; HC10/2850, ZNA, however, it has not been recorded whether the wife petitioned for its execution.

Saʿad was ordered to provide, he deemed it unsuitable to house two wives and ruled for Zayana to stay in her own house as previously. In a second visit to a new house, the court found the house satisfactory but household items were far below standard. There was no mattress on the bed, although Sh. Saʿīd considered the set of cooking utensils complete. Given these deficiencies and Saʿad's failure to provide maintenance, Sh. Saʿīd pronounced a *faskh* six months after the case was opened in May 1952.[32] If, however, a suitable dwelling was provided, the *kadhi* expected the wife to return to the husband. Contingent on her return, *kadhi* Sh. ʿUmar entitled a wife to a poor man's maintenance, clothes, and accommodation or to a *faskh* if the husband failed to provide any of these rights in 1955. Possibly immediately after Sh. ʿUmar read the judgement to the litigants, the wife must have refused to return to the husband. After signing the judgement and without giving a different date, the *kadhi* added that because of her refusal, she was not entitled to any of these rights or a *faskh*.[33]

Although *kadhi*s acted on the husband's proven failure to provide maintenance, they did not necessarily entitle wives to a dissolution after three days as provided under Shafiʿi law. This indicates that they challenged what they perceived as women's precipitate attempts to dissolve their marriages.[34] *Kadhi*s' reluctance to order a *faskh* after three days and demand of wives' insistence on divorce attests to their belief in marriage as a key social institution, which should not be dissolved arbitrarily. Shafiʿi *kadhi* Sh. Ṭāhir explained to a wife, whose husband was impoverished and hiding, that she would not get a *faskh* if the husband were only in arrears with maintenance for three days. But as he was in arrears for months, he ordered a *faskh*.[35] *Kadhi*s either dissolved the marriage in the judgement or entitled the wife to apply for dissolution if the husband failed to comply with the judgement within a specified period. Wives seem to have applied for and/or obtained the execution of *faskh* within months following the judgement. The *kadhi* would not grant a *faskh* in the case of physical desertion if the wife had been left with adequate maintenance. If the wife's obedience

[32] HC10/2881, ZNA. Cf. Chapters 5 and 9.

[33] HC10/3202, ZNA.

[34] Cf. Stiles, "'There Is No Stranger to Marriage Here!'," where she argues that *kadhi*s seek to sustain marriages.

[35] HC10/15, ZNA.

was confirmed, the *kadhi* would order the seizure of any movable and immovable property of the husband to pay off his maintenance debts. In the *kadhi*'s courts, the husband's role as a provider was enforced with no exceptions if the wife could prove her obedience.[36] Jurists' ideals of the dependent obedient wife and her unfettered right to maintenance were enforced and socioeconomic realities, in which the wife contributed to the household income, were consistently ignored. Although removed from reality, this legal precept offered women a way to negotiate divorce.

Understanding the Preponderance of *khul*ʿ

While previous studies addressing divorce in Swahili societies have suggested a high divorce rate, actual divorce figures are mostly obscure.[37] Margaret Strobel gives the figure of "one divorce for every two marriages." Janet Bujra, doing research in a village on an island off the northern Kenyan coast in the 1960s, indicates that 59.7 percent of marriages contracted and registered between 1951 and 1957 ended in divorce by 1965. In 1950, the Shafiʿi *kadhi* in Zanzibar Town, Sh. ʿUmar, estimated that 80 percent of Zanzibari marriages ended in divorce, while John Middleton noted that the divorce rate among the Hadimu was above 70 percent in 1958.[38] Given the high divorce rate along the Swahili coast, it is instructive to question which type of divorce predominated. Touring East Africa in 1961, J. S. Trimingham portrayed *kadhi*s as rigid interpreters of women's grounds for divorce and suggested women's difficulties in getting a divorce in court, pointing to female counterstrategies, such as deserting husbands, and the frequency of divorce for a consideration.[39] Similarly, scholar

[36] J. N. D. Anderson, *Islamic Law*, 74; cf. Tucker, *In the House of the Law*, 75, where she asserts that she found no record of the court's refusal to confirm women's rights to maintenance.

[37] Ingrams, *Zanzibar*, 220, 492; Landberg, "Kinship and Community," 148, 167–68; Romero, *Lamu*, 139; J. N. D. Anderson, *Islamic Law*, 74; Hirsch, *Pronouncing and Persevering*, 59; Middleton, *The World of the Swahili*, 124–25; Mirza and Strobel, *Three Swahili Women*, 10.

[38] Strobel, *Muslim Women*, 88; Bujra, "Production, Property, Prostitution," 28n30; J. N. D. Anderson, *Islamic Law*, 74n5; Middleton, *The World of the Swahili*, 217n11.

[39] Trimingham, *Islam in East Africa*, 139. He must refer to *khul*ʿ when he explains that if the husband files for *faskh*, the payments are on the wife's family.

of Islamic law J. N. D. Anderson noted in 1950 that "divorce for a consideration is exceedingly common."[40]

While these reports by contemporaries suggest the preponderance of *khul*ʿ, scholars have subsequently paid little attention to these hints and corroborated an understanding of women's exposure to arbitrary repudiation and difficulties of obtaining a divorce. Patricia Romero hints at men's excessive use of their right to repudiation in Lamu, suggesting that their lack of treating marriage seriously was reflected in divorce statistics.[41] Laura Fair reasons that from the 1910s to the 1930s Zanzibari women were "systematically undermined" when suing for divorce, as even in cases in which a legal grounds for divorce existed, they were ordered to return to their husband.[42] In the case to which she refers, *kadhi* Sh. Ṭāhir (initially) ordered the wife, Mgeni, to return to her husband. Being a Shafiʿi *kadhi*, he could not, as Fair reasons, dissolve the marriage on the grounds of cruelty. The initiative of Mgeni's *wakīl* to sue for maintenance rather than divorce, interpreted by both Mgeni and Fair as undermining Mgeni's claim, was actually a common strategy to obtain a divorce.[43] The case sample I have drawn on, supported by divorce certificates, does not suggest that *kadhi*s were unwilling to grant women a divorce but indicates that they mostly offered women the opportunity to buy their divorce.

The results of many *khul*ʿ negotiations out-of-court are recorded in the divorce registers and belie the common understanding that *khul*ʿ is initiated by the wife and merely accepted by the husband. These records further strongly question the preponderance of *ṭalāq* (see Table 8.1).[44] Even if we bear in mind that *ṭalāq* was rarely decided in court, the fact that divorce by *khul*ʿ comprises 67 percent of the sample of divorce

[40] J. N. D. Anderson, *Islamic Law*, 74.

[41] Romero, *Lamu*, 173. In Lamu, 95 percent of the divorce cases from the 1970s (?), which Le Guennec-Coppens analysed, actually were repudiations (idem, "L'instabilité conjugale," 236).

[42] Fair, *Pastimes and Politics*, 202.

[43] HC8/86, ZNA, original in Arabic and English.

[44] This corroborates findings from other parts and time periods of the Muslim world. See, for example, Tucker, *Women in Nineteenth Century-Egypt*; idem, "Ties That Bound"; Peirce, *Morality Tales*; idem, "'She Is Trouble'"; Rapoport, *Marriage, Money and Divorce*; Welchman, *Beyond the Code*, 249; Appendix VII, 385. Tucker thus describes *khul*ʿ as a "very ordinary occurrence" (idem, *Women, Family, and Gender*, 109).

TABLE 8.1. *Types of Divorce in Zanzibar Town*

Year	*Ṭalāq*	*Khulʿ/Mubāraʾa*	*Faskh*	Number of Sample
1925	30	70	0	344
1930	25	75	0	100
1935	24	75	1	100
1940	20	80	0	100
1945	18	81	1	100
1950	43	57	0	99
1955	47	52	0	99
1960	59	41	0	100
Total	32	67	0	1,042

Source: Sample of divorce certificates from *Mambo Msiige*. Numbers are given in percentages; due to rounding, totals may not equal 100 percent. The data for 1925 comprise all divorces registered in Zanzibar Town. The random samples for the remaining years cover the months of January until December, save for 1930, which lacks the register for February.

registers indicates the predominance of *khulʿ* in town.[45] The almost complete absence of *faskh* is unusual and suggests that *kadhi*s may not have recorded them in the divorce registers but only in the court records.

The most complex form of dissolving a marriage, *khulʿ*, in which the wife has to compensate the husband refusing to release her for free, reveals best the material implications of divorce. The translation of *khulʿ* as "divorce at the instigation of the wife" or "by mutual consent" may be misleading. *Khulʿ* was not necessarily initiated by the wife and was at times ordered by *kadhi*s, known as "judicial *khulʿ*".[46] Unlike judicial dissolution in court, or *faskh*, the husband must consent to *khulʿ*, which, under Shafiʿi and Ibāḍī laws, is irrevocable, unless the

[45] Although Sh. ʿUmar held that the vast majority of marriages ended in *khulʿ* in 1950, Table 8.1 indicates a noticeable decline in *khulʿ* by 1950 continuing to 1960. The reasons for this decline remain to be explored.

[46] See Lucy Carroll, "Qurʾan 2:229 'A Charter Granted to the Wife'? Judicial *Khulʿ* in Pakistan," *Islamic Law and Society* 3, no. 1 (1996): 91–126; Oussama Arabi, "The Dawning of the Third Millennium on Shariʿa: Egypt's Law no.1 of 2000, or Women May Divorce at Will," *Arab Law Quarterly* 16, no. 1 (2001): 2–21; Lynn Welchman, "Family, Gender, and Law in Jordan and Palestine," in *Family, Gender, and Law in a Globalizing Middle East and South Asia*, ed. Kenneth M. Cuno and Manisha Desai (Syracuse: Syracuse University Press, 2009), 138–43.

spouses stipulate otherwise.[47] The consequences of *khulʿ* are rendered obvious by Swahili speakers, who refer to it as *kununua talaka*, "to buy a divorce", rather than by the legal term "*khuluu.*" This material aspect becomes even clearer by contrasting *khulʿ* to its counterpart *ṭalāq*, locally known as *kuachwa bure*, "to be released without paying". As the financial loss *khulʿ* entailed was usually considerable, this chapter shows that *ṭalāq*, although it may not have been consensual, was actually the type of divorce that preserved women's financial rights by entitling them to receive any outstanding debts from the husband.[48]

Whereas *ṭalāq* and *faskh* may have entailed material losses on the wife, the forgoing of her financial rights and/or payments to the husband were at the centre of *khulʿ* and *mubāraʾa*. I introduce the term "*mubāraʾa*," as it was explicitly mentioned in the divorce registers of 1945 and 1950. It is a variant of *khulʿ* and may have been used to differ between the nature and amount of compensation. The exact meaning of the two terms varies. *Khulʿ* should imply that the wife returns her prompt dower and waives her right to her deferred dower, whereas *mubāraʾa* refers to husband and wife releasing each other from any remaining obligations.[49] The difference between *khulʿ* and *mubāraʾa* is that the former implies the return of the dower and possibly adding to it, and the latter consists of a mere release of mutual rights and duties.[50]

As divorce registers provided for the type of divorce to be registered, from at least 1945 onwards registrars additionally attempted to distinguish between *khulʿ* and *mubāraʾa*. While registering the exact type of divorce would have enabled women to claim their rights and prevented husbands from exploiting their wives' willingness to divorce, not all registrars mastered these legal subtleties. The terminological intricacies of *khulʿ* and *mubāraʾa* were at the centre of the bargaining for divorce between Musa b. Suleiman and Khadija bt. ʿAli at the district court of

47 Berg, *Minhādj*, vol. II, 416; Aḥmad b. Ḥamad al-Khalīlī, *Fatāwā al-nikāḥ*, 2nd ed. (Muscat, Oman: Ministry of Religious Endowments and Affairs, 2003), 348.

48 See Hallaq, *Shariʿa*, 190.

49 Interview with Sh. Abdalla Suleiman Jumbe, 22 June 2004; HC10/84, ZNA.

50 Schacht, *Introduction to Islamic Law*, 164. The question of initiation and intent is inherent in the differentiation given by Dawoud Sudqi El Alami and Doreen Hinchcliffe, *Islamic Marriage and Divorce Laws of the Arab World* (1996; repr., London: Kluwer Law International, 1998), 27. These technical terms and their precise meanings are usually not part of everyday discourse but of scholarly debates.

Chwaka in 1934. The husband claimed that a *khulʿ* for Rs. 100 had been registered, whereas the wife had agreed to a divorce by forgoing the remainder of her dower, Rs. 50, and one month's maintenance, Rs. 10. *Kadhi* Sh. Ṭāhir explained this discrepancy with the registrar's ignorance of the difference between *khulʿ* and *mubāraʾa*. He confirmed the wife's claim that she forwent her rights, thus a *mubāraʾa*, which the registrar wrongly termed *khulʿ*.[51]

A dispute over the form of *mubāraʾa* further arose in a case of 1936 between Ame b. Rajabu and Aisha bt. Simai. The value of the *mubāraʾa* was not indicated on the divorce certificate, and, referring to *Minhāj al-ṭālibīn* by thirteenth-century Shafiʿi scholar al-Nawawī, *kadhi* Sh. Ṭāhir argued that a *mubāraʾa* of unknown value was void and revocable. He further quoted from *Kitāb fatḥ al-muʿīn*, which says that a *mubāraʾa* is irrevocable and not valid unless both parties regard it as firm. Based on this, Sh. Ṭāhir ruled for the wife's return to the husband, who claimed to have revoked the *mubāraʾa*, which the wife did not deny.[52] Rather than trying to establish the value of the *mubāraʾa*, Sh. Ṭāhir concentrated on referring to variant opinions of the Shafiʿi school and pointed to its undenied retraction.

The idea of compensating the husband for the wife's (arbitrary) wish to end her marriage is intrinsic to Islamic legal doctrines, but men exploited this provision in light of economic difficulties and the cost of marriage. A coercive form of *khulʿ*, in which the husband asked the wife for money without her desiring a separation, known as *kuandikia pesa*, "to write (a divorce) for money", came into use at least from 1900 onwards.[53] It was most likely inspired by mainland customary law, under which the wife had to return her bridewealth to the husband if she wanted to dissolve the marriage.[54] At the time when men blamed

51 HC10/84, ZNA.

52 HC5/536, ZNA, original in Arabic and English.

53 It is thanks to Erin Stiles' contemporary research that I could make out the existence of this type of divorce in the records and thus predate its existence. Pat Caplan also refers to this type of divorce in Mafia Island (idem, "Law and Custom," 206). On forced *khulʿ* in the Ottoman Empire, see Zarinebaf-Shahr, "Women, Law, and Imperial Justice," especially 92–93; for the Mamluk period, see Rapoport, *Marriage, Money and Divorce*, 72–73.

54 See Lovett, "Elders, Migrants and Wives;" Marjorie Mbilinyi, "Women's Resistance in 'Customary' Marriage: Tanzania's Runaway Wives," in *Forced Labour and Migration: Patterns of Movement within Africa*, ed. Abebe Zegeye and Shubi Ishemo (London: Hans Zell, 1989), 211–54.

elders of dower inflation, in 1944, ʿAziza bt. Hamed al-Marjebi alleged that her husband forced her to forgo her dower in writing, even though he had agreed in court to give her "her rights." Based on a piece of paper saying ʿAziza forwent her deferred dower, Shs. 100, and household items, the *mudir* had issued a divorce certificate. As ʿAziza brought witnesses for the duress under which she agreed to this *khul*ʿ, *kadhi* Sh. Saʿīd b. Rashīd al-Ghaythī declared the *khul*ʿ character of the divorce void, and, without explicitly stating so, seems to have confirmed that a revocable *ṭalāq* occurred between the spouses.[55] Thus the husband still had the option of taking ʿAziza back. In another case of 1944, in which the husband only agreed to a reconciliation if his wife signed over her house and provided a power of attorney for her share of inheritance, the same *kadhi* ruled for a *faskh* as the husband admitted his neglect of conjugal duties.[56]

The socioeconomic importance of *khul*ʿ and men's abusive conduct are aptly reflected in Hemedi, who gives us insight into the dialectic between local norms and Islamic law.

> People [that is, husbands] often say to their wives "I will not divorce you unless you return me my property"; or they deliberately treat the wife badly and when she complains they say "I want my property; I want my property" always the same words so that the woman has no peace. This is very wrong and totally forbidden. Others divorce their wives and recall them not out of affection, but because when they gave the divorce they omitted to demand the property. [...] This happens very often in this country [Tanganyika] and it is entirely wrong; it is utterly forbidden by the Law of Islam because the property demanded is that given at the time of the marriage [...] What is allowed by the Sharia is Khului. Khului is for a husband and wife to separate for consideration given by the wife or by another person to the husband, whether that consideration is the same as that given by the husband at the time of the marriage or more or less.[57]

As Hemedi elucidates, the monetarisation of marital relations seems to have been too deeply entrenched in many men for them to consider that it is reprehensible to ask for more than the dower.[58] Among East

[55] HC10/1403, ZNA.
[56] HC10/1276, ZNA. Cf. Peirce, *Morality Tales*, 232.
[57] Hemedi, *Nikahi*, 9–10.
[58] Cf. El Alami and Hinchcliffe, *Islamic Marriage*, 28; Tucker, *Women, Family, and Gender*, 97.

African scholars and in Zanzibari practice, compensation was interpreted in material terms generally rather than as exclusively monetary. Unlike maintenance debts, which *kadhi*s enforced in cash, *khul'* could be achieved by offering any type of property, an object, payment, or a service. In order to be divorced from her husband, Mgeni bt. Ja'far forwent furniture, a trinket, two gold bangles, and four gold foot rings in addition to the deferred dower, Rs. 80.[59] Equally, Hilal b. Sheikhan al-Riyami, a shopkeeper, claimed a considerable list of household items as an alleged part of the *khul'* from his wife in 1953.[60]

While *khul'* was husbands' preferred form of divorce, as "[m]ost husbands were deterred, first and foremost, by the financial costs of divorce [that is, repudiation],"[61] other ways of ending marriage suited husbands less, possibly were less well known, and, correspondingly, were less commonly used. These are delegated divorce, conditional or suspended divorce, *īlā'*, *ẓihār*, and *li'ān*.[62] When J. N. D. Anderson asked the Zanzibari *kadhi*s in the 1950s about these alternative ways of dissolving a marriage, they replied that *īlā'*, *ẓihār*, and *li'ān* were practically unknown and delegated divorce was rare. Yet suspended divorce was common.[63] The condition on which the divorce hinged was usually not stipulated in the marriage contract but arose from a spouse's grievance and could work to the advantage of either spouse.[64] Tellingly, a condition put by husbands was that the wife should forgo her dower. When Siha (?) bt. Muhammad al-Mu'amari

59 HC10/43, ZNA. See El-Busaidy, *Ndoa na talaka*, 33–34; Hemedi, *Nikahi*, 10.

60 HC10/3004, ZNA.

61 Rapoport, *Marriage, Money and Divorce*, 70.

62 El Alami and Hinchcliffe, *Islamic Marriage*, 25; Hemedi, *Nikahi*, 15. On delegated divorce, see Berg, *Minhādj*, vol. II, 429–31.

63 J. N. D. Anderson, *Islamic Law*, 74. *Īlā'* means that the husband swears an oath not to have intercourse with his wife. After four months, the wife can petition the court for divorce. I have not come across any record of *īlā'*. If the husband declares that his wife has become for him as untouchable as the back (Ar. *ẓahr*) of his mother, this is called *ẓihār* and requires a heavy expiation that can be enforced by a *kadhi*. The effect of *ẓihār* is that the husband is forbidden to have intercourse with his wife, which may equal a repudiation or be without legal effect according to Shafi'i jurists (Berg, *Minhādj*, vol. II, 427). If the husband accuses his wife of adultery and thus denies paternity, as Muhammad b. 'Ali did in his divorce paper (see above), this procedure is called *li'ān*. See El Alami and Hinchcliffe, *Islamic Marriage*, 25–27; Hemedi, *Nikahi*, 22–26; Schacht, *Introduction to Islamic Law*, 164–65.

64 Interview with Sh. Ahmed Mohamed Saleh Ba Kathir, 27 January 2004; cf. Tucker, *In the House of the Law*, 101–108.

sued Muhammad b. Salim al-Muʿamari for her dower, Qirsh 100, in 1900, he claimed he had divorced her on the condition that she forwent everything. Siha's understanding was that he divorced her first and took her back on this condition. It is unclear why Siha sued for her dower, as she admitted before the *kadhi* that she had forgone it. The husband then took her back in the *kadhi*'s presence.[65] The condition that the wife should forgo her dower also emerged in the correspondence between a husband in Bagamoyo and *kadhi* Sh. ʿUmar during 1954 and 1955.[66]

However, not all conditions of divorce related to money. Bilal b. Juma, "slave of the government," had imposed on himself the condition that if he beat his wife, she would be divorced. In court Bilal refused to take the oath to confirm that he had not beaten her. He thereby confirmed the beating and thus the divorce was established.[67] In 1900, ʿAbdallah b. Khatib told his wife Chambua (?) bt. Saʿid that if she left his house, then she would be divorced. She left and the divorce was affected.[68] Most likely both parties were former slaves. In 1919, *kadhi* Sh. Ṭāhir registered Sheikha bt. Hassan's conditions of divorce as follows: she would be divorced if the husband beat her, did not provide two pieces of clothing every month, or came home after 11 P.M. After agreeing to these conditions, the husband admitted to have broken one of them, which was confirmed by witnesses. He then pronounced the divorce in the presence of Sh. Ṭāhir.[69]

Material Underpinnings of Divorce: Negotiating the Cost of Remarriage

Given the complementary rights and duties of husband and wife in a Muslim marriage, Zanzibari spouses had gendered perceptions of divorce and accordingly adopted different strategies to dissolve marital

[65] Entry #259, 26 Jumādā II 1318/21 September 1900, HC28/29, ZNA. The same condition was stipulated in HC9/62; HC9/131; HC9/134; Entry #634, no number, 2 Jumādā II [1319]/15 September 1901, HC28/29, ZNA. See also Bakari, *Customs of the Swahili*, 131.

[66] HC10/3097, ZNA, original in English and Swahili.

[67] No entry #, no number, 7 Shawwāl 1320/6 January 1903, HC28/29, ZNA. Cf. Chapter 9.

[68] Entry #190, no. 136, 3 Jumādā I 1318/29 August 1900, HC28/29, ZNA.

[69] HC9/65, ZNA.

ties. Women's strategies hinged on suing for outstanding debts from their husbands, such as the dower and maintenance. If such a claim was established, the *kadhi* would then issue a decree that not only entitled the wife to collect this debt from her husband but may also have included the condition that the marriage would be terminated if the husband failed to comply with the *kadhi*'s decree. Thus filing a claim for outstanding dower and/or maintenance was often an initial step towards obtaining a divorce. Another reason that at least some manumitted wives invoked during the abolition of slavery was the lack of *kafāʾa* between them and their slave husbands. Husbands, on their part, invoked the wife's duty to obedience and tended to counter maintenance claims by declaring their wives disobedient, in which case they forfeited their right to maintenance. In legal terms, wives' claims for maintenance were reciprocated, if not preempted, by husbands' petitions for restitution of conjugal rights.

In 1955, J. N. D. Anderson wrote that

> [h]usbands, whose wives run away or prove recalcitrant may, of course, bring suits for "obedience" (restitution of conjugal rights) before either the Shāfiʿī or Ibāḍī Qāḍī; and judgement will, where suitable, be given accordingly. No such judgements, however, are now forcibly executed in Zanzibar by dragging the wife back to the marriage home or reinforced by committing her to prison – although the latter was allowed until comparatively recently.[70]

Restitution of conjugal rights claims and the option of using police force to return a wife to her husband, or incarcerating her, were intrinsic to Islamic law in the view of colonial observers like Anderson. As historian of the Middle East Kenneth Cuno convincingly demonstrated, however, these concepts were colonial innovations.[71] As colonial authorities sought to maintain what they perceived as the patriarchal family, they were drawn into a power struggle between African elders, men, and women, who all used these authorities to enhance their

[70] J. N. D. Anderson, *Islamic Law*, 73.

[71] Kenneth Cuno, "Disobedient Wives and Neglectful Husbands: Marital Relations and the First Phase of Family Law Reform in Egypt," in *Family, Gender, and Law in a Globalizing Middle East and South Asia*, ed. Kenneth M. Cuno and Manisha Desai (Syracuse: Syracuse University Press, 2009), 3–18. See also Marie Rodet, "'Le délit d'abandon de domicile conjugal' ou l'invasion du pénal colonial dans les jugements des 'tribunaux indigènes' au Soudan français, 1900–1947," *French Colonial History* 10 (2009): 151–70; Tucker, *Women, Family, and Gender*, 74–75.

socioeconomic positions. In opening a restitution of conjugal rights claim, men utilised the colonial government to bolster their authority in the household. The *kadhi* played a key role in this power structure. If the wife admitted that there was no legal reason for her disobedience, without exception he ordered her to return to the husband.[72] *Kadhi*s followed the colonial script and did not draw on legal discourse to question the use of force to return the wife to the husband. Thus in 1931, *kadhi* Sh. Ṭāhir issued a warrant for Khadija bt. Maftah in execution of a restitution of conjugal rights claim. The marriage ended in *khul*ʿ before the arrest was executed.[73]

As claims such as restitution of conjugal rights, maintenance, and dower were part of bargaining strategies that may have resulted in an agreement on the terms of divorce, the legal category in which these claims were filed does not necessarily reveal the actual outcome of the case. Cases from the register of 1900 to 1903 show the bargaining potential for divorce, with spouses making additional claims and counterclaims before the *kadhi* or *kadhi*s. In 1900, Ridawa (?) bt. Hassan, a Comorian, sued her husband ʿAli b. Hajj, a Hadimu, for Riyal 140. ʿAli acknowledged her right but claimed he was impoverished. The short summary of this case does not reveal the full story but we can piece together that in a previous judgement, Sh. Rashīd b. Sālim al-Ghaythī had ordered ʿAli to hand over the crop of his *shamba* to Ridawa until he would have paid off his debt. On appeal, the *kadhi*s in the Court for Zanzibar and Pemba confirmed this judgement, ruling that ʿAli should keep the *shamba* himself and give his wife the crops according to her demand, as she found the seizure of the *shamba* difficult. *Kadhi*s accommodated women's requests for specific arrangements only if they deemed them compatible with shariʿa. Ridawa then sued ʿAli for maintenance and falling short of conjugal duties, which was confirmed by the *kadhi*s and suggests her aim of dissolving the marriage.[74]

[72] Wives were ordered to return to their husband in HC5/536; HC8/86; HC9/112; HC9/136; HC10/45; HC10/79; HC10/1141; HC10/1198; HC10/2833; HC10/2843; HC10/2910; HC10/3202; HC10/3612; HC10/5533; HC10/5534; No entry #, no number, 22 Rajab 1320/24 October 1902; No entry #, no number, 7 Shaʿbān 1320/8 November 1902, HC28/29, ZNA.

[73] HC10/45, ZNA.

[74] Entry #120, no number, 18 Ṣafar 1318/16 June 1900, HC28/29, ZNA.

Although after 1908 *kadhi*s reminded parties of the rules of procedure, which impeded litigants to raise additional claims and to amend the nature of the plaint, divorce bargains remained relatively flexible.[75] In 1944, *kadhi* Sh. Saʿīd b. Rashīd al-Ghaythī confirmed Mtumwa bt. Nassor's right to maintenance, clothes, and proper accommodation. In the following court sessions, the couple debated the delay in the husband's payment of maintenance. After the husband settled his debt, Mtumwa returned to him. Yet, in the last entry of 17 January 1945, *kadhi* Sh. Saʿīd recorded that the couple agreed to separate through *khulʿ*. Mtumwa forwent the deferred dower, Shs. 100, and Shs. 60 (of maintenance?), to which the court had entitled her, while her husband paid the court costs, Shs. 63.[76] This case is indicative of divorce negotiations at the time and also shows *kadhis'* equation of fault with financial liabilities.

The bargaining between husband and wife revolved around their differing perceptions of what constituted a divorce.[77] A typical pattern consisted of a husband claiming the return of a disobedient wife who argued that they were divorced. In 1909, a former slave filed for restitution of conjugal rights, alleging that the father of his wife had demanded a divorce. The wife's understanding was that she had got a *khulʿ* for Rs. 14 six years ago. This interpretation suited her aim of marrying another man, which she had done three years after the divorce. According to her first husband, he remarried her one year after their divorce for the same amount of dower he had paid previously. The *kadhi*, however, confirmed the *khulʿ*, as both parties corroborated its occurrence.[78]

An important female strategy were suits for deferred dower, which enabled wives to raise other issues, such as non-provision of

75 Cf. Richard Roberts, "Representation, Structure and Agency," 400, on the impact of procedure on grievances.

76 HC9/136, ZNA. As this case shows, most divorce negotiations were informal and spouses mainly used the court to formalise the result. Cf. Rapoport, *Marriage, Money and Divorce*, 74.

77 Erin Stiles argues that the removal of the wife's goods and her subsequent return to her natal family may be the only way a wife can indicate her new status. In spite of gendered experiences of divorce, Stiles does not find evidence of gender differences in understanding divorce. Idem, *Islamic Court*, Chapter 3; idem, "'There Is No Stranger to Marriage Here!,'" 582–98.

78 HC9/97, ZNA.

maintenance, to support their final aim of getting a divorce.[79] In 1955, Amne bt. Salum b. Sa'id al-Hadrami sued Naji b. Sultan for her deferred dower, Shs. 200, past maintenance for nine months at Shs. 90 per month, future maintenance at Shs. 3 per day, and clothes worth Shs. 20 per quarter, or dissolution of the marriage. *Kadhi* Sh. 'Umar ordered Naji to pay the deferred dower and entitled Amne to a poor man's maintenance at Shs. 2 a day, two clothes every three months, and a suitable dwelling. As Amne admitted that she had left Naji without his permission, Sh. 'Umar did not grant an order for past maintenance. About two months after the judgement, Amne applied for *faskh* as, despite her willingness to return to Naji, he had failed to comply with the order. Although the course of events seems to have been favourable to Amne's intention of getting a divorce, she had to renounce her deferred dower and half of the costs before Naji divorced her in court.[80]

Non-provision of maintenance as a grounds for divorce served not only poor women, who may have sought to provide for themselves by contracting a new marriage, but also women who lived in financial ease. Asha bt. Simai obtained an order for maintenance and her dower, Shs. 36, in 1936. As her husband, Ame b. Rajab, could not pay the debt, he divorced her in court before *kadhi* Sh. Sa'īd b. Nāṣir al-Ghaythī, possibly at the instigation of the latter. Asha remarried a couple of months after the divorce, presumably shortly after she had completed her *'idda*. She was exempt from paying court fees, which indicates that she was poor, and serial marriage may have been her way of maintaining herself.[81] At the opposite end of the economic scale, in 1901 Salima bt. Yusuf sued Suleiman b. Madai for maintenance, which comprised the wage of her *khādima* for six months and the rent for her house for five years. Her husband, in turn, sued her for Rs. 120 that he gave on her behalf as security to an Indian. She, however, alleged that this was her dower. Clearly, Salima was not a poor woman and although the outcome of the case has not been recorded, her intention of suing her husband appears to have been motivated by ending the marriage rather than merely by recovering her debts.[82]

[79] Cf. Agmon, "Women, Class, and Gender," 489.
[80] HC10/3238, ZNA.
[81] HC5/536, ZNA, original in Arabic and English.
[82] Entry #584, no number, 13 Rabī' II [1319]/29 July 1901, HC28/29, ZNA.

Movements of people across the northwestern Indian Ocean also shaped marriages, providing opportunities for both genders. Labour migration and travels made husbands go back and forth between the islands of Zanzibar and Pemba, the East African coast, and Oman and may have affected marriage negatively, as these movements entailed the geographical separation of spouses.[83] While the mobility of Zanzibar's population included every social group, and possibly the majority of travellers were members of lower social strata,[84] wives rarely joined husbands during travels and sojourns outside Zanzibar Island. Although the geographical separation of a couple might have strained the relationship, it was at the same time an opportunity women used to end their marriages, albeit not always successfully. In 1943, Mtumwa bt. Athmani sued Hamadi b. Khamisi for maintenance, clothes, and a proper dwelling. Unable to recall when she got married, Mtumwa explained she first lived with Hamadi in Miafuni in Zanzibar Town. Then they moved to Pemba, where they lived for four or five years. When Hamadi started to travel to Tanga on the Mrima coast, where he stayed for a couple of months before returning to Pemba, Mtumwa decided to leave for Zanzibar. *Kadhi* Sh. Saʿīd b. Rashīd al-Ghaythī, however, found no reason for her departure from Pemba. He declared her claim void, ordering her return to her husband.[85]

Lack of maintenance due to the husband's prolonged absence was a grounds for Shafiʿi and Ibāḍī *kadhi*s to dissolve a marriage.[86] Zaynab bt. Mabruk, freed slave of Salim b. Sulayman al-Marhubi, claimed in 1900 that her husband had been absent for seven years, without leaving her maintenance or a *wālī*, or legal guardian, to take care of her affairs. The *kadhi*s in the Court for Zanzibar and Pemba referred her claim to the sultan, who pronounced a divorce.[87] If a wife asked for a dissolution because of the husband's lack of maintenance due to his lengthy absence, the judgement was phrased in a formulaic way and

[83] Cf. Lovett, "Elders, Migrants and Wives," 289.

[84] Prestholdt, *Domesticating the World*, 97–99.

[85] HC10/1198, ZNA. For wives taking advantage of their husband's prolonged absence, see also HC8/67; HC10/20; HC10/3253, ZNA. Usually the husband's reasons for travelling remain elusive, save in one instance in which we know that he was a sailor (HC10/48, ZNA).

[86] Hemedi, *Nikahi*, 29.

[87] Entry #22, no number, 25 Dhū l-Qaʿda 1317/27 March 1900, HC28/29, ZNA.

was contingent on an oath, confirming her hypothetical obedience if her husband had maintained her. The *kadhi*s did not grant a dissolution unless two witnesses testified that the husband had neither left maintenance nor property.[88]

Records of judicial dissolutions suggest that if a wife, such as Zaynab, obtained a divorce in the absence of her husband, she was unable to access her deferred dower, as the handing over of the entire dower upon marriage was exceptional at the time. The loss of the deferred dower occurred in addition to her renunciation of any other claims of debts, mostly maintenance.[89] Sakina bt. Ashur al-Bahrani filed for *faskh* in 1959 due to her husband's non-provision of maintenance for two months. She had left the matrimonial home in Dar es-Salaam on the understanding that she would be divorced. As the husband neither provided maintenance nor divorced her, Ibāḍī *kadhi* Sh. Muḥammad Sālim al-Rawwāḥī pronounced a *faskh* in the husband's absence, which implied that Sakina forwent the remainder of her dower of an unspecified amount.[90] When *kadhi* Sh. ʿAbdallāh Ṣāliḥ al-Farsī dissolved a marriage in the husband's absence in 1961, the wife forwent a complete set of household items, a bed, and nineteen months of maintenance debts.[91] Since in the majority of cases wives forwent the deferred dower, it lacked the value as a post-divorce source of maintenance that Muslim jurists ascribed to it.

In addition to suing for the dissolution of marriage on the grounds of lack of maintenance, lack of *kafāʾa* between the spouses appeared as a legitimate grounds for divorce, particularly in the years following the abolition of slavery. Among the social changes in the first half of the twentieth century, the abolition of slavery was a major force in restructuring the social landscape, shaping family and marital relations. Islamic law provides for the manumission of slaves through contractual manumission or by the owner. A woman who became

[88] HC9/63; HC9/72; HC9/84; HC9/130; Entry #22, no number, 25 Dhū l-Qaʿda 1317/27 March 1900; Entry #43, no number, 17 Dhū l-Ḥijja 1317/17 April 1900, HC28/29, ZNA. In HC9/110, ZNA, the husband was present in court but had been on the Mrima coast for the last three years. One month after the case opened in 1901, Sh. Burhān dissolved the marriage due to the husband's failure to appear again in court and to pay his maintenance debt.

[89] HC10/15; HC10/3295; HC10/3705; HC10/3731; HC10/5570, ZNA.

[90] HC10/3731, ZNA.

[91] HC10/5570, ZNA.

manumitted other than by contract during her marriage to a slave could ask for the dissolution of her marriage within the framework of *kafāʾa*.[92] If freed slave women pursued this right, they could thus achieve more geographical mobility, seek new employment opportunities, and re-create their social identities, manifest in the assertion of control over their sexuality. In 1903, Mwajuma, the freed slave of Mwanafaika (?) bt. ʿUthman, sued her husband for pretending to be free when they married, while in fact he was a slave and thus unlike her. The husband countered that his wife knew and accepted his social status. As he claimed to have witnesses in Mkokotoni, the *kadhi* ordered the hearing of these witnesses and sought permission from the master for representation in court. Alas, here the record discontinues.[93] Two years later, *kadhi* Sh. Burhān declared the marriage between a slave and a former slave as void, ruling that *kafāʾa* was the obligation of the guardian and the right of his ward at the time of contract.[94] In both cases, *kadhi*s applied the status of slave after abolition.

Aiming to end their marriages, women's strategies could take other sophisticated forms. According to her husband, Mbuku bt. Juma cunningly tricked him into divorce in 1921. She made him write a triple divorce contingent on her release of her dower. She took each divorce paper to a scribe who read it to her. Returning to her husband, she explained both times that she had not been divorced yet so that he wrote a third paper, equating a triple and thus irrevocable divorce. The debate in court hinged on the intention of the husband. The husband claimed that he had neither pronounced the divorce nor intended it. *Kadhi* Sh. Ṭāhir held that the *khulʿ* occurred, as the husband did not stipulate the wife's acceptance as a condition. He refuted the arguments of the husband's *wakīl* that two criteria of the validity of *khulʿ* were missing, pronunciation and intent. Sh. Ṭāhir confirmed the *khulʿ* as for him, writing was necessarily an expression of intention.[95]

Seeking treatment and sick care were other strategies that wives applied to end their marriages for good, as they provided justifiable

92 Berg, *Minhādj*, vol. II, 367–68.
93 No entry#, no number, 19 Dhū l-Qaʿda 1320/17 February 1903, HC28/29, ZNA.
94 HC9/117, ZNA. See Chapter 6.
95 HC9/134, ZNA. Cf. Stiles, "When Is a Divorce a Divorce?" for an identical ruse applied more recently.

reasons to return to their natal families.[96] In response to her husband's claim for restitution of conjugal rights, Mgeni bt. Hamid al-Saʿudi argued that she had left him to receive traditional healing and stayed with the daughter of her mother's uncle. She refused to go to hospital as suggested by her husband.[97] Fifty years earlier, in 1909, Mchawi also explained her desertion of her husband by seeing a traditional healer.[98] In neither case did the *kadhi* accept the wife's argument and ordered her return. Yet when Mtumwa bt. Nassor returned to her parents for giving birth in 1944, *kadhi* Sh. Saʿīd b. Rashīd al-Ghaythī confirmed her right to maintenance during that period. Mtumwa had informed her husband by letter about the birth of his child, asking him to come and take her back to his house.[99] Another *kadhi*, Sh. ʿAlī b. Muḥammad, entitled Safi bt. Saburi to a divorce in 1921, as her husband owed her maintenance and clothes for the past three years even though she had not stayed with him. When Safi had fallen ill, her father had invited her to stay at his house and her brother testified to her husband's permission.[100]

Mtumwa's and Safi's cases suggest that *kadhi*s weighed their judgements according to the evidence produced in support of claims. While the wife's relatives tended to support her stay at her natal family because she was sick or took care of a sick family member, some husbands turned her absence into a suit for disobedience.[101] Yet, ultimately, neither the court nor the husband could force a wife to join her husband if she refused to do so.

The recalcitrant wife puzzled *kadhi*s and officers, as she defied male ideals of submissiveness and, in more pragmatic terms, cooperation. In 1955, Mwajuma bt. Ayub sued her husband for past and future maintenance or divorce. As she admitted to having left the matrimonial home without the husband's consent and defied any attempt at reconciliation, "much to the surprise of the Mudir who expressed that

96 Hemedi, *Nikahi*, 35.
97 HC10/3612, ZNA.
98 HC9/90, ZNA.
99 HC9/136, ZNA. Cf. Hemedi, *Nikahi*, 35.
100 HC9/133, ZNA. See also HC9/129, ZNA.
101 See HC8/67, ZNA, where the wife used a permitted visit to desert her husband. One woman did not return to her husband after delivery (HC10/5533, ZNA). According to a witness, another wife did not return to the husband after visiting a sick relative (HC10/2881, ZNA).

it did not appear that the Plaintiff was in favour of any peaceful settlement," she was not entitled to maintenance or a dissolution.[102] In such a case, her option would have been to buy her divorce. In 1909, Ibāḍī *kadhi* Sh. ʿAlī b. Muḥammad tried in vain to make an independently minded wife return to her husband. Niya Njema, whose name means "good intention," categorically turned down the *kadhi*'s concessions, which made him conclude that she was not fond of her husband, Mzee b. Ameir, and neither force nor detention would make her change her mind. Sh. ʿAlī suggested to Mzee that "it is best for you that she gives to you what you gave to her [that is, that she returns the prompt dower] and that you divorce her and take another wife." The husband agreed, adding that he had given her various sums of money, Rs. 10, Rs. 22, and Rs. 8. Niya Njema confirmed that she had received her prompt dower, Rs. 10, and Rs. 22 for maintenance but denied the receipt of another Rs. 8. Sh. ʿAlī then ordered Mzee to accept Rs. 32 as *khul*ʿ and to divorce her. Mzee agreed and a paternal relative of Niya Njema became liable for the payment. A week later, Niya Njema handed over the said amount to Mzee, who then divorced her before Sh. ʿAlī.[103] Based on *kadhi*s' interpretation of fault and compensation, they made wives pay for the independence they sought.

*Kadhi*s implemented husbands' demands for compensation from their wives so they could raise the dower for another wife.[104] This idea of using *khul*ʿ to enable serial marriage is not unique to Zanzibar. Aharon Layish has described this as "customary *khul*ʿ" in Libya. Customary *khul*ʿ differs from shariʿa *khul*ʿ, as the return of the dower, or a sum in addition to the dower, is contingent on the wife's remarriage and occurs at that time. The wife may negotiate the customary *khul*ʿ herself and her father may help raise the amount, but in most cases her agnatic relatives and her husband achieve the arrangement. Layish sees customary *khul*ʿ as a compromise between shariʿa, under which

102 HC10/3202, ZNA, original in English. Cf. Chapter 6. The *mudir* of Mkokotoni mediated between the spouses. For disobedience cases that resulted in *khul*ʿ and in which the wife was initially ordered to return to her husband, see HC5/536; HC8/86; HC9/124; HC9/136; HC10/20; HC10/45; HC10/1141; HC10/2833, ZNA.

103 HC9/83, ZNA.

104 In the French Soudan, a husband also claimed reimbursement as his wife wanted a separation for no apparent reason. See Rebecca Shereikis, "From Law to Custom: The Shifting Legal Status of Muslim *Originaires* in Kayes and Medine, 1903–13," *Journal of African History* 42, no. 2 (2001): 270.

the wife is a party to divorce negotiations, and custom, under which she is a passive participant.[105] While in Libya the wife's new husband paid for her *khul'*, in Zanzibar the wife's *khul'* payment enabled her husband to take another wife. In both cases dire financial straits seem to account for these arrangements, which were sanctioned, and in Zanzibar even encouraged, by *kadhis*.

Although *kadhis* suggested women bought their divorce, they took debts of husbands towards them seriously and, at least occasionally, also questioned legal gender roles. They could order the attachment of property to pay off dower and past maintenance debts, even though husbands had already divorced their wives. In 1901, *kadhi* Sh. Burhān did not support a rebellious (Ar. *'aṣīy*) husband who wanted to pay his maintenance debts in instalments and provided for a *faskh* after one month if the husband failed to pay. The divorce was affected as stated.[106] Disobedience is a legal category of female behaviour,[107] yet in this case, Sh. Burhān was clearly irritated by the husband's rebellious conduct. His colleague Sh. Ṭāhir ordered the sale of a former husband's house as he failed to pay Rs. 40, the remainder of the dower, which the *kadhi* had ordered him to pay in monthly instalments of Rs. 2.[108] The same *kadhi* reminded a husband of the financial liabilities arising from marriage. Following a judgement for maintenance and the dower, which Sh. Ṭāhir had passed against him, Issa b. 'Ali wrote to the resident magistrate for assistance on 4 August 1938. Issa wanted "to get his money from his wife," as he was very poor and unable to pay for a summons.[109] Sh. Ṭāhir opposed Issa's petition for exemption from court fees. In this case of restitution of conjugal rights, the *kadhi*

105 Aharon Layish, "Customary *Khul'* as Reflected in the *Sijill* of the Libyan *Shari'a* Courts," *Bulletin of the School of Oriental and African Studies* 51, no. 3 (1988): 428–39.

106 HC9/110, ZNA.

107 Tucker, *Women, Family, and Gender*, 73–74.

108 HC10/58, ZNA. *Kadhis* also enforced wives' claims for husbands' debts in HC10/752; HC10/1010; HC10/1276; HC10/3001; HC10/3295; HC10/3302; HC10/3447; HC10/3537; HC10/3731; Entry #120, no number, 18 Ṣafar 1318/16 June 1900; Entry #138, no. 69, 6 Rabī' I 1318/3 July 1900; Entry #764, no. 225, 23 Shawwāl [1319]/2 February 1902; No entry #, no. 549, 17 Rabī' I [1320]/24 June 1902, HC28/29, ZNA.

109 Issa b. Ali to Resident Magistrate, 4 August 1938, AX8/2, ZNA.

reasoned, how would Issa be able to feed his wife if he could not even pay the fees?[110]

Women's willingness to divorce required funding, leading to the important question how they were able to afford *khulʿ*. Unlike *faskh*, *khulʿ* can be achieved or paid by someone other than the wife (her father, for instance) if the husband accepts the offer. Several cases recorded that kin, guardians, and patrons initiated *khulʿ* or became liable for its payment.[111] One interviewee stated that she was able to buy her divorce with money her husband gave her, that is, the dower or part of it. Another woman recalled that her paternal aunt gave her money to compensate her husband upon divorce.[112] As discussed in Chapter 7, it is also likely that women drew on brothers to raise the amount for *khulʿ*. Hence there is little evidence to support J. S. Trimingham's observation that the wife's kin were unwilling to support compensation payments, but there is considerable evidence to confirm that *khulʿ* may have entailed hefty payments from them, enabled by instalments and delay in payment.[113] Even if women did not have the necessary resources themselves, they were at least able to raise them with the help of socioeconomic networks among kin. The frequency of divorce, or *khulʿ* to be precise, clearly defies jurists' ideal of the wife's economic dependency on the husband.[114]

110 Sh. Tahir, 9 August 1938, AX8/2, ZNA, original in English.

111 HC9/86; HC9/90; HC9/97; HC9/98; HC9/124; HC10/45; HC10/1010; HC10/3612, ZNA. In 1960, Sh. ʿAbdallāh Ṣāliḥ al-Farsī ruled that Tatu bt. Mgana had to return to her husband, Seif b. Khamis, or that her father should pay Seif Shs. 300 as promised so he might divorce her. The *kadhi* thus established that *khulʿ* could be offered and paid by someone other than the wife. This order against the father, who was not party to the suit, entailed a rebuke by Chief Justice G. M. Mahon (HC10/5533, ZNA). In an Ottoman context, Peirce suggests that brothers were crucial to enabling *khulʿ* (idem, *Morality Tales*, 231). Also in colonial northern Nigeria wives frequently relied on kin to compensate the husband (J. N. D. Anderson, *Islamic Law*, 209).

112 Interviews with Bi Mwanaidi Makame Ameir, 24 June 2004; Bi Bahati Ramadhani Juma, 27 March 2004.

113 Trimingham, *Islam in East Africa*, 139; HC9/62; HC9/86; HC9/90; HC9/98; HC9/124; HC10/20; HC10/43; HC10/45; HC10/1010; HC10/2833; HC10/3612; Entry #190, no. 136, 3 Jumādā I 1318/29 August 1900, HC28/29, ZNA. The *liwali* El-Busaidy further points to the problem of elders and women getting indebted, pawning items to buy a *khulʿ* (idem, *Ndoa na talaka*, 34–35).

114 Cf. Rapoport, *Marriage, Money and Divorce*, 6.

In spite of its economic implications, in most cases *khulʿ* was the only way for women to end their marriage and the amount of money they thereby lost could be substantial. In 1943, Jokha bt. Saʿid b. Muhammad al-Salimi paid her husband Muhammad b. Nassor b. Muhammad al-Kindi Shs. 300 and forwent Shs. 180, originally suing him for Shs. 150.[115] At the lower end of the socioeconomic ladder, Fadila bt. Simba forwent a (maintenance?) debt of Rs. 37 and her deferred dower, Rs. 20, when her husband divorced her in court, even though she had obtained a decree that ordered her husband to pay his debt in a previous session in 1919.[116] In a case of 1909, Mwamini, a freed slave, had to refund the dower to her second husband, Khamis, a dependent (Ar. *tābiʿ*), or, rather, former slave, of ʿAbdallah b. Muhammad al-Rawwahi, as it appeared that she had another husband on the Mrima coast.[117] Mwamini sold her belongings, crockery worth Rs. 6, and her *wālī* agreed to pay the remainder of the dower, Rs. 20 (of which she alleged to have received only Rs. 12) in monthly instalments. Khamis demanded the return of the dower, "since it had been an expense."[118]

Husbands' perception of marriage as an expense is attested in divorce cases of the first half of the twentieth century. Men struggled to cover the costs marriage entailed, with some even deferring payment of the prompt dower.[119] Regardless of their social background, most men applied for paying off debts in instalments under the supervision of the court.[120] The fact that restitution of conjugal rights cases as well as suits for maintenance and dower tended to result in *khulʿ* confirms men's drive for material compensation. Musa b. Muhammad, for instance, a Swahili-Shirazi and cultivator, explicitly said in his plaint for restitution of conjugal rights in 1960 that if his wife refused to

115 HC10/1141, ZNA.

116 HC9/60, ZNA.

117 If a woman was given into marriage to two husbands by different guardians, she was not considered as adulterous (Hemedi, *Nikahi*, 2–3).

118 HC9/98, ZNA.

119 Entry #764, no. 225, 23 Shawwāl [1319]/2 February 1902; No entry #, no. 549, 17 Rabīʿ I [1320]/24 June 1902, HC28/29, ZNA. See also Ingrams, *Zanzibar*, 237.

120 HC9/127; HC10/42; HC10/58; HC10/3537; Entry #120, no number, 18 Ṣafar 1318/16 June 1900; Entry #138, no. 69, 6 Rabīʿ I 1318/3 July 1900; Entry #180, no. 118, 24 Rabīʿ II/20 August 1900; No entry #, no number, date of hearing 20 Ṣafar 1321/18 May 1903, HC28/29, ZNA.

return, he wanted her to refund the dower of Shs. 300, clothes, and all household items so he might divorce her.[121] Also ʿAbdallah b. Sheilab was very firm in his request for the refund of the dower when his wife, who had deserted him in 1947, refused to return during his restitution of conjugal rights suit of 1952. As the wife admitted not to have Shs. 300, which he demanded for a *khul*ʿ, she offered to sell her furniture to raise this amount. The court consequently attached her property but then agreed that she paid the amount in instalments and cancelled the sale of her furniture.[122] Thus, a wife's *khul*ʿ debt was enforced with the same rigidity as a husband's maintenance debt.

Although husbands' insistence on the return of their wives is discouraged in socioreligious terms,[123] across the social hierarchy, they came to perceive their wives' value in material rather than companionate terms. If a man insisted on the return of his wife after she had refused him, it emphasised his underlying economic motivation. Velten's *Desturi za Waswahili* records the custom that the husband should leave the wife half of the possessions in the marital home and an amount of money upon repudiation.[124] In the interior of Tanganyika, Schacht noted that husbands frequently made gifts to their wives outside the marriage settlement.[125] Such an exceptional arrangement, attesting to the husband's generosity, arose from the dissolution of the marriage between Zena bt. ʿAbdallah and Rajab b. Juma in 1906. He gave her money, paid the (deferred) dower and maintenance, and left her the house they coowned before divorcing her in the presence of *kadhi* Sh. Burhān.[126]

How money drove negotiations among all actors in court, including the *kadhi*, is clearly demonstrated by a case of 1909 involving two former slaves. ʿAbdallah b. ʿUbayd sued Tausi bt. Mchanakhayri for restitution of conjugal rights as she had gone to her family without his permission. She countered that he had beaten her. When she demanded

121 HC10/5534, ZNA.
122 HC10/2833, ZNA.
123 See the introduction to this chapter; interviews with Sh. Abdalla Suleiman Jumbe, 24 March 2004; Sh. Ibrahim Mtoro and Sh. Hamid Musa Mlomri, 22 December 2003.
124 Velten, "Sitten und Gebräuche," 63; Middleton, *The World of the Swahili*, 130.
125 Schacht, "Notes on Islam," 110.
126 HC9/128, ZNA.

a divorce, he asked for "his right," meaning the return of his investment in the marriage. After a reconciliation attempt, Tausi argued before *kadhi* Sh. ʿAlī b. Muḥammad that ʿAbdallah owed her maintenance and had received money to divorce her. ʿAbdallah's concise reply in court was, "I want my wife." *Kadhi* Sh. ʿAlī offered a special maintenance contribution and special clothes, which Tausi refused; all she wanted was a divorce. Given the spouses' irreconcilable attitudes, Sh. ʿAlī suggested a *khulʿ* at this point, phrased as follows: "That is between you and him. [If] you have come to terms with something, [then] agree on it, and this is demanded and this is the law." The couple agreed on Rs. 40 and Tausi gave her husband her house as security until she handed over the amount. Because she managed to pay the amount the same day, ʿAbdallah divorced her in court.[127] As illustrated by Sh. ʿAlī, *kadhi*s may have considered material items as an enticement for reconciliation. But they also requested security from both genders in case of illiquidity.

The monetarisation of marital relations seems to have increased the diverging understanding of divorce between husband and wife, which revolved around her intention to remarry and his difficulties in raising a new dower. Remarriage potentially offered women financial security and certainly respectability and accounts for their determination to obtain a divorce. Their tendency to remarry (immediately) after completing the *ʿidda* was indicated in a judgement of *kadhi* Sh. Saʿīd b. Rashīd al-Ghaythī in 1952, when he explicitly stated that the wife had no right to remarry after he had refused to acknowledge the husband's divorce.[128]

The relative ease with which marriage was dissolved, both in and out-of-court, counters contentions, such as by Jan Knappert and J. N. D. Anderson, that a Muslim wife lived in constant anxiety of repudiation and that her life focussed on retaining the love of her husband.[129]

[127] HC9/89, ZNA. In a case of 1920, in which the wife sued for divorce on the grounds of cruelty and offered a *khulʿ*, *kadhi* Sh. Ṭāhir achieved a reconciliation by making the husband hand over Rs. 30 to her as compensation for "forcibly incurring danger to her"(HC9/131, ZNA).

[128] HC10/2843, ZNA.

[129] Knappert, "Social and Moral Concepts," 58; J. N. D. Anderson, "The Eclipse of the Patriarchal Family in Contemporary Islamic Law," in *Family Law in Asia and Africa*, ed. J. N. D. Anderson (London: George Allen & Unwin, 1968), 221.

In Zanzibar, repudiation essentially remained a threat rather than husbands' preferred way of ending a marriage,[130] with concerns about women's claims of debts frequently driving them to bargain for *khul*ʿ. Women's grounds for divorce were clearly limited but were not rigidly interpreted by the *kadhi*s. A well-described strategy was that the wife used to make her husband's life so unbearable that he would divorce her.[131] Yet husbands used the same initiative to make wives miserable so that they in turn offered their husband a *khul*ʿ.[132] In addition to socioeconomic motivations, women simply preferred other partners or were tired of husbands. To be merely tired of one's husband (Sw. *kuchoka*) was a legitimate reason for divorce. However, the *kadhi* would have made the wife pay for this grounds of divorce.[133]

Conclusion

Drawing on Islamic and customary laws, women in Zanzibar Town initiated divorce with the support of both *kadhi*s and kin. *Kadhi*s offered women legal recourse primarily by considering the evidence and contradictions in claims, but they also responded to changing social circumstances by adapting legal doctrines. This suggests that divorce was not merely a discourse about men collaborating with the state, as scholars have argued in several case studies for the colonial period.[134] I would argue that the underlying moral discourse was an

130 Cf. Rapoport, *Marriage, Money and Divorce*, 70–72.

131 For examples of wives who tricked their husbands into divorcing them, see Patricia W. Romero, "Mama Khadija: A Life History as Example of Family History," in *Life Histories of African Women*, ed. Patricia W. Romero (London: The Ashfield Press, 1988); Mirza and Strobel, *Three Swahili Women*. In colonial Buha, women also tried to make their presence intolerable to the husband who would then end the marriage by asking for the return of the bridewealth (Lovett, "Elders, Migrants and Wives," 317). Wives could also provoke a divorce by refusing marital and household duties (Rapoport, *Marriage, Money and Divorce*, 73).

132 In the Copperbelt of the early 1960s, husbands made their wives suffer so they would sue for divorce. See Sally Engle Merry, "The Articulation of Legal Spheres," in *African Women and the Law: Historical Perspectives*, ed. Margaret Jean Hay and Marcia Wright (Boston: Boston University, 1982), 88.

133 El-Busaidy, *Ndoa na talaka*, 36. Cf. Stiles, *Islamic Court*, 196, where she concludes that Zanzibari women seeking divorce in court nearly always get one by buying it.

134 See Chanock, *Law, Custom and Social Order*; Lovett, "Elders, Migrants and Wives;" Mbilinyi, "Women's Resistence," 211–54; Schmidt, "Patriarchy, Capitalism, and the Colonial State."

Islamic social discourse about female protection and a legal discourse about fault, coloured by the socioeconomic pressures particularly of the early and late colonial period. Given the respectability that marriage bestowed on women and men, the importance of being married and protected outweighed any stigmatisation of divorcees. The universality of serial marriage is born out in marriage registers, which predominantly recorded marriages of women who had been married previously. Because of the increasing difficulties that husbands faced in providing the dower, *kadhi*s made wives compensate husbands in order to keep solid the social fabric, of which serial marriage was a central component. This suggests that *kadhi*s sought a solution for the benefit of the entire community rather than individuals.

A key concept of a Muslim marriage, the husband's role as the sole provider, enabled wives to instigate the dissolution of their marriage. Court records provide little context to explain why wives sought divorce. In some cases, it appears that the wife must have had a new partner in mind, as a remarriage occurred soon after her divorce. The frequency of divorce suggests that most wives were financially independent within marriage. They regarded *khul*ʿ as an investment in remarriage, which they rarely sought for financial support but for social respectability and affection.

An important factor of the relative ease with which partners seemed to split was the arranged nature of marriage. Custom prevented women and men from eschewing the tie that elders wanted them to forge. Yet because of the arranged nature of marriage, Zanzibari society accepted that once daughters and sons had obeyed their parents' wish, they sought means to mould marriage in their individual interests, also considering the option of divorce. Hence in many cases, marriage was but a temporary compliance, defying elders' plans of securing socioeconomic interests.

Regarding the material implications of divorce, the evidence only occasionally reveals how women raised the money with which they compensated their husband or which resources allowed them to generously renounce their deferred dower and maintenance debts. We know that, at least sometimes, these resources were relatives; sometimes wives borrowed money or sold property. *Khul*ʿ arrangements seem to have been an essential component of the prevailing "culture of indebtedness,"[135] in which money tied people together but also disrupted networks of trust. In the first half of the twentieth century, Zanzibaris did not question the option of divorce, but female and male understandings of its nature differed considerably. *Kadhis* facilitated the separation of spouses, showing the interconnectedness of legal, economic, and social dimensions, with remarriage being the aim of all actors.

135 Thomas F. McDow, "Where Credit Is Due: Zanzibar and the Limits of Indian Ocean Cosmopolitanism" (Paper presented at the workshop Shifting the Meaning: Time, Space, Connectivity and its Challenges in the Western Indian Ocean, Berlin, May 21–23, 2007).

PART III

9

The *Kadhis*, Ethnicity, and the Perpetuation of Master–Slave Relations

In 1945, almost fifty years after the abolition of slavery in the protectorate, a woman called Panya bt. Fundi asked in disbelief whether a master could inherit from his slave. Pursuing Panya's question, this chapter examines Islam, ethnicity, and the perpetuation of master–slave relations as the main vectors in the processes of inclusion and exclusion during the first half of the twentieth century. It propounds that two key tools for the social exclusion of slaves, their assumed kinlessness and illegitimate descent, help explain irreconcilable differences between them and their former masters. In the nineteenth century, ethnicity tended to coincide with an individual's degree of Islamisation. This categorisation, however, became blurred when ethnicity started to replace religion as the principle exclusionary marker. The processes that upheld the fundamental divide between freeborn and slave in the nineteenth century were replaced by an increasingly politicised ethnic identification during the first half of the twentieth century. Although former slaves and their descendants continued to maintain economic and social relations with their patrons within the evolving colonial class-based society, these relations point to fundamental differences in their understanding of social roles. These differences were politically exploited and made most apparent during the pogroms of the revolution in 1964. The *kadhis* were active agents in the process of ethnicisation, as differences in litigants' social, including ethnic, origin affected their judgements.

Slavery and Mechanisms of Social Inclusion and Exclusion

The expansion of commercial networks in the late eighteenth and early nineteenth centuries formed the basis for the Bū Saʿīdī dynasty's plantation economy, which depended on the socioeconomic system of slavery and was running firmly by the 1840s.[1] Slave owners were not uniform in terms of either social or ethnic background, with slaves adding value to their owners as personal dependants as much as labourers. Slave accumulation was not limited to wealthy plantation owners but also included men with little means, such as Mohammed Ramji, a milk seller, who provided for the manumission of his slaves upon his death, and women, who seem to have constituted a considerable proportion of slave owners. One Bint Kibari, wife of Usen b. Hamisi of Chwaka (most likely a fisherman or cultivator), bought a little girl, about eight years old, who was stolen from the Mrima coast in 1897.[2] Due to the increasing difficulties of many peoples on the coast and in the interior to cover their basic needs, individuals pawned members of kin, many of whom were taken to Zanzibar as slaves.[3] However, under Islamic law, individuals cannot be pawned but may serve as guarantors.

Wealthy Arabs, immigrants from Oman and their descendants, were the archetypical slave owners who sought to enhance their wealth, social esteem, and even piety through slaves. If they treated their slaves generously, these slaves were least likely to apply for a deed of freedom in court, as, for reasons of piety and prestige, their chance to be

[1] Frederick Cooper has provided the most detailed analysis of the establishment of the plantation economy (idem, *Plantation Slavery*, Chapter 2). See also Abdul Sheriff, "The Slave Mode of Production Along the East African Coast, 1810–1873," in *Slaves and Slavery in Muslim Africa*, vol. II, *The Servile Estate*, ed. John Ralph Willis (London: Frank Cass, 1985), 161–81.

[2] AB71/9, ZNA. For examples of female slave owners, see AB71/9; HC5/229; HC5/312; HC9/116; HC9/123; HC9/126; HC9/130; HC10/15; Entry #43, no number, 17 Dhū l-Ḥijja 1317/17 April 1900; Entry #220, no. 192, 20 Jumādā I 1318/15 September 1900; No entry #, no number, date of hearing 20 Ṣafar 1321/18 May 1903, HC28/29, ZNA. Cf. M. Reda Bhacker, *Trade and Empire in Muscat and Zanzibar: Roots of British Domination* (London: Routledge, 1992), 132.

[3] On the transition from pawning to slavery among the Mijikenda on the Kenyan coast, see Fred Morton, "Pawning and Slavery on the Kenya Coast: The Miji Kenda Case," in *Pawnship, Slavery, and Colonialism in Africa*, ed. Paul E. Lovejoy and Toyin Falola (Trenton, NJ: Africa World Press, 2003), 239–54. The issue of pawning is also thematised in Abdulrazak Gurnah, *Paradise* (London: Penguin, 1995).

manumitted by their owner was generally high. The indigenous, mostly agriculturalist, peoples of Zanzibar, the Hadimu and the Tumbatu, also had *suria*s and slaves as an agricultural workforce, such as Juma b. Khamis, described as "*khādim al-Tumbatu*,"[4] the slave of a Tumbatu. The social networks and offers of patronage of this second group of slave owners were less appealing and potent than those of Omani plantation owners, who were at the top of the social hierarchy. A third category of slave owners was formed of relatively poor craftspeople and petty traders, individuals barely socially superior to their slaves and thus extremely dependent on them.[5] Adopting their owner's concept of lavishness and social display, slaves themselves bought slaves as a way of compensating for their inferior status. Bahati bt. Baraka was a freed slave of Farhan, who himself was a freed slave of sayyid Nasir b. Saʿid.[6] Also, Mlange bt. Ngoro was the concubine of a slave and used to accompany the master of her master on journeys.[7]

Slaves were inherited from one generation to the next, from male heirs to female and vice versa. Most importantly, gender was not an impediment to asserting control over dependants. While Jonathon Glassman suggests that neither women nor slaves were full human and social beings in patriarchal Swahili institutions, Margaret Strobel points to the fact that the categories of slave and female did not necessarily coincide, as some women were slave owners.[8] Frederick Cooper also acknowledges the social acceptability of women as slave owners. He juxtaposes the Muslim matriarch and the secluded Muslim woman who could further increase her social status by accumulating dependants.[9] Although women acted under the constraints of purdah, slave ownership and property transactions in general show that women and men were equal economic actors. Thus the patriarchal structure

4 No entry #, no. 161, [8 Jumādā II 1320?/11 September 1902], HC28/29, ZNA.

5 Cf. Lyne, *Zanzibar*, 184; Prestholdt, *Domesticating the World*, 121.

6 HC5/312, ZNA, original in Arabic and English. On (former) slaves purchasing slaves themselves, see also McMahon, *Slavery and Emancipation*, 13, 42–43; Prestholdt, *Domesticating the World*, 142.

7 HC5/547, ZNA, original in English. Cf. Chapter 7.

8 Glassman, "The Bondsman's New Clothes," 292–93; Strobel, *Muslim Women*, 43.

9 Frederick Cooper, *From Slaves to Squatters*, 21–22; idem, "Islam and Cultural Hegemony;" idem, *Plantation Slavery*, 227.

FIGURE 9.1. Group of female ex-slaves. Courtesy of ZNA.

of the coastal societies should be understood as an ideal image rather than the actual social fabric.

Like their owners, slaves did not form a uniform socioeconomic group with common interests; some of them enjoyed considerable mobility in socioeconomic and geographical terms.[10] The English consulate records of freed slave sailors and travellers give evidence of hundreds of women and men who travelled as contract workers to places like Arabia and India and then returned to Zanzibar. The differentiation of slaves depended on their skills and space of work. Skills

[10] See Suzanne Miers and Igor Kopytoff, eds., *Slavery in Africa: Historical and Anthropological Perspectives* (Madison: University of Wisconsin Press, 1977), 48–49; Humphrey J. Fisher, *Slavery in the History of Muslim Black Africa* (London: Hurst, 2001), 177; William Gervase Clarence-Smith, *Islam and the Abolition of Slavery* (London: Hurst, 2006), 2–3. On the four categories of slaves and their ambiguous, constantly shifting boundaries, see Glassman, "The Bondsman's New Clothes," 290–91. Janet Ewald argues that the forced mobility of slave labour explains why slavery flourished in the nineteenth-century northwestern Indian Ocean. Idem, "Crossers of the Sea: Slaves, Freedman, and other Migrants in the Northwestern Indian Ocean, c. 1750–1914," *American Historical Review* 105, no. 1 (2000): 69–91.

such as craftsmanship and trading increased the status of slaves. Those being closer to their owners, thus in the house, were valued higher than those working on plantations. Receiving better treatment, house slaves were less likely to seek freedom.[11] *Mtumishi*s belonged to the category of house slaves, like *suria*s, and were trusted by their mistresses and masters. Among the most trusted slaves were *mzalia*s, slaves born in the owner's house. Female *mzalia*s worked there but also accompanied their mistress or their master's wife to social gatherings and travelled with her. The role of a male *mzalia* was similar; he washed his master's clothes, did shopping, and, if he was a trained craftsperson, he was allowed to keep the profit he made but might have given a part to his owner.[12] Another category of slaves, *kibarua*s, was hired out for labour on a daily wage.[13] While domestic slaves had the closest relations to owners, those being labourers in town had most independence.[14]

*Suria*s illustrate both the fluidity in the categories of slaves and the dependency of slaves on their masters. Called "Mamebwana" or "Mamebibie," mother of the master's son or daughter, a *suria* derived her improved social status towards her fellow slaves from her master and her offspring.[15] When she had given birth to her master's child, she could no longer be sold and became free upon her master's death. She could thus access any legacy set aside for her by her master.[16]

[11] *Africa: Correspondence Respecting Slavery and the Slave Trade in East Africa and the Islands of Zanzibar and Pemba*, no. 6 (London: Harrison & Sons, 1902), 4. On skilled artisans, see Frederick Cooper, *From Slaves to Squatters*, 186–87. Slaves were conscious of the different categories of their work and distinguished among themselves accordingly (Prins, *The Swahili-Speaking Peoples*, 69–70).

[12] Velten, "Sitten und Gebräuche," 71–74; Bakari, *Customs of the Swahili*, 172. Bakari defines a *mzalia* as one whose mother came from the interior and had a child with another slave. There was a distinction between first-generation and second-generation *mzalia*s, with the status of the seventh generation being that of a free person (idem, *Customs of the Swahili*, 170).

[13] Glassman, "The Bondsman's New Clothes," 291. Some of these slaves gave part of their daily income to their masters. The independence with which they acted could raise suspicion about their social status (Bennett, *History of the Arab State*, 118; Vianello and Kassim, *Servants of the Sharia*, 40–41).

[14] Frederick Cooper, *Plantation Slavery*, 184.

[15] Interviews with Bi Amina Abdulrahman Mahmud, 19 June 2004; Bi Mwanaidi Makame Ameir, 3 April 2004.

[16] See EI^2, s.v. "*umm al-walad*," and further s.v. " *'abd*." For the Swahili coast specifically, see Velten, "Sitten und Gebräuche," 73; Frederick Cooper, *Plantation Slavery*,

FIGURE 9.2. Imagined *suria*. Courtesy of ZNA.

Although the child of a *suria* followed her or his father's social status and was thus free, this did not necessarily imply that *suria*s and their children were socially accepted. When Riadu bt. ʿUthman made it clear in 1909 that she was like a child to Addi b. Juma al-Zarʿa and not his *suria*, she hinted at the common practice of having a *suria* and at the negative connotation the status of *suria* implied.[17]

Along the coast differences existed with regard to the status of concubines. In Lamu, people believed that a slave mother contaminated her master's offspring, which accounted for the ambivalent status of her children.[18] In Zanzibar, *suria*s themselves tried to hide their status. In non-elite families, children of concubines tended to be stigmatised.

195–99. The Ibāḍī rules provide that an *umm al-walad* remains a slave save that the heirs have no right over her (Velten, "Sitten und Gebräuche," 73). On the Ibāḍī regulations for *suria*s, see further ʿAbdallāh b. Ḥumayyid al-Sālimī, *Jawhar al-niẓām fī ʿilmī al-adyān wa-l-aḥkām*, 2 vols., 11th ed. (s.l.: Sulayman and Ahmad al-Salimi, 1989), 327–31.

[17] HC9/82, ZNA, original in Arabic and English. Cf. below and Chapter 6. See also McMahon, *Slavery and Emancipation*, 209–18.

[18] Frederick Cooper, "Islam and Cultural Hegemony," 286–87.

Yet in the sultan's and *kadhi*s' families it was perfectly acceptable to have a *suria* as a mother. Fatma, the wife of *kadhi* Sh. Ṭāhir, for instance, was the child of a *suria*. *Kadhi*s such as Sh. Burhān had concubines, which illustrates that concubinage was socially and legally entrenched.[19]

Regardless of their ambiguous status in society, concubines seem to have been popular among men of all backgrounds since they enhanced their prestige and did not require the material investment due to wives. As in the case of Mlange bt. Ngoro, discussed in Chapter 7, masters perceived *suria*s' geographical mobility and kinlessness as an advantage, as the latter made them more dependent on their master.[20] Laura Fair, and Margaret Strobel more obliquely, have accounted for the vastly practised institution of concubinage as a decisive factor in the adaptability of ethnic identities.[21] I would stress the fact that because *surias* did not require a dower, this constituted men's underlying economic reason for concubinage. Ethnically "mixed" relations were a by-product of concubinage rather than its aim, as Chapter 6 has demonstrated that marriage between different races remained socially unacceptable.[22]

As Frederick Cooper has argued, the personal bond between master and slave, which characterised pre-nineteenth-century slavery, changed with the establishment of plantation slavery, which needed a more rigid underpinning and a more coercive form of master–slave relationship.[23] The emerging cleavage between the Omani oligarchy, or, more precisely, slave owners, and their slaves was informed by the understanding that a slave was socially excluded from those who were freeborn and had to remain so unless his or her master decided otherwise. The perception of slaves as producers further implied that they did not

[19] Interviews with Bi Mwanaidi Makame Ameir, 3 April and 24 June 2004; Bi Amina Abdulrahman Mahmud, 2 May 2004. See Miers and Kopytoff, *Slavery in Africa*, 33; Prestholdt, *Domesticating the World*, 140–41.

[20] Cf. Chanock, *Law, Custom and Social Order*, 165; Miers and Kopytoff, *Slavery in Africa*, 29.

[21] Fair, *Pastimes and Politics*, 97–99; Strobel, *Muslim Women*, 48–51.

[22] Cf. Bakari, *Customs of the Swahili*, 175.

[23] Frederick Cooper, *Plantation Slavery*, 6, 255; idem, "Problem of Slavery," 112. See also Glassman, "The Bondsman's New Clothes," 286, 298. Slave owners could coerce their slaves by corporal punishment and selling them at any time (Niese, *Personen- und Familienrecht*, 43–44).

have a right or the space to have families and participate in social institutions.

Different perceptions between master and slave as to the possibility of doing away with the divide between free persons and slaves account for an underlying and persistent tension in their relationship, which was compounded by Islamic doctrines. Although slaves succeeded in negotiating their terms of participation, as Jonathon Glassman and others have clearly demonstrated, there remained an unbridgeable difference in the conception of the role of the master and the slave between these two groups of actors. The authority and social superiority of the master was attached to his power of manumitting slaves and his advancement in religious education and practice, hence in civilisation, of which Islam formed the underlying structure on the coast. Slaves and slave owners constantly struggled over and navigated between Islamic ideals of equality and Swahili notions of social hierarchy. The equality of all Muslims purported by the Qurʾan put the hierarchical order of Swahili societies at stake.[24]

Although Islamic doctrines do away with inequalities among Muslims based on race and social origin, at the same time they offer an inherent potential for differentiation based on notions of piety and social norms.[25] Differences in religious practices and knowledge were distinguishing criteria in Zanzibari society during the nineteenth and the twentieth centuries. Religion originally was the dividing line between master and slave, and between civilised and uncivilised, and thus ideologically separated the Muslim coast from the non-Muslim interior. In the late nineteenth century, the English explorer John Hanning Speke reported how slaves bought in Zanzibar were circumcised, taught to distinguish between clean and unclean animals, learned some Arabic words, and went on the hajj.[26] This attests to some effort by masters to introduce slaves to their religion, such as by making them understand the Islamic principle of ritual cleanliness; it also attests to

[24] See Kresse, "'Swahili Enlightenment?'," 297.

[25] For an exploration of this contradiction in the Swahili context, see Jonathon Glassman, "Stolen Knowledge: Struggles for Popular Islam on the Swahili Coast, 1870–1963," in *Islam in East Africa: New Sources, (Archives. Manuscripts and Written Historical Sources. Oral History. Archaeology), International Colloquium, Rome, 2–4 December 1999*, ed. Biancamaria Scarcia Amoretti (Rome: Herder, 2001).

[26] Speke 1863, xxv–vi, xxviii, cited in Fisher, *Slavery*, 65.

the efforts of slaves to adopt their masters' religion to enhance their status.

Slaves sought social inclusion through adopting and consequently adapting the social code of Islam, through which they accessed a means towards becoming equal to their owners.[27] By converting to Islam, slaves could diminish the inferiority of their status and explore Islam's tools of universality and equality for their own ends. The huge appeal of Islam, at least theoretically, was its compatibility with any ethnic origin and descent. The largest ethnic groups among Ng'ambo residents, Yao, Makonde, Zaramo, and Nyamwezi, were either born Muslim or converted soon after reaching Zanzibar.[28] Most Nyasa, Yao, and Manyema arrived as slaves, while Zaramo were both migrants and slaves. The distinction between slave descendants, mainland migrants, and indigenous islanders would become crucial in politicised rhetoric by the 1930s.[29] As discussed in Chapter 4, among those who addressed the *kadhi*'s courts were many former slaves and immigrants from the mainland who sought to express their belonging to a Muslim community and their religious equality by seeking not only legal redress at a core Islamic institution but also social inclusion through it.

The enslaver achieved the cultural subordination of the enslaved through his or her loss of ancestry.[30] Masters and mistresses stressed slaves' status as outsiders by giving them names distinct from their own and those of the indigenous population. To achieve this purpose, they invented names (Sw. *majina ya kupangapanga*),[31] as only free-born people could have names from the Qur'an. Slaves were given names of days of the week (Juma), precious stones (Almasi, Feruz), and synonyms of the material value they brought their masters, such

27 Cf. Frederick Cooper, *Plantation Slavery*, 215–18; idem, *From Slaves to Squatters*, 165; idem, "Islam and Cultural Hegemony," 276. On the social exclusion of ex-slaves who continued with non-Islamic practices, see Patricia Romero, "'Where Have All the Slaves Gone?' Emancipation and Post-Emancipation in Lamu, Kenya," *Journal of African History* 27, no. 3 (1986): 507. Sufism often served for the religious articulation of slaves. See August Nimtz, *Islam and Politics in East Africa: The Sufi Order in Tanzania* (Minneapolis: University of Minnesota Press, 1980).

28 Myers, "Reconstructing Ng'ambo," 136.

29 Glassman, *War of Words*, 108–23.

30 Frederick Cooper, "Problem of Slavery," 124.

31 Interviews with Bi Amina Abdulrahman Mahmud, 19 June 2004; Bi Hadija Nasoro Ibrahim, 17 June 2004. In a similar vein, on the mainland slaves were not addressed by their name but by "you" (Bakari, *Customs of the Swahili*, 173).

as benefit and profit (Faida), the cost (Arobaini), or what their masters hoped they would bring them, like blessing (Baraka, Heri).[32] Bi Amina Abdulrahman Mahmud remembers *kadhi* Sh. Burhān's slaves as Mama Andikalo (Mother "Write It"), Mama Hairudi (Mother "It Does Not Return"), Mama Hayasemeki (Mother "It Cannot Be Said"), and Mama Sitoambia (Mother "I Cannot Say").[33] Bearing names of an inanimate nature, slaves were constantly reminded that their owners did not regard them as human beings but as things. Moreover, owners did not allow slaves to take their name, as this would have enhanced the slave's social status.[34] In Zanzibar, the strong embeddedness of an increasingly chattel-like master–slave relationship preempted the possibility of a slave being called the son of his master.

To enhance social integration, slaves adopted respectable Islamic names upon manumission. A list of slaves freed between 1874 and 1907 shows both invented and Qur'anic names, names of the Prophet's family and his companions like Amina, Fatuma, Isa, and Omar.[35] Muhammad al-Swahili[36] chose the name of the Prophet when he was freed. Runaway slaves and criminals were also known for changing their names and others did so without any apparent reason.[37] As shown below in the discussion of the impact of bureaucratisation on ethnicisation, names served only as contextual and temporary indications of identities.

Although slaves appropriated markers of status of the *mwungwanas*, such as by adopting Islam, accumulating slaves and objects, and changing their names upon manumission, the stigma of illegitimacy and kinlessness was a mechanism that impeded the social mobility of ex-slaves decades after the abolition. The freeborn associated "the

[32] Frederick Cooper, "Islam and Cultural Hegemony," 289; Prestholdt, *Domesticating the World*, 122, 135; Vianello and Kassim, *Servants of the Sharia*, 41.

[33] "Mother" is used here for respect. Interviews with Bi Amina Abdulrahman Mahmud, 2 May, 19 May, and 19 June 2004; Bi Hadija Nasoro Ibrahim, 17 June 2004.

[34] Interviews with Bi Amina Abdulrahman Mahmud, 19 June 2004; Bi Mwanaidi Makame Ameir, 3 April 2004. Also deeds of sale from Brava usually mention slaves as chattel or speaking things rather than by their names (Vianello and Kassim, *Servants of the Sharia*, 60). However, ex-slaves' adoption of their former owner's name has been recorded in Lamu and Massawa (Romero, "'Where Have All the Slaves Gone?,'" 508; Miran, *Red Sea Citizens*, 254).

[35] AB71/9, ZNA. Cf. Vianello and Kassim who have found that slaves were given Muslim names by their owners (idem, *Servants of the Sharia*, 41).

[36] Entry #196, no. 150, 6 Jumādā I 1318/1 September 1900, HC28/29, ZNA.

[37] Bakari, *Customs of the Swahili*, 14–15.

kinless slave" with illegitimacy, as a child, whose father's name was unknown, was illegitimate.[38] *Sheha* Salih Pandu Sheha ascribed illegitimacy, and thus lack of genealogy, to the status of slaves in an inheritance case of 1940. The father of the female plaintiff was a slave, who, to the concern of *sheha* Salih, had not married "among us" and fathered an indecent woman. In addition to the freeborn and their descendants drawing a persistent divide between themselves and those of slave origin, they regarded slaves as a group among themselves who did not procreate.[39] By recognising slaves as individuals lacking any social ties, owners claimed the right to rebuild these ties from scratch and ensured the dependency of their slaves on them.

Slaves confirmed their masters' understanding of the kinless slave to achieve social integration. Rehani b. Ngoro, for instance, had told his masters that he had no relatives in Zanzibar, while others testified that he had siblings on the island. According to the son of his master, Rehani provided for the grandchildren of his master to inherit.[40] The master narrative invented by slave owners suggests that slaves were taken to Zanzibar bare of all ties to relatives and were thus socially dependent on both their fellow slaves and their masters, who provided them with a new social identity. On the one hand, the understanding of the freeborn that slaves did not have kin was disadvantageous, as it impeded slaves from establishing claims of inheritance from kin. On the other hand, slaves used this understanding as it integrated them more firmly into their owner's family and social networks.

Court records suggest that in some instances siblings were enslaved; according to the marriage register, *khādima* Binti Seif Hamud, still defined as a slave in 1930, was given into marriage by her father.[41] In 1934, Mawlidi bt. Sudi told the court that she lived on the *shamba*

[38] Interview with Sh. Abdalla Suleiman Jumbe, 22 June 2004.

[39] HC10/741, ZNA. For masters' insistence on the absence of kin ties of their slaves, see also HC5/547; HC10/1451, ZNA; interviews with Rashid Omar Sharif, 9 April 2004; Bi Mwanaidi Makame Ameir, 3 April and 24 June 2004; Bi Hadija Nasoro Ibrahim, 24 April 2004. On the meaning of the slave family for slaves and slave owners, see Frederick Cooper, *Plantation Slavery*, 220–25. That slave women indeed had children is established by McMahon, *Slavery and Emancipation*, 56–57.

[40] HC5/547, ZNA, original in English. See Chapter 7. Also in Lamu, most ex-slaves pointed out that they were both kinless and landless (Romero, "'Where Have All the Slaves Gone?,'" 509).

[41] HC5/547; HC5/575; HC10/741; HC10/1451, ZNA. The presence of a brother or sister of a former slave is also alleged in HC5/312, ZNA; Sample of Marriage Registers, 1930, *Mambo Msiige*. See also McMahon, *Slavery and Emancipation*, Chapter 6.

of *kadhi* Sh. Saʿīd b. Rashīd al-Ghaythī as he was her master, while her father lived near this *shamba*.[42] These networks of kinship were certainly not vast, but, exceptionally, some slaves might have had a familiar person and protection available in an otherwise oppressive and exploitative social environment.

The notion of kin and the social importance attached to its absence are key explanatory factors in understanding Zanzibar's social history of the nineteenth and twentieth centuries. The pivotal strategy of slaves to achieve social integration was through fictive kinship of their master's kin group.[43] The term "*jamaa*" was used to indicate membership in a social network rather than kinship, and (former) slaves defined themselves as *jamaa* of their master in situations such as court proceedings, in which they sought to be recognised through their owner's respected social status.[44] Other references to servile status shortly after the abolition of slavery were less euphemistic. Nafasi, *khādima* of *kadhi* Sh. Aḥmad b. Sumayṭ, sued Mwaliza bt. Saʿid, freed slave of Mzee b. Muallim, for Rs. 30, the remainder of the value of a house.[45] Another record reveals that with the permission of her mistress, one Safarani sued for divorce because of her husband's continuous absence.[46] Even more intriguingly, in another case Muhammad b. ʿAbdallah allowed his slave to represent himself in court so he could sue *sharīf* Muhammad b. ʿAbdallah for Rs. 10, house rent.[47] Unless a case of sharing the same name, this suggests that the slave obtained permission to sue his own master.

The complex roles of slaves and ex-slaves in court are further captured in an entry of 1904, which reveals that a certain Feruzi b. Songoro was represented in court by a *wakīl*, who was called ʿAbdallah b. Juma and was a *mawlā* of al-Jahadim, one of the Omani kin groups. Feruzi was probably either of slave origin or from one of the indigenous peoples of the islands and drew on the services of a *mawlā*,

42 HC10/79, ZNA.

43 See Frederick Cooper, *Plantation Slavery*, 194, 214. See also Miers and Kopytoff, *Slavery in Africa*, 39–40, on how the master's socioeconomic position affected the opportunities of slaves.

44 HC5/547, ZNA, original in English. This case refers to the *jamaa* of the notorious Zanzibari slave trader Tippu Tip.

45 No entry #, no. 82, 17 Dhū l-Qaʿda 1320/15 February 1903, HC28/29, ZNA.

46 Entry #43, no number, 17 Dhū l-Ḥijja 1317/17 April 1900, HC28/29, ZNA.

47 No entry #, no. 92, 19 Dhū l-Qaʿda 1320/17 February 1903, HC28/29, ZNA.

a former slave socially defining himself as belonging to an Omani.[48] That one Zaynab bt. Mabruk presented herself as manumitted slave of Salim b. Suleiman al-Marhubi suggests that she expected to enhance a favourable outcome of her claim by referring to her former master.[49] In addition to slave owners' responsibility for the treatment of slaves in case of illness, providing building material and clothes as well as acting as guardians in marriage,[50] slaves obtained considerable advantages when they were part of their owners' *jamaa*. They could bargain for the type of labour they would engage in, would have easier access to land and *wakīl*s, and would be allowed to represent themselves in court.

The Abolition of Slavery and Its Socioeconomic Ramifications

As plantations were a vital component of the economic structure of the protectorate, the colonial government sought to achieve the abolition of slavery in a way that would cause least disruption to the existing system. The measures adopted for the suppression of slavery prior to the enactment of the Abolition Decree of 1897 were directed against the traffic in slaves rather than the elimination of domestic slavery.[51] There was no consensus among colonial officials as how to achieve abolition. Abolitionists in England were in favour of more immediate measures than officers on the ground, such as Lloyd Mathews, first minister to the sultan from 1891 to 1901, and Arthur Hardinge, consul and administrator general from 1895 to 1901. Both were good friends with the ruling elite and afraid that abolition would uproot the socioeconomic foundation of the protectorate, thus causing the Arab oligarchy to turn against the British. Their recognition of Arab interests materialised in their advocacy of the gradual abolition of slavery.[52]

48 HC9/115, ZNA. A few months later, ʿAbdallah b. Juma also appeared as *wakīl*, *mawlā* of al-Jahadim (HC9/120, ZNA).

49 Entry #22, no number, 25 Dhū l-Qaʿda 1317/27 March 1900, HC28/29, ZNA.

50 Bakari, *Customs of the Swahili*, 171; Frederick Cooper, *Plantation Slavery*, 163–64.

51 Memorandum on slavery, n. d., AB71/4, ZNA.

52 AB71/4, ZNA; Hollingsworth, *Zanzibar under the Foreign Office*, 135, cited in Lofchie, *Zanzibar*, 60. For an account of British ideologies towards slavery, see Frederick Cooper, *From Slaves to Squatters*, Chapter 2.

Sultan Ḥamūd made an important concession to the British by issuing the decree abolishing the legal status of slavery in 1897. This decree provided for claims between former masters and slaves to be taken to district courts and entitled ex-masters to compensation. It also stipulated that concubines could ask for the dissolution of the relationship to their master on the grounds of cruelty.[53] The series of abolition decrees was completed with the Slavery Decree of 1909, which allowed former slaves to claim compensation until December 1911. The grounds on which a former slave could claim compensation were her or his inability to earn a living and the ex-master's or mistress's refusal of the support that she or he previously had to provide (food, accommodation, and sick care). The decree of 1909 did not grant concubines – although they were technically free – the right to leave their master, unless they were prepared to forgo their rights.[54]

As Islamic law only recognises manumission by the owner, any deed of freedom slaves obtained in court was void for Muslims. Hence the fact that some slaves sought manumission in court as others were emancipated by their masters created friction among slaves. Slaves manumitted by their owner initially despised the so-called slaves of the government.[55] This term appears to have had two meanings: literally, that the slave had obtained freedom in court and, metaphorically, that the slave was pursuing social rights by claiming work from the manumitter, the government.[56] Many older ex-slaves especially had to turn to the government for help, demanding work.[57] Thus appealing to colonial officers for protection, the client–patron relationship continued.

Although slavery was finally abolished in 1909, social notions of clientage persisted along the coast. Generosity was an essential feature

[53] Decree 1 Dhū l-Qaʿda 1314/7 April 1897, BA14/25, ZNA.

[54] Decree No. 11 of 1909, BA14/1, ZNA.

[55] *Africa: Correspondence Respecting Slavery*, 22.

[56] For the literal meaning see ibid.; Frederick Cooper, *From Slaves to Squatters*, 76. On the work demands towards the manumitter, see Lyne, *Zanzibar*, 186–87; *Africa: Correspondence Respecting Slavery*, 15; Hardinge to the Marquess of Salisbury, 9 April 1900, Private papers, Sir John Gray, Add. 7739, box 25, CUL. *Mateka* was the Swahili term used for slaves freed in court – a term that originally designated slaves who were emancipated by Europeans from slave ships (Frederick Cooper, *From Slaves to Squatters*, 76; Glassman, *Feasts and Riot*, 107–108).

[57] Abd Hamid, "Unfinished Business," 160; Salim, *Swahili-Speaking Peoples*, 114.

of the qualities of patrons and a means of tying dependants to them, such as by allowing them to squat on their land.[58] Patronage prevailed when descendants of former slaves did not get married without the permission of the descendants of their former masters, and concubinage with the female descendants of former slaves was continuously practised.[59] The duty of giving daughters of clients and squatters into marriage continued at least until 1950, when the marriage registers recorded that two patrons acted as guardians in marriage.[60]

Patronage also manifested itself in form of estate owners paying for the funeral of labourers dying at work, noted as late as 1957.[61] Additionally, former slave owners became liable for their ex-slaves to show their continuous potency. They acted as guarantors, went on bail, and gave testimony in favour of their clients in court.[62] Vice versa, former slaves were willing to act as witnesses for their owners' descendants.[63] From the point of view of the patron, ongoing relations with clients provided for the exercise of power, authority, and social duty, whereas for the clients they opened an opportunity to demand rights. The interchangeability of the partners in this symbiosis resembles a seesaw, well exemplified by the term "*mawlā*," which can refer to both mistress/master and slave.[64] Islam, the religion of the slave owners and ideological foundation of their economic system, in social terms represented a status to which slaves and former slaves aspired. Yet at the same time, Islamic doctrines justified their social and

58 Generosity, if not to say lavishness, was noted by Western observers (Lloyd Mathews to Arthur Hardinge, 17 March 1899, Private papers, Sir John Gray, Add. 7739, box 13, CUL; British Resident Rankine to Philip Cunliffe-Lister, 16 January 1933, CO 618/55/19, NAK; Lyne, *Zanzibar*, 222). On squatting as a frequent act of piety, see Bakari, *Customs of the Swahili*, 176.

59 Schacht, "Notes on Islam," 111–12. On the social ties between the descendants of freed slaves and those of the former master regarding wedding and funeral ceremonies, see Prins, *The Swahili-Speaking Peoples*, 70.

60 Sample of Marriage Registers, 1950, *Mambo Msiige*; see also Frederick Cooper, *From Slaves to Squatters*, 91.

61 Bennett, *History of the Arab State*, 218.

62 HC5/229, original in English; HC9/67; HC9/69; HC9/124; HC10/15; Entry #634, no number, 2 Jumādā II [1319]/15 September 1901, HC28/29, ZNA.

63 HC9/119; HC10/48, ZNA. In Lamu, former slaves supported former masters with food, helped them financially, and also worked for them (Romero, "'Where Have All the Slaves Gone?,'" 502, 506, 511).

64 For the etymology of this term and its historical use in Muslim societies, see *EI*², s.v. "*mawlā*."

physical exploitation.[65] The moral economy invoked by slaves, peasants, and workers during protests also played out in court, where options of suing social superiors enabled slaves to differentiate themselves from their fellows.[66]

The relationship between former slaves and owners primarily continued for economic reasons, exemplified in the following case. On 10 March 1900, Faraji b. Abeidi, freed slave of Mwana Tumu bt. Kombo, bought a *shamba* for $27 from Khelef b. ʿAli al-Mawli. When Faraji died in 1918, his wives claimed his estate, two *shamba*s. In court they learned that their late husband had sold one *shamba* to Mwana Asha bt. ʿUmar, a paternal niece of his mistress, and that the other was in the hands of an Indian, Ismail D(a)ramsi. The economic relations among these three were not recent, as Faraji had previously sued Mwana Asha for a debt, and Ismail D(a)ramsi had advanced credit to Faraji for coconuts he bought from his *shamba*s. When Faraji bought the second *shamba* he borrowed Rs. 100 from Ismail, for which the latter wanted Faraji's other *shamba* as security. Faraji, however, could not mortgage it, as he had already written it over to Mwana Asha, who would stand surety for the loan.[67] Although relations ranged from male ex-slaves acting as representatives for their former mistresses to mistresses acting as guarantors for their slaves, the complexity of the economic relations between Faraji and his mistress suggests that the advancement of credit through fictitious transfers of property was the most important aspect in the perpetuation of their ties.

*Kadhi*s were instrumental in upholding post-abolition master–slave relations. For *kadhi*s as Muslims and members of the local elite, slavery was an intrinsic and uncontestable part of the social fabric. When

[65] Cf. François Constantin, "Leadership, Muslim Identities and East African Politics: Tradition, Bureaucratization and Communication," in *Muslim Identity and Social Change in Sub-Saharan Africa*, ed. Louis Brenner (Bloomington: Indiana University Press, 1993), 39–40.

[66] No entry #, no. 5020, 29 Ṣafar [1320]/6 June 1902; No entry #, no number, 25 Rajab 1320/27 October 1902; No entry #, no. 92, 19 Dhū l-Qaʿda 1320/17 February 1903, HC28/29, and possibly HC5/229, ZNA, original in English.

[67] HC5/229, ZNA, original in English. Faraji appeared as "slave of Binti Kombo Bajuni" on the deed of sale in 1900. These transactions are known as *bayʿ al-khiyār* and explored by Bishara, "Sea of Debt"; McMahon, *Slavery and Emancipation*, 102–103.

*kadhi*s adjusted their judgements to the social status of the litigants, the difference between freeborn and slave was the most decisive one. In court, former slaves were usually identified by their social status, thus as "slave of the government," "*khādim* of x," or "freed slave of y." "As one judge remarked: 'It is not a little startling that in a Mombasa Court in 1922 one can still hear such phrases as "she is my slave," "the owner of a slave" spoken apparently in all seriousness.'"[68] Giving testimony about disturbances in Zanzibar in 1936, *kadhi* Sh. Ṭāhir stated that one of its instigators, "Sheni is a Swahili and is considered an Arab slave. Because he has got a job from the Government he pretends he is an important person, but they know that he was once an Arab slave."[69] He thereby bluntly indicated his understanding of slaves as being inferior beings. So did *kadhi* Saʿīd b. Rashīd al-Ghaythi in 1941, when he referred to Feruz as slave of Sh. Saʿid b. Nasir al-Khanjiri in a letter to the latter.[70] When talking to each other, former slave owners still referred to their clients as slaves as late as the 1940s. Both in Mombasa and in Zanzibar, *kadhi*s applied Islamic legal principles that gave former masters shares of inheritance from the estate of their ex-slaves.

*Kadhi*s' continuous application of the master–slave relationship was linked to their ownership of slaves, which made them likely to sympathise with other slave owners and their descendants, many of whom were their equals in social rank. The equation of high social status with ownership of a considerable number of slaves is embodied in the Amawī family. *Kadhi* Sh. ʿAbd al-ʿAzīz b. ʿAbd al-Ghanī al-Amawī (1838–1896) had eleven female slaves, among whom was at least one *suria*. As a pious Muslim, he arranged for the manumission of these slaves upon his death. His son Sh. Burhān also owned slaves, about six to ten slaves from the mainland (Nyasa, Yao, Nyaturu, and Manyema) and a *suria* who he must have acquired himself, as he did not inherit his father's slaves. The *yaya* of his son Mohamed was one of his slaves.[71] Yet *kadhi*s were not unanimous in their approach to slavery. Among

68 Strobel, *Muslim Women*, 51.
69 Interrogation of Sh. Tahir bin Abibakr al-Amawi, CO 618/65/9, NAK.
70 HC10/761, ZNA.
71 Interviews with Bi Amina Abdulrahman Mahmud, 2 May, 19 May, and 19 June 2004.

the Ibāḍī *kadhi*s, Sh. ʿAli b. Msellum al-Khalasy openly opposed the abolition of slavery in 1909.[72] His colleague Sh. ʿAlī b. Muḥammad al-Mundhirī, however, endorsed the emancipation of slaves by non-Muslims and supported the right of the government to dismiss *kadhi*s if they failed to comply with this regulation.[73]

The complicity between *kadhis* and judges in perpetuating the divide between former slave owners and slaves is revealed by inheritance claims. In 1945, in a letter to the secretary of the African Association, the aforementioned Panya bt. Fundi posed the revealing question whether a master could inherit from his slave ("Can a master heris [sic] slave?").[74] She was puzzled and angered by the fact that decades after the abolition of slavery, the descendants of former masters were entitled to the estate of former slaves of their family. Shortly after Panya had inherited the estate of her maternal aunt, Tabia bt. Sudi, ʿAbdallah b. Nasor al-Miskeri sued for his share in this estate. He claimed that the deceased was his maternal aunt and *yaya*, as his mother, Hali ya Watu bt. Sudi, a Manyema and the *suria* of his father, was the sister of the deceased. ʿAbdallah's witnesses testified to the kinship between him and the late Tabia according to what they had heard from the deceased herself. As Panya's witnesses gave evidence based on hearsay, Ibāḍī *kadhi* Sh. Saʿīd b. Rashīd al-Ghaythī ruled that the evidence of ʿAbdallah received precedence.[75] Thus for Sh. Saʿīd, Panya's kinship to Tabia was not established. Ibāḍī rules, like other schools of law, declare that an illegitimate child can inherit from his or her mother but not from the father. By declaring ʿAbdallah illegitimate, the *kadhi* confirmed his right to inherit "from his mother by virtue of lineage."[76] Concubinage was a widespread and lawful practice before abolition. It is revealing that by 1945, it was construed as illegitimate,

[72] Pouwels, *Horn and Crescent*, 191.

[73] Strobel, *Muslim Women*, 52.

[74] Panya to the Honorary Secretary, The African Association, 8 June 1945, HC5/575, ZNA, original in English. For a discussion of this question in West Africa's Niger Bend, see Hall, *History of Race*, 238.

[75] Panya's two witnesses claimed to know the deceased personally from Nyamwezi country, while one of ʿAbdallah's witnesses got to know the relationship between the deceased and ʿAbdallah from his and ʿAbdallah's father (HC10/1451, ZNA).

[76] Memorandum by Sh. Saʿid b. Rashid, n. d., HC5/575, ZNA, original in Arabic and English. In a case of 1940, the same *kadhi* held an allegation of illegitimacy as detestable (HC10/741, ZNA).

which ran counter to the general reluctance to acknowledge any illegitimate descent, and thus entitled to inheritance. The *wakīl*s of both Panya and ʿAbdallah agreed that the latter was the maternal nephew of Tabia and therefore a legitimate heir. In his appeal judgement, John Gray reiterated that an illegitimate child could only inherit from his or her mother and confirmed the *kadhi*'s judgement. No one, including Judge Gray, doubted that the legitimate child of a *suria* and her master was entitled to inherit from his mother, termed illegitimate offspring in post-abolition discourse. For Panya, however, the son of a slave owner and a slave remained a master.[77]

I would argue that, in addition to Frederick Cooper's elaboration of the continuation of master–slave relations via access to land and food, claims of inheritance were contentious manifestations of patronage and clientage. It seems that the social networks of security, selling and buying, representation and witnessing in court as well as acting as guarantors and guardians in marriage continued to be shaped to a great extent by relations among individuals, while the importance of relations between individuals and the state increased simultaneously. Justin Willis has advanced the crucial argument that Mombasa's social structure at the end of the nineteenth century was still based on individual's relationships to other individuals rather than to the state.[78] During the colonial period men and women increasingly identified along the lines of class, as Frederick Cooper and Laura Fair have accounted for. Fair argues that landowners' demands for higher rent partly explain the identification of Ng'ambo residents as a class, "the poor." Yet it seems that an emerging class identity did not completely replace the previously preponderant social ties along clientage.[79] Whether men and women identified themselves as members of a class or as patrons and clients depended on whether they sought to benefit from the colonial state or individual networks.

Kadhi's Courts and the Ethnicisation of Social Identities

Scholarly debates about social identities in Zanzibar have been dominated by arguments for the precolonial existence of a racial

77 HC5/575, ZNA, original in Arabic and English.
78 Willis, *Mombasa*, 74.
79 Fair, *Pastimes and Politics*, 111.

consciousness on the one hand and its emergence in the course of the colonial period on the other.[80] Frederick Cooper observed that coastal peoples were not free from a colour bias that, for instance, was reflected in the different prices paid for slaves. Yet he asserted that race was not indicative of a person's status or group affiliation prior to the establishment of the colonial state.[81] Alamin Mazrui and Ibrahim Noor Shariff have argued that racial categories became more rigid under colonial rule, while Laura Fair has shown how Zanzibaris utilised these categories for their own advantage.[82] It is now well established that the colonial state overemphasised the correlation between ethnic identities and economic roles, thereby contributing to a reification of identities. While earlier scholarship paid more attention to the agency of the colonial state, most recently, Jonathon Glassman has foregrounded the role of Zanzibari intellectuals in promoting racial ideas in the first half of the twentieth century.[83]

Conscious changes in identities to raise one's esteem have been documented since the midnineteenth century, when slaves adopted the term "*uungwana*," or freeborn. With this term being appropriated by the socially marginalised, the freeborn adopted the more prestigious identification "*ustaarabu*." While *uungwana* is a Swahili term of Bantu origin, *ustaarabu* equates civilisation with Arabisation and thus locates the ideal of social origin in the Arab world rather than the Muslim world more broadly. Thereby, the freeborn created a new barrier between themselves and (freed) slaves, who would find it difficult to amend their lack of genealogy – a social stigma that implied

80 Pearce has advanced the non-existence of a racial hierarchy prior to British rule (idem, *Zanzibar*, 158). For a historical analysis that deemphasises ethnicity in Pemba, see McMahon, *Slavery and Emancipation*.

81 Frederick Cooper, *Plantation Slavery*, 124, 167–68, 267. For a nuanced archaeological approach to nineteenth-century identity formation, see Sarah Croucher and Stephanie Wynne-Jones, "People, Not Pots: Locally Produced Ceramics and Identity on the Nineteenth-Century East African Coast," *International Journal of African Historical Studies* 39, no. 1 (2006): 107–24.

82 See Alamin M. Mazrui and Ibrahim Noor Shariff, *The Swahili: Idiom and Identity of an African People* (Trenton, NJ: Africa World Press, 1994); Fair, *Pastimes and Politics*.

83 Glassman, *War of Words*.

the lack of a protector. Given the opposition of freeborn and slave, the absence of slave descent became crucial to claiming Arabness.[84]

As claims of Middle Eastern descent became the most prestigious form of social identity, the trend in adopting and creating Arab *nisbas* gained increasing popularity in the twentieth century.[85] This trend proved more of a psychological remedy and a mechanism for moving up the social ladder than an accurate reproduction of paternal descent. The creation of a *nisba* was a tool of social assimilation as was the adoption of a Muslim name. In this endeavour, people created names that evoked desirable places.[86] Likewise, they used ethnicities as proper names, such as by Amur b. Mshirazi and Mwarabu al-Swahili (literally: the Arab-Swahili).[87] As Trimingham argued, the lack of an acceptable *nisba* stigmatised mainlanders who otherwise had become assimilated into coastal society,[88] whereas the adoption of Shirazi origin, for instance, increased their social esteem.

The Shirazi identity came to embody landownership in the twentieth century, particularly from the 1920s onwards when claims of Arab and Shirazi origin became more common, partly, due to government policies of taxation and property ownership and, more importantly, due to ethnicisation driven by Zanzibari intellectuals.[89] By the 1940s, and possibly earlier, the distinction between those of island and those

84 See Prestholdt, *Domesticating the World*, 140–42; Glassman, *Feasts and Riot*; idem, "Slower Than a Massacre: The Multiple Sources of Racial Thought in Colonial Africa," *American Historical Review* 109, no. 3 (2004): 720–54; idem, "Sorting Out the Tribes"; Trimingham, *Islam in East Africa*, 146; Pouwels, *Horn and Crescent*, 73–74. For newspaper discourses on *ustaarabu*, see Katrin Bromber, "*Ustaarabu*: A Conceptual Change in Tanganyikan Newspaper Discourse in the 1920s," in *The Global Worlds of the Swahili: Interfaces of Islam, Identity and Space in 19th and 20th-Century East Africa*, ed. Roman Loimeier and Rüdiger Seesemann (Berlin: Lit Verlag, 2006), 67–81.

85 Cf. Pouwels, *Horn and Crescent*, 129–30.

86 See Landberg, "Kinship and Community," 68; Prestholdt, *Domesticating the World*, 135.

87 HC10/55; Entry #181, no. 135, 24 Rabīʿ II 1318/20 August 1900, HC28/29, ZNA. On the Arabisation of patronyms, see also Willis, *Mombasa*, 188–89, 191. Cf. further Glassman "Sorting Out the Tribes," 411, where he briefly discusses conventions and choices by people in listing their names.

88 The invention of genealogies towards Arab descent was noted by Trimingham in 1964 (idem, *Islam in East Africa*, 144, 147).

89 Fair, *Pastimes and Politics*, 36, 39, 51–53. In *War of Words*, Glassman challenges the material incentive argument by placing emphasis on locally induced ethnicisation.

of mainland origin became reinforced via the adoption of a Shirazi identity, which implied stressing one's roots as an indigenous islander as opposed to being an immigrant from the mainland. By that time, colonial policies had broadened their previous non-native–native discourse to encompass more racial categories.[90]

Court cases confirm the identification of those referring to themselves as Shirazi, Tumbatu, or Hadimu through land ownership, either by suing for such or by listing their occupation as agriculturalists.[91] In 1902, Salama bt. ʿAli, a Tumbatu, sued ʿAli b. Khamis, a Swahili, for three papers: her mother's deed of manumission, the deed for a *shamba* that her father bought, and a paper containing details about the legacy of her father.[92] While the relationship between the two litigants remains unaccounted for, Salama clearly tried to lay claim to land rights and access resources. She supported this claim by referring to herself as Tumbatu, an identity she might have taken on herself or inherited from her father who had engaged in the transaction of land.

The adoption of a Shirazi identity proves that the predominance of Middle East–Arab values lingered on. In addition to the increase of those who identified themselves as Shirazi, court records as well as marriage and divorce registers attest to the continuous use of a Swahili identity among at least a small number of people.[93] When in the 1940s many people changed both their ethnic identity and their name, the ideal was to become more Arab, particularly as the term "Hadimu" is said to derive from the local Arabic term for slave, *khādim*.[94] During the nineteenth century, "Swahili" implied being Muslim, speaking Swahili and being freeborn of mixed African–Arab ancestry from any urban trade centre on the East African coast. In the later nineteenth

90 See Glassman, "Sorting Out the Tribes," 403–404. Abdul Sheriff and Chizuko Tominaga argue that class frictions across ethnic groups rather than racial divide account for the revolution (idem, "The Ambiguity of Shirazi Identity," 1–37).

91 HC10/1156; HC10/2822; HC10/2906; HC10/3033; HC10/3535; HC10/3552; HC10/5534, ZNA. This identification may be inferred in HC10/2884; HC10/3284; HC10/3302; HC10/3447, ZNA.

92 No entry #, no number, 7 Shaʿbān 1320/8 November 1902, HC28/29, ZNA.

93 HC10/42; HC10/48; HC10/761; HC10/981; HC10/1370; HC10/1451; HC10/2906; HC10/3097, ZNA. The plaintiff and the two defendants claimed a Swahili-Shirazi identity in HC10/5534, ZNA.

94 Frederick Cooper, *From Slaves to Squatters*, 286; Ibrahim Fokas Shao, "Land Tenure System and Land Reform in Zanzibar (1830s–1978)" (MA diss., University of Dar es-Salaam, 1978), 15.

century, the Hadimu and the Swahili became distinct in terms of residence and work. The Hadimu came to identify themselves as the indigenous peasants occupying the southeastern part of Zanzibar Island, whereas the Swahili became associated with freeborn Muslim Africans living in town. At the turn of the twentieth century, "Swahili" became a euphemism for slaves and ex-slaves, who had adopted coastal values such as Islam and *ustaarabu*.[95]

Drawing on precolonial consciousness of race and assertions of the fluidity of social identities, I would argue that the *kadhi*'s courts entrenched ethnic consciousness by pinning down litigants' social and ethnic origins. In addition to the increase of people in identifying themselves as Shirazi, which Glassman interprets as laying claim to Arabness,[96] I suggest that the continuous identification of Swahili offered an identity less directly associated with landownership but more with belonging to the coast in general, while simultaneously offering a *nisba*.[97]

Regardless of colonial attempts to bureaucratise ethnicity, men and women continuously applied a contextual understanding of their social and ethnic identities.[98] Instances of individuals changing their identity within the colonial bureaucracy and in front of colonial officers show that these attempts were unsuitable to the preponderance of multiple identities. In 1905, Mashavu bt. Musa appeared in the court records as both Tumbatu and Hadimu. In this restitution of conjugal rights case, Mashavu's two ethnicities seem to have been irrelevant to the case in which *kadhi* Sh. Burhān had to determine the validity of her marriage.[99] In a court record of 1942, Salima bt. Suleiman appeared as

[95] Fair, *Pastimes and Politics*, 35–36. See also Strobel, *Muslim Women*, 2, on "Swahili" as a euphemism for slave. For debates on Swahili identities, see Mazrui and Shariff, *The Swahili*; David Nurse and Thomas Spear, *The Swahili: Reconstructing the History and Language of an African Society, 800–1500* (Philadelphia: University of Pennsylvania Press 1985); W. Arens, "The *Waswahili*: The Social History of an Ethnic Group," *Africa* 45, no. 4 (1975): 426–38; Eastman, "Who Are the Swahili?"; James de Vere Allen, *Swahili Origins: Swahili Culture and the Shungwaya Phenomenon* (London: James Currey, 1993).

[96] Glassman, *War of Words*, 55. See also Frederick Cooper, *From Slaves to Squatters*, 158–72; Fair, *Pastimes and Politics*, 30–31, 36, 51–52.

[97] The three main founders of the National Party of the Sultan's Subjects considered themselves as Swahili (Lofchie, *Zanzibar*, 151).

[98] Cf. Fair, *Pastimes and Politics*; Glassman, "Sorting Out the Tribes," 401–403.

[99] HC9/121, ZNA.

Hadimu, which was crossed out and replaced by Shirazi,[100] most likely upon Salima's denial of being a Hadimu. For reasons unrecorded not only ethnicities but also patronyms were adjusted. After Saʿad Msellem al-Riyami's wife sued him for maintenance or divorce in May 1952, he swore an affidavit in March 1953 saying that his *nisba* so far had been given as al-Riyāmī but actually was al-Bū ʿAlī.[101]

Traditional practices account for children not being named at a specific time and receiving a new name after circumcision or if a misfortune occurred.[102] Mwana Khamis was known as Matata (literally: problem) after her jaundice but adopted the respectable name of Mwana Khamis as an adult; her sister changed her name from Chausiku, a name that bore the signs of slavery, to Mwana Idi. Their father was of mainland origin and most likely a freed slave.[103] One Asiya, also known as Akupalo bt. Salim b. Khamisi, a Shirazi, knew Salim b. Khamisi b. Mgeni, also a Shirazi who she claimed was her father, as Mwinyiabudu. Asiya's mother also had two names, Mtumwa, suggesting slave origin, and Mwana Mkuwa bt. ʿAli. After Asiya's misfortune, arguably a disease, her name was changed from Akupalo to Asiya.[104] The common habit of having two names was acknowledged by *kadhi* Sh. Muḥammad Sālim al-Rawwāḥī in a judgement of 1961.[105] Change of name indicates efforts to hide slave origin and to stress Islamic identity. *Kadhi*s, less familiar with names of mainland origin, tended to Arabise names, such as when Safarani appeared as Zafrān in the record,[106] while some women and men chose Islamic names for social integration and used those in court rather than the names by which they were known to kin and friends.

In addition to the fluidity of names, those of ethnic identities was an impediment to the establishment of claims in court, as *kadhi*s rejected arguments based on contradictory evidence. The aim of the colonial state to rule the protectorate along racial categories is reflected in its

[100] HC10/1010, ZNA.
[101] HC10/2881, ZNA. Cf. Chapters 5 and 8.
[102] Bakari, *Customs of the Swahili*, 14–15.
[103] HC10/48, ZNA.
[104] HC10/1435 ZNA. On the fluidity of names, see also HC10/3631, ZNA.
[105] HC10/3535, ZNA, original in English.
[106] Entry #43, no number, 17 Dhū l-Ḥijja 1317/17 April 1900, HC28/29, ZNA. On the Arabisation of non-Arabs to facilitate their participation in Indian Ocean trade networks, see Bishara, "Sea of Debt," 131–35.

increasing attention to the assertion of ethnicity, applied by the Arab elite in the administration and the courts. Yet court records bearing the litigant's ethnic identity and/or *nisba* indicate the importance of locating individuals in the social hierarchy well before the British provided for the registration of ethnicities. By the 1930s, racial categorisations were reflected in court in printed forms with rubrics for recording litigants' ethnic identities. By that time, it was rare for names to be listed without any reference to an ethnic identity, with *kadhi*s possibly calling witnesses and evidence to establish it.

Being part of the colonial machinery, the *kadhi*'s courts became active agents of the increasing ethnicisation of Zanzibari society. In 1933, the debate about *kabila*, or ethnicity, dominated the argumentation in a case heard before *kadhi* Sh. Ṭāhir, who asked for a certificate to confirm the Arab genealogy of Amur b. Mshirazi. The *kadhi* found the evidence satisfactory but held that "[d]ue to their *kabila* Shangani they are not Arabs, they are from *ahl* Swahili in Kenya as it is common."[107] Sh. Ṭāhir clearly applied his own perception of ethnic stratification, reinforced by the colonial social order of which he formed part. Thus *kadhi*s may have ruled against litigants who failed to provide an ethnically satisfactory genealogy. Litigants' social background had previously informed *kadhi*s' judgements, such as to determine shares of inheritance and ascertain equality between spouses. Given the increased range of ethnic identities and seeking to protect the status of the Muslim elite, *kadhi*s applied their and the colonial administration's racial hierarchy in which Arabs and indigenous islanders predominated over immigrants and former slaves.

As the entire bureaucratic apparatus was based on the assumption that Islamic law and custom governed the daily life of the people in the Zanzibar Protectorate, non-Muslims felt encouraged to adopt a Muslim identity, while colonial officers' association of certain mainland groups with Christianity and traditional religion made it more difficult for them to do so. The colonial bias in favour of the Arab and, more importantly, the colonial equation of Arab with Muslim was made explicit by Judge Reed, when he confirmed in 1925 that one Rupia b. Khamis was entitled to the residuary of an estate as there

[107] HC10/55, ZNA. Presumably Amur hailed from Shanga in the Lamu archipelago, thus "Shangani." See also HC10/741, ZNA.

were "no other Arabs of the father's side."[108] Ironically, Rupia was a freed slave and thus not an Arab in colonial view.

As "natives" were Muslim according to the colonial legal doctrine, there were no provisions for administering their estate according to any other than Islamic law. When a Sukuma woman, who was married according to Islamic law, left an estate, her heirs claimed she was not Muslim. The contested religious identity of the deceased became a concern to a *mudir*, who wanted to ensure the lawful division of this estate in 1962. The same *mudir* believed that the marriage of a Makonde couple, who appeared before him to settle a dispute, was wrongfully registered as Muslim.[109] The service of Arabs, who had their own biassed understanding of Islamic and ethnic (in)compatibility, in the colonial administration was an obstacle to be overcome by those who sought inclusion. Arabs contested mainlanders' claims to Muslim identity on ethnic grounds, although, theoretically, the word of a person who claimed to be Muslim had to be accepted. By the 1960s, the ethnicisation of Islam had become rampant.

Even though the Arab elite contested the degree to which former slaves could absorb Islamic principles, the evidence of oath taking questions their monopoly over Islam. As the most efficient component of Islamic rules of procedure, oath taking serves as an excellent index of Islamisation and demonstrates that slaves, who were not considered proper Muslims by the ruling strata, had absorbed the meaning of accepting or declining an oath. The process of oath taking entirely relies on a Muslim's conscience. The oath taker swears that he or she acts according to what is right, accepting that Allah will punish any wrongdoing. When Mchanakheir, *khādima* of Musa b. Hajj, sued Khamis b. Vuai for the dower, Rs. 20, and other unspecified rights from the estate of her husband in 1902, he acknowledged the dower debt but denied any other rights. As she could not provide proof for her inheritance claim, the *kadhi* ordered Khamis to take the oath to confirm that he did not know about any outstanding rights other than the dower. Khamis returned the oath to Mchanakheir and thereby confirmed her claim.[110] In another case of 1903, Bilal b. Juma, "slave of the government" and

[108] Minutes of appeal, H. Reed, 2 May 1925, HC5/312, ZNA.
[109] *Mudir maghrib* to district commissioner, 30 November 1962, AK13/41, ZNA.
[110] No entry #, no. 5020, 29 Ṣafar [1320]/6 June 1902, HC28/29, ZNA.

husband of Sitara, *khādima* of Mzee Musa, refused to take the oath in order to confirm that he had not beaten his wife. His refusal confirmed the beating and the divorce.[111] Hence an Islamic consciousness, though not necessarily advanced legal knowledge, was prevalent among those who addressed the courts. This suggests that already at the turn of the twentieth century, Islamisation was more extensive than acknowledged by the elite, who had created notions of religious impurity of slaves and their descendants to claim cultural and religious superiority towards converts from these groups.[112]

Changes in ethnic consciousness between the precolonial period, when men and women were classified according to their genealogy or lack thereof, and the late colonial period, when ethnicity became a central criterion of identity, are apparent. The increasing ethnic consciousness was informed by omnipresent official requests to state one's ethnicity and the continuous importance of descent, established as a marker of social status in the nineteenth century. Asserting an ethnic identity could compensate lack of genealogy. The emphasis of the ruling groups on ethnicity as an exclusionary marker became more pronounced from the early twentieth century onwards, after the criteria of inclusion and their articulation changed with the abolition of slavery and the increase in labour migration.

Racial Nationalism and Political Participation

The articulation of ethnic identities went hand in hand with the formation of political associations. After the end of World War I, the colonial government intended to give the population, over whom they ruled via the sultan, a restricted right to political representation. Hence in 1926, two governing councils were created. The first was the legislative council (LEGCO), which was presided over by the British resident and included as unofficial members three Arabs, two non-mainland Africans, two Asians, and a European. The second was the executive council, headed by the sultan. At that time, nascent nationalism was manifest on the island. The Arab Association and the Indian National

[111] No entry #, no number, 7 Shawwāl 1320/6 January 1903, HC28/29, ZNA. Cf. Chapter 8.

[112] Frederick Cooper, "Problem of Slavery," 122, 124.

FIGURE 9.3. Legislative council, 1960s. Courtesy of ZNA.

Association, formed after the abolition and just before World War I, respectively, preceded the formation of African associations, which emerged in the 1930s.[113] These associations led to the formation of the first political parties, implying that they were initially organised along racial lines. While Michael Lofchie locates the origins of anticolonial sentiment exclusively in the Arab Association, Jonathon Glassman has shown more recently that African intellectuals played a crucial role in the articulation of racial nationalism by the end of World War II.[114]

[113] The African Association and the Shirazi Association were founded in 1934 and 1939, respectively (Lofchie, *Zanzibar*, 99–100).

[114] See ibid., 150–51 and Chapter 5, on the emergence of Arab nationalism. On the importance of African intellectuals and first nationalists in the instrumentalisation of ethnicity in Zanzibar, see Glassman, *War of Words*; idem "Sorting Out the Tribes"; idem, "Slower Than a Massacre;" idem, "Creole Nationalists and the Search for Nativist Authenticity in Twentieth-Century Zanzibar: The Limits of Cosmopolitanism," *Journal of African History* 55, no. 2 (2014): 229–247. For Tanganyika, see Brennan, *Taifa*.

After World War II, the handing over of power to the sultan became foreseeable, but it was not until 1957 that the first elections took place. In that year, Sh. Ameir Tajo, a member of LEGCO since 1946, and others achieved the merger of a fraction of the Shirazi Association with the African Association, thus forming the Afro-Shirazi Party. Its counterpart, the Zanzibar Nationalist Party, evolved from the National Party of the Sultan's Subjects in 1955, supposedly driven by peasants but actually by Arab nationalists.[115]

Zanzibaris used their membership of these political associations to pursue their rights and achieve dispute resolution, whereas officials buttressed the authority of the leaders of ethnic communities to establish law and order. When Panya bt. Fundi, as discussed above, felt deprived of her share of inheritance, she addressed the African Association, whose secretary then wrote to the chief justice on her behalf.[116] To support the claim of Mlange bt. Ngoro and Yasmin bt. Kahunga in 1939, the head of the Wamanyema Community appeared as witness for them.[117] In 1940, the court called one of the leaders of the Shihiris or Hadramis to mediate in a dispute between two litigants of South Yemeni origin,[118] while in 1964, the Mkwajuni Branch of the Afro-Shirazi Party served as point of reference for Khamis Haji to understand why his wife got a divorce in court in 1960. The chief *kadhi* then replied to the chairman of the branch that the wife obtained a divorce on the grounds of non-provision of maintenance.[119]

Interracial relations were already tense before World War II when indebtedness strained Arab–Asian relations.[120] During the 1920s and 1930s, the phenomenon of mortgaging and fictitious sales was paramount.[121] Yet the case of Faraji above suggests that this was the culmination of a long-term practice that revealed the hitherto latent antagonism between indebted plantation owners (mostly Arab and

115 Lofchie, *Zanzibar*, 153–54; Glassman, *War of Words*, 127.

116 Panya to the secretary of the African Association, 8 June 1945, and the African Association to chief justice, 11 June 1945, HC5/575, ZNA.

117 HC5/547, ZNA, original in English. See Chapter 7 for a discussion of this case.

118 HC5/561, original in English, and HC10/64, ZNA.

119 HC10/3705, ZNA.

120 On the causes of indebtedness, colonial interference, and how this affected Arab-Asian relations, see Lofchie, *Zanzibar*, 101–102, 104–26; Bishara, "Sea of Debt".

121 Middleton and Campbell, *Zanzibar*, 46–47.

Shirazi), Indians, who primarily functioned as moneylenders, and Africans (indigenous islanders, ex-slaves, and mainland migrants), who also emulated the prevailing culture of indebtedness. Indians were not targeted during pogroms before the revolution and immediately after, as newspapers like *Afrika Kwetu* provided historical essays portraying them in a neutral role. They claimed that Indians came as businesspeople and neither helped nor harmed Africans, whereas they blamed the Arabs for the enslavement of the majority of the population and the lingering antagonism between ex-masters and slaves.[122] Yet paradoxically, regardless of the African hatred borne against Arabs, the markers of cultural superiority were still inspired by Arab-Islamic values.

By the 1950s, no dimension of social behaviour remained politically neutral and racial antagonism dominated everyday life. Therefore, a "neutral," unifying identity became an urgent demand. Arab intellectuals became aware of the detrimental impact of associating Arabs with slave owners and prominent Arab nationalists, like Ahmed Lemki, stressed a "Zanzibari" identity to overcome this bias.[123] Local and colonial policies played their role in creating and nourishing strife as much as subordinating elements of the Bū Saʿīdī social structure and its ethnic regime based on descent, which clashed with ex-slaves' and immigrants' understanding of their social and economic roles. This boiled down to incompatible interests and an explosive mixture.

Violence was not unknown to Zanzibari history. Discontent had been expressed previously in riots, which occurred in 1928, 1936, and 1951. The courthouse, a symbol of colonial power, was used to proclaim a jihad during the Kiembe Samaki riots in July 1951. The jihad was preceded by the government's acquisition of land for the airport, which also included the site of a mosque. The evacuation of the mosque was dropped, but the gradual expropriation of land in conjuncture with the arrest of villagers refusing to inoculate their cattle against rinderpest culminated in the riots of 1951.[124] In 1954, the call

[122] Glassman, "Sorting Out the Tribes," 421.

[123] See Lofchie, *Zanzibar*, 141–42, 183–84.

[124] Clayton, *Zanzibar Revolution*, 36–37. On the background to these riots, see further Lofchie, *Zanzibar*, 147–50; Glassman, *War of Words*, 125–27; Report by Sir John Gray on the Civil Disturbances in Zanzibar on 30 July, 1951, dated 26 October 1951, Private papers, Sir John Gray, Add. 7739, box 31, CUL.

of jihad was reiterated in the newspaper *al-Falaq*, causing the British to bring the first seditious case against a Zanzibari newspaper.[125] Riots also occurred after the elections of 1957 and 1961, and 1958 witnessed economic boycotts.[126] Conventional analyses identified as the most prominent factors underlying the racial violence the British racial quota of communal representation in the governing bodies and the colonial policy of preserving the Omani oligarchy at the expense of Indians and Africans. In fact, Arab and African nationalists instrumentalised ethnicity to advance their political agendas, culminating in the revolution of 1964.[127]

Islamic Discourses on Difference

The coloniser's equation of Arab with Muslim and its application by the ruling elite, religious and political, administrators and *kadhi*s, fostered Arabisation and Islamisation.[128] Invoking Arabness was also an important component of being a patron. The continuous esteem of Arab values was one of the reasons why patron–client relations continued throughout the colonial period. While Zanzibaris' ethnic identification changed over time, the underlying and potentially unifying religious system on which their society was based, Islam, also underwent changes. An indicative question of changes in Muslim consciousness pertains to what defined a Muslim as such and, consequently, who represented which knowledge of Islam?

Access to Islamic knowledge varied among Arabs of the nineteenth century, slaves and their descendants, indigenous islanders, and immigrants from the mainland. The social and geographical origin of Muslims determined their understanding and practice of Islam as much as it shaped their ethnic identity. Because former slaves and immigrants seemed less knowledgeable about Islamic law, they were excluded from

[125] Lawrence E. Y. Mbogoni, "Censoring the Press in Colonial Zanzibar: An Account of the Seditious Case against *al-Falaq*," in *In Search of a Nation: Histories of Authority & Dissidence in Tanzania*, ed. Gregory H. Maddox and James L. Giblin (Oxford: James Currey, 2005), 198–215.

[126] Lofchie, *Zanzibar*, 184–85.

[127] Glassman, *War of Words*.

[128] Cf. Layish, *Divorce in the Libyan Family*, 185, where he argues that *kadhi*s were key actors in Islamisation, as they were constantly interacting with the population.

the ruling elite. The aforementioned Yasmin bt. Kahunga, for example, a former slave, wanted to be considered as maternal relative in an estate claim, although there was no way she could have excluded those above her in rank of inheritance.[129] The fact that, under Shafiʿi law, a Muslim woman cannot appoint whoever she wants as a guardian identified Addi b. Juma b. al-Zarʿa as not being part of the Muslim elite, which was compounded by the Tumbatu ethnic identity an Arab lady placed on him. His *nisba* attests to his effort to adopt Arab descent, as *zaraʿa* means to cultivate in Arabic and likely was a literal translation of his occupation.[130] François Constantin's hypothesis that prestige is directly related to social utility (ideological and symbolic resources) explains the Arab elite's exclusive yet contested hold over religious and practical knowledge.[131]

Changes in religious discourse from the nineteenth to the midtwentieth centuries show an increasing differentiation of religious practices and thus a stronger basis for intolerance and narrower definitions of what constituted being a "good" Muslim. In the nineteenth century, the ruling Ibāḍī Bū Saʿīdī dynasty and particularly sayyid Saʿīd had been noted for their religious tolerance. These observations were made by non-Muslim travellers and British officers, such as at the memorial service for First Minister Lloyd Mathews, when "even rigid Mahommedans [were] saying fervent 'Amens' at the end of Christian prayers."[132] Even if these impressions were exaggerated, they indicate that there was no widespread animosity based on differences of religion. For most of the nineteenth century, the religious monopoly of the ruling elite went relatively unchallenged and was expressed through their pious patronage of slaves.

When men and women from a mainland or non-Muslim environment sought integration and clientage via conversion to Islam, the criteria of being a proper Muslim shifted. This had already occurred around the midnineteenth century, when the criteria of nobility

[129] HC5/547, ZNA, original in English. See Chapter 7.

[130] HC9/82, ZNA, original in English and Arabic. See above and Chapter 6.

[131] François Constantin, "Social Stratification on the Swahili Coast: From Race to Class?," *Africa* 59, no. 2 (1989): 152.

[132] *Africa: Correspondence Respecting Slavery*, 15. Muslims enthusiastically saying "Amen" must have seen a resemblance to "*āmīn*" in Islamic prayers.

became linked to Arab descent and freed slaves appropriated the term "*uungwana*" for themselves. The basic tenets of Islam, such as praying five times a day and fasting in Ramaḍān, and the application of the categories of forbidden and lawful were obvious signs of being Muslim. Yet more subtle signifiers of Muslim identity remained hidden to the newly converted. Praying, in the case of women at home, was an uncontested expression of being Muslim.[133] When the scope of leisure activities increased, women's piety demanded that they would not go to the cinema or go out on their own. In the 1950s, it was unacceptable for a proper Muslim woman not to do her prayers, not to fast in Ramaḍān, or to participate in dance activities.[134] The prohibition on consuming alcohol under Islamic law was a parameter of distinction between Muslim and non-Muslim throughout the period under study, but the defining characteristic of a "good Muslim" became more nuanced over time. In 1909, sobriety defined a good Muslim from a bad one.[135] Yet the same parameter entailed clear racial connotations when it was debated in the 1950s, as shown below.

These shifting conceptions of the "good Muslim" became entrenched in the racialised political discourse at its height in the late 1950s and early 1960s, for which Islam "provided some of the language with which the intelligentsia constructed their chauvinist rhetoric."[136] Zanzibari newspapers represented readerships divided along racial lines, which equally reflected different interpretations of Islamic legal discourse. Questions about whether it was sinful to drink alcohol and whether it was appropriate to take a photo for a passport or to display pictures at home would likely not have been raised among readers who had been raised in Arab-Muslim families in previous generations or among readers of the newspaper *al-Falaq*, the mouthpiece of the Arab Association and medium of pan-Islamic and pan-Arab discourse.[137] The African readership of *Afrika Kwetu* and *Mwongozi*,

133 Women's prayer space in mosques was mostly created in the post-revolution era.

134 This social understanding is advanced in HC10/3325, original in English; HC10/3612, ZNA. See Chapter 3.

135 HC9/82, ZNA, original in Arabic and English.

136 Glassman, "Slower Than a Massacre," 745.

137 These questions were posed in *Mwongozi*, 22 October 1948. For an account of pan-Islamic and pan-Arab discourse of Ibāḍī intellectuals in Zanzibar, see Amal N.

however, which debated these issues, reshaped and contested the ideas of the religious elite, who had been identified as Arab since the nineteenth century.

The potential of equality in Islam disappeared in the face of racism under which ethnic identities were consciously and contextually constructed. In 1949, ʿAli b. Awadh Ferej, a Hadrami, described his maternal grandmother, a *suria*, as Swahili:

> She was a Swahili. There is a difference of opinion as to whether a Shirazi is an Arab. They are descended from Persians. A Mtumbatu is not an Arab. Watumbatu are Africans. They say they are of Asiatic descent but Arabs do not accept this. Comorians are not Arabs. They do not belong to the Qureysh [the kinship group of the Prophet]. [...] A learned man [a Muslim scholar], who is not an Arab, is not the equal of an Arab.[138]

ʿAli's understanding of Swahili was the meaning of the term that emerged in the late colonial period, a person of mixed origin living on the coast. Moreover, his careful distinction between Arab and African reflects the belief of the Arab intelligentsia and the colonial administration in Arab superiority. While Arab values were openly adopted prior to the rise of nationalism, the elevation of Arabness above Africanness was henceforth the subconscious benchmark for the integration of the socially marginalised.

The interrelation of the processes of Islamisation and ethnicisation is manifest in the concept of *kafāʾa*. As shown in Chapter 6, ethnicity became an important criterion of *kafāʾa*, which suggests that in post-abolition Zanzibar adherence to Islam was less disputed but that a Muslim's ethnic background determined his or her inclusion within or exclusion from the community. In 1909 Saʿid b. ʿAbdallah, a fiddle player at the sultan's court, explained that he did not understand marrying in the Arab way, but he knew how to do it in the Swahili way. Thus he wondered whether this would enable him to contract a marriage between an Arab woman and a Tumbatu man.[139] Obviously for Saʿid, the performance of a marriage ceremony differed among

Ghazal, *Islamic Reform and Arab Nationalism: Expanding the Crescent from the Mediterranean to the Indian Ocean (1880s-1930s)* (London: Routledge, 2010).

[138] HC5/582, ZNA, original in English.

[139] HC9/82, ZNA, original in Arabic and English. Cf. above and Chapter 6.

Arabs and Swahilis, with the first being more knowledgeable in shariʿa requirements.

Ethnicisation also permeated the question of consuming alcohol, which by 1952 had become enmeshed with more overtly racial tones. Responding to concerns about the increasing consumption of alcohol among Muslims, the authors of an article in *Afrika Kwetu* insisted that this habit should be ended among all Muslims, not only Africans. Their response implicitly acknowledged the existence of a firm division between Muslims along racial lines. Similarly, they reasoned if alcohol permits were to be introduced, they should be applied to every person irrespective of religion and colour. Asking for bars selling alcohol to be closed and turned into shops and for an embargo on the import of alcohol, they adopted a more radical approach to the matter than *kadhi* Sh. ʿAbdallāh Ṣāliḥ al-Farsī. Another sinful matter that had not been addressed from the point of view of the authors of the article was "some persons who walk and speak in girlish way – so sinful a thing and sight."[140] For them, transgendering was incompatible with being Muslim.

By the 1950s, being Muslim was further qualified by one's ethnic and social identity. The Muslim community was less ethnically and socially uniform and highly sensitised to any issues that would cause further friction. In 1957, an article published in *Afrika Kwetu* made the government anxious enough to start a file on the society that stood behind it. The article used Islamist rhetoric which must have worried the government, as it criticised the predominance of materialism in society, the lack of humanity, and the widespread disregard of Muslim duties, such as the proper burial of the dead. Its authors disapproved of Muslims' expectations of material payment in this world, where money would be spent on silly things (Sw. *mambo ya uzushi*), rather than of reward in the hereafter. The article also invoked the equality of all Muslims and purported that neither slavery nor social hierarchy (Sw. *uungwana*) existed in Islam. It further disapproved of the practice of slave descendants praying in a different part of the mosque during the Friday prayer. Moreover, the authors objected to Muslims prostrating before other human beings, worshipping graves, and using

140 "Islams are Forbidden to Drink Liquior it is Sinful [sic]" in the English, and "Islamu Haramu Kulewa?" in the shorter Swahili version (*Afrika Kwetu*, 17 April 1952).

the mosque like a coffee shop.[141] By insisting on the equality of all Muslims, while attesting to the existence of non-Islamic divisions and materialist attitudes within Zanzibari society, these debates show the extent to which colonial policies and racial nationalism polarised the common basis of Islam.

Conclusion

British colonial officers and *kadhi*s recognised slavery as an intrinsic institution of Zanzibari society. By affirming slaves' kinlessness and illegitimate descent, they perpetuated the marginalisation of their descendants in the post-abolition era. Former slaves wanted to prove ties of kinship to claim social and economic rights but failed to do so because of the notion of kinlessness that masters had created and slaves had confirmed prior to abolition. Islamic legal principles applied by the *kadhi*s left the descendants of slaves tainted and struggling for social inclusion. By the 1950s, their anger was manifest in demands for racial and social equality among Muslims. The ethnicisation of Islam, which replaced the dividing line between slave and free of the nineteenth century, arose from the colonial categorisation of the sultan's subjects into racial groups and the efforts of the partially excluded (slave descendants, immigrants, and those lacking Arab genealogy) to compensate for the lack of prestigious descent with a *nisba* derived from an ethnicity. Most importantly, this process was catalysed by racialised ideas of African and Arab nationalists. Zanzibaris' identities remained fluid throughout the colonial period, yet were inscribed into racialised nationalism and the colonial political economy.

Nationalist rhetoric and the creation of a colonial social order in which socioeconomic status was determined by ethnicity blurred the fact that many slave owners were women and indigenous islanders. Slavery had permeated men and women among all social and ethnic groups in Zanzibar, while the distinction between islanders and mainlanders gained in importance after abolition. There clearly were common interests and social ties among those who defined their identity through access to land and considered themselves Shirazi. Yet an emerging class-consciousness did not completely replace older social

[141] "The Young Muumin Society," *Africa Kwetu*, 26 December 1957.

networks of clientage, which now showed obvious signs of friction. Patrons and clients joined hands in non-material social duties, such as guardianship in marriage and representation in court, but competed against each other in the increasingly racialised struggle for resources.

Conclusion

After the revolution of 1964, Ibāḍī law was removed from the legal system and Swahili became the official language of the *kadhi*'s courts. The esteem in which *kadhi*s were held diminished, and oral sources suggest that bribery prevails among them today.[1] Within the post-revolution judiciary, *kadhi*s are accused of ignoring procedure and omitting their administrative duties. Their legal tradition, spanning centuries, was expunged with a revolutionary change in politics, which sought a complete rupture with the Arab past. The revolutionary government branded Arabs as slave owners who had subjugated the African population and deprived them of their land and freedom. The action of the new rulers in arbitrarily excising anything Arab from the judiciary caused greater alienation of the Islamic legal system from both the *kadhi*s and the population than had already occurred under British rule. While the consequences of the legal reforms under the revolutionary government remain to be explored, it is striking that notions of the *kadhi*s' arbitrariness in adjudication and negligence of procedure from the early colonial period were revived after the end of colonial rule.

How important were the *kadhi*'s courts to Zanzibar's cosmopolitan population in the first half of the twentieth century? Although not every Muslim man and woman sought redress at these courts, I have argued for their popularity and their significant role in facilitating and

[1] Interviews with Bi Faida Salim Babu, 22 March 2004; Bi Mwajuma Mzee Mhina, 17 March 2004; Omar Barwani, 27 December 2003.

denying social mobility. *Kadhis* were shaped by their socioeconomic environment and understanding of being servants of Islamic law, while their assessment of litigants' moral integrity was equally determined by the latter's social and also ethnic background. These social etymologies were intrinsic to Islamic law yet experienced intensification and hardening through the bureaucratisation of the judiciary. *Kadhis* and judges were steeped in legal traditions whose workings and aims partly differed. Islamic law, which had served the peoples and trade networks of the Indian Ocean since the seventh century, was slowly substituted by colonial decrees underpinning a capitalist global economy and eventually transforming the protectorate into a nation-state. Yet in spite of British admiration of and preference for shariʿa over unwritten customary law, it failed to fully meet their legal, moral, and economic standards. Applying a double standard, the British were concerned with maintaining social order by acknowledging patriarchal Muslim rule while excoriating it at the same time. Informed by an understanding of restricted female agency, colonial interference in Islamic law was characterised by ambiguity and contradiction. If women benefitted from colonial enactments pertaining to marriage, it was rather a by-product of the government's primary aim to maintain social order. Most importantly, it was the structure and substance of Islamic law that enabled women and the socially marginalised to bring claims to the *kadhi*'s courts.[2]

Before the revolution, Zanzibaris could consult either a Shafiʿi or an Ibāḍī *kadhi*. Although this choice was limited in practice, as the number of Ibāḍī *kadhis* decreased and necessitated longer journeys for litigants, the option gave women the possibility of manoeuvring between legal doctrines. Exploring Shafiʿi and Ibāḍī doctrines, women were able to seek the dissolution of their marriage as well as to contract marriages. Marriage was the central institution that bestowed respectability on women and men and initiated them into adulthood. This initiation, however, was supervised by elders, who chose the partner for their child and negotiated the dower. I have argued that elders' arrangements of marriage entailed the continuous prevalence of endogamy and that, drawing on Islamic legal doctrines, neither spouses nor elders regarded marriage as a union lasting for life.

[2] Cf. Tucker, *Women, Family, and Gender*, 18.

The institution of marriage was shaped by wider social and economic change, causing tensions between men and women as well as juniors and seniors in the transition from the nineteenth to the twentieth centuries. The dower as an effect of a Muslim marriage served as a tool for women to bargain for divorce but constituted the main reason why husbands clung to their wives. When men sued for restitution of conjugal rights and insisted on wives paying for their divorce, they appeared to be motivated by a perception of marriage as a material investment. We should understand the preponderance of divorce for a consideration in relation to the social importance of marriage and the cost it involved for men. Husbands were exploited by elders and, in turn, they exploited wives upon divorce.

The abolition of slavery and the mounting debts of plantation owners repositioned women in the social and economic order. By the late colonial period women increasingly had access to education and thus more options for providing for themselves. Some former slave women sought respectability by marrying free men. Women from respectable families, whose fathers and brothers could no longer provide for them, faced choices in negotiating competing needs to hold onto their respectability and to maintain themselves. Their preferred option seemed to be marrying a socially inferior but economically superior man. Women consciously and deliberately referred to being under their husband's tutelage and thus switched between registers of respectability to defend and improve their social status. The legal doctrines that served as tools for negotiating social status clearly did not operate within a socioeconomic vacuum.

I have explored the relationships between spouses, among kin, and between patrons and clients by referring to the abolition of slavery as the turning point of Zanzibar's twentieth-century history. This emphasis should not belie other changes that happened over the twentieth century, which, however, appear to have affected relations among these groups of actors to a lesser degree. It was abolition that enabled an increased range of actors, most prominently former slaves, to struggle for citizenship, claiming participation in social institutions and material assets in court. We know from previous studies that former slaves acquired property as a strategy for climbing the social ladder. Court records indicate dense activities of selling and buying, masking the advancement of credit, between slaves and masters and, subsequently, patrons and clients in the post-abolition era. Woven into the emerging class structure, patron–client relations provided clients with financial security, with patrons acting as guarantors and creditors, and offered patrons possibilities for the assertion of social and economic power. Yet patrons also needed clients as creditors if they faced financial difficulties. In largely securing mutual benefit, patron–client relationships operated flexibly, serving the economic aims of both partners within the political economy of the colonial state.

The most powerful assertions of patronage in post-abolition Zanzibar were claims for the inheritance of former slaves, to which masters are entitled under Islamic law. Questioning the legal status of ex-slaves and their descendants as free subjects of the sultan, these claims attest to persistent fundamental differences in relations between former masters and slaves. Inheritance cases further indicate that in spite of colonial legal reforms, *kadhi*s found it difficult to extricate themselves from a legal tradition endorsing the masters' right to inherit from slaves. Both *kadhi*s and judges believed that patrons were entitled to their share from their client's estate. The British concept of Zanzibar as an Arab state permeated the judiciary and the colonial political economy. It created legal categories based on ethnic and economic criteria and *kadhi*'s court records suggest that ethnicity and descent were more significant in impeding and enabling socioeconomic participation than gender. These records further yield evidence that women as well as the poor continuously and successfully pursued claims in the *kadhi*'s courts throughout the colonial period.

In the struggle for social inclusion, former slaves seem to have held advantages over immigrants on account of their recourse to networks of clientage. Marital relations and clientage in the nineteenth century were defined by social status, as determined by descent and being free or slave. Lacking a respectable *nisba*, former slaves continued to face social exclusion after abolition. With the increasing influence of ethnicity on social relations, adopting ethnic labels as *nisba*s compensated for lack of ancestry but at the same time provided a new grounds for the exclusion of large numbers of mainland immigrants. An ethnic consciousness clearly existed prior to British rule, but it was the interplay between the ethnic categories entrenched by the coloniser and those created by the colonised that drove Zanzibari society apart.

Appendix
Distribution of Cases[1]

Kadhis in Chronological Order	Period from which Cases Originate	Breakdown of Cases Per Year	*Kadhis*' Cases in Total
Sh. Aḥmad b. Sumayṭ Shafiʿi (1861–1925) *kadhi* from 1888 to 1925	1909	1909 [2]	2
Sh. Burhān b. ʿAbd al-ʿAzīz al-Amawī Shafiʿi (1861–1935) *kadhi* from 1890/91 to 1932	1901–1919	1901 [1] 1904 [3] 1905 [9] 1906 [4] 1909 [1] 1919 [2]	20

(*continued*)

[1] This table is based on the cases classified as HC9, HC10, and HC5 in the ZNA. As HC5 are appeal cases, I attributed them to the *kadhi* who originally adjudicated the case. I have not included the HC28/29 cases and the HC8 appeal cases in the breakdown. Due to their status as appeal cases, the HC8 cases were heard by two *kadhis* and a judge, while the entries in HC28/29 rarely mention the name of the *kadhi*. Two HC9 cases are not included in this table as they were heard in the Court for Zanzibar and Pemba, like the HC8 cases. Thus the overall number of cases in this breakdown does not equal the total of cases considered in this study (see Tables 3.1 and 4.1). The dates of *kadhis* are taken from Bang, *Sufis and Scholars*; Lacunza Balda, "Investigation into Some Concepts"; Loimeier, *Between Social Skills*; *Zanzibar Protectorate, Administrative Report, 1930*; AX1/1; AX1/3; BA82/44; HC26/18, ZNA.

(continued)

Kadhis in Chronological Order	Period from which Cases Originate	Breakdown of Cases Per Year	*Kadhis*' Cases in Total
Sh. ʿAlī b. Muḥammad al-Mundhirī Ibāḍī (1866–1925) *kadhi* from at least 1903 to 1925	1909–1921	1909 [4] 1917 [1] 1919 [1] 1920 [2] 1921 [1]	9
Sh. ʿAbd al-Raḥīm b. Maḥmūd Mngazija Ibāḍī (1872–1936) *kadhi* from at least the 1910s to 1936	1911	1911 [2]	2
Sh. Ṭāhir b. Abī Bakr al-Amawī Shafiʿi (1877–1938) *kadhi* from at least 1907 to 1938	1909–1938	1909 [1] 1914 [1] 1919 [6] 1920 [2] 1921 [2] 1925 [1] 1926 [1] 1927 [1] 1930 [1] 1931 [2] 1932 [3] 1933 [1] 1934 [2] 1937 [1] 1938 [1]	26
Sh. Muḥammad b. Khamīs al-Bū Saʿīdī Ibāḍī (d. 1930) *kadhi* from 1897 to 1930	1928	1928 [2]	2
Sh. Gharīb b. ʿAlī al-ʿAwfī Ibāḍī (d. 1934) *kadhi* from 1930 to 1934	1931–1934	1931 [1] 1932 [1] 1934 [1]	3
Sh. Saʿīd b. Nāṣir al-Ghaythī Ibāḍī (d. 1942) *kadhi* from at least 1931	1934–1941	1934 [1] 1939 [1] 1940 [2] 1941 [1]	5

Kadhis in Chronological Order	Period from which Cases Originate	Breakdown of Cases Per Year	*Kadhis*' Cases in Total
Sh. Sa'īd b. Rashīd al-Ghaythī Ibāḍī (1882–1954) *kadhi* from 1942 to 1953	1942–1952	1942 [2] 1943 [2] 1944 [5] 1945 [2] 1951 [3] 1952 [6]	20
Sh. 'Umar b. Aḥmad b. Sumayṭ Shafi'i (1886–1973) *kadhi* from 1937 to 1959	1940–1959	1940 [2] 1943 [2] 1944 [2] 1949 [1] 1952 [3] 1953 [4] 1954 [5] 1955 [5] 1956 [1] 1957 [2] 1959 [2]	29
Sh. Muḥammad Sālim al-Rawwāḥī Ibāḍī (b. 1909) *kadhi* at least until 1962	1955–1959	1955 [1] 1956 [3] 1958 [4] 1959 [4]	12
Sh. 'Abdallāh Ṣāliḥ al-Farsī Shafi'i (1912–1982) *kadhi* from 1953 to 1967	1960	1960 [5]	5
Sh. Hādī b. Aḥmad al-Ḥaddār Shafi'i (b. 1921) *kadhi* from 1953 to 1964	1956	1956 [1]	1

Bibliography

Oral Sources

Sh. Abdalla Suleiman Jumbe, 26 October 2003, 24 March, and 22 June 2004, Milimani (Kiembe Samaki)
Sh. Ahmed Mohamed Saleh Ba Kathir, 27 January 2004, Chuini
Bi Amina Abdulrahman Mahmud, 2 May, 19 May, and 19 June 2004, Msikiti Barza
Bi Aziza Sharif Issa, 26 April 2004, Baghani
Bi Bahati Ramadhani Juma, 27 March 2004, Mpendae
Bi Fadhila Mohamed Hasan, 30 March and 11 June 2004, Mwembemakumbi
Bi Faida Salim Babu, 22 March and 26 June 2004, Karakana
Bi Hadija Nasoro Ibrahim, 24 April and 17 June 2004, Baraste Kipande
Bi Hadiya Rashidi Ali, 13 June 2004, Makadara
Bi Halima Abdalla Jafar, 13 February, 13 April, and 27 May 2004, Vikokotoni
Sh. Hamid Musa Mlomri, 22 December 2003, High Court, Zanzibar Town
Sh. Ibrahim Mtoro, 22 December 2003, High Court, Zanzibar Town
Juma Bakari Mfaume, 28 May 2004, Kwahani-Mwembenjugu
Bi Maua Azizi Mbarak, 16 March and 9 June 2004, Kiembe Samaki
Bi Mwajuma Mzee Mhina, 17 March 2004, Sebleni
Bi Mwanaidi Makame Ameir, 3 April and 24 June 2004, Mwembenjugu
Omar Barwani, 27 December 2003, Baghani
Rashid Omar Sharif, 9 April 2004, Hurumzi
Bi Rehema Abbasi Rajabu, 11 May 2004, Baghani
Saidi Haji Yusuf, 9 February 2004, Saateni
Bi Salme Shaban Hilal, 27 April and 25 May 2004, Kikwajuni
Seif Hemedi Musa, 7 May 2004, Baghani

Archival Sources

Zanzibar

Zanzibar National Archives
Mambo Msiige, Zanzibar Town

United Kingdom

The National Archives, Kew
Cambridge University Library, Royal Commonwealth Society
School of Oriental and African Studies, University of London, Manuscript Collection

Unpublished Sources

Abd Hamid, Hamidin. "Unfinished Business: The Implementation of the Land Titles Ordinance in Coastal Kenya, 1908–1940s." PhD diss., SOAS, University of London, 2000.

Bishara, Fahad Ahmad. "A Sea of Debt: Histories of Commerce and Obligation in the Indian Ocean, c. 1850–1940." PhD diss., Duke University, 2012.

Lacunza Balda, Justo. "An Investigation into Some Concepts and Ideas Found in Swahili Islamic Writings." PhD diss., SOAS, University of London, 1989.

Landberg, Pamela Weaver. "Kinship and Community in a Tanzanian Coastal Village (East Africa)." PhD diss., University of California, Davis, 1977.

Lovett, Margot Louise. "Elders, Migrants and Wives: Labor Migration and the Renegotiation of Intergenerational, Patronage and Gender Relations in Highland Buha, Western Tanzania, 1921–1962." PhD diss., Columbia University, 1996.

McDow, Thomas F. "Where Credit Is Due: Zanzibar and the Limits of Indian Ocean Cosmopolitanism." Paper presented at the workshop Shifting the Meaning: Time, Space, Connectivity and Its Challenges in the Western Indian Ocean, Berlin, May 21–23, 2007.

McDow, Thomas F. "Arabs and Africans: Commerce and Kinship from Oman to the East African Interior, c. 1820–1900." PhD diss., Yale University, 2008. ProQuest (ATT 3317172).

Mwakimako, Hassan Abdulrahman. "Politics, Ethnicity and Jostling for Power: the Evolution of Institutions of Muslim Leadership and Kadhiship in Colonial Kenya, 1895–1963." PhD diss., University of Cape Town, 2003.

Myers, Garth Andrew. "Reconstructing Ng'ambo: Town Planning and Development on the Other Side of Zanzibar." PhD diss., UCLA, 1993.

O'Malley, Gabrielle E. "Marriage and Morality: Negotiating Gender and Respect in Zanzibar Town." PhD diss., University of Washington, 2000.

Purpura, Allyson. "Knowledge and Agency: The Social Relations of Islamic Expertise in Zanzibar Town." PhD diss., CUNY, 1997.

Shao, Ibrahim Fokas. "Land Tenure System and Land Reform in Zanzibar (1830s–1978)." MA diss., University of Dar es-Salaam, 1978.

Published Sources

Government Publications

Africa: Correspondence Respecting Slavery and the Slave Trade in East Africa and the Islands of Zanzibar and Pemba, No. 6. London: Harrison & Sons, 1902.
Annual Report of the Provincial Administration, 1957. Zanzibar: Government Printer, 1958.
Annual Reports on the Social and Economic Progress of the People of the Zanzibar Protectorate, 1931–1938. London: His Majesty's Stationery Office, 1932–1939.
Supplement to the Official Gazette Zanzibar 1928, Vol.XXXVII-No.1897, 2 June 1928.
Supplement to the Official Gazette Zanzibar 1928, Vol.XXXVII-No.1898, 9 June 1928.
Zanzibar Law Reports. Vol. 1. Compiled by Sir William Murison and S. S. Abrahams. London: Waterlow & Sons Ltd., 1919.
Zanzibar Protectorate. Administrative Reports, 1915–1931. Zanzibar: Government Printer, 1916–1932.

Periodicals

Afrika Kwetu
al-Falaq
Mwongozi

Articles and Books

Abdal-Rehim, Abdal-Rehim Abdal-Rahman. "The Family and Gender Laws in Egypt during the Ottoman Period." In *Women, the Family, and Divorce Laws in Islamic History*, ed. Amina El Azhary Sonbol, 96–111. Syracuse: Syracuse University Press, 1996.
Agmon, Iris. "Women, Class, and Gender: Muslim Jaffa and Haifa at the Turn of the Twentieth Century." *International Journal of Middle East Studies* 30, no. 4 (1998): 477–500.
Agmon, Iris. "Text, Court, and Family in Late-Nineteenth-Century Palestine." In *Family History in the Middle East: Household, Property and Gender*, ed. Beshara Doumani, 201–28. Albany: State University of New York Press, 2003.
Agmon, Iris. *Family and Court: Legal Culture and Modernity in Late Ottoman Palestine*. Syracuse: Syracuse University Press, 2006.

Ahmed, Leila. *Women and Gender in Islam: Historical Roots of a Modern Debate*. New Haven: Yale University Press, 1992.

Akarlı, Engin Deniz. "Law in the Marketplace: Istanbul, 1730–1840." In *Dispensing Justice in Islam: Qadis and their Judgments*, ed. Muhammad Khalid Masud, Rudolph Peters, and David S. Powers, 245–70. Leiden: Brill, 2006.

Allen, James de Vere. *Swahili Origins: Swahili Culture and the Shungwaya Phenomenon*. London: James Currey, 1993.

Allman, Jean, and Victoria Tashjian. *"I Will Not Eat Stone": A Women's History of Colonial Asante*. Portsmouth, NH: Heinemann, 2000.

Allott, Antony N. "The Future of African Law." In *African Law: Adaptation and Development*, ed. Hilda Kuper and Leo Kuper, 216–40. Berkeley: University of California Press, 1965.

Alpers, Edward. "'Ordinary Household Chores': Ritual and Power in a Nineteenth-Century Swahili Women's Spirit Possession Cult." *International Journal of African Historical Studies* 17, no. 4 (1984): 677–702.

Alshech, Eli. "'Do Not Enter Houses Other Than Your Own': The Evolution of the Notion of a Private Domestic Sphere in Early Sunni Islamic Thought." *Islamic Law and Society* 11, no. 3 (2004): 291–332.

Anderson, J. N. D. "Recent Reforms in the Islamic Law of Inheritance." *International and Comparative Law Quarterly* 14, no. 2 (1965): 349–65.

Anderson, J. N. D. "The Eclipse of the Patriarchal Family in Contemporary Islamic Law." In *Family Law in Asia and Africa*, ed. J. N. D. Anderson, 221–34. London: George Allen & Unwin, 1968.

Anderson, J. N. D. *Islamic Law in Africa*. 1955. Reprint with a new preface, London: Frank Cass, 1970.

Anderson, J. N. D. "Reforms in the Law of Divorce in the Muslim World." *Studia Islamica* 31 (1970): 41–52.

Anderson, Michael R. "Islamic Law and the Colonial Encounter in British India." In *Institutions and Ideologies: A SOAS South Asia Reader*, ed. David Arnold and Peter Robb, 165–85. Richmond: Curzon, 1993.

Anderson, Michael R. "Legal Scholarship and the Politics of Islam in British India." In *Perspectives on Islamic Law, Justice, and Society*, ed. Ravindra S. Khare, 65–91. Lanham: Rowman & Littlefield, 1999.

Arabi, Oussama. "The Dawning of the Third Millennium on Shariʿa: Egypt's Law no.1 of 2000, or Women May Divorce at Will." *Arab Law Quarterly* 16, no. 1 (2001): 2–21.

Arens, W. "The *Waswahili*: The Social History of an Ethnic Group." *Africa* 45, no. 4 (1975): 426–38.

Askew, Kelly M. "Female Circles and Male Lines: Gender Dynamics along the Swahili Coast." *Africa Today* 46, no. 3/4 (1999): 67–102.

Ayany, Samuel G. *A History of Zanzibar: A Study in Constitutional Development, 1934–1964*. Nairobi: East African Literature Bureau, 1970.

Bakari, Mtoro bin Mwinyi. *The Customs of the Swahili People: The Desturi za Waswahili of Mtoro bin Mwinyi Bakari and Other Swahili Persons*. Ed. and trans. by J. W. T. Allen. Berkeley: University of California Press, 1981.

Bang, Anne K. *Sufis and Scholars of the Sea: Family Networks in East Africa, 1860–1925*. London: Routledge Curzon, 2003.
Bang, Anne K. "Another Scholar for All Seasons? Tāhir b. Abī Bakr al-Amawī (1877–1938), qādī of Zanzibar, c. 1900–1933." In *The Global Worlds of the Swahili: Interfaces of Islam, Identity and Space in 19th and 20th-Century East Africa*, ed. Roman Loimeier and Rüdiger Seesemann, 273–88. Berlin: Lit Verlag, 2006.
Bang, Anne K. "Cosmopolitanism Colonised? Three Cases from Zanzibar, 1890–1920." In *Struggling with History: Islam and Cosmopolitanism in the Western Indian Ocean*, ed. Edward Simpson and Kai Kresse, 167–88. New York: Columbia University Press, 2007.
Bang, Anne K., and Knut S. Vikør. "A Tale of Three *shambas*: Shāfiʿī-Ibāḍī Legal Cooperation in the Zanzibari Protectorate, Part I." *Sudanic Africa* 10 (1999): 1–26.
Bang, Anne K., and Knut S. Vikør. "A Tale of Three *shambas*, Part II." *Sudanic Africa* 11 (2000): 1–24.
Becker, C. H. "Materialien zur Kenntnis des Islam in Deutsch-Ostafrika." *Der Islam* 2 (1911): 1–48.
Becker, Felicitas. *Becoming Muslim in Mainland Tanzania, 1890–2000*. Oxford: Oxford University Press, 2008.
Bennett, Norman R. *A History of the Arab State of Zanzibar*. London: Methuen, 1978.
Benton, Lauren. *Law and Colonial Cultures: Legal Regimes in World History, 1400–1900*. Cambridge: Cambridge University Press, 2002.
Berg, L. W. C. van den. *Minhādj aṭ-ṭālibīn. Le guide des zélés croyants. Manuel de jurisprudence musulmane selon le rite de Chāfiʿī*. Vols. II–III. Arabic text, published at the order of the government, trans. and annotation by L. W. C. van den Berg. Batavia: Government Press, 1883–84.
Bhacker, M. Reda. *Trade and Empire in Muscat and Zanzibar: Roots of British Domination*. London: Routledge, 1992.
Biersteker, Ann. "Language, Poetry, and Power: A Reconsideration of 'Utendi wa Mwana Kupona.'" In *Faces of Islam in African Literature*, ed. Kenneth W. Harrow, 59–77. Portsmouth, NH: Heinemann, 1991.
Bissell, William Cunningham. *Urban Design, Chaos, and Colonial Power in Zanzibar*. Bloomington: Indiana University Press, 2011.
Boddy, Janice. *Civilizing Women: British Crusades in Colonial Sudan*. Princeton: Princeton University Press, 2007.
Brennan, James R. *Taifa: Making Nation and Race in Urban Tanzania*. Athens: Ohio University Press, 2012.
Brockelmann, C. *Geschichte der Arabischen Litteratur*. Second supplement. Leiden: E. J. Brill, 1938.
Bromber, Katrin, ed. *The Jurisdiction of the Sultan of Zanzibar and the Subjects of Foreign Nations*. Trans. by Katrin Bomber. Würzburg: Ergon Verlag, 2001.
Bromber, Katrin. "Who are the Zanzibari? Newspaper Debates on Difference, 1948–1958." In *Space on the Move: Transformations of the Indian Ocean*

Seascape in the Nineteenth and Twentieth Century, ed. Jan-Georg Deutsch and Brigitte Reinwald, 75–89. Berlin: Klaus Schwarz Verlag, 2002.

Bromber, Katrin. "Ustaarabu: A Conceptual Change in Tanganyikan Newspaper Discourse in the 1920s." In *The Global Worlds of the Swahili: Interfaces of Islam, Identity and Space in 19th and 20th-Century East Africa*, ed. Roman Loimeier and Rüdiger Seesemann, 67–81. Berlin: Lit Verlag, 2006.

Brown, Beverly B. "Islamic Law, Qadhis' Courts and Muslim Women's Legal Status: The Case of Kenya." *Journal of Muslim Minority Affairs* 14, no. 1/2 (1994): 94–101.

Bujra, Janet M. "Production, Property, Prostitution. 'Sexual Politics' in Atu." *Cahiers d'études africaines* 17, no. 1 (1977): 13–39.

Burton, Richard F. *Zanzibar: City, Island, and Coast*. Vol. I. London: Tinsley Brothers, 1872.

Caplan, Pat. *Choice and Constraint in a Swahili Community: Property, Hierarchy, and Cognatic Descent on the East African Coast*. London: Oxford University Press, 1975.

Caplan, Pat. "Gender, Ideology and Modes of Production on the Coast of East Africa." *Paideuma* 28 (1982): 29–43.

Caplan, Pat. "'Law' and 'Custom': Marital Disputes on Northern Mafia Island, Tanzania." In *Understanding Disputes: The Politics of Argument*, ed. Pat Caplan, 203–21. Oxford: Berg, 1995.

Carroll, Lucy. "Qurʾan 2:229 'A Charter Granted to the Wife'? Judicial *Khulʿ* in Pakistan." *Islamic Law and Society* 3, no. 1 (1996): 91–126.

Chanock, Martin. "Making Customary Law: Men, Women, and Courts in Colonial Northern Rhodesia." In *African Women and the Law: Historical Perspectives*, ed. Margaret Jean Hay and Marcia Wright, 53–67. Boston: Boston University, 1982.

Chanock, Martin. *Law, Custom and Social Order: The Colonial Experience in Malawi and Zambia*. Cambridge: Cambridge University Press, 1985.

Chanock, Martin. "A Peculiar Sharpness: An Essay on Property in the History of Customary Law in Colonial Africa." *Journal of African History* 32, no. 1 (1991): 65–88.

Christelow, Allan. "The Muslim Judge and Municipal Politics in Colonial Algeria and Senegal." *Comparative Studies in Society and History* 24 (1982): 3–24.

Christelow, Allan. *Muslim Law Courts and the French Colonial State in Algeria*. Princeton: Princeton University Press, 1985.

Christelow, Allan. "The Transformation of the Muslim Court System in Colonial Algeria: Reflections on the Concept of Autonomy." In *Islamic Law: Social and Historical Contexts*, ed. Aziz al-Azmeh, 215–30. London: Routledge, 1988.

Christelow, Allan. "Theft, Homicide, and Oath in Early Twentieth-Century Kano." In *Law in Colonial Africa*, ed. Kristin Mann and Richard Roberts, 205–23. Portsmouth, NH: Heinemann, 1991.

Christelow, Allan, ed. *Thus Ruled Emir Abbas: Selected Cases from the Records of the Emir of Kano's Judicial Council.* East Lansing: Michigan State University Press, 1994.
Christelow, Allan. "Islamic Law and Judicial Practice in Nigeria: An Historical Perspective." *Journal of Muslim Minority Affairs* 22, no. 1 (2002): 185–204.
Clancy-Smith, Julia. "Islam, Gender, and Identities in the Making of French Algeria, 1830–1962." In *Domesticating the Empire: Race, Gender, and Family Life in French and Dutch Colonialism*, ed. Julia Clancy-Smith and Frances Gouda, 154–74. Charlottesville: University Press of Virginia, 1998.
Clarence-Smith, William Gervase. *Islam and the Abolition of Slavery.* London: Hurst, 2006.
Clayton, Anthony. *The Zanzibar Revolution and Its Aftermath.* London: Hurst, 1981.
Comaroff, John, and Simon Roberts. *Rules and Processes: The Cultural Logic of Dispute in an African Context.* Chicago: University of Chicago Press, 1981.
Constantin, François. "Le saint et le prince: Sur les fondements de la dynamique confrérique en Afrique orientale." In *Les voies de l'islam en Afrique orientale*, ed. François Constantin, 85–109. Paris: Karthala, 1987.
Constantin, François. "Social Stratification on the Swahili Coast: From Race to Class?" *Africa* 59, no. 2 (1989): 145–60.
Constantin, François. "Leadership, Muslim Identities and East African Politics: Tradition, Bureaucratization and Communication." In *Muslim Identity and Social Change in Sub-Saharan Africa*, ed. Louis Brenner, 36–58. Bloomington: Indiana University Press, 1993.
Cooper, Barbara M. "Reflections on Slavery, Seclusion and Female Labor in the Maradi Region of Niger in the Nineteenth and Twentieth Centuries." *Journal of African History* 35, no. 1 (1994): 61–78.
Cooper, Barbara M. *Marriage in Maradi: Gender and Culture in a Hausa Society in Niger, 1900–1989.* Portsmouth, NH: Heinemann, 1997.
Cooper, Frederick. *Plantation Slavery on the East Coast of Africa.* New Haven: Yale University Press, 1977.
Cooper, Frederick. "The Problem of Slavery in African Studies." *Journal of African History* 20, no. 1 (1979): 103–25.
Cooper, Frederick. *From Slaves to Squatters: Plantation Labor and Agriculture in Zanzibar and Coastal Kenya, 1890–1925.* New Haven: Yale University Press, 1980.
Cooper, Frederick. "Islam and Cultural Hegemony: The Ideology of Slave-owners on the East African Coast." In *The Ideology of Slavery in Africa*, ed. P. E. Lovejoy, 270–307. London: Sage, 1981.
Cooper, Frederick, and Ann Laura Stoler, eds. *Tensions of Empire: Colonial Cultures in a Bourgeois World.* Berkeley: University of California Press, 1997.
Coulson, N. J. *A History of Islamic Law.* Edinburgh: Edinburgh University Press, 1964.

Coulson, N. J. *Succession in Islamic Family Law*. Cambridge: Cambridge University Press, 1972.

Coulson, N. J. *Conflicts and Tensions in Islamic Jurisprudence*. 1969. Reprint, Kuala Lumpur: The Other Press, 2006.

Croucher, Sarah, and Stephanie Wynne-Jones. "People, Not Pots: Locally Produced Ceramics and Identity on the Nineteenth-Century East African Coast." *International Journal of African Historical Studies* 39, no. 1 (2006): 107–24.

Cuno, Kenneth M. "Disobedient Wives and Neglectful Husbands: Marital Relations and the First Phase of Family Law Reform in Egypt." In *Family, Gender, and Law in a Globalizing Middle East and South Asia*, ed. Kenneth M. Cuno and Manisha Desai, 3–18. Syracuse: Syracuse University Press, 2009.

Dickerman, Carol. "The Use of Court Records as Sources for African History: Some Examples from Bujumbura, Burundi." *History in Africa* 11 (1984): 69–81.

Dickerman, Carol. "African Courts under the Colonial Regime: Usumbura, Ruanda-Urundi, 1938–1962." *Canadian Journal of African Studies* 26, no. 1 (1992): 55–69.

Doumani, Beshara. *Rediscovering Palestine: Merchants and Peasants in Jabal Nablus, 1700–1900*. Berkeley: University of California Press, 1995.

Eastman, Carol. "Who Are the Swahili?" *Africa* 41, no. 3 (1971): 228–36.

Eastman, Carol. "Women, Slaves, and Foreigners: African Cultural Influences and Group Processes in the Formation of Northern Swahili Coastal Society." *International Journal of African Historical Studies* 21, no. 1 (1988): 1–20.

El Alami, Dawoud Sudqi, and Doreen Hinchcliffe. *Islamic Marriage and Divorce Laws of the Arab World*. 1996. Reprint, London: Kluwer Law International, 1998.

El-Busaidy, Hamed bin Saleh. *Ndoa na talaka*. 1958. Reprint, Nairobi: East African Literature Bureau, 1962.

Elmasri, F. H. "Sheikh al-Amin bin Ali al-Mazrui and the Islamic Intellectual Tradition in East Africa." *Journal of Muslim Minority Affairs* 8, no. 2 (1987): 229–37.

Ewald, Janet J. "Crossers of the Sea: Slaves, Freedman, and other Migrants in the Northwestern Indian Ocean, c.1750–1914." *American Historical Review* 105, no. 1 (2000): 69–91.

Fair, Laura. "Dressing Up: Clothing, Class and Gender in Post-Abolition Zanzibar." *Journal of African History* 39, no. 1 (1998): 63–94.

Fair, Laura. *Pastimes and Politics: Culture, Community, and Identity in Post-Abolition Urban Zanzibar, 1890–1945*. Athens: Ohio University Press, 2001.

Farsy, Abdallah Salih. *Seyyid Said bin Sultan*. Zanzibar: Mwongozi Printing Press, [1942].

Farsy, Abdallah Salih. *The Shafi'i ulama of East Africa, c.1830–1970: A Hagiographic Account*. Trans., ed., and annotated by R. L. Pouwels. Madison: University of Wisconsin, 1989.

Fisher, Humphrey J. *Slavery in the History of Muslim Black Africa*. London: Hurst, 2001.

Gerber, Haim. "Social and Economic Position of Women in an Ottoman City, Bursa, 1600–1700." *International Journal of Middle East Studies* 12, no. 3 (1980): 231–44.

Gerber, Haim. *State, Society, and Law in Islam: Ottoman Law in Comparative Perspective*. Albany: State University of New York Press, 1994.

Ghazal, Amal N. *Islamic Reform and Arab Nationalism: Expanding the Crescent from the Mediterranean to the Indian Ocean (1880s–1930s)*. London: Routledge, 2010.

Glassman, Jonathon. "The Bondsman's New Clothes: The Contradictory Consciousness of Slave Resistance on the Swahili Coast." *Journal of African History* 32, no. 2 (1991): 277–312.

Glassman, Jonathon. *Feasts and Riot: Revelry, Rebellion, and Popular Consciousness on the Swahili Coast, 1856–1888*. Portsmouth, NH: Heinemann, 1995.

Glassman, Jonathon. "Sorting out the Tribes: The Creation of Racial Identities in Colonial Zanzibar's Newspaper Wars." *Journal of African History* 41, no. 3 (2000): 395–428.

Glassman, Jonathon. "Stolen Knowledge: Struggles for Popular Islam on the Swahili Coast, 1870–1963." In *Islam in East Africa: New Sources. (Archives. Manuscripts and Written Historical Sources. Oral History. Archaeology). International Colloquium, Rome, 2–4 December 1999*, ed. Biancamaria Scarcia Amoretti, 209–25. Rome: Herder, 2001.

Glassman, Jonathon. "Slower Than a Massacre: The Multiple Sources of Racial Thought in Colonial Africa." *American Historical Review* 109, no. 3 (2004): 720–54.

Glassman, Jonathon. *War of Words, War of Stones: Racial Thought and Violence in Colonial Zanzibar*. Bloomington: Indiana University Press, 2011.

Glassman, Jonathon. "Creole Nationalists and the Search for Nativist Authenticity in Twentieth-Century Zanzibar: The Limits of Cosmopolitanism." *Journal of African History* 55, no. 2 (2014): 229–247.

Gleave, R., and E. Kermeli, eds. *Islamic Law: Theory and Practice*. London: I. B. Tauris, 1997.

Gocking, Roger. "British Justice and the Native Tribunals of the Southern Gold Coast Colony." *Journal of African History* 34, no. 1 (1993): 93–113.

Goody, Jack, and S. J. Tambiah. *Bridewealth and Dowry*. Cambridge: Cambridge University Press, 1973.

Gower, Rebecca, Steven Salm, and Toyin Falola. "Swahili Women since the Nineteenth Century: Theoretical and Empirical Considerations on Gender and Identity Construction." *Africa Today* 43, no. 3 (1996): 251–68.

Gray, John. *History of Zanzibar from the Middle Ages to 1856*. London: Oxford University Press, 1962.

Groff, David. "The Dynamics of Collaboration and the Rule of Law in French West Africa: The Case of Kwame Kangah of Assikasso (Côte d'Ivoire),

1898–1922." In *Law in Colonial Africa*, ed. Kristin Mann and Richard Roberts, 146–66. Portsmouth, NH: Heinemann, 1991.

Gundara, Jagdish S. "British Extraterritorial Jurisdiction in Nineteenth Century Zanzibar." *Africa Quarterly* 23, no. 3/4 (1983): 10–27.

Gurnah, Abdulrazak. *Paradise*. London: Penguin, 1995.

Hall, Bruce S. *A History of Race in Muslim West Africa, 1600–1960*. Cambridge: Cambridge University Press, 2011.

Hallaq, Wael. "The *qāḍī's dīwān* (*sijill*) before the Ottomans." *Bulletin of the School of Oriental and African Studies* 61, no. 3 (1998): 415–36.

Hallaq, Wael B. *Shariʿa: Theory, Practice, Transformations*. Cambridge: Cambridge University Press, 2009.

Hanak, Irmi. *Gericht–Sprache–Macht: Überlegungen zur Realisierung von Dominanzverhältnissen in und durch sprachliche Kommunikation am Beispiel des Familiengerichts in Zanzibar*. Vienna: Afro-Pub, 1994.

Hanretta, Sean. *Islam and Social Change in French West Africa: History of an Emancipatory Community*. Cambridge: Cambridge University Press, 2009.

Hay, Margaret Jean. "Women as Owners, Occupants, and Managers of Property in Colonial Western Kenya." In *African Women and the Law: Historical Perspectives*, ed. Margaret Jean Hay and Marcia Wright, 110–23. Boston: Boston University, 1982.

Hay, Margaret Jean, and Marcia Wright, eds. *African Women and the Law: Historical Perspectives*. Boston: Boston University, 1982.

Hemedi, Ali bin. *Nikahi: A Handbook of the Law of Marriage in Islam*. Trans. by J. W. T. Allen. s.l.: s.n., 1934.

Hirsch, Susan F. "Kadhi's Courts as Complex Sites of Resistance: The State, Islam, and Gender in Postcolonial Kenya." In *Contested States: Law, Hegemony and Resistance*, ed. Mindie Lazarus-Black and Susan F. Hirsch, 207–30. New York: Routledge, 1994.

Hirsch, Susan F. *Pronouncing and Persevering: Gender and the Discourses of Disputing in an African Islamic Court*. Chicago: University of Chicago Press, 1998.

Ho, Engseng. *The Graves of Tarim: Genealogy and Mobility across the Indian Ocean*. Berkeley: University of California Press, 2006.

Hodgson, Dorothy L., and Sheryl McCurdy. *"Wicked" Women and the Reconfiguration of Gender in Africa*. Portsmouth, NH: Heinemann, 2001.

Hoffman, Valerie J. "The Articulation of Ibadi Identity in Modern Oman and Zanzibar." *Muslim World* 94, no. 2 (2004): 201–16.

Hoffman, Valerie J. "In His (Arab) Majesty's Service: The Career of a Somali Scholar and Diplomat in Nineteenth-Century Zanzibar." In *The Global Worlds of the Swahili: Interfaces of Islam, Identity and Space in 19th and 20th-Century East Africa*, ed. Roman Loimeier and Rüdiger Seesemann, 251–72. Berlin: Lit Verlag, 2006.

Hollingsworth, L. W. *Zanzibar under the Foreign Office, 1890–1913*. London: Macmillan, 1953.

Hooker, M. B. *Legal Pluralism: An Introduction to Colonial and Neo-Colonial Laws*. Oxford: Oxford University Press, 1975.

Ibn Battuta. *Travels in Asia and Africa, 1325–1354*. Trans. and selected by H. A. R. Gibb. New York: Augustus M. Kelley, 1969.

Ibrahim, Abdullahi Ali. *Manichaean Delirium: Decolonizing the Judiciary and Islamic Renewal in the Sudan, 1898–1985*. Leiden: Brill, 2008.

Imber, Colin. *Ebu's-su'ud: The Islamic Legal Tradition*. Edinburgh: Edinburgh University Press, 1997.

Ingrams, W. H. *Zanzibar: Its History and Its People*. London: H. F. & G. Witherby, 1931.

Jeppie, Shamil, Ebrahim Moosa, and Richard Roberts, eds. *Muslim Family Law in Sub-Saharan Africa: Colonial Legacies and Post-Colonial Challenges*. Amsterdam: Amsterdam University Press, 2010.

Kandiyoti, Deniz. "Islam and Patriarchy: A Comparative Perspective." In *Women in Middle Eastern History: Shifting Boundaries in Sex and Gender*, ed. Nikki R. Keddie and Beth Baron, 23–42. New Haven: Yale University Press, 1991.

Kapteijns, Lidwien. "Government Qadis and Child Marriage in Aden: Ethnography in the Aden Archives." *International Journal of African Historical Studies* 37, no. 3 (2004): 401–34.

al-Khalīlī, Aḥmad b. Ḥamad. *Fatāwā al-nikāḥ*. 2nd ed. Muscat, Oman: Ministry of Religious Endowments and Affairs, 2003.

Kingdon, H. E. *The Conflict of Laws in Zanzibar*. Zanzibar: Government Printer, 1940.

Kirkman, James, ed. "The Zanzibar Diary of John Studdy Leigh, Part I." *International Journal of African Historical Studies* 13, no. 2 (1980): 281–312.

Kirkman, James, ed. "The Zanzibar Diary of John Studdy Leigh, Part II." *International Journal of African Historical Studies* 13, no. 3 (1980): 492–507.

Knappert, Jan. "Social and Moral Concepts in Swahili Islamic Literature." *Africa* 40, no. 2 (1970): 125–36.

Kresse, Kai. "'Swahili Enlightenment?' East African Reformist Discourse at the Turning Point: The Example of Sheikh Muhammad Kasim Mazrui." *Journal of Religion in Africa* 33, no. 3 (2003): 279–309.

Kyomuhendo, Grace B., and Marjorie K. McIntosh. *Women, Work, and Domestic Virtue in Uganda, 1900–2003*. Oxford: James Currey, 2006.

Landberg, Pamela. "Widows and Divorced Women in Swahili Society." In *Widows in African Societies: Choices and Constraints*, ed. Betty Potash, 107–30. Stanford: Stanford University Press, 1986.

Lawrance, Benjamin N., Emily Lynn Osborn, and Richard L. Roberts, eds. *Intermediaries, Interpreters, and Clerks: African Employees in the Making of Colonial Africa*. Madison: University of Wisconsin Press, 2006.

Layish, Aharon. "Customary *Khul'* as Reflected in the *Sijill* of the Libyan *Sharī'a* Courts." *Bulletin of the School of Oriental and African Studies* 51, no. 3 (1988): 428–39.

Layish, Aharon. *Divorce in the Libyan Family: A Study Based on the* sijills *of the* sharī'a *Courts of Ajdābiyya and Kufra*. New York: New York University Press, 1991.

Lazreg, Marnia. *The Eloquence of Silence: Algerian Women in Question.* New York: Routledge, 1994.
Le Cour Grandmaison, Colette. "Rich Cousins, Poor Cousins: Hidden Stratification among the Omani Arabs in Eastern Africa." *Africa* 59, no. 2 (1989): 176–84.
Lee, Christopher J. "The 'Native' Undefined: Colonial Categories, Anglo-African Status and the Politics of Kinship in British Central Africa, 1929–38." *Journal of African History* 46, no. 3 (2005): 455–78.
Lee, Christopher J. "*Jus Solis* and *Jus Sanguinis* in the Colonies: The Interwar Politics of Race, Culture, and Multiracial Legal Status in British Africa." *Law and History Review* 29, no. 2 (2011): 497–522.
Le Guennec-Coppens, Françoise. "L'instabilité conjugale et ses conséquences dans la société Swahili de Lamu (Kenya)." In *Transformations of African Marriage*, ed. David Parkin and David Nyamwaya, 233–45. Manchester: Manchester University Press, 1987.
Le Guennec-Coppens, Françoise. "Qui épouse-t-on chez les Hadrami d'Afrique orientale: Les réseaux d'alliances." In *Les Swahili entre Afrique et Arabie*, ed. Françoise Le Guennec-Coppens and Pat Caplan, 145–62. Paris: Karthala, 1991.
Lofchie, Michael F. *Zanzibar: Background to Revolution.* Princeton: Princeton University Press, 1965.
Loimeier, Roman. "Patterns and Peculiarities of Islamic Reform in Africa." *Journal of Religion in Africa* 33, no. 3 (2003): 237–62.
Loimeier, Roman. *Between Social Skills and Marketable Skills: The Politics of Islamic Education in 20th century Zanzibar.* Leiden: Brill, 2009.
Lydon, Ghislaine. *On Trans-Saharan Trails: Islamic Law, Trade Networks, and Cross-Cultural Exchange in Nineteenth-Century Western Africa.* Cambridge: Cambridge University Press, 2009.
Lyne, Robert Nunez. *Zanzibar in Contemporary Times: A Short History of the Southern East in the Nineteenth Century.* London: Hurst & Blackett, 1905.
Mahmood, Saba. *Politics of Piety: The Islamic Revival and the Feminist Subject.* Princeton: Princeton University Press, 2005.
Mann, Kristin. *Marrying Well: Marriage, Status and Social Change among the Educated Elite in Colonial Lagos.* Cambridge: Cambridge University Press, 1985.
Mann, Kristin. "The Rise of Taiwo Olowo: Law, Accumulation, and Mobility in Early Colonial Lagos." In *Law in Colonial Africa*, ed. Kristin Mann and Richard Roberts, 85–107. Portsmouth, NH: Heinemann, 1991.
Mann, Kristin. *Slavery and the Birth of an African City: Lagos, 1760–1900.* Bloomington: Indiana University Press, 2007.
Mann, Kristin, and Richard Roberts, eds. *Law in Colonial Africa.* Portsmouth, NH: Heinemann, 1991.
Martin, B. G. "Notes on Some Members of the Learned Classes of Zanzibar and East Africa in the Nineteenth Century." *African Historical Studies* 4, no. 3 (1971): 525–45.

Martin, Esmond Bradley. *Zanzibar: Tradition and Revolution*. London: Hamish Hamilton, 1978.

Masud, Muhammad Khalid, Rudolph Peters, and David S. Powers. "Qādīs and their Courts: An Historical Survey." In *Dispensing Justice in Islam: Qadis and their Judgments*, ed. Muhammad Khalid Masud, Rudolph Peters, and David S. Powers, 1–44. Leiden: Brill, 2006.

al-Māwardī, Abū Ḥasan. *al-Aḥkām as-Sulṭāniyyah. The Laws of Islamic Governance*. Trans. by Asadullah Yate. London: Ta-Ha, 1996.

Mazrui, Alamin M., and Ibrahim Noor Shariff. *The Swahili: Idiom and Identity of an African People*. Trenton, NJ: Africa World Press, 1994.

Mbilinyi, Marjorie. "Women's Resistance in 'Customary' Marriage: Tanzania's Runaway Wives." In *Forced Labour and Migration: Patterns of Movement within Africa*, ed. Abebe Zegeye and Shubi Ishemo, 211–54. London: Hans Zell, 1989.

Mbogoni, Lawrence E. Y. "Censoring the Press in Colonial Zanzibar: An Account of the Seditious Case against *al-Falaq*." In *In Search of a Nation: Histories of Authority & Dissidence in Tanzania*, ed. Gregory H. Maddox and James L. Giblin, 198–215. Oxford: James Currey, 2005.

McClintock, Anne. *Imperial Leather: Race, Gender and Sexuality in the Colonial Contest*. New York: Routledge, 1995.

McDow, Thomas F. "Being Baysar: (In)flexible Identities in East Africa." *The MIT Electronic Journal of Middle East Studies* 5 (2005): 34–42. http://web.mit.edu/cis/www/mitejmes/

McIntosh, Marjorie K. *Yoruba Women, Work, and Social Change*. Bloomington: Indiana University Press, 2009.

McMahon, Elisabeth. *Slavery and Emancipation in Islamic East Africa: From Honor to Respectability*. Cambridge: Cambridge University Press, 2013.

McMahon, Elisabeth, and Corrie Decker. "Wives or Workers? Negotiating the Social Contract between Female Teachers and the Colonial State in Zanzibar." *Journal of Women's History* 21, no. 2 (2009): 39–61.

Meriwether, Margaret L. *The Kin Who Count: Family and Society in Ottoman Aleppo, 1770–1840*. Austin: University of Texas Press, 1999.

Mernissi, Fatima. *Beyond the Veil: Male-Female Dynamics in Modern Muslim Society*. Revised ed. London: Saqi Books, 2003.

Merry, Sally Engle. "The Articulation of Legal Spheres." In *African Women and the Law: Historical Perspectives*, ed. Margaret Jean Hay and Marcia Wright, 68–89. Boston: Boston University, 1982.

Messick, Brinkley. *The Calligraphic State: Textual Domination and History in a Muslim Society*. Berkeley: University of California Press, 1993.

Middleton, John. *The World of the Swahili: An African Mercantile Civilization*. New Haven: Yale University Press, 1992.

Middleton, John, and Jane Campbell. *Zanzibar: Its Society and Its Politics*. London: Oxford University Press, 1965.

Miers, Suzanne, and Igor Kopytoff, eds. *Slavery in Africa: Historical and Anthropological Perspectives*. Madison: University of Wisconsin Press, 1977.

Miran, Jonathan. *Red Sea Citizens: Cosmopolitan Society and Cultural Change in Massawa*. Bloomington: Indiana University Press, 2009.

Mir-Hosseini, Ziba. *Marriage on Trial: A Study of Islamic Family Law*. Revised ed. London: I. B. Tauris, 2000.

Mirza, Sarah, and Margaret Strobel, eds. *Three Swahili Women: Life Histories from Mombasa, Kenya*. Trans. by S. Mirza and M. Strobel. Bloomington: Indiana University Press, 1989.

Mommsen, W. J., and J. A. De Moor, eds. *European Expansion and Law: The Encounter of European and Indigenous Law in 19th and 20th Century Africa and Asia*. Oxford: Oxford University Press, 1991.

Moore, Sally Falk. *Law as Process: An Anthropological Approach*. London: Routledge & Kegan Paul, 1978.

Moore, Sally Falk. *Social Facts and Fabrications: 'Customary' Law on Kilimanjaro, 1880– 1980*. Cambridge: Cambridge University Press, 1986.

Moors, Annelies. *Women, Property and Islam: Palestinian Experiences, 1920–1990*. Cambridge: Cambridge University Press, 1995.

Moors, Annelies. "Debating Islamic Family Law: Legal Texts and Social Practices." In *Social History of Women and Gender in the Modern Middle East*, ed. Margaret L. Meriwether and Judith E. Tucker, 141–75. Boulder, CO: Westview Press, 1999.

Morton, Fred. "Pawning and Slavery on the Kenya Coast: The Miji Kenda Case." In *Pawnship, Slavery, and Colonialism in Africa*, ed. Paul E. Lovejoy and Toyin Falola, 239–54. Trenton, NJ: Africa World Press, 2003.

al-Mughayrī, Saʿīd b. ʿAlī. *Juhaynat al-akhbār fī tārīkh zinjibār*. 2nd ed. Muscat, Oman: Ministry of Heritage and Culture, 1986.

Mwakimako, Hassan. "The *ʿulamāʾ* and the Colonial State in the Protectorate of Kenya. The Appointment of *shaykh al-islām sharīf* ʿAbd al-Raḥmān b. Aḥmad Saggaf (1844–1922) and Chief Kadhi Sh. Muhammad b. ʿUmar Bakore (c.1932)." In *The Global Worlds of the Swahili: Interfaces of Islam, Identity and Space in 19th and 20th-Century East Africa*, ed. Roman Loimeier and Rüdiger Seesemann, 289–315. Berlin: Lit Verlag, 2006.

Mwangi, Kuria. "The Application and Development of Sharia in Kenya: 1895–1990." In *Islam in Kenya. Proceedings of the National Seminar of Contemporary Islam in Kenya*, ed. Mohamed Bakari and Saad S. Yahya, 252–59. Nairobi: Mewa, 1995.

Nicholls, C. S. *The Swahili Coast: Politics, Diplomacy and Trade on the East African Littoral, 1798–1856*. London: George Allen & Unwin, 1971.

Niese, Richard. *Das Personen- und Familienrecht der Suaheli. (Ein Beitrag zur vergleichenden Rechtswissenschaft)*. Berlin: Georg Pintus, 1902.

Nimtz, August H. *Islam and Politics in East Africa: The Sufi Order in Tanzania*. Minneapolis: University of Minnesota Press, 1980.

Noorani, Yaseen. "Normative Notions of Public and Private in Early Islamic Culture." In *Harem Histories: Envisioning Places and Living Spaces*, ed. Marilyn Booth, 49–68. Durham: Duke University Press, 2010.

Nurse, Derek, and Thomas Spear. *The Swahili: Reconstructing the History and Language of an African Society, 800–1500*. Philadelphia: University of Pennsylvania Press, 1985.

O'Fahey, R. S. "The Office of 'Qadi' in Dar Fur: A Preliminary Inquiry." *Bulletin of the School of Oriental and African Studies* 40, no. 1 (1977): 110–24.

O'Fahey, R. S. "'Small World': Neo-Sufi Interconnexions between the Maghrib, the Hijaz and Southeast Asia." In *The Transmission of Learning in Islamic Africa*, ed. Scott S. Reese, 274–88. Leiden: Brill, 2004.

Pearce, Major F. B. *Zanzibar: The Island Metropolis of Eastern Africa.* London: T. Fisher Unwin, 1920.

Peirce, Leslie. "'She Is Trouble . . . and I Will Divorce Her': Orality, Honor, and Representation in the Ottoman Court of ʿAintab." In *Women in the Medieval Islamic World: Power, Patronage, and Piety*, ed. Gavin R. G. Hambly, 269–300. New York: St. Martin's Press, 1999.

Peirce, Leslie. *Morality Tales: Law and Gender in the Ottoman Court of Aintab.* Berkeley: University of California Press, 2003.

Peletz, Michael G. *Islamic Modern: Religious Courts and Cultural Politics in Malaysia.* Princeton: Princeton University Press, 2002.

Peters, Rudolph. *Crime and Punishment in Islamic Law: Theory and Practice from the Sixteenth to the Twenty-first Century.* Cambridge: Cambridge University Press, 2005.

Peterson, Derek R. "Morality Plays: Marriage, Church Courts, and Colonial Agency in Central Tanganyika, ca.1876–1928." *American Historical Review* 111, no. 4 (2006): 983–1010.

Pouwels, Randall L. *Horn and Crescent: Cultural Change and Traditional Islam on the East African Coast, 800–1900.* Cambridge: Cambridge University Press, 1987.

Powers, David S. "Orientalism, Colonialism, and Legal History: The Attack on Muslim Family Endowments in Algeria and India." *Comparative Studies in Society and History* 31, no. 3 (1989): 535–71.

Powers, David S. "Kadijustiz or Qāḍī Justice? A Paternity Dispute from Fourteenth-Century Morocco." *Islamic Law and Society* 1, no. 3 (1994): 332–366.

Prestholdt, Jeremy. "On the Global Repercussions of East African Consumerism." *American Historical Review* 109, no. 3 (2004): 755–81.

Prestholdt, Jeremy. *Domesticating the World: African Consumerism and the Genealogies of Globalization.* Berkeley: University of California Press, 2008.

Prins, A. H. J. *The Swahili-Speaking Peoples of Zanzibar and the East African Coast (Arabs, Shirazi and Swahili).* London: International African Institute, 1961.

Rapoport, Yossef. *Marriage, Money and Divorce in Medieval Islamic Society.* Cambridge: Cambridge University Press, 2005.

Rathbone, Richard. "Law, Lawyers and Politics in Ghana in the 1940s." In *Contesting Colonial Hegemony: State and Society in Africa and India*, ed. Dagmar Engels and Shula Marks, 227–47. London: British Academic Press, 1994.

Reese, Scott S. "Tales Which Persist on the Tongue: Arabic Literacy and the Definition of Communal Boundaries in Sharīf ʿAydarūs's Bughyat al-Āmāl." *Sudanic Africa* 9 (1998): 1–17.

Reese, Scott S., ed. *The Transmission of Learning in Islamic Africa*. Leiden: Brill, 2004.
Reese, Scott. *Renewers of the Age: Holy Men and Social Discourse in Colonial Benaadir*. Leiden: Brill, 2008.
Roberts, Richard. "Representation, Structure and Agency: Divorce in the French Soudan during the Early Twentieth Century." *Journal of African History* 40, no. 3 (1999): 389–410.
Roberts, Richard. *Litigants and Households: African Disputes and Colonial Courts in the French Soudan, 1895–1912*. Portsmouth, NH: Heinemann, 2005.
Roberts, Simon, ed. *Law and the Family in Africa*. The Hague: Mouton, 1977.
Rodet, Marie. "'Le délit d'abandon de domicile conjugal' ou l'invasion du pénal colonial dans les jugements des 'tribunaux indigènes' au Soudan français, 1900–1947." *French Colonial History* 10 (2009): 151–70.
Romero, Patricia W. "'Where Have All the Slaves Gone?' Emancipation and Post-Emancipation in Lamu, Kenya." *Journal of African History* 27, no. 3 (1986): 497–512.
Romero, Patricia W. "Possible Sources for the Origin of Gold as an Economic and Social Vehicle for Women in Lamu." *Africa* 57, no. 3 (1987): 364–76.
Romero, Patricia W. "Mama Khadija: A Life History as Example of Family History." In *Life Histories of African Women*, ed. Patricia W. Romero, 140–58. London: The Ashfield Press, 1988.
Romero, Patricia W. *Lamu: History, Society, and Family in an East African Port City*. Princeton: Marcus Wiener, 1997.
Rosen, Lawrence. *The Anthropology of Justice: Law as Culture in Islamic Society*. Cambridge: Cambridge University Press, 1989.
Ruete, Emily. *Memoirs of an Arabian Princess from Zanzibar*. Zanzibar: The Gallery Publications, 1998.
Sabean, David Warren. "The History of the Family in Africa and Europe: Some Comparative Perspectives." *Journal of African History* 24, no. 2 (1983): 163–71.
Sachau, Eduard. "Das Gutachten eines Muhammedanischen Juristen über die Muhammedanischen Rechtsverhältnisse in Ostafrika." *Mittheilungen des Seminars für Orientalische Sprachen. Afrikanische Studien* 1, no. 3 (1898): 1–8.
Sadgrove, Philip. "From Wādī Mīzāb to Unguja: Zanzibar's Scholarly Links." In *The Transmission of Learning in Islamic Africa*, ed. Scott S. Reese, 184–211. Leiden: Brill, 2004.
Salim, A. I. *The Swahili-Speaking Peoples of Kenya's Coast, 1895–1965*. Nairobi: East African Publishing House, 1973.
al-Sālimī, ʿAbdallāh b. Ḥumayyid. *Jawhar al-niẓām fī ʿilmī al-adyān wa-l-aḥkām*. 2 vols. 11th ed. s.l.: Sulayman and Ahmad al-Salimi, 1989.
Schacht, Joseph. *An Introduction to Islamic Law*. Oxford: Clarendon Press, 1964.
Schacht, Joseph. "Notes on Islam in East Africa." *Studia Islamica* 23 (1965): 91–136.

Schmidt, Elizabeth. "Negotiated Spaces and Contested Terrain: Men, Women and the Law in Colonial Zimbabwe, 1890–1939." *Journal of Southern African Studies* 16, no. 4 (1990): 622–48.

Schmidt, Elizabeth. "Patriarchy, Capitalism, and the Colonial State in Zimbabwe." *Signs* 16, no. 4 (1991): 732–56.

Shadle, Brett L. "'Changing Traditions to Meet Current Altering Conditions': Customary Law, African Courts and the Rejection of Codification in Kenya, 1930–60." *Journal of African History* 40, no. 3 (1999): 411–31.

Shadle, Brett L. "Bridewealth and Female Consent: Marriage Disputes in African Courts, Gusiiland, Kenya." *Journal of African History* 44, no. 2 (2003): 241–62.

Shadle, Brett L. *"Girl Cases": Marriage and Colonialism in Gusiiland, Kenya, 1890–1970*. Portsmouth, NH: Heinemann, 2006.

Shaham, Ron. "Judicial Divorce at the Wife's Initiative: The Sharīʿa Courts of Egypt, 1920–1955." *Islamic Law and Society* 1, no. 2 (1994): 217–57.

Shaham, Ron. "Custom, Islamic Law, and Statutory Legislation: Marriage Registration and Minimum Age at Marriage in the Egyptian Sharīʿa Courts." *Islamic Law and Society* 2, no. 3 (1995): 258–81.

Shaham, Ron. *Family and the Courts in Modern Egypt: A Study Based on Decisions by the Sharīʿa Courts, 1900–1955*. Leiden: Brill, 1997.

Shereikis, Rebecca. "From Law to Custom: The Shifting Legal Status of Muslim *Originaires* in Kayes and Medine, 1903–13." *Journal of African History* 42, no. 2 (2001): 261–83.

Sheriff, Abdul. "The Slave Mode of Production Along the East African Coast, 1810–1873." In *Slaves and Slavery in Muslim Africa*. Vol. II, *The Servile Estate*, ed. John Ralph Willis, 161–81. London: Frank Cass, 1985.

Sheriff, Abdul. *Slaves, Spices and Ivory in Zanzibar: Integration of an East African Commercial Empire into the World Economy, 1770–1873*. London: James Currey, 1987.

Sheriff, Abdul, and Chizuko Tominaga. "The Ambiguity of Shirazi Identity in the History & Politics of Zanzibar." *Christianity and Culture* 24 (1990): 1–37.

Siddiqui, Mona. "Law and the Desire for Social Control: An Insight into the Hanafi Concept of *Kafāʾa* with Reference to the Fatawa ʿAlamgiri (1664–1672)." In *Feminism and Islam: Legal and Literary Perspectives*, ed. Mai Yamani, 49–68. Reading, UK: Ithaca Press, 1996.

Sonbol, Amina El Azhary. Introduction to *Women, the Family, and Divorce Laws in Islamic History*, ed. Amina El Azhary Sonbol, 1–20. Syracuse: Syracuse University Press, 1996.

Stiles, Erin E. "Buying a Divorce in Zanzibar."*ISIM Newsletter* 10 (2002): 33.

Stiles, Erin E. "When Is a Divorce a Divorce? Determining Intention in Zanzibar's Islamic Courts." *Ethnology* 42, no. 4 (2003): 273–88.

Stiles, Erin E. "'There Is No Stranger to Marriage Here!': Muslim Women and Divorce in Rural Zanzibar." *Africa* 75, no. 4 (2005): 582–98.

Stiles, Erin E. *An Islamic Court in Context: An Ethnographic Study of Judicial Reasoning*. New York: Palgrave Macmillan, 2009.

Stockreiter, Elke E. "'British *kadhis*' and 'Muslim judges': Modernisation, Inconsistencies and Accommodation in Zanzibar's Colonial Judiciary." *Journal of Eastern African Studies* 4, no. 3 (2010): 560–76.

Stockreiter, Elke E. "Child Marriage and Domestic Violence: Islamic and Colonial Discourses on Gender Relations and Female Status in Zanzibar, 1900–1950s." In *Domestic Violence and the Law in Colonial and Postcolonial Africa*, ed. Emily Burrill, Richard Roberts, and Elizabeth Thornberry, 138–58. Athens: Ohio University Press, 2010.

Stockreiter, Elke E. "Materialism, Contention, and Rebellion: The Changing Demands on Marriage in Colonial Zanzibar." In *Domestic Tensions, National Anxieties: Global Perspectives on Modern Marriage Crises*, ed. Kristin Celello and Hanan Kholoussy. Oxford: Oxford University Press, forthcoming.

Stoler, Ann Laura. *Carnal Knowledge and Imperial Power: Race and the Intimate in Colonial Rule*. Berkeley: University of California Press, 2002.

Stoler, Ann Laura. *Along the Archival Grain: Epistemic Anxieties and Colonial Common Sense*. Princeton: Princeton University Press, 2009.

Strobel, Margaret. *Muslim Women in Mombasa, 1890–1975*. New Haven: Yale University Press, 1979.

Swartz, Marc J. "Religious Courts, Community and Ethnicity among the Swahili of Mombasa: An Historical Study of Social Boundaries." *Africa* 49, no. 1 (1979): 29–40.

Swartz, Marc J. *The Way the World Is: Cultural Processes and Social Relations among the Mombasa Swahili*. Berkeley: University of California Press, 1991.

Tanner, R. E. S. "The Relationships between the Sexes in a Coastal Islamic Society: Pangani District, Tanganyika." *African Studies* 21, no. 2 (1962): 70–82.

Tanner, R. E. S. "Cousin Marriage in the Afro-Arab Community of Mombasa, Kenya." *Africa* 34, no. 2 (1964): 127–38.

Thomas, Lynn M. *Politics of the Womb: Women: Reproduction, and the State in Kenya*. Berkeley: University of California Press, 2003.

Trimingham, J. Spencer. *Islam in East Africa*. Oxford: Clarendon Press, 1964.

Tucker, Judith E. *Women in Nineteenth-Century Egypt*. Cambridge: Cambridge University Press, 1985.

Tucker, Judith E. "Ties That Bound: Women and Family in Eighteenth- and Nineteenth-Century Nablus." In *Women in Middle Eastern History: Shifting Boundaries in Sex and Gender*, ed. Nikki R. Keddie and Beth Baron, 233–53. New Haven: Yale University Press, 1991.

Tucker, Judith E. *In the House of the Law: Gender and Islamic Law in Ottoman Syria and Palestine*. Berkeley: University of California Press, 1998.

Tucker, Judith E. *Women, Family, and Gender in Islamic Law*. Cambridge: Cambridge University Press, 2008.

Vaughan, J. H. *The Dual Jurisdiction in Zanzibar*. Zanzibar: Government Printer, 1935.

Velten, C. "Sitten und Gebräuche der Suaheli." *Mittheilungen des Seminars für Orientalische Sprachen. Afrikanische Studien* 1, no. 3 (1898): 9–85.

Vianello, Alessandra, and Mohamed M. Kassim, eds. *Servants of the Sharia: The Civil Register of the Qadis' Court of Brava, 1893–1900*. 2 vols. Leiden: Brill, 2006.

Vikør, Knut. *Between God and the Sultan: A History of Islamic Law*. London: Hurst, 2005.

Welchman, Lynn. *Beyond the Code: Muslim Family Law and the Shariʿa Judiciary in the Palestinian West Bank*. The Hague: Kluwer Law International, 2000.

Welchman, Lynn. "Family, Gender, and Law in Jordan and Palestine." In *Family, Gender, and Law in a Globalizing Middle East and South Asia*, ed. Kenneth M. Cuno and Manisha Desai 126–44. Syracuse: Syracuse University Press, 2009.

Werner, Alice. "The Utendi of Mwana Kupona." *Harvard African Studies* 1 (1917): 147–81.

White, Luise. *The Comforts of Home: Prostitution in Colonial Nairobi*. Chicago: University of Chicago Press, 1990.

Wilkinson, John C. *The Imamate Tradition of Oman*. Cambridge: Cambridge University Press, 1987.

Willis, Justin. *Mombasa, the Swahili, and the Making of the Mijikenda*. Oxford: Clarendon Press, 1993.

Yazbak, Mahmoud. "Minor Marriages and *khiyār al-bulūgh* in Ottoman Palestine: A Note on Women's Strategies in a Patriarchal Society." *Islamic Law and Society* 9, no. 3 (2002): 386–409.

Zaman, Muhammad Qasim. *The Ulama in Contemporary Islam: Custodians of Change*. Princeton: Princeton University Press, 2002.

Zarinebaf-Shahr, Fariba. "Women and the Public Eye in Eighteenth-Century Istanbul." In *Women in the Medieval Islamic World: Power, Patronage, and Piety*, ed. Gavin R. G. Hambly, 301–24. New York: St. Martin's Press, 1999.

Ze'evi, Dror. "The Use of Ottoman Shariʿa Court Records as a Source for Middle Eastern Social History: A Reappraisal." *Islamic Law and Society* 5, no. 1 (1998): 35–56.

Index